The Future Global Challenge

The Future Global Challenge:

A Predictive Study of World Security, 1977–1990

Neville Brown

ROYAL UNITED SERVICES INSTITUTE
FOR DEFENCE STUDIES
WHITEHALL, LONDON SW1A 2ET

CRANE, RUSSAK & COMPANY, INC.
NEW YORK

First published in Great Britain, 1977
by Royal United Services Institute for Defence Studies
Whitehall, London SW1A 2ET

© RUSI, 1977

ISBN   0   88516   038   1

Distributed by Seeley Service and Cooper Ltd
196 Shaftesbury Avenue, London WC2 8JL

Published in the United States by
Crane, Russak & Company, Inc.
347 Madison Avenue, New York, N.Y. 10017

Crane, Russak ISBN 0-8448-1256-0
LC 77-82865

Printed in the United States of America

DEDICATED
To the late Anthony Crosland
With thanks for encouragement and example

Contents

Preface

Any explosion, in the strict meaning of the word, progressively diminishes in ferocity the further its shock wave travels in time and space from the point of origin. But those who attempt to gauge the "knowledge explosion" that effectively began with the Renaissance advise us it has been getting faster constantly. They say that around the time of the Napoleonic wars the sum total of human knowledge was doubling every half century. By 1950 the interval was ten years and by 1970 five. Similarly, it is reckoned that more than 90 per cent of all the scientific knowledge possessed by Man today has accumulated since 1945. Thus well over 90 per cent of all articles in medical journals have been published since then.

Arguably, however, this acceleration cannot continue so very much longer. We move ever closer to the natural limits of significant knowledge in quite a number of fields; and also to the limits of human comprehension, computer-aided or otherwise.

Even so, we are bound to find it more and more difficult to keep pace with our own advances. Taking the Baconian axiom that knowledge itself is power, we are generating for ourselves as a world community a massive challenge in the harnessing and application of this general power. For the overriding need of Man today is to retain a commanding overview—to demonstrate, if you like, that both the pen and the spoken word can yet be mightier than the automated data bank.

The analysis which follows is one person's attempt to come to terms with this problem in the critical arena of international security affairs. Maybe the fact that the work in question has largely been carried out in Britain has been of singular advantage. For the British were, to a far greater extent than any other people, the founding fathers of the modern world. And lately their country has been, much more visibly than most, a case-study in the multiple crisis of adjustment this world is passing through.

As regards terminology, there is not a lot to say. The phrase "order of magnitude" is accorded its formal mathematical meaning, i.e. a close to tenfold change or difference. Also, a billion is taken throughout to be a thousand million (10^9) and a trillion a million million (10^{12}). In other words, French and American usage is followed as opposed to traditional British which would have them as 10^{12} and 10^{18} respectively.

Then again, because United Nations statistics are drawn on heavily, the tonnages cited are very generally metric, a metric ton being a little less than the customary British long ton and about 10 per cent more than the American short ton. A conversion to tons per year from barrels of petroleum per day is given as a footnote to Chapter 7(c).

Money values are nearly always given in United States dollars. In mid-September 1973 (which cannot be far from the median date for the fiscal data deployed herein) the exchange rate was 2·41 dollars to the pound. As we go to the press, the rate is 1·73 but climbing. In fact, of course, this rate has not always been an exact reflection of current comparative prices.

Warmest thanks are extended to the staff of the RUSI, particularly Miss Jenny Shaw who tackled with her usual felicity the arduous task of editing. Also to the three ladies who once again transposed my palaeographic longhand into elegant typescript: Ms Marjorie Davies, Jill Fowler and Joan Sweby. Also to three people, each of whom read the typescript from start to finish and made many sharp comments: Mr James Walsh, my father, and my wife, Yu-ying.

Nor would this study have been possible without the advice so abundantly accorded me by specialists in the various fields covered. They include permanent officials in Washington, London and Stockholm. They also include the following private persons: Michael Belton, David Chambers, Paule Chicken, Robin Curtis, Ken Davey, Sir Kingsley Dunham, Martin Easteal, Ian Fells, Sir Christopher Foxley-Norris, John Fremlin, Philip Hanson, Henry Maddick, Janet Marsh, Sir Claus Moser, David Pasteur, Henry Scott, David Shepperd and David Wightman. All gave of their expertise most generously and always without prejudice to whatever wider inferences might be drawn.

Accordingly, I would wish to absolve them even more explicitly than is normal in such circumstances from any responsibility for the synoptic appreciation made as a result of what has been, after all, a many-sided study. By the same token, this appreciation can in no wise be held to encapsulate any kind of collective RUSI viewpoint.

January 1977   *Neville Brown*

Part I

The Salient Issues

1

The Contemporary Global Turbulence

Fortunately, simple extrapolation of a pre-existing trend is a crude and unreliable technique for predicting the future. Were it not, one could hold out no prospect of effective disarmament or even arms control this side of the year 3000, let alone 1990.[1] Thus since 1945 there have been no multilateral agreements on disarmament. Furthermore, whilst progress on arms control may have appeared considerable during the second half of this period, it has been almost entirely cosmetic as opposed to substantial.

The first such cosmetic exercise was the Antarctic Treaty which came into force in 1961 and precluded the militarisation of this barren and inclement continent. Why should anybody wish to militarise it? Whatever kind of military facility is contemplated— submarine pens, nuclear test facilities, master radars, internment camps, staff colleges, . . . —the answer always is that it would be far cheaper and more convenient to build them elsewhere. In World War II the Germans put some weather stations in Greenland. Duly, the Allies sent small raiding parties against them. But the brave and resourceful men on each side often felt constrained from coming to mortal grips with one another because, in that awesome setting, internecine human conflict seemed almost trivial.[2] And Antarctica is every bit as grim as Greenland.

All that can really be said for this 1961 treaty is that it contains a provision precluding the use of the Antarctic as a dumping ground for nuclear waste. By the same token, the case in favour of the 1963 treaty banning nuclear tests either underwater or anywhere above the Earth's surface is almost entirely ecological. This Partial Test Ban has not prevented over 500 more nuclear tests being conducted. Nor has it stopped another two or three nations from joining the military "nuclear club" in the interim.

Then again, when commonsense tests of comparative cost are applied, the notion of military emplacements on the Moon fails by a

3

wide margin. Therefore, those provisions of the Outer Space Treaty of 1967 which prohibit the location on the Moon (or other celestial bodies) of any weapons of mass destruction were, in reality, otiose. Nor dare one be more positive about the parallel provisions which state that no such objects shall be placed in orbiting satellites, given that any such departure would exacerbate greatly the problem of command and control. Needless to say, too, similar caveats have to be entered against the 1971 treaty prohibiting the placing of nuclear weapons and other weapons of mass destruction "on the Sea-Bed and the Ocean Floor and in the Subsoil Thereof".

Two or three weeks after the initial signatures of the Outer Space Treaty came those of the Treaty of Tlatelolco, by which Latin America was to be kept a nuclear free zone. Yet, unlike the Non-Proliferation Treaty of the following year (the imperfections of which are outlined in Chapter 10), Tlatelolco did not forbid unequivocally the development of nuclear explosives by non-nuclear states, this being an option in which both Argentina and Brazil had become actively interested. Indeed, these two countries only signed the treaty on the understanding that they could develop and explode for peaceful purposes nuclear charges, including types well suited to use as warheads.

To dismiss without further ado the 1972 convention banning the development, production and stockpiling of bacteriological and toxic weapons would be too cavalier. Even so, this measure is not so big and firm a step forward as it looks at first sight. Thus, like several of the other agreements here noted, it has yet to be signed—let alone ratified—by quite a number of countries. In this case, the absentees early in 1976 included the following: Algeria, China, France, Israel, Libya, the Sudan and Uganda. Moreover, in this case, too, external monitoring is usually difficult.

Nor is it easy to be much more positive about the several bilateral arms control agreements between the USA and the USSR. Let us consider recent moves in the Strategic Arms Limitation Talks (SALT), by far and away the largest part of this particular dialogue. At their summit meeting in Vladivostok in November 1974, President Ford and Mr Brezhnev agreed that their negotiating teams should work out, if possible before the end of the following year, a new agreement to run from 1977 until the end of 1985. The nub of this SALT 2 was to be that each side would retain echelons of strategic missiles and of strategic bombers closely comparable to their existing forces. Since qualitative improvements were allowed for, however, this meant that the numbers of warheads deployed could rise quite considerably. Besides all of which, the negotiators are—as of January 1977—deadlocked on some key matters of implementation.

In the absence of effective disarmament and arms control, the world has been getting more heavily armed. Of this some indication is provided by the Stockholm studies of cumulative defence expenditures. These show annual world totals, in billions of United States dollars and at 1970 prices and exchange rates, as rising from *c.* 131 in 1960 to 212 in 1972 and 214 in 1975. For countries other than those in NATO and the Warsaw Pact, the rise was from 14 in 1960 to 40 in 1972 and 47 in 1975. For the Middle East, in particular, the trend was from one in 1960 to 5·4 in 1972 and 13 in 1975.[3]

Even at a purely econometric level, of course, such essays in comparison pose technical problems that are not entirely surmountable. Differential movements in exchange rates, salaries and prices are not at all easy to correct for, especially in an era of economic turbulence. Defence budgets are not all defined the same way, as witness the Soviet exclusion of a good deal of military-oriented research.

Nevertheless, the calculations here cited surely confirm an augmentation and diffusion of military strength between 1960 and 1972. Furthermore, the virtual levelling off in global budgetary outlays recorded between 1972 and 1975 is probably consonant with further advances in war-waging capability. True, some increase in real salaries has to be allowed for. On the other hand, even a steady or slowly shrinking expenditure on equipment items may mask a continual process of inventory expansion and modernisation. One current example is the constant growth in the strategic nuclear deterrents of the Superpowers. Another may be the spread of supersonic warplanes among the air arms of the newly developing world. In 1960 four of them operated such machines. Thirty-three did in 1972 and ten more by 1975.

What is more, there are strong indications that inhibitions about turning armed might to political advantage are once again on the wane. Needless to say, the conflicts in the Eastern Mediterranean are well to the fore in this perceived trend. In 1958, 1964 and 1967 pressure from the United States and Britain effectively dissuaded Turkey from landing troops on Cyprus. In 1974 it did not. In 1958 several hundred people were killed or injured in inter-sectarian strife in the Lebanon. Since 1975 several tens of thousands have been.

Then again, in 1967 President Nasser broke a solemn pledge he had given the Eisenhower administration ten years before not to evict United Nations troops from the Sinai. The ensuing war was wider than in 1956; and this time Israel struck unilaterally and, having succeeded, refused meekly to withdraw. Throughout the next six years the authority of the United Nations was flouted on all sides more often than could ever be listed, whilst acts of insurgent terror and other irregular operations were carried out far beyond the recognised zone of confrontation. In 1973 the Arabs pursued much bolder military, to say nothing of economic, strategies than ever before whilst Israel burst into Africa for the first time. In this context the Entebbe raid of 1976 appears almost as part and parcel of a grimly logical progression.

In like manner, India and Pakistan waged war in 1971 in a much more full-blooded fashion than in 1965. Indonesia took over Portuguese Timor in 1975 with less compunction than it had done Dutch New Guinea in 1962. The terror campaign launched by the IRA in Ulster in 1969 has proved to be quite the most ruthless Ireland has known since the birth pangs of the Irish Free State. The second Indo-China war was peculiarly horrendous in scale and character, the chief indicators being the rampant use of selective assassination by one side and the extravagant use of firepower by the other. Meanwhile, the widespread emergence of what threatened to become dispro-portionately effective cells of urban insurgency induced dozens of governments to resort the more freely to forceful interrogation and other illiberal techniques of internal security.

No doubt instances could be cited that lend themselves to a contrary inference. All the same, most of the comparisons indicated above are more or less of like with like. This being so, it is hard to avoid the conclusion that something of a cult of *force majeure* is once more gaining ground in world affairs, not least among smaller countries acting in single-minded advancement of highly specific interests. Precedent readily spawns precedent in this televisual age. Nobody any longer holds out the great hopes of the United Nations as peacekeeper which some entertained in the late 1950s and early 1960s. Increased social tensions also contribute to this trend and so does deepening moral confusion. The treacherous seizure by the Communists of Hue during the Tet truce in Vietnam in 1968 led to three times as many civilians being massacred as did the Nazi blitz against Guernica in 1937; and, in the case first mentioned, many of the victims were individually done to death with gratuitous sadism. Yet world anguish over this outrage against the ancient Annamese capital was not one ten thousandth of what the previous generation had felt apropos the virtual destruction of the Holy City of the Basques. Nor, for that matter, does anyone give a fig these days for formal declarations of war, a propriety that still mattered to some people in 1939. In certain respects, the modern world does have a remarkably strong moral conscience. Yet this can be curiously tentative and partial on the central issue of lethal violence.

What is more, it requires no great imagination to see how all this shades into a broader manifestation of diminishing moral restraint— the global crime wave. Not that the evidence on this score is at all easy to marshal systematically. Crime statistics remain notoriously unreliable for many territories, and for many others—notably those of the Communist world—are not released at all. Nor could the definitions of crime ever be standardised universally. Where, for example, does banditry end and insurgency begin?

Nor, in fact, does such analysis as can be carried out invariably endorse the depressing conclusion that the escalation is everywhere relentless. In many areas, the urban crime wave seems considerably worse than the rural. Yet even urban crime waves can be at least temporarily reversed, as notably happened with crimes of violence in Calcutta and in Washington, DC, in the early 1970s.

Inchoate though the total picture is, however, it does seem to reflect a more or less continuous rise in crime (not least violent crime) more or less world-wide and throughout the thermonuclear era. Sadly, too, this trend has not infrequently gone hand-in-hand with a widespread amelioration in what have classically been regarded as the underlying causes of crime: primary poverty, inequality, inadequate social services and so on. Sweden affords one clear example[4] and Britain another. Thus, having fallen by a gratifying 16 per cent in the period 1951 to 1955, recorded crime levels in England and Wales have risen so steadily ever since as to be today a good five times what they were in the depths of the inter-war slump. Neither does the combination of a marginal increase in population plus an apparently large rise in the reporting rates in some districts do so very much to modify the picture thus presented. Under such circumstances, no review of the prospects for world peace, least of all one that endeavours to be proscriptive in some measure, ought to ignore this almost incessant groundswell.

Of especial concern, of course, has been the pronounced upsurge of violence among young people, meaning the teenagers in particular. In the 1950s this was chiefly manifest in the general rise in aimless delinquency typified by the *halbstarken* in West Germany, the street gangs in New York and the *stilyaga* groups the Soviet authorities regularly condemned. A fresh dimension was added in the next decade with the use of muscle power—or worse—for the impatient pursuit of political ends, by no means least in those societies which had customarily been regarded as sufficiently open and democratic to avoid that sort of thing. More often than not, a significant proportion of the muscle flexers themselves were the New Left scions not of the poor but of the upper middle class. And with this phenomenon came a sharp recrudescence in literature and the visual arts of a cult of all the less licit and more egotistical forms of violence.

Among the ugliest manifestations of this trend, especially in the United States and Britain, has been the *kulturkampf* sporadically waged by certain of the more fascistic elements within the New Left to destroy, by muscular as well as vocal violence, the free speech not merely of those public figures it regards as racially prejudiced but even of those genetic scientists who place unusually heavy emphasis on innate factors (as opposed to environmental) as determinants of intelligence.

The chosen bone of contention has been the insistence of this school of thought on treating as a legitimate subject for discussion the observed differences in average Intelligence Quotient between various ethnic groups, even though—on any rational analysis—these findings do not really lend support to race discrimination. The repressive onslaughts against its freedom of expression are generally deemed to have been sparked off by an article published in the *Harvard Educational Review* in 1969 by Arthur Jensen, a mild-mannered professor at Berkeley. In the wake of its publication, he was subject to sustained harassment and intimidation as an alleged Hitlerian. William Shockley and H. J. Eysenck are among the other academic alumni who have regularly been pilloried on this score. Also, on supposedly related grounds, the great German animal ethologist, Konrad Lorenz.

Still, it would be grotesquely unjust to take the above as wholly characteristic of the youth revolt that upsurged so dramatically in the middle 1960s. Against it might be set, for example, the rather utopian but utterly fair-minded idealism of Amnesty International and the

Minority Rights Group, to cite two London-based groups that were not integral to the youth revolt but which certainly drew encouragement from it.

Yet it cannot be denied that eruptions of muscular and vocal intolerance of the kind described above have usually been facilitated by the dumb acquiescence of most of the vast peer group in question. Nor that this dumbness has itself been the product of the veritable kaleidoscope of self-contradictory and ill-assorted ideas and values into which emergent youth found itself being drawn: "global villages", "the theology of liberation", "repressive tolerance", dogmatic optimism, permissive conformism, acupuncture, drugged alienation, "situation ethics", affluent insurgency, "the medium as the message", progressive deschooling, libertarian Marxism, "love-ins", painless adventure, ego-trips to nowhere, muscular neutralism, charismatic terrorism, ... Ten years ago the permutations seemed endless and mostly bizarre.

Not that the chaos was ever as complete as it appeared. On the contrary, a substantial part of the above cacophony did achieve, however dubiously, a measure of political orchestration. It did so through the political emergence of the New Left.

One says "dubiously" because, diffuse and fissiparous though its leadership has always been, the warmed-over Marxism with which this purportedly forward-looking movement is informed has consistently, albeit unwittingly, recapitulated just about all the propositions Jean-Jacques Rousseau, an amoral egomaniac if ever there was one, incorporated into his anti-cosmopolitan and pre-Romantic political philosophy in the years leading up to the French Revolution of 1789. And it is, in fact, with the fall of the Bastille that July that Mankind enters the age of "total war": mass mobilisation, ideological commitment and global strategy.

Thus, the New Left would endorse to the hilt Rousseau's famous axiom that "Man is born free, and everywhere he is in chains". Also his hatred of such despotisms as have deep historical roots; his admiration of emotional commitment to organic nationalism; and his frequent manifestations of impatience with minority rights and individualistic liberalism, an impatience that led him on to proclaim that men must "be forced to be free".

All the same, the key to the parallel here being drawn lies in the similarity between Rousseau's abstract notion of the "general will" and the New Left's unswerving conviction that they know better than ordinary mortals what ordinary mortals really want. Every member of the community is required by Rousseau to surrender himself utterly to this general will. Yet he gives us few clues to its identity save that it is "always constant, unalterable and pure"! Disturbing though the thought would be to both Rousseau and the New Left, in the above can be seen the conceptual tap-root of the xenophobic totalitarianism of Robespierre, Hitler and Stalin. This is because it enables such men to claim that they, and they alone, personify the general will. As the late Carl Gustav Jung had a fictional yet archetypal radical say, "Starting from unlimited freedom, I arrive at unlimited despotism". It is a culmination which can clearly be seen in miniature in the fascisto-Marxist cast of mind possessed by those who harass Jensen and his colleagues.

Whether on balance it be judged harmful or beneficent, however, the youth revolt was not the only dimension in the mounting turbulence in human affairs so evident by the end of the 1960s. Another was the way in which inflation had started to accelerate well before the sharp increases in oil prices at the close of 1973.

As much can be gauged from a UN consumer price index in which the 1970 average is taken as a 100. The median annual figure for Australia rose from 91 in 1967 to 123 in 1973. In other words, a nine point increase in 1967 to 1970 was followed by a 23 point one in the next three year period. Meanwhile, the Federal German rise was from 93 to 119; the French from 85 to 120; the British from 85 to 128; and the Japanese from 84 to 124. The Israeli acceleration was relatively steep, from 90 to 152 whilst that of the United States was only moderate.[5] As the above record more or less confirms, Federal Germany's will to curb inflation is exceptionally deeply ingrained. Yet only a few years before, the eight per cent annual rate being registered there by the summer of 1973 would have been considered uncomfortably high, at least by any country in the OECD zone.[6]

In modern times, academics have been prone to neglect the border zones between politics and sociology on the one hand and economics on the other. This being so, the exact linkages between socio-political causes and economic effects generally remain indeterminate. Nevertheless, many people have sensed that the quickening of price rises in the recent past owed quite a lot to a more rapid loosening of social cohesion as a whole. The fact that countries like Israel or Japan, which are not normally seen as deficient in social solidarity, have suffered in this regard as much as most does not disprove the point as here made. It merely shows that a total explanation would need to adduce other considerations as well.

Certainly, no one could deny that, during the decade prior to the Yom Kippur war, the industrial labour force became more restive more or less throughout the West, the most concrete manifestation being the spread of industrial action. Comparing 1969–73 with 1964–68, we find that in virtually every Western country save the Irish Republic there was a rise in the average number of working days thereby lost per year and per 1,000 employees, according to figures released by the International Labour Office. True, the calculation for both Sweden and West Germany remained below 100 and for France (1968 excepted), Holland and Japan below 300. But Britain and Australia rose to c. 1,000 from c. 225 and c. 400 respectively. The USA's rise was from just over 1,100 to just under 1,400 and Canada's from 1,150 to 1,700. Worst was the Italian increase, from 1,000 to 2,200.[7]

Closely related to this trend was a more marked concentration of militancy at local or shop-floor level. Thus in 1969, for the first time since the war, wildcat strikes became widespread in the Federal German Republic as workers defied management and even their own unions in a bid to win their share from an unexpected economic boom.[8]

Subject to the usual caveat about the pattern being by no means identical from country to country, one could also see certain aspirations being aired much more generally than hitherto. The humanisation of the working environment was one. More consultation by management was another. A devolution of trade union power towards the shop-floor was a third. In some cases, too, a disposition to use industrial action to further wider political objectives became more evident.

But all this did not mean that the union activists were losing interest in what had traditionally been their prime concerns: real wages and occupational status. On the contrary, there were signs that a new generation of trade union leaders—at once more intellectual and more aggressive—would weld the old and the new themes together to produce a synthesis for radical social challenge.

Robert J. Hawke, the thrusting ex-Rhodes Scholar who was elected president of the Australian Council of Trade Unions in 1969, could be taken as a harbinger in this respect. For, at least at the outset, he strongly insisted that his trade union movement had a right to use industrial action to influence national policies in general. A collateral trend has been the growing contact between the Communist-controlled and non-Communist trade unions in Western Europe.

Still, the more extreme manifestations of industrial militancy are never guaranteed a swelling chorus of popular approval. On the contrary, both they and sustained campus radicalism are always liable soon to invoke countervailing pressures from a "great silent majority" apprehensive about the undermining of legitimate authority. Furthermore, there has been a certain amount of evidence from national hustings these last few years of this backlash effect. Perhaps the clearest was the general election held in France several weeks after the grand confrontation, in the factories and on the campuses, of May 1968. The maintenance of civil order became the central campaign issue, and the result was a decisive swing to the Right.

Whatever the mechanics of a particular situation, however, the tendencies just examined should be regarded as part of something much more diverse and universal. This is what the late Adlai Stevenson identified as "the revolution of rising expectations".

The first point to make about this revolution is that it is social or cultural as opposed to straight economic. The distinction is important because the economists are prone to focus on the pressure put on goods and services by the growth in what they call "effective demand" —i.e. spending power or, if you like, disposable income. In the short-term, the problem these days is indeed largely one of ensuring that disposable income does not run too far ahead of the output of goods and services. But in the longer-term, the problem is one of ensuring that disposable income manages to keep abreast of rising expectations. Whilst the former is essentially an economic matter, the latter is sociological.

Not that we have to assume that material expectations are some-how predestined to rise indefinitely and everywhere. The attitudes and policies of national elites—and especially the political leadership—always have some bearing on the situation. Then again, in nearly all the advanced democracies the incidence of industrial militancy (strikes and large pay claims) diminished during 1974 and 1975. It was as though, as it dawned on people that—because of the energy crisis—material advance might henceforward be harder to sustain, they *ipso facto* became less concerned about it. Then again, another strong thrust beneath the youth revolt which welled up in the 1960s was the counter-culture: the search for "an alternative society" in which the quest for personal fulfilment remained vigorous but in which the accent had shifted away from material goods and duly costed services produced in ever-greater abundance by large-scale technology and scientific management. Though this counter-culture has always been especially in evidence in certain of the more *avant-garde* localities in the United States, it has ramified and does concern itself with limiting the demands made by Man on a strictly finite Spaceship Earth.

Yet each and every one of the aforesaid influences may prove to be only local or minor modulations of the basic theme which is rising material expectations. Thus these last 12 months Britain has often been cited as a model of wage restraint in the face of national economic adversity. Yet no one can tell how far this moderation is due to anticipation of the material benefits of one very special factor—to whit, North Sea oil. Nor can anyone be quite certain at this stage that it will not, in any case, collapse in a wages and salaries explosion well before this "black gold" comes fully on stream. Nor should anyone forget that, in the months before the current incomes policy was imposed, industrial peace was being maintained only by the repeated concession of truly massive wage increases.

Nor does the anti-materialism of the counter-culture seem set to make any very deep and lasting impression anywhere. The movement in question has lately been on the wane; and it has always owed much to the kind of affluent romanticism typified by the "Sunset Strip" in California. In addition, its declared ideology has been, thus far at any rate, every bit as shallow and confused as that of its cousin, the New Left. It can well be argued, for example, that the creation of an infrastructure suitable for the alternative society it dreams of would require programmes of capital reconstruction so vast and complex as to necessitate innumerable technological breakthroughs and the most comprehensive bureaucratic control. So much for its rejection of materialistic managerialism.

Besides which, all across the newly developing world[9] the revolution of rising expectations has acquired far too strong a momentum to be much retarded by influences such as the above. The cardinal explanations are almost painfully simple. To live longer and in better health is self-evidently good. So are most of the basic welfare advantages of life in the affluent West.

What is more, the impact made by this ineluctable truth is constantly being reinforced by another. This is that the real income gap between the poorer peoples and the affluent West is already so wide that it is set to widen more and more in absolute terms. Granted, precise comparisons between expenditure patterns as contrasting as those of, say, Sweden and India are inherently impossible. Nevertheless, it would not be far wrong to say that a per capita rise in Swedish real income of, let us say, two per cent would be equivalent volumetrically to one of the order of 75 per cent in the case of India.

Fairly enough, some stress that a peasant in the Punjab usually does not relate his consumption norms to those obtaining in Stockholm. His concern is with the income difference between himself and his parents or elder brother. Inevitably, however, the urban implosion discussed in Chapter 6 will bring ever greater numbers of ordinary people in Afro-Asia and Latin America into more direct contact with what will be, in fact, a rosy-coloured version of Western affluence; and this at the same time as it deprives them of the customary compensations of village life.

Then there is the prospective use of satellites in orbit as relay points for regular sound and televisual broadcasts to all parts of the world. Already a televisual signal sent via a satellite might be received on an antenna perhaps five feet in diameter; and such an antenna, plus a requisite frequency converter, could probably be mass produced for installation on domestic TV receivers for about $200 apiece. What is more, eventually—maybe by 1990—such sets should be able to pick up these transmissions without the adaptation just described. Under these circumstances, it may no longer be possible for any territory to insulate itself from the big wide world. In the meantime, international civil aviation is virtually certain to expand constantly in spite of the high fuel costs now obtaining.[10]

Among the many countries with at least one TV set per 50 inhabitants by the early 1970s were Mauritius, El Salvador and Jordan. Thus we could well find, much to our embarrassment, that those very countries and communities in which deprivation is exceptionally deep-seated may be peculiarly prone to sample the good life in this vicarious manner. In many cases, too, they are likely to prove in the 1980s prime growth areas for the international tourist trade; and that is a renowned medium of cultural change, especially among the host peoples. For all these various reasons, nobody who is prepared to exercise themselves about world security in the 1980s or beyond can afford to ignore the revolution of rising expectations. Nor the economic circumstances that will shape our response to it.

Notes

1. Arms control does not embrace force reductions as such: its concern is with instituting checks on further numerical expansion, technical development, or tactical deployment.

2. Colonel Bernt Balchen, *War Below Zero*, Houghton Mifflin, Boston 1944 and Douglas Liversidge, *The Third Front*, Souvenir Press, London 1960.

3. *SIPRI Yearbook 1976*, Almqvist and Wiksell, Stockholm 1976. Table 6A, 1. SIPRI is the Stockholm International Peace Research Institute.

4. See Chapter 3.

5. *UN Monthly Bulletin of Statistics*, Vol. XXVIII No. 11, November 1974, Table 60.

6. OECD stands for Organisation for Economic Cooperation and Development. This consultative consortium of states was formed in 1961 out of the old Organisation of European Economic Cooperation of Marshall Plan days. But it now includes among its full members Australia, Finland, Japan and New Zealand.

7. *The Economist*, 4 January 1975.

8. Eric Jacobs, *European Trade Unionism*, Croom Helm, London 1973, p. 160.

9. Throughout this analysis the term "newly developing" is preferred to "underdeveloped" precisely because it conveys a sense of dynamic change.

10. See Chapter 26.

2

New Parameters for Strategy

Historically the British school of strategy placed comparatively little emphasis on the security implications of economic and social change. Agreed, the evolution of the empire was guided in some measure by a need to safeguard commerce and to secure access to such materials as cotton, gold and oil. True also that, in neither of the two world wars which dominated the first half of this century, was the United Kingdom slow to perceive the counter-economic potentialities of naval blockade and strategic bombing. Even so, the United Kingdom has never been imbued with a sense of war as a continuation of politics (and vice versa) at all akin to that which has informed successive despotisms in continental Europe.

For one thing, the Pacification of the Highlands and the recurrent miseries of Ireland apart, the British Isles themselves have been remarkably free, for centuries past, from social unrest of such a scale and character as to pose an internal security problem. Their insularity has enabled them to enjoy relative immunity from outside interference of the kind which, especially during times of rapid change, may all too easily precipitate within a national society a vicious polarisation of basic attitudes.

Thus not even during the political-cum-religious civil war between Cavaliers and Roundheads during the 1640s, did England experience anything remotely approaching the horror of the Thirty Years' War in Germany or the earlier religious strife in the Low Countries and France. Moreover, as religious struggles gave way to secular, this habit of restraint survived. The General Strike of 1926 petered out almost as soon as it had begun. In the 1930s the Fascists never became the force internally they did in many parts of the continent. Nor in the 1940s did the Communists. The campus revolt of recent years at no time reached a pitch comparable to some attained elsewhere. Even the British Empire waxed and waned with far less upheaval than its scale and diversity might have led one to expect. Small wonder that even such 20th century prophets as B. H. Liddell-Hart and J. F. C. Fuller have tended to see strategy very predominantly in military operational terms.[1]

Singular though its experience may have been, however, it is not just in Britain that the socio-economic dimension to strategy has been played down unduly. Modern strategic science evolved as a distinct academic discipline principally in order to assist those who operate in the defence and diplomatic fields. As a result, it has usually been rather too preoccupied, throughout the Western world, with deterrence and with military and political crises.

A high-profile illustration of the imbalances thus occasioned is inadvertently afforded us by the Indian subcontinent. Strategic analysts have often weighed the likely consequences of India's armed forces acquiring "the Bomb". Yet rarely do they reflect on the possibly far-reaching strategic reverberations of it experiencing one or more of these developmental setbacks: an acute economic crisis; the breaking away of one or more states or regions; an administrative collapse in Calcutta or some other urban centre.

Nor again do strategists qua strategists look much at economic and social change in, say, Tibet, Nepal, Sikkim, Bhutan and Nagaland—change that cumulatively could make the Himalayas much less of a barrier-line than they have been historically. Nor, indeed, did any contemplate in advance, or even much in retrospect, the geopolitical ramifications of the secession of the eastern wing of Pakistan. Nor are they now much exercised about the future internal stability of either the residual Pakistan or Bangladesh.

To my mind, a striking particular example of this uneven vision was furnished by the closure of the Suez Canal from 1967 to 1975. Although this situation put a grave incremental strain on the always fragile economies of countries like Pakistan and India, there was a disposition to discuss its strategic implications exclusively in terms of the way in which it inhibited the movement of Soviet warships and supply vessels between the Mediterranean and the Indian Ocean. No matter that when you have a navy as superfluously large in relation to legitimate requirements as do the Russians, a bit of extra steaming time can, more often than not, be something of an attraction!

Then again, a similar dichotomy to the one here identified has lately been prevalent in popular discussion of global affairs. Not infrequently, one has heard it said that, whereas in the 1950s the prime threat to Mankind came from the nuclear bomb, in the 1970s and beyond it will come from the population explosion.

Surely, however, only a little reflection is required to perceive that each is but a facet of the general problem of international violence. A nuclear war could yet turn out to be the process whereby the human race, or some large portion of it, effects a "population crash" comparable to the ones which, according to the zoologists, have occasionally terminated phases of rapid growth in other branches of the animal kingdom.

Not that one ought to give even oblique endorsement to lurid apprehensions, derived from more traumatic aspects of our remoter past, of embattled hordes desperate for more territory and with nothing to lose but their nuclear warheads. The truth of the matter is that, at least since the frontiers of the great European expansion finally closed around the world, instances of ineluctable competition for "living space" as a root cause of war have been few and far between. Thus the *lebensraum* theories formulated by certain fascist regimes before World War II were altogether too weak on empirical evaluation, logical analysis and even internal consistency to appear as much other than deliberate exercises in anti-intellectualism.

Imperial Japan serves as perhaps the most damning refutation of the "living space" hypothesis. From 1885 emigration had been systematically encouraged by the authorities after having been banned for several centuries to preserve cultural purity. In 1895 Taiwan and Korea had been acquired by force. Between 1931 and 1933 the vast, underpopulated and potentially rich territory of Manchuria was forcibly turned into the puppet state of Manchukuo. And in 1933 the total emigration to there from the home islands reached what was to prove its peak for one year of 27,000, even this modest figure being registered only through the push of a persistent depression at home and the pull of semi-mystical notions about the "open spaces of North Manchuria".

By 1941 the total number of Japanese living anywhere abroad had grown to a mere 3,000,000; and only 60 per cent of these were in Taiwan, Korea and Manchukuo, the rest being mainly in the Western Hemisphere. On the other hand, the population of the Japanese home islands had risen from c. 30,000,000 in 1885 to 50,000,000 in 1920 and 73,000,000 in 1941, this mounting pressure on living space being accepted or even—as in Fascist Italy and Nazi Germany—encouraged by successive governments. In the very year the Pearl Harbor strike was launched the Tojo administration introduced specific measures to promote large families.

In other words, demographic factors made only an indirect and decidedly ambiguous contribution to Japanese expansion. By the same token, we would do well to view with scepticism all the recent pronouncements to the effect that the crude menace of demographic overspill from China is impelling the USSR towards genuine *détente* in Europe.[2] Shades here of the "Yellow Peril" that so obsessed Kaiser Wilhelm and others at the time of the Boxer Rising.

Still, none of this proves that Dean Rusk was entirely wrong to warn us in 1968 that land hunger might be a direct and repeated source of strife by the 1980s were the population explosion to slide out of control in the interim.[3] Even this last 20 years or so, it has been possible to identify conflicts to which this factor has made a substantial contribution. Thus the fierce border clashes (known as "the football war") associated with the infiltration into Honduras in 1969 of 250,000 people from a desperately overcrowded El Salvador (450 per square mile: 1972) was an exceptionally clear-cut instance in Latin America. Extensive emigration by the Ibos from their badly congested heartland in the Eastern Region of Nigeria set the scene for the communal tensions which culminated in the Nigerian civil war of 1967–70. Palestinian insistence on a "right of return" has long been a central feature of the Arab–Israel conflict. Overcrowding of the tribal reserves is one determinant of the South African situation. The periodic armed strife within Sukarno's Indonesia evidently owed much to demographic imbalance: the twin islands of Java and Madura embrace but seven per cent of the land area of that vast archipelago yet had, according to the 1962 Census, about two-thirds of the population.[4]

Closely analogous to seeking population outlets is the desire to command sources of food and raw materials. Throughout the Age of Mercantilism in the 17th and 18th centuries, the struggle to achieve this via annexation or in some other hard-and-fast way was a recurrent *casus belli*. On various subsequent occasions, not least during World War II, the same concern has led to the further extension of armed conflict.

Undoubtedly, the securing of oil supplies was a principal aim of the Suez expedition of 1956. Five years later British forces deployed to Kuwait in moderate strength after a claim by General Kassem that this fabulously oil-rich sheikhdom really belonged to Iraq. Three times in the last 20 years the Royal Navy and the Icelandic coastguard service have been locked in dour, albeit non-lethal, confrontations over fishing rights. At least a *prima facie* case can be made for saying that gaining access to readily workable uranium ores plus certain other material sources, was a prime motive behind Soviet imperialism in Eastern Europe from 1944 onwards. Tin and rubber accentuated the importance, as perceived on each side, of the campaign against insurgent terrorism in Malaya from 1948 onwards. The attempted secessions of Katanga in the Congo and later of "Biafra" in Nigeria were made at once more feasible and less acceptable by their reserves of non-ferrous ores and oil respectively.

Considered overall, however, the wish physically to ensure the continued availability of primary products seems not to have been a dominant cause of armed conflict in the nuclear era as yet. On the other hand, some of the bellicose talk engendered by the sudden 1973 energy crisis did sound ominous. Enough so to make one think that the battles shortly afterwards between China and South Vietnam for control of the Paracel Islands, and hence of whatever oil deposits may lie off their shores, heralded a new and even more savage mercantilist era.

Still, the full emergence of such a pattern would itself be confirmation that the breakdown of world civilisation was already far advanced. More immediately significant is the general propensity of governments that feel insecure on the domestic front, perhaps because of sustained but lop-sided development or maybe economic recession, to "export their tensions" via aggressiveness towards outsiders. An example often singled out is the way in which, during the Sukarno era, the tensions within Indonesia found expression in external as well as internal conflict, the two examples being the absorption of West Irian and the ill-starred attempt to "crush Malaysia". Another instance may be Ho Chi Minh's explicit underwriting of the Viet Cong's campaign from 1960 onwards.[5]

The struggle against Israel has repeatedly been used, obliquely or otherwise, to justify authoritarian measures within Egypt, Syria and—in a more hesitant fashion—Jordan. Conversely, many Zionists freely acknowledge that Israel's constant encompassment by well-armed foes helps keep her national solidarity and dynamism at high levels and, in addition, permits the indefinite postponement of some awkward questions about ultimate identity. Above all, the propensity of the Soviet Union to externalise its contradictions may become more pronounced as the 1980s progress.[6]

In a speech delivered in Montreal in May 1966, Robert McNamara, one of the few public figures who has regularly attempted to bridge the gap between development studies and strategic studies alluded to above, examined the general correlation between average living standards and the incidence of organised violence. He said that 32 of the 38 states listed by the World Bank as "very poor" (i.e. average annual incomes then below $100) had "suffered significant conflict" since 1958. So had 69 per cent of the poor nations and 48 per cent of those with middle incomes. Yet of the 27 nations designated as rich (i.e. at least $750 per capita per annum), only one had experienced major internal upheaval.[7]

One does not have to share what is at times an overweening faith in quantification on Mr McNamara's part to be disturbed by his analysis. Nor does one have to accept, any more than he would himself, income per head as the sole yardstick of development or even as the most reliable one in every single case.

Nor, indeed, should the argument that economic and social change is relevant to modern strategy be construed to read that it, and it alone, is the very bedrock of it. The shifting military balance is usually at least as fundamental in a given situation. Historically, countless societies have been vanquished on the field of battle by protagonists no more populous than themselves and conspicuously less advanced in terms of social philosophy and material well-being. Not infrequently, of course, the sheer envy of the less advanced has been a cardinal predatory motive.

Today the correspondence between overall development and a capability against armed attack from without is approximate, to put it mildly. Furthermore, even vulnerability to insurgency is by no means just a function of imbalances in economic, social or political development—a simple but necessary thought to which we must return in Chapter 12.

In order to appreciate just how multifarious the cause-and-effect interplay between economic and military circumstances can be in a backward territory caught up in global turmoil, it may be useful to revert to the Indian subcontinent and take a particular look at Bengal, starting with the Japanese occupation of nearby Burma in 1942. For this so badly disorganised the regional rice market that, when climatic adversity struck the following year, 1,500,000 Bengalis died in India's first famine for more than three decades. Hoarding and other patterns of maldistribution contributed materially to this outcome. But these in their turn were largely due to the extent to which both the civil administration and the railway system were tied down by the continuing war effort.[8] Mercifully, the failure of the

Imperial Japanese Army's offensive towards Imphal in 1944 precluded Tokyo's unleashing, in the aftermath of the famine, the strong streak of violence long evident in radical Bengali nationalism.

Tensions between the Hindu and Moslem communities in Bengal were a factor in the decision to partition the subcontinent on its accession to independence in 1947, a partitioning in which East Bengal became East Pakistan. Four thousand people had died in Calcutta alone in August 1946 in riots blatantly encouraged by the local Moslem League leaders; and serious communal disturbances were to recur in both parts of rural Bengal in 1949 and again in 1950. In the meantime, the two wings of Pakistan showed no sign of generating a sense of common identity. Instead, resentment smouldered. One result was to stultify what could have been an important experiment by President Ayub Khan in a kind of pyramidal guided democracy. Another was to compromise considerably the link-pin role of Pakistan in the cordon of interlocking alliances that John Foster Dulles forged in the 1950s for the containment of Russia and China.

Then, in 1970, the interaction between economic and political instability reached danger point. A freakish and horrendous cyclone smote the ill-protected delta lands of the Ganges–Brahmaputra confluence, killing hundreds of thousands outright and ruining much invaluable land; and, as a direct consequence, the crisis of political confidence between East and West Pakistan deepened.

Things finally erupted in 1971 as military rule overseen from a full 1,000 miles away in Rawalpindi became desperate and hence repressive, thereby obliging several million East Pakistanis to take refuge across the Indian border. That December the scenario became one of full-scale hostilities between the Indian and Pakistani armed forces, the swift upshot being the secession of East Pakistan to become Bangladesh. But possessed of an economy that would have been over-stretched at the best of times and which was now debilitated by the ravages of war and also by a drought which was to kill another half million, the new state sank into a morass of corruption and political violence. Meanwhile, extrapolation of the growth rate of the Bangladeshi population suggested that, by the end of the century, it could more than double to reach 165 million—i.e. 3,000 per square mile, or five per acre! Alas, the spectre of the gruesome Malthusian checks (war, disease and so on) drew yet closer when a further 300,000 died of malnutrition brought on by the severe floods of 1974.

Little wonder that by then the very name Bangladesh had become a by-word for destitution and hopelessness. Nor that August 1975 witnessed a take-over by exasperated though confused army officers. Since then, this new regime has quarrelled bitterly with New Delhi over the extremely delicate though crucial question of flood control in the delta lands; and it has been seeking to rebuild, on a piecemeal basis, its pan-Islamic links with Rawalpindi. Throughout this continuing sequence of dramas, the interaction between economics, sociology, politics, internal security and grand strategy has been diverse and interminable.

Mercifully, the same cannot really be said of the North Atlantic region, at any rate not since the rise and fall of Hitler. The shadow of primary poverty has everywhere been receding. For this and other reasons, factional confrontations, whether communal or otherwise, have generally been less sharply delineated and therefore not so bitter and persistent. Above all, collective security geared to nuclear deterrence has, as a rule, virtually precluded the USSR or any other state from exploiting domestic weakness by direct intervention. You could say, in fact, that the nuclear bomb has done for Western Europe since 1945 what the Straits of Dover did for England across nearly 1,000 years. It has cut to a minimum the scope either for outright aggression or for polarising interference.

Still, it might be extremely foolish, for a whole complex of reasons, to assume that so blessed a situation is going to hold good all through the 1980s. If so, we would do well to study the recent fortunes of those parliamentary democracies that already stand very exposed to various forms of armed violence applied by or through neighbouring states less free and affluent than themselves.

Israel is the example that comes most readily to mind; and, as this study will more than once insist, its salient position is indeed very critical, not just in its own terms but for the Western world as a whole. At the same time, however, this position is decidedly singular. Its landward limits are, to quite an exceptional extent, lines of separation rather than contact. Yet within those *de facto* borders relatively large Arab populations live under occupation.

This being so, it may be more broadly relevant to look at Singapore, a bustling city-state that still looks set to emerge as a node of Asian affluence as the 1980s progress. At the same time as he is masterminding an economic drive, however, Prime Minister Lee Kuan Yew is ever more firmly imposing the national mould of cultural conformism he extols as the "rugged society".

Undoubtedly, this imposition has some positive connotations for the common weal. But neither could anybody deny that it involves much restrictive manipulation of the press and other means of expression. Hence the retention by Lee's People's Action Party of all the 65 seats in parliament.

Some of his more acid critics would say that Lee Kuan Yew discarded a pristine zeal for pure democracy a bit too easily as he himself drew near the premiership.[9] Another ingenious hypothesis is that this brilliant product of Cambridge imbibed whilst there rather too much of its traditional Platonism. But surely the most essential point is that Lee's struggle to keep his island the calm epicentre of the South-East Asian cyclone was bound to be a desperate one these last 15 years or so.

After all, most of his critics care not to recall how serious were the stresses caused throughout the incipient Federation of Malaysia, of which Singapore was a founder member, by the violent *konfrontasi* waged by Sukarno of Indonesia between 1963 and 1966. Nor that hundreds were killed or wounded on Singapore island in inter-communal riots (probably encouraged from without) in 1964. Nor that, throughout the late 1960s, Lee warned repeatedly, albeit vainly, against Western attitudes towards South-East Asian security oscillating too violently. In short, the Singaporean experience should be seen in all humility as a classic study of the difficulties inherent in trying to preserve even a tolerably open polity when one is set amidst a much more extensive and populous zone in which confusion, frustration and envy are endemic. As such it appears as something of a microcosm of the situation the Western world as a whole could face if the 1980s were to go thoroughly sour.

But to argue thus, and to refer specifically to territories as far-flung as Bangladesh and Singapore, is to suggest another vital characteristic in any Grand Strategy for the future. This is that be it conceived in global terms. On first examination, of course, this proposition is so axiomatic as to be positively banal. Even in the 1930s international tension and violence proved liable to switch from the Far East to Europe and back again with horrifying ease. Since then the world has shrunk a good deal and, by 1990, will have done so further. Already we must surely be at a stage in which virtually every point on Earth is of some strategic importance to virtually every other, Antarctica perhaps excepted.

Political terror is one phenomenon that has come repeatedly to transcend physical and legal boundaries and, in so doing, to bridge great distances: Israel alone has been under terrorist attack in locations as far apart as Bangkok, Entebbe and Washington. Much macabre credit is due to the transformation in global communications effected by air travel and by television. Also perhaps to the near uniqueness of the terrorist mentality with its curiously egocentric altruism, rationalised and reinforced by fascist or fascisto-Marxist ideology. Being each a member of so exclusive a genre, both politically and psychologically, the activists are impelled to seek one another out in all four corners.

But the obverse side of this coin is that virtually all governments everywhere have at least a *prima facie* interest in limiting the incidence of terrorism everywhere else. Thus the cooperation even of countries like Cuba was obtained in curbing the wave of aerial hijacking that suddenly erupted world-wide in the wake of the Middle East war of 1967. According to the International Institute for Strategic Studies, there were 29 attempted hijacks in 1974, eight of them successful, as against 82 in the peak year of 1969 of which 70 were pulled off. In the absence of a measure of international collaboration on such matters, the customarily "open societies" of the West might be obliged, on this account alone, to limit freedom and invade privacy much more extensively than now.

In like manner, the evolving global framework of multilateral nuclear deterrence is intermeshed quite closely. Policy changes by the USA could affect the nuclear postures of India and Japan, and hence of China, and so of Russia, and thereby of the USA itself! Correspondingly, the freedom of navigation on the High Seas may not be preserved indefinitely unless dozens of states will that it should be.

Then again, there has been a tendency historically for the embroilment of one or more Great Powers in a localised conflict situation to affect profoundly their respective postures across the world at large. An especially direct connection occurs when such a state retaliates forcefully in some distant theatre for a particular adversary initiative it finds intolerable yet is unable to cope with on the spot. Thankfully, this geostrategic gambit (which might best be entitled Limited World War) can be quite heavily discounted in 1977. But it has been apparent in the recent past and might all too readily become so again (see Chapter 21).

To all of which should be added various problems that are hardly encompassed by Grand Strategy as such but which do impact on the closely associated themes of law and order within states and intercourse between them. Big crime syndicates often ramify as extensively as do the networks of political terror. Curtailing the heroin culture in the West is deemed to depend heavily on the cooperation of the distant lands in which the opium is grown. Some aspects of atmospheric pollution are best tackled on the global plane. By 1990 the pollution of the major oceans may be a burgeoning issue in diplomacy.

Even so, it may be far from easy to insist throughout what could be the increasingly stressful decade or so ahead that peace is indivisible. For one thing, the statement as made is not absolutely true. Thus that arbitrary occupation, in 1975, by Indonesia of Portuguese Timor did not exercise the world at large anything like as much as would a Soviet invasion of Finnmark. Nor should it have done.

For another, even though the proposition in question may be essentially true, it is unlikely to be steadily perceived as such by popular or even elite opinion. At the best of times, those who rule democracies tend to be considerably reluctant to involve themselves in the security affairs of, to paraphrase Neville Chamberlain in 1938, some faraway country of which they know nothing. Furthermore, in the aftermath of Vietnam and certain other disillusioning and well-televised episodes, a bitter reaction against "globalism" has lately taken place almost throughout the West, not least among articulate youth. Likewise, during the 1980s anxiety about internal stress coupled with disappointment with the situation of the newly developing world (again oft-dramatised on television) could easily induce a profound syndrome of introspection and retrenchment.

How alluring and yet misguided responses of this sort may be can be seen by brief reference to the well-known study William and Paul Paddock wrote a decade ago, just at the start of the current swing against "globalism". Apprehending the advent by 1975 of an era of major and repeated famines, the authors enunciated a strategy of "triage" for the distribution of, in particular, American food aid. What this entailed was the division of the newly developing world into three classes of country on the basis of the relative Malthusian pressures and the responses being evoked. The first was comprised of those states (e.g. Egypt, Haiti and India) adjudged beyond redemption already. The second included those (e.g. Pakistan and Tunisia) thought able to survive provided they receive enough aid. Lastly, some (e.g. Libya) were deemed set to make headway irrespective of aid.

Needless to say, the Paddock brothers duly advocated a concentration of aid on the intermediate grouping.[10] Yet just a few years later this simple division of the world into the damned and the saved or savable seems wrong-headed on at least four counts. Probably we now attach more importance to the world economic order as a determinant of the fortunes of individual states. This apart, we are less certain than we were before what the best indicators of economic prospects are. In so far as we are sure, we would now be unlikely to single out Egypt and India as beyond economic redemption. Parallel objections could, of course, be raised to similarly rigid parcellations in the political and military spheres.

Limited though its notion of strategy may have been in other ways, the basic precept that strategy must be global to be effective can fairly be identified as the *sine qua non* of the United Kingdom's traditional approach. After all, it is well over two centuries since a Prime Minister in London averred that Canada could be won on the plains of Germany. One would like to think, too, that another respect in which Britain may still be equipped to set something of an example within the Western Alliance is in the steady maintenance of a broad political consensus apropos key external policies. Certainly, its time-honoured preference for evolution rather than revolution and for pragmatism rather than dogma would seem to favour this.

At all events, a large measure of consensus, on all questions appertaining to international security, will be desirable both within and between the member states of the Western Alliance. One object is simply to preclude a migration to the extremes of Left and Right, extremes which often share (as Eysenck argued many years ago) a temperamental proclivity towards autocratic close-mindedness. Another is to minimise the risk of paralysing conflicts of aim and purpose in times of international crisis. A third is to bring to bear on the formulation of Grand Strategy a far wider range of talents and perceptions than is available when that strategy remains some kind of factional preserve. There may not be a need for grander coalitions but there is for more extensive dialogue.

Here a cardinal consideration is that, thanks to the extraordinary fluidity of the social and cultural scene in modern times, the old dichotomy between Right and Left has often seemed less meaningful than before, not least in regard to matters that have implications for peace and stability. Among the major issues which have cut sharply across the Right–Left divide in recent years in Britain, for instance, are the following: membership of the Common Market, devolution for Scotland and Wales, a statutory prices and incomes policy, a military presence East of Suez, the Arab–Israel dispute, Vietnam and capital punishment. An associated phenomenon, in Britain and several other Western countries, is the emergence or resurgence of middle-of-the-road third force parties.

Still, the fact remains that the electorates of the parliamentary democracies, young no less than old, continue overwhelmingly to classify their own political options in Left-versus-Right terms. For good or ill as each citizen conceives it, the former continues to be more closely identified with public ownership, welfare provision, egalitarian wealth distribution and educational reform, civil public expenditure, regional economic planning, worker's participation, tough legislation against sex- or race-discrimination, a liberal penal code in other respects, foreign economic aid and anxieties about nuclear deterrence. Nor would it be wise to assume that we have heard the last of the old understanding that social democrats are more likely than conservatives to tolerate inflation in a quest for fuller employment. To all of which most observers would certainly add that the latter have a deeply ingrained scepticism about the prospects for any very rapid and sustained improvement in international morality; and this leads them never to doubt that Defence is always something to take very seriously.

One essential point is that a Grand Strategy sufficiently comprehensive to cope with what may well be the uniquely grave challenge of the 1980s needs elements from both sets of attitudes. Another is that any such strategy needs to be rooted in a shared conviction that constitutional democracy based on personal liberty is a superior form of government which should be not only upheld but extended. That it does matter whether individuals can express their opinion without being either shouted down or reported by an informer. Also whether they are free to see the "other side of the hill" through travel and free access to information. Also that their labour should not be forced nor electoral choice denied them.

These things do matter not only because, if the word "progress" means anything, they must represent a higher civic morality. They matter, too, for the plain pragmatic reason that, if their preservation or attainment is not accepted as a core aim of national development, then this development is itself liable to become hopelessly convoluted. To provide ever more people with motor-cars without progressively easing travel restrictions is to set up a dangerous contradiction. So is to educate them without affording scope for political participation. Any regime that is committed to economic and social advance must *ipso facto* be committed to liberal democracy, at least as an ultimate goal. The only alternative is to become progressively more repressive—a course that, in this shrinking world, can lead only to menace for its neighbours and disaster for itself.

Notes

1. For a stimulating critique of this circumscription see Correlli Barnett, *Strategy and Society*, Manchester University Press, Manchester 1975.
2. E.g. Harrison E. Salisbury, *The Coming War Between Russia and China*, Secker and Warburg, London 1969. Chapter 9.
3. *The Times*, 12 January 1968.
4. See the author's "Underdevelopment as a threat to world peace", *International Affairs*, Vol. 47 No. 2, April 1971 pp. 327–39.
5. P. J. Honey, *Communism in North Vietnam*, MIT Press, Cambridge 1963. Chapter 4.
6. See Chapter 14 *et alia*.
7. *Documents on American Foreign Relations 1966*, Council on Foreign Relations, New York 1967, pp. 251–4.
8. Sir Henry Knight, *Food Administration in India, 1939–47*, Stanford University Press, Stanford 1954, p. 102.
9. T. J. S. George, *Lee Kuan Yew's Singapore,* André Deutsch, London 1973. Chapter 7.
10. William and Paul Paddock, *Famine—1975!*, Weidenfeld and Nicolson, London 1968. Chapter 9.

3

The Fragility of Freedom

In the political *melée* that is the modern world the sundry forces of repression face innumerable counter-pressures. Many of these are directed towards the liberalisation from the inside of the scores of unabashedly authoritarian regimes currently in being. Others seek to curb the autocratic tendencies which sporadically arise—from various quarters—within the liberal democracies themselves. Yet all these strivings within states should be set in the context of a wider aim. This is an evolution of international society such that the progressive extension of freedom is precluded neither by economic stagnation or recession nor by aggression and war.

But this leads on to what may be one of the most crucial questions of our time. Might not the democracies of the West be so distracted henceforward by mounting internal dissent that they are unable to address themselves to global challenges with the constancy these may demand? Might not this be, in fact, a decidedly negative aspect of the economic and social dimensions of strategy referred to in Chapter 2? Or are there grounds for optimism?

Let us concede straightway that, when we examine national responses to military threats historically, no simple correlation is to be discerned between the internal situation prior to hostilities and the patriotic solidarity subsequently evinced. Students of the origins of World War I have often remarked on the suddenness with which domestic political tensions dissolved—not least so in Great Britain—as soon as the battles loomed. Likewise, some 25 years later the mere fact that nations like Poland and Greece had lately been subject to acute internal stress did not prevent their effecting a lion-hearted solidarity in the face of the predatory dictatorships. Nor could a structural analysis of social and economic trends hope to explain the alteration in the British national mood between the autumn of 1938 and the summer of 1940.

Then again, the freely acknowledged reality that Israel is plagued by major philosophical and social discordances has not meant it lacks cohesion whenever its very survival is in doubt. Rather the reverse, one might say. Nor are these by any means the only examples that could be cited of the cohesive effects of major and overt threats from without.

Even in what one may term classic crisis situations, however, this particular relationship between cause and effect has not always been manifest. Thus, throughout the half decade or so that culminated in the catastrophe of June 1940, France's resolve to defend itself had continually been sapped by a sharp polarisation within the political spectrum between Left and Right extremists. Nor did this resolution return in the hour of decision.

Besides, the threats we in the West face to our survival in the nuclear age tend to present themselves more gradually and less directly than heretofore. The decisive issues may be harder to identify; and so, as a rule, are the points of no return. As often as not, indeed, the specific challenges mainly stem from broad alterations in the global scene as opposed to the belligerency of an individual nation or bloc.

By the same token, even when conflicts become military in character, these may not seem so obviously of prime importance as they did in, say, the great struggles of 1914–18 and 1939–45. Accordingly, the will to prosecute them may prove less stable. The serious defeat suffered by the United States in Vietnam was basically the result of a collapse of will in 1967–68; and that emanated from an interaction between, on the one hand, bitter domestic tensions over cultural change and ethnic identity and, on the other, mounting scepticism on the part of the American people at large as to the strategic relevance of a territory of which most of them had never previously heard.

To take another example, supposing the desperate inflationary crisis that stared the United Kingdom in the face in the middle of 1975 had culminated in financial collapse. How bright would have been the outlook for those of us who regard the defeat of the Celtic fascist and fascisto-Marxist insurgency in Ulster as vital to the preservation of parliamentary democracy anywhere in the British Isles and, by extension, anywhere in Western Europe? Surely, the resultant social malaise would have been such that our notions about dangerous precedents and chain reactions would have stood little chance against the "Give Ireland back to the Irish" reflex.

In short, appropriate responses to the intricate and manifold external challenges the West will repeatedly encounter through the 1980s and beyond will considerably depend upon the parliamentary democracies preserving over time great tenacity of purpose and flexibility of tactics. But in order to achieve this combination they will need to be able to contain or subsume at least tolerably well the tendencies towards alienation and militant dissent within themselves. Otherwise their attitude towards international security affairs is all too likely to be characterised by long phases of equivocation and procrastination punctuated by sudden bouts of overreaction. In essence, this is what Britain's Defence White Paper for 1976 was getting at with its admonition that "the social and economic problems now facing the West could, if not satisfactorily resolved, have consequences for the external security of Western countries".[1]

If one is looking for a single test case of the viability of liberal democracy in advanced industrial nations in the late 20th century, Sweden is the best to take despite its formal neutrality and relatively small population. One reason for saying this lies in the quality of the established data base. Another is that official circles in Stockholm have lately become considerably attuned to futuristic perspectives. Thus, on the initiative of Prime Minister Olaf Palme, a working party was set up in May 1971, under the chairmanship of Mrs Alva Myrdal, to report on various future prospects within the country. Two years later a Secretariat for Future Studies was established under the auspices of the Cabinet Office.

More directly germane, however, is the significance of the Swedish nation as a whole as a vanguard of the future. Material living standards now average the highest in the world and the income distribution is exceptionally even. The pressure of population on the fine natural landscape is even lower than it is across the USA: another circumstance that ought to be conducive to diminished stress—e.g. through wide recreational opportunities. During its 45 years of Social Democrat rule, the country acquired a great reputation as a spearhead of modernity in attitudes and institutions, especially as regards education and social welfare. Moreover, there has been throughout this century a conspicuous infrequency of mass protest, violent or otherwise. The clear implication is that, were liberal democracy to fail in Sweden, there might be precious little hope for it anywhere else.

The strictures levelled against Sweden over the years by its Old Right and, more recently, by its New Left bifurcate into two main contentions. The one is that burgeoning affluence has caused a progressive erosion of social motivation, the accent being placed increasingly on aimless hedonism. The other is that the society in question is suffocating itself within a cocoon of social conformity.

Predictably enough, the riposte has been made that these lines of criticism lead in diametrically opposite directions and so cancel each other out, at least more or less.[2] Yet whether they really do is a moot point. Intense conformity and low motivation can, in fact, go together all too easily.

Certainly, some of the recognised indicators point to a sense of rootlessness which may remain vague but which has been getting more pervasive: an expression, if you like, of expectations running ahead of satisfactions. Not that any categoric conclusions should be too glibly drawn. Almost certainly, for instance, far too much has been made by foreigners of the relatively high suicide rate recorded. National statistics are hard to compare in this grey area and there are, in any case, sharp differences in social tolerance towards it. All the same, there may be something in the contention that, in Sweden, gifted individualists are peculiarly prone to take this way out.[3] And such people are, or should be, the very salt of liberal democracy.

Next let us consider recourse to sedatives and stimulants other than the three stock perennials: alcohol, kaffein and tobacco. As in other modern societies, whilst the immoderate use of barbiturates and the like by older people does occasion some concern, it is recourse to drugs among the young that gives rise to most discussion and study, not only as a clinical problem in its own right but also as a symptom of social malaise. As early as 1950 the consumption of morphine had become quite common as had the sniffing of paint thinners and the like. During the late 1960s the taking of cannabis became quite widespread; and in those years, too, perhaps 10,000 people (i.e. 1 in 800 of the total population) were enmeshed in a hard-drug culture.

Since 1967 studies of this problem have been conducted annually on a nationwide sample (c. 50,000 strong) of 18-year-old conscripts. According to the 1973 findings, c. 17 per cent had tried narcotics (chiefly cannabis) at least once whilst 25 per cent had "sniffed" at least once and 12 per cent had used tranquillisers. Meanwhile, an investigation on school pupils in their 16th year revealed that 12 per cent of the boys and 14 per cent of the girls had tried cannabis or other drugs. In the bigger cities, however, these national averages were much exceeded. A survey of Stockholm schools around this time showed every third pupil to have taken drugs on one or more occasions.

The point about these behaviour patterns among Swedish youth is not that they betoken imminent social collapse. Nor is it that they are burgeoning rampantly. Neither statement could fairly be made. What can and must be said, on the other hand, is that their prevalence is disappointing in relation to the progress Sweden has made towards the elimination of deprivation and injustice.

Exactly the same applies to the figures for certain types of crime. Here we stand indebted to the Institute for Criminal Science at the University of Stockholm for the historical and trans-Scandinavian comparisons it has conducted systematically and in depth. As regards murder and other serious acts of violence, the Swedish record is not at all bad. Between 1860 and 1925, in fact, the incidence dropped 75 per cent. But since 1960 or so, a gradual yet continual increase has occurred.

Much more alarming, however, is the big escalation in theft these last 25 years. Around 1850 a long downward trend had set in, the only perturbation of note coming in the late 1860s when stealing became a standard response to the last of the traditional famines. Accordingly, the incidence of this kind of anti-social practice was remarkably low a century later.

Yet in the interval petty larceny, and also breaking and entering, have become commonplace, youths in their early teens being the main culprits. Likewise, the passing of bogus cheques, largely by young people, has been on the increase. Then again, in Stockholm in the late 1960s the frequency of bank robberies (which, in 1950, were virtually unknown there) rose sharply to a level of one a fortnight or so—seemingly to mock the euphoric confidence with which many of these banks had recently been redesigned on an open-plan basis! The total number of criminal offences recorded by the police throughout the country rose from 162,000 in 1950 to 572,000 in 1972.

On the industrial front, the number of days lost through strikes is still extraordinarily low. Unfortunately, the same cannot be said of absenteeism, the other sure yardstick of alienation. According to calculations made by the Central Bureau of Statistics in 1960 an average of 3·8 per cent of those in employment absented themselves for one reason or another. By the end of the ensuing decade, the figure had almost doubled.

One pertinent factor, both in industry and elsewhere, is that the progressive concentration of effective decision-taking about economic and social matters has proceeded even further in Sweden than in some of the other advanced industrial democracies. A salient example is the remarkably comprehensive and exact determination of wage rates through direct negotiations conducted at national level between the respective federations of employers and wage-earners. Vast hypermarkets are another. So are the huge housing schemes, with their high-rise configurations and community heating systems. So is the marked acceleration of the industrial merger rate which began in 1959 and continued through the 1960s.

With all these centralising pressures has gone a curiously strong tendency towards a consensus of stated belief. Virtually all the politicians to whom one talks treat burgeoning affluence, social peace and economic security as the absolute virtues. Likewise, few are disposed to challenge the principle of no-streaming within the all but universal system of state comprehensive schools. Correspondingly, both official and educational circles (and, of course, the media) are thoroughly permeated by the given precept of Equality.

Certainly, it does appear that, in the Swedish educational debate in particular, the standard arguments in favour of Equality have gone unduly by default. Thus the report of an Alva Myrdal working group, set up in 1968 by the Social Democratic party and the Swedish Confederation of Trade Unions, adopted without compunction a strategy of the direct approach in this important sphere. We were advised that "All instruction . . . should be designed so that students may participate in the decisions about form and content" (p. 62), the schools serving "as a lever in the process of democratising the whole of working life" (p. 63). For one thing, "Traditional assumptions about male and female roles must be eliminated from the textbooks" (p. 64). So must nationalist or regional bias. Furthermore, "The grading system must be replaced as far as possible by individual reporting on how students are progressing in their studies" (p. 61).[4]

What is so conspicuously lacking in this by no means unrepresentative appraisal is any great concern for that dimension of Equality whereby individuals receive enough hard information to enable them to make their own judgments about prevailing orthodoxies. A similar disregard is evident in the low priority accorded History in Swedish schools. Agreed, there is room for debate as to what mix of historical topics is most relevant to a nation that is small, formally non-aligned, and trans-industrial. Even so, when solid historical fact is discounted heavily, there is bound to be some substance in Roland Huntford's acid stricture that phrases about the development of "an independent and critical way of thinking" become Newspeak for collective thought conditioning.[5] In other words, the social consensus achieved is too synthetic to be healthy.

But there is a further danger inherent in the sterility of dialecticism *in vacuo*. This is that, sooner or later, it will be made more real by focusing on the most fundamental question of all: how worthwhile is any scholastic education? At first sight, this is not too much of a hazard in contemporary Sweden. After all, in 1972 no fewer than 93 per cent of all pupils stayed on at school beyond the compulsory period. Nevertheless, educationists in Stockholm make no bones about the unhappiness evident in the higher grades throughout the country; and some of them predict that by the 1980s there will be a considerable debate nationally about whether school (at any rate, secondary school) should be compulsory at all.

Inevitably, sundry points of comparison with the recent experience of other Western nations spring readily to mind. Nor does one have to be a compulsive prophet of doom to see that certain of the trends towards social atomisation could not be continued indefinitely without terminating in a major crisis for democracy. For, almost by definition, they would then culminate in a collapse of national cohesion and will; and this, in its turn, would lead either to a Marxian revolution (stimulated, in all probability, from without) or else to an illiberal backlash so extreme as to destroy the precepts of an open society.

Given that the atomising processes have had quite their biggest influence among the young, the implications for military security are already a subject for active debate. The question has been posed succinctly in a study by Major-General Nils Sköld, an officer who ranks as one of Scandinavia's best-known defence intellectuals and who has been designated the next chief of the Swedish defence staff. He predicates that the modern industrial scene is characterised increasingly by social equality and the specialist division of labour. Moreover, this evolution has been closely paralleled by changes in the nature of war, more reliance perforce being placed on the morale and initiative of small groups. So the issue becomes, in essence, the motivational one of how to reconcile a basic and continuing requirement for strict obedience with an emergent need, throughout all ranks and all phases of an individual's military career, of fuller personal involvement and sharing of responsibility.[6]

The ascendant influence within the Swedish armed forces of the egalitarian response to this dilemma is evident in manifold ways. All major breaches of discipline are dealt with, in peacetime, in civil courts. The time-honoured dichotomy between commissioned and non-commissioned personnel has been replaced by a simple rank gradation. Salutes are normally exchanged only with direct superiors. Little attention is paid to anything akin to what used to be known as Swedish drill. A lot of attention is paid to the operation of consultative machinery for all ranks and at all levels; and with this goes, of course, a great concern with welfare provisions—e.g. soldiers training in the far North can usually fly down to Stockholm every other week-end. Another possibility actively being mooted is the introduction of a common programme of basic training for all categories of recruit.

Those who endorse this approach insist that the armed forces must indeed be closely in accord with the structure and ethos of society at large. Moreover, they would insist that, to judge from at least some of the relevant criteria, the effect on peacetime motivation has been on balance good in the Swedish situation. Even so, a legitimate doubt must remain as to how far such a trend could go in any army without having manifestly deleterious effects on cohesion and fighting spirit.

When all is said and done, however, the future in Sweden or anywhere else will not be—nay, could not be—a straight extrapolation of the recent past. The interaction of given trends is too complex for that; and the impact of what the statisticians might call random factors is liable to be too great. Among the latter might be the contribution of prominent individuals. The emergence somewhere or other of a new Churchill in the sphere of Grand Strategy or of a new Keynes or Myrdal in the social sciences might enhance enormously the prospects for the survival of liberal democracy.

Across most of the world, however, the problem is not the survival of democracy: it is its creation. Moreover, this process is likely to prove but a false dawn whenever the economic and social bedrock and the administrative infrastructures are unable to support what is, after all, a decidedly optimistic philosophy of government. The current political crisis in India highlights this simple truth all too well.

Unfortunately, we are now in a phase of considerable uncertainty as to how best to guide the dynamic state of ecological disequilibrium we are pleased to call "economic and social development". Until the early 1960s, the prevailing assumption seemed to be that this development would always broadly replicate what was then read as the general Western experience ever since the onset in Britain of the Industrial Revolution. Continual economic growth, based largely on industrial investment, would be its central feature; and this would ensure a progressive increase in welfare all round and hence in social contentment.

Now, the prevailing disposition is to attach more importance to all those cultural and other influences on growth which are not encompassed by formal economic theory. Likewise, more scepticism can be discerned than heretofore about the prospects (even on optimum assumptions about such vital contributory factors as international aid and world trade) for a smooth path of balanced development leading to something like Alfred Tennyson's mid-Victorian vision of a "land of settled government" in which "Freedom slowly broadens down from precedent to precedent".

For one thing, no polity on this Earth is entirely free from social cleavages, whilst often the effect of basic development—at least in its initial stages—is to exacerbate these rather than heal them. In particular, the economic advance of newly developing states may accentuate inter-communal friction by bringing different ethnic groups into closer and—as it may well turn out—more abrasive contact. Thus weak minorities just within the geographical or psychological periphery of some new nationalism find it ever harder to retain their corporate identity in the face of progressively more effective cultural aggression and material pressures. To look at this from a slightly different angle, growing numbers of them are finding it more and more difficult to decide whether they want to. The Nagas in Assam and the Kurds in the borderlands around the Upper Euphrates are two examples from areas which strategically are exceptionally sensitive.

Another burgeoning pattern is hostility towards minorities which have customarily enjoyed a quasi-exclusive hold on key positions in commerce and related activities. Thus Indians and Levantines are vulnerable to this challenge in various parts of Black Africa and the Caribbean. So are the Overseas Chinese in South-East Asia. So were the Ibos in pre-1967 Nigeria.

Another thrust, which could well wax stronger as time goes by, is towards the partial or total displacement of such tribal or communal groups as have achieved an overweening dominance within the political and administrative establishment of a given country: the

Javanese in Indonesia and, much more explicitly and comprehensively, the Malays in Malaysia have been neighbouring examples.

Nor is it only the privileged ethnic groups, and the social classes with which they may or may not coincide, that find their material advantages and—perhaps even more precious—their role identity threatened by developmental change. So, too, may the male sex! For it remains true to say that, in many parts of Afro-Asia, one of the aspects of life which most astonishes an observer fresh from the West is the lowly position of women. Often, they do more than their fair share of the donkey work. They tend to be excluded from collective leisure activities. Matrimonial legislation is frequently biased in favour of men. Above all, customary social structures hold women down simply through their very explicit definition of the respective roles of each sex.

Not that the female situation is either uniform or immutable. On the whole, for instance, the horizons for women in West Africa are wider than in East, a difference not unconnected with urbanisation having deeper roots in the former region.[7] Virtually everywhere, too, an emancipatory revolution has got quietly under way. Even in Saudi Arabia—the supreme bulwark of fundamentalist Islam—girls have started to attend school whilst in Indonesia half the magistrates and in bustling Singapore a quarter of the senior officials are said to be females these days.[8]

The connotations for the full extension of democracy are obvious. What may need emphasis, however, is that, as they gather pace, such changes will accelerate still further the revolution of rising material expectations. On the one hand, women will be ever freer to express their material wants; and, on the other, many men will yearn at least subconsciously for something to offset the erosion of their time-honoured dominance. Indeed, the whole attitude of the menfolk towards modernisation may be coloured considerably by the emergent challenge from the "weaker sex". Will they evince a positive response towards this and related matters or will they merely relapse into bitter ambivalence? At all events, the almost total neglect of this dimension in development studies is becoming increasingly hard to condone.

In some localities even today, one of the most serious of the more strictly institutional barriers to rapid and balanced economic development is inequity in land ownership and control. This may reflect itself in various facets of the overall problem: the degree of security accorded tenants by law and custom; the scale and character of the rentals; the burden of chronic indebtedness; the social role of the landlords and so on. But as true an index as any is the landless peasant class as a proportion of the total rural population. Among the areas in which the percentage is ominously in excess of 40 are North-East Brazil, Java, Central Luzon, Nepal and various districts within the Indian subcontinent, such Central American republics as Guatemala and El Salvador, and parts of the Middle East. So, until lately, was Ethiopia.

As regards prospective remedies, "the weight of the evidence is in favour of granting ownership to individual landholders or rights to individual land-use within a group holding ownership".[9] In other words, forced collectivisation is best avoided.

What makes the internal challenges faced by the newly developing countries look the more awesome is that practically all of them are, albeit to varying degrees, what Gunnar Myrdal terms "soft states": polities unable to achieve proper border control and administrative cohesion. Corruption is widespread everywhere and seems almost everywhere to be on the increase. Furthermore, it is becoming less and less easy to explain away graft and nepotism as merely expressive of traditional extended family or localist ties and obligations. Therefore, when either econometricians or political scientists elaborate models of development from which this variable is excluded, they are guilty of false perfectionism.

What may be of transcendent importance in generating or preserving an adequate sense of commitment among the governing elites of any state is the existence of a well-defined and estimable national identity. Sometimes, the stresses of a war of independence have served to temper an emergent nation's character in a manner appropriate to the subsequent battle for development. Algeria, China, Israel, North Vietnam, Yugoslavia and, in a sense, Nigeria are or were cases in point. Obversely, however, almost all this list figures, too, in the alternative debate about optimum size, a debate to which we should now turn.

Five or ten years ago received opinion was that the smaller of the younger states tended to be suffused with a peculiarly strong dynamic. Israel, North Vietnam and Singapore were regularly taken as examples. At the same time, the fragmentation of India was widely thought inevitable if not desirable. In a nutshell: "It is the smaller, more compact countries that seem better fitted to confront the tasks of development and it is the larger ones that lag behind".[10]

Yet today the very opposite seems more generally true, at least in prospect. Brazil, Indonesia, Nigeria and Zaïre are cited elsewhere in this study as having particularly good economic prognoses. China has started to "stand on two feet" in various senses. And now Algeria "may be about to explode from rags into relative riches" thanks to its resource base and "the surprising dynamism of the top bureaucracy".[11]

However, as several of the territories just mentioned have shown over the years, simple geographical determinism of this or any other sort is an inadequate framework for description, still less of prediction. Among the other relevant parameters is the prevailing political philosophy. And quite the most distinctive political phenomenon of the 20th century has been mass mobilisation through a neo-Rousseau revolutionary ideology that "promises to each person the opportunity to begin anew with a fresh set of life-chances" based on social restratification and a new general vision. The puritan virtues of industry, sobriety and abstinence are extolled to the full in a frenetic struggle towards an ultimate utopia in which "abundance, personal dignity and natural benevolence will be the conditions of life".[12]

Leadership and control are provided by a ramifying party structure imbued with a political religion laced with socialistic semantics yet charismatically geared to the life and recorded thoughts of its leading figure, the presumed personification of the "general will". Invariably, too, the armed services are well to the fore, although the professional cadres tend to be encompassed by militia and other paramilitary penumbrae which help to keep them locked into the revolution in word and deed. Social and private life is totally politicised, individuality being dismissed as mere egotism or affectation. Authorised comment is always suffused with themes like crisis and attack. Facts are subordinated to consciousness and the past to the future.

As Nazi Germany demonstrated all too clearly, such a system may in its heyday tap a remarkable amount of social energy, not least through its appeal to the more primitive traits of group behaviour. Accordingly, it may well have functional advantages for a society in the early stages of modernisation. But, in the medium-term, what chance do such regimes stand of avoiding a vicious spiral of alienation and repression, a political contradiction that may be contained only, if at all, by a growing belligerency in external policies? As the 1980s progress, this question may come to seem more and more germane to the general situation in Afro-Asia.

Historically, political religions have never been more than a crude approximation to social reality and have rarely, if ever, been consistent within themselves. Nor does the contribution made to this genre of thought (or, indeed, to social philosophy in the round) by Afro-Asia these last few decades do much to qualify this verdict. For one thing, the works in question have all too often been merely the episodic soliloquisings of the venerated autocrats. Gamel Abdul Nasser's *The Philosophy of the Revolution* and the successive political testaments of Kwame Nkrumah were disturbing cases in point.

Needless to say, in the absence of suitable guidelines for liberalisation, revolutionary regimes may soon become too brittle. Thus they are peculiarly prone to the emergence of political generation gaps because of the rapid change they induce and because of the stress they lay on the mass involvement of youth. The big danger is that with a waning of the pristine authority of the political religion itself will go the growth of bureaucratisation, factionalism and graft; and this decay will, in its turn, lead to ever-worsening alienation throughout society, not least among the young. Hence the ever more frenetic recourse to authoritarianism within and belligerency without of which Stalin's Russia was an extreme, but not uninstructive, example.

Seeing that the political religion of Marxist Communism may lately have enjoyed something of a revival—thanks to the advent of the New Left and now its more concrete gains in Angola, Cambodia, Laos and Vietnam—it may be appropriate to look at one or two case studies of its ability to galvanise a people to social reconstruction and yet, as and when the time is ripe, to transmute itself into a more relaxed and empirical mode of government. One relatively encouraging test case may be Yugoslavia whilst China might, in due course, prove to be another. All the same, it may be more appropriate to discuss these countries in Chapters 16 and 17 respectively and to concentrate for the moment on Castro's Cuba and Allende's Chile.

Fidel Castro acceded to power in 1959. By the early 1970s, Cuba's gross national product was perhaps 30 per cent below the 1958 level, due to a marked decline in the sugar industry in the face of climatic adversity and utter mismanagement. In the interval, too, Cuba had sunk deeply into debt to the USSR whilst many consumer goods had become virtually unobtainable by the population at large.

Naturally, this dismal economic performance made systematic repression the more imperative. Thus in 1970 a Vagrancy Law was enacted whereby any male between the ages of 17 and 60 who had done no work for a fortnight or more became liable to two years' hard labour unless he could furnish a convincing excuse. In 1973 various youth organisations were absorbed into a new paramilitary youth movement, the *Ejercito Juvenil de Trabajo*. That same year, too, the judiciary was brought under much tighter political control.

And well before these sinister events, the Cuban revolution had tarnished itself thoroughly by its generalised brutality towards political dissenters, Left as well as Right. By the late 1960s, the total number executed apparently ran into several thousands whilst tens of thousands more languished as political prisoners in varying degrees of discomfort and obscurity.[13] Meanwhile, the deification of Castro proceeded apace.

Against all this, the die-hard apologists for Cuba set some big steps taken in the spheres of education and public health. Also the declared objective of Castro and Guevara: to create, in due course, a "new man" who would be aggressively committed to a rural and very close-knit community life and be, too, both willing and able to dispense with "that vile intermediary, money".

Yet even the positive achievements and visions had been sullied by the martial and pervasive authoritarianism. What is more, they had often been warped by the supercharged but utterly arbitrary personality of Fidel Castro himself. For instance, it seems largely thanks to the peculiar intensity of his anti-urban bias that the city of Havana, once lovely in many aspects, has been studiedly neglected by his government.

Quite possibly Cuba will do rather better, economically at any rate, in the years immediately ahead. Even if it does, however, it will still have demonstrated once again the unsuitability to the fast-moving modern world of the standard Marxist recipe. At best, this is likely to achieve constructive results only after many precious years have been wasted. In the meantime, the erstwhile clarion calls of revolutionary idealism are all too liable to become the official credo of a new class system, more clearly stratified and rigidly structured than ever.[14]

Suffice to add that one would not be justified in placing anything like the entire blame on the United States for the early diversion, not to say perversion, of the Fidelist experiment. For Castro's own temperament required "if possible, a situation where he could pose, or remain, as the rebel chief. . . . surrounded by enemies".[15] Within a fortnight of gaining power, he was publicly daring the Americans to send in the Marines. Within a few months, he had pitched his movement decisively towards dictatorship, ostensibly to frustrate the "enemies of the revolution". Yet thus far the official attitude of Washington towards his regime had been distinctly non-committal.

To all intents and purposes, this pattern recapitulated itself in 1975. Henry Kissinger's declaration in March that America was moving in "a new direction" on Cuba was followed by some weeks of cautious but sustained effort to prepare the economic and political bases for a reconciliation. Yet Fidel Castro chose that very time to reopen his subversive account, notably in Angola. It all looks disturbingly like a fascisto-Marxist Big Brother perpetually yearning for bogey figures, without as well as within. The ultimate lesson of Cuba is that the world will not become more peaceful if more of it passes into the hands of charismatic paranoiacs.

What then is the lesson of Chile? The standard question to start with is to what extent United States interference in the said country's internal affairs helped to generate the gravitation to extremes which culminated, in September 1973, in viciously uncompromising counter-revolution. Certainly, this interference was multifarious and extensive. Thus, in March 1972 the American columnist Jack Anderson disclosed that the International Telephone and Telegraph Company (ITT) had sought to instigate a military coup to prevent the avowedly Marxist Dr Salvador Allende forming a minority government in the weeks following the 1970 election. In September 1974 came the revelation that the CIA had distributed a million dollars among Allende's opponents to try and influence the 1970 poll, and another seven million over the next three years to try and "destabilise" his government. Meanwhile, United States economic aid had tapered off.

More central to the Chilean situation, however, were the grave contradictions inherent in Allende's own position. Only a man of his charm, commitment and political acumen could have sustained as long as he did the attempt to pursue a constitutional path to socialism, whilst relying on the backing of Leftists interested not in what they scorned as *electoralismo* but in forcing a pre-revolutionary breakdown of the body politic. At the very outset, Allende himself was threatening to "paint Santiago with blood" should Congress seek to deny him the Presidency. This he was doing in an endeavour to ride a tiger of Left extremism which even then was freely resorting to violence in both town and country in order to accelerate, and thereby disrupt, the process of evolutionary reform. One of his first concrete acts was to recognise the Castro regime in Cuba. Subsequently, a huge Cuban Embassy staff in Santiago became the main fount of scores of armed cells throughout Chile and perhaps elsewhere. To cap everything, in July 1973 a workers' militia was formed, ostensibly under the auspices of the *Centre Unico de Trabajaderes* (CUT): the Chilean equivalent of the TUC. This at the very time when Allende himself was struggling desperately to rebuild some sort of national consensus to restore social peace and cope with an inflation rate of 300 per cent per annum.

What makes Allende's Chile of special interest and concern is that it was one of the few countries of any size which, on 1972 estimates of annual per capita income, lay in the intermediate 401 to 600 dollar bracket. In more particular respects, too, it bore the hallmarks of developmental transition. Already it had a relatively large middle class. Though the land reform legislation enacted in 1967 had undoubtedly been too gradualistic, it could not be dismissed as a mere charade.[16] Above all, the body politic was imbued with a solid tradition of parliamentary democracy and military neutrality.

Accordingly, Allende's ill-fated essay in Popular Front politics contains lessons of direct relevance not only to the newly developing states of Latin America and elsewhere but also to Western Europe. It indicates, for one thing, how oscillatory and contingent a Marxist commitment to peaceful change is likely to be, especially in an age of increasing turbulence.

In Western Europe, of course, the problem is compounded by the overhanging might of the USSR and the ambivalence towards it of the region's indigenous Communists. At the individual level, a most instructive pointer is afforded us by the career of Palmiro Togliatti, for many years the leader of the Italian Communist Party (PCI) and the man generally credited with having loosened considerably Moscow's grip on it. As early as June 1956, for instance, he voiced doubts about the Soviet road to socialism as fundamental as any raised in that quarter today. In an interview published in the non-communist journal *Nuovi Argomenti*, he said he had found Khrushchev unconvincing when, in his famous "secret speech", he had suggested that the abuses of the Stalin era stemmed, in essence, from the personality defects of this one man. Togliatti contended that such apologetics evaded the true problem "which is why and how Soviet society could reach and did reach certain forms alien to the democratic way, and to the legality it had set itself, even to the point of degeneration".

As it stands, this contention is every bit as radically revisionist as anything Enrico Berlinguer has said these last few years. What is more, in a memorandum drafted on holiday in Yalta a few days before his sudden death in August 1964, Togliatti reiterated it plainly. Yet, taken as a whole, the document in question clearly betokens the umbilical cord of love–hate linking its author to the Russian revolution. It calls on Moscow to speed up the abolition of "the limitations on personal and democratic freedoms installed by Stalin" in order to secure what is credulously termed "a return to Leninist democracy". Furthermore, and even though this text freely acknowledges that Maoism does make a strong appeal to an agrarian strand within the PCI, it goes on to urge all concerned "not to cease for one minute from the polemic against the principles and policy of the Chinese".

Granted, subtlety is called for in the conduct of this polemic. But this is explicitly in order to further "the unity of all Socialist forces" against a "reactionary imperialism" led by a United States supposedly being impelled ever further Rightwards by Barry Goldwater: "It is impossible to think of excluding the Chinese Communists from this unity. . . . Our whole fight against the Chinese position must be a function of the battle for unity . . .". Similarly double-edged is the emphasis on the needful acceptance on all sides of differences between the various "Socialist countries".[17]

What one cannot overlook is that, in times of great tension anywhere, the spirit of rational criticism is liable to be engulfed by an upwelling of "tribal" emotion. And we must assume in this connection that many tens of thousands of Communist Party members in Italy and elsewhere still retain deep-down an emotional attachment to the Soviet Union. Certainly, as much was apparent in the obituary tribute by Togliatti to Stalin published in *Pravda* in 1953, "Stalin's work lives and triumphs. Those who just now are predicting possible deviations from his teachings and commandments, . . . are stupid and miserable provocateurs".

Nor can we take for granted that what one may characterise as the Togliatti disjunctions will automatically fade away as the generation that knew the pristine hopes for the Russian revolution passes on. All too often, the reaction of Communists in the West to, for instance, the invasion of Czechoslovakia in 1968 has been to treat it as a tactical blunder on the part of a few men in the Kremlin rather than what it blatantly was: a devastating exposure of a most dangerous contradiction in the whole Marxist–Leninist theory of development (see Chapter 14). Furthermore, all the other elements within the far Left—both Old and New—are usually immersed in Marxian confusion to at least the same extent. Hence their recurrent proneness to form up behind the Communist Party in Popular Front alliances. To which one must add that if (as is likely) the world becomes more stressful in the 1980s, this propensity may be accentuated.

Entry once more by the Communists into parliamentary government in such Western European countries as Italy, France or Spain would not lead immediately or inevitably to the death of liberal democracy. What it would do, however, is to open up a new front in the global struggle between this democracy and totalitarianism. The conflict on this front is likely to be bitter and perhaps decisive; and it may well continue through 1990, the terminal date chosen for the main part of this study.

Notes

1. *Statement on the Defence Estimates 1976*, Cmnd 6432 HMSO, London 1976, p. 9.
2. Lars Gustafsson, *The Public Dialogue in Sweden*, Norstedts, Stockholm 1964, p. 16.
3. Roland Huntford, *The New Totalitarians*, Allen Lane, London 1971. Chapter 2.
4. Alva Myrdal *et alia Towards Equality*, Prisma, Stockholm 1971.
5. *The New Totalitarians*, op. cit.
6. Nils Sköld, *Defence Policy for the 1970s and '80s*, The Ministry of Defence, Stockholm 1974, pp. 60–3.
7. Kenneth Little, *African Women in Towns*, Cambridge University Press, London 1973, p. 189.
8. "Tasting Power: The New Asian Women", *Newsweek*, 23 September 1974.
9. Doreen Warriner, *Land Reform in Principle and Practice*, The Clarendon Press, Oxford 1969, p. 434.
10. Max Beloff, *The Beatty Memorial Lectures at McGill*, George Allen and Unwin, London 1968, p. 45.
11. Norman Macrae, "Socialist Revolutionaries at Take-off Point", *The Economist*, 13 April 1974.
12. David E. Apter, *The Politics of Modernization*, University of Chicago Press, Chicago and London 1965, Chapter 10.
13. Hugh Thomas, *Cuba*, Eyre and Spottiswoode, London 1971, pp. 1460–1.
14. René Dumont, *Is Cuba Socialist?* André Deutsch, London 1974. Chapter 9.
15. Thomas, op. cit., p. 1058.
16. Doreen Warriner, op. cit., Chapter IX.
17. For the full text see *The Annual Register of World Events in 1964*, Longmans, London 1965, pp. 510–12.

4

How Helpful is Prediction?

Since we can here discount all the more obvious forms of utopianism and millenarianism because they are essentially proscriptive rather than predictive, it would be fair to say that, in the last 100 years before the nuclear era dawned, speculation among the intelligentsia about the world's future was dominated by historicism: the belief that the operation of cause and effect in social and political affairs can be encompassed by some tolerably straightforward theorem which is itself susceptible to definitive verification. Taken as a whole, however, historicism is decidedly on the wane today. One may doubt whether even the Marxists read Hegel any more. Certainly nobody bothers with Spengler. Even the magisterial erudition of the late Arnold Toynbee is heavily discounted except, one gathers, in Japan.

Nevertheless, there is one major school of historicism which has flourished anew these last ten years or so, not least in Western European universities and within revolutionary movements in the newly developing world. This is, of course, Marxism. However, to acknowledge what may, in any case, prove a transient revival need not be to endorse even its philosophy of knowledge. The key tenet that the totality of historical experience lends itself to inductive analysis and hence unerring extrapolation was shot to pieces by Sir Karl Popper a full generation back.[1] The Dialectic, a concept Marx borrowed rather self-consciously from Hegel, is a truism placed on so high and ornate a pedestal as to become an absurdity. Furthermore, in most other respects the philosophical basis of Marxism is vintage Victoriana.

Nor does Marxism stand up to empirical tests at all well, not even when these focus on the European scene Marx and Engels knew best. Modern research has exposed as all too crudely dogmatic sundry judgments about such historical episodes as the English civil war of the 1640s. Similarly, previsions of the increasingly pauperised masses of the advanced industrial nations periodically rushing to the barricades to secure elementary justice for their starving children have become little more than grist for ritual humour among second-year undergraduates. Lenin's attempt to put some flesh on Marx's skeletal ideas about colonialism derives its not inconsiderable prestige less from the fact that some devotees have actually read it than from the contrary reality that many more have not. To read is to become more aware of Lenin's debt to J. A. Hobson, a liberal economist who concerned himself little with Marx and whose impassioned condemnation (in 1902) of empire-building drew succour from a conviction that it was not an absolutely inevitable outgrowth of capitalism in crisis.[2]

Nor does Marxism–Leninism look any more cogent when viewed on a broader canvas. The obsession with private property as *the* fount of power, wealth and status is decidedly pre-electronic as well as pre-Stalin. Marx's vision of life beyond the great divide of revolutionary upheaval is analogous in its rosy vacuity to that characteristic of the numerous millenarian cults History has spawned. His episodic disquisitions on primitive communism are but a continuation of the "noble savage" myth. He bothered little about the relations *between* (as opposed to *within*) advanced states, be they socialist or otherwise.

What is more, Marx failed in his later years to hedge his original formulations with any qualifications sufficiently fundamental to invalidate the above critique. So did virtually all his mainline disciples from Engels through to Trotsky and beyond. Nor has Maoism yet proved itself to be a coherent and durable departure. Nor would the New Left appear to have produced so far any thinker of enduring stature. All things considered, it is hardly surprising that the Marxist expression of "historical inevitability" in practice lapses into degenerative and, indeed, fascistic modes with a regularity that is both depressing and alarming.

Ostensibly at any rate, the opposite end of the spectrum of prediction to that represented by the historicists is that occupied by the reflective individualist, heavily reliant on a few plain truths as revealed by personal observation and intuition. The turbulent 20th century has produced various such figures: Aldous Huxley, George Orwell, Yevgeny Zamyatin to name just three. But in all probability most people would still acclaim H. G. Wells as the doyen of this genre. Accordingly, his work stands as a fair measure of its strengths and limitations, not least in respect of the evolution of technology for peace and war.

Occasionally he has flashes of almost uncanny prescience as when in *The World Set Free*, published in 1913, he postulates the outbreak of atomic warfare soon after the requisite technical breakthrough in 1953: "Power after power . . . went to war in a delirium of panic, in order to use their bombs first. . . . By the spring of 1959 from nearly two hundred centres. . . roared the unquenchable crimson conflagrations of the atomic bombs . . .". Even so, Wells' interest in military science as such was too lay and too episodic to yield any very definitive results. Instead he oscillated between a blimpish insensitivity to change and a skittish indifference to continuity.

His successive attitudes to air power bear this judgment out only too well. Let us look first at two books he published in the first decade of this century, the decade which saw the historic flights of Orville Wright (1903) and Louis Blériot (1909). Both in *Anticipations* (1901) and in *The War In the Air* (1908) he does accord to this dimension of warfare an overriding importance that does broadly correspond with our subsequent experience. However, he foresees the exercise of air power as being through massed echelons of fighting balloons "as thick as starlings in October". The kind of flying machines we know much better are conceded little more than a "guerrilla" role.

Likewise, although in *The Shape of Things to Come* (1933) Wells does visualise the massive use of aeroplanes in counter-city bombardment, his preliminary struggles for supremacy between rival air fleets tend to be altogether too drawn out. Thus he has the German air force take over a year, in the early 1940s, to overcome the Polish.[3] Finally, in 1941, he is taken to task by George Orwell for declaiming at the beginning of that year, one in which the *blitzkrieg* was to be carried to Crete and to Moscow, how "The German air power has been largely spent. It is behind the times and its first-rate men are mostly dead or disheartened or worn out".[4] A precursor this of more recent manifestations of olympian euphoria about, for instance, the Soviet technological lag and the inability of the Arabs to operate anything from an oil embargo to a SAM-6.

In the arena of social and political thought, too, the tireless Wells chops and changes. But he does so here in a much more controlled fashion. The alternation is between pessimism and optimism and is, first and foremost, a symptom of his awareness of how narrow the divide between tragedy and triumph has become for Man.

Some measure of the full scope of his idiosyncratic vision can be gleaned from a more extensive perusal of *Anticipations* (Chapman and Hall, London, 1902). In this synoptic prediction for the end of the century then beginning, Wells contended that the diffusion of urban settlement would have more or less obliterated the contrast between countryside and town, in England in particular (pp. 63–4 in the fifth edition); and with this diffusion would come a greater variegation of industry, agriculture and residential zoning. At the same time, however, greater physical mobility would promote various homogenizing tendencies—e.g. the erosion of the vocabulary, idiom and inflections of local dialects.

A residue of "unemployable" paupers will always be around as casualties of progress (p. 82). But the echelons of domestic servants will shrink dramatically (p. 111) even though the middle classes as a whole will considerably expand, mainly thanks to the growth of the service trades. In Britain, at any rate, a good war or two will be needed to raise the status of the scientist and engineer above that of a "performing animal" (p. 154). Everywhere, mounting moral confusion will threaten national stability and hence international peace.

By 1935 the United States is likely to overhaul Britain in naval and mercantile terms. But concurrently the rising challenge of Germany, naval as well as military, should effect a "synthesis of the English-speaking peoples" (p. 258). Yet, once German aggressiveness has been shattered or weakened in a series of wars, the destiny of Western Europe will lie in a federalism based on the six states that stretch across the Rhine valley, six states that cannot but become a single economic entity in the course of the next 50 years (p. 241). Unfortunately, however, this "splendid" entity is bound to retain "her Irelands of unforgettable wrongs" (p. 260): pseudo-revivals of petty nationalisms espoused by literary quacks.

Pan-Latinism is deemed a non-starter since it lacks a core area. Pan-Slavism can hardly fair much better, given the cultural orientation of both Bohemia and Poland towards the West plus the fact that the political centre of gravity of Russia itself is manifestly swinging eastwards, away from St. Petersburg. Notionally she may extend her sphere of influence over China though a deeper reality is likely to be that the remarkable Japanese people will effect a synthesis with the Chinese in defence of their common culture (p. 243 and 247). Altogether the odds are long against "the existence of a great Slavonic power" (p. 252) in 2000 AD.

Meanwhile, the biggest danger for Mankind as a whole is that the world-wide spread of Democracy would prove "but the first impulse of forces that will finally sweep round into quite a different path"

(p. 146). The countervailing hope had to be that a vast expansion and reform of Education would be able, acting in conjunction with other forces, to promote a new and universal spirit.

Probably, most people would agree that from our present vantage point, three-quarters of the way down the century, this spread of shot looks like hitting quite a number of targets. Therefore, it must be rated a remarkable personal achievement, considering the acute ambient difficulties its fledgling author laboured under. We may be thankful that this tradition of free-ranging speculation on the part of nimble-minded amateurs did survive, through men like Huxley and Orwell, the passing of Wells himself in 1946.

Still, this approach to prediction was by then being complemented or supplanted by what the sanguine called "objective" mathematical techniques. The vigorous germination of statistics as an applied science, plus a growing demand for macro-economic planning in order to avoid another world crash, gave a big boost to econometrics, as witness the seminal work of Colin Clark on national income measurement. In like manner, the exigencies of World War II stimulated Operational Research greatly; and from this stem both modern war gaming and systems analysis.

These last two decades futurology has drawn much succour from strategic studies. Each sphere of interest is interdisciplinary and has to embrace omnibus questions about the preservation of a modicum of peace and liberty within the confines of Spaceship Earth. What strategic studies has done for futuristic speculation is to gear it to current debate and decision-making more closely than before. In return the latter has helped the former to regain some of its pristine vitality by stretching beyond the esoterics of deterrent philosophy and the enigmas of the Cold War.

Herman Kahn is, of course, the archetypal expression of this new symbiosis between prediction and strategy. In addition, he and his colleagues at the Hudson Institute well reflect the creative tension being generated within futurology itself between mathematical projections and free-ranging speculation.

A bullish attitude towards economic and technological change, though not necessarily towards progress in a broader or profounder sense, is a salient attribute of work from this quarter. Particular attention has been drawn to the regional growth prospects in the 1970s and 1980s for Eastern and Southern Europe, parts of Latin America (e.g. the São Paulo–Rio axis), and the Pacific rimland of

Asia.[5] France and South Korea are two countries that have lately received special commendation.

Nor have Kahn and his colleagues allowed themselves to be deflected by the ripples of the energy crisis. Crash programmes for coal, oil shale and tar sands could, they have averred, fend this threat off quite quickly. Therefore, provided we are not talked into a crisis by the pessimists, we can still look forward to the world-wide abolition of absolute poverty by 2099 AD and to a situation a century later in which the then inhabitants of this planet (perhaps some 15 billion strong) will enjoy average incomes of $15,000 a year at 1972 prices.

Whilst optimism of this sort is by no means exceptional among contemporary futurologists, it is also very far from universal. Perhaps the most contentious example of the contrary view is *The Limits to Growth*, the outcome of a project sponsored by the Club of Rome (a somewhat exclusive but decidedly interdisciplinary forum founded in 1968 to study our evolving global system) and conducted by the Systems Dynamics group at the Massachusetts Institute of Technology. In the course of this work computerised studies were done of the changes, basically exponential[6] in character, to be observed or predicted between 1900 and 2100 AD in five of the main factors in world economic development: population, agricultural production, natural resources, industrial production and pollution.

The forecast that emerges is sombre, especially for our grandchildren. In the World Model Standard Run the global system is accorded—a shade generously in the view of the MIT team itself—250 years worth of all non-replenishable resources in 1970 and at the 1970 usage rates. No major change is postulated in the physical, economic or social relationships that historically have governed Man's exploitation of this planet. Thanks to accelerating resource depletion, per capita output of food and industrial products starts to fall early in the 21st century. By 2050 each is well below half its 1970 level and so a precipitate decline in population has set in.

Nor is this scenario much improved by doubling the resource base predicated for 1970. On the contrary, the population crash sets in rather earlier as a result of a dramatic increase in pollution! In short, swift and drastic alterations in Mankind's collective attitudes will be imperative if an eco-catastrophe is to be avoided.[7]

On the other hand, strong objections have been raised to the heuristic use on the global plane of econometric macro-models.

3

Moreover, many of these have been levelled against *The Limits to Growth* specifically, a concentration of effort that may or may not reflect this book's stature and seminal power. Thus *The Economist* forcefully attacked its obsession with the inelasticities of supply that must appear eventually in every particular line of economic development but which are, in practice, almost invariably offset by the development of substitutes.[8] Previously, a team at the Shell Research Laboratory in Amsterdam had queried the use in a pilot study of an aggregate index for pollution; and it had stressed, too, the undue sensitivity of some of the world models to marginal changes in the data base.

Similar reservations about this brain-child of the Club of Rome were expressed in an overall evaluation of it at the Science Policy Research Unit of the University of Sussex. And, in the light of these and other difficulties, the categoric character of some of the main conclusions were adjudged unfortunate. As the introductory chapter of the Sussex report has it, "The computer fetishist endows the computer model with a validity and an independent power which altogether transcend the mental models which are its essential basis".[9]

Nor is it at all clear that mathematical prediction yields very satisfactory results even when applied to national economies rather than global and to the shorter-term rather than the longer. Sir Alec Cairncross, for five years the head of Her Majesty's Government's economic service, has affirmed a need for systematic forecasting as an aid to multilateral communication within Whitehall and also as a framework of reference for policy decisions and their subsequent monitoring. Nevertheless, he goes on to remind us how readily forecasts may be compromised by sudden discontinuities or singular events and by the way key interactions may vary over time.

To which potential pitfalls is to be added what he terms the Jonah Syndrome: a sense that it may be prudent always to urge immediate action to stave off an allegedly impending disaster because, should the supposedly mortal threat never actually present itself, everybody will be too relieved to abuse the prophet of woe.[10] Maybe we should set against this consideration, however, the bias towards sanguineness that Chancellors of the Exchequer, being political animals, may impose on the final verdict. Thus over the period 1969–73, Treasury predictions of Britain's gross domestic product in the ensuing financial year were overestimated by an average of 1·4 per cent, a rather critical margin in terms of planning. Several monographs from the Institute of Economic Affairs have cast considerable doubt on the results being achieved overall in central forecasting.[11]

Nor is the situation much easier in the realms of science and technology. For one axiom we have to reckon with is that it is impossible to predict fundamental discovery: if one can predict a discovery, it cannot be fundamental. Work now in progress in such fields as astronomy, climatology, sub-nuclear physics, genetics, parapsychology and ecology is liable at almost any time to cast entirely fresh light on the nature of Man's total environment and his relation to it. On the other hand, such findings are usually slow to work their way into the public consciousness in Britain or anywhere else.

The impact of technological advance is, of course, more tangible and immediate. What is more, it is logically possible to predict it. All the same, it is also possible for serious errors to be made especially by rumbustious enthusiasts with a surfeit of imagination. Thus among the possibilities seriously canvassed for 1969 (i.e. a decade ahead) in Herman Kahn's first major study were controlled thermo-nuclear energy—*alias* fusion power—and nuclear submarines capable of 85 knots.[12]

Nevertheless, our current state of knowledge does permit us to make with confidence quite a number of technical predictions, not least in spheres appertaining to strategy. For instance, we can now say that, whilst fusion power is very likely to come on tap one day, that day is extremely unlikely to dawn this side of the year 2015 (see Chapter 26). Clearly, too, military electronics is destined to make massive strides these next ten to 15 years. Then again, the pronounced technical economies of scale associated with hovercraft, at any rate in the maritime environment, mean that the maximum displacement of these craft will soon exceed 2,000 tons.

But what is loosely described as cultural change is a sight harder to fathom, partly because it does not lend itself at all well to quantifica-tion. Thus Robert Nisbet has piquantly perceived a sharp diminution of humour across the United States "ranging from the spontaneous laughter no longer heard across the land to the kind of writing that America was once so rich in".[13] He may well be right and not only apropos his own country. Yet who could put this proposition to any statistical test? And who could reduce to the same arithmetical melting pot all the semi-ponderables and downright imponderables that determine individual contentment and social harmony? Enough may have been said above about the enigmas of contemporary Sweden to show such questions to be unanswerable.

To all of which must be added the rider that if such computations are impracticable in retrospect, they border on the ludicrous if applied prognostically. Nobody could thus have predicted, for example, the sweeping radicalisation of the teenage offspring of the upper middle classes that became one of the central social and political realities in various Western countries during the middle to late 1960s. Nor, as has already been noted, can the emergence of good leadership be foretold. The hour does not invariably bring forth the man. Neither do the years invariably sustain him.

But none of these considerations amounts to anything like an absolute objection to synoptic appreciations of the future, least of all if these are arrived at through open-ended debate rather than by some methodologist trying to play God. The first rejoinder to make is that, whether one is forecasting the human future or tomorrow's weather, the feasibility of the exercise fluctuates markedly with the current situation; and, as may be inferred from Chapter 21, the late 1970s may be quite an appropriate time to essay this art. Besides which, the serious purpose of all such intellectual explorations ought to be to influence and not just anticipate. The merit of cautionary forecasts, in particular, ought to be judged by the extent to which they turn out to be self-defeating prophecies.

What must be said, too, is that just about every thinking person in the modern Western world is, in fact, looking ahead continually in regard to society at large as well as to his own situation. However, if this is not done overtly and with tolerable coherence, there will be a vague but probably strong bias towards the view that something close to the *status quo* will be preserved in many respects. Yet the one great constant of modern life is flux. The sole thing 1987 or 1997 can be depended on not to do is to replicate at all closely 1977.

Certainly the drift of governmental thinking in various capitals seems to be along these lines. In the field of strategic studies this has been especially true, a state of affairs that does much to explain the rapid expansion of the discipline in question. Recently Cairo and Tehran have joined, at least tentatively, the growing list of capitals with officially-sponsored centres for strategic studies. Reputedly, Whitehall has a predilection in favour of playing things by ear. Nevertheless, three-year costings of the British defence budget were introduced as early as 1957. In 1960 these became five-year and in 1964 ten.

In our ten-year costings may perhaps be seen a pointer to the time-perspective needed to ensure that prediction is at once efficacious and relevant. There is much to be said against futurology being as preoccupied as heretofore with the year 2000 and the century thereafter. As the 10th century of the Christian era drew to a close, a groundswell of belief was generated that its termination would see the end of the world: "Satan will soon be unleashed because the thousand years have been completed".[14] In this day and age, however, we ought surely to entrance ourselves less with the symbolism of perfect numbers and so be free to fix our gaze on whatever point in the future is pragmatically the most convenient. At this juncture, that is likely to be, for the great majority of purposes, less than 23 years ahead. Thirteen probably represents a sensible upper limit.[15]

Notes

1. *The Open Society and Its Enemies*, George Routledge, London 1945, Vol. II, Chapter 25.
2. J. A. Hobson, *Imperialism*, George Allen and Unwin, London 1938 edition, p. 302.
3. H. G. Wells, *The Shape of Things to Come*, Hutchinson, London 1933, pp. 202–19.
4. "Wells, Hitler and the World State", in George Orwell *Critical Essays*, Secker and Warburg, London 1946, pp. 83–8.
5. Herman Kahn and B. Bruce-Briggs, *Things to Come*, Macmillan, New York 1972, Chapter III.
6. Exponential means increasing by a constant percentage each year.
7. Donella H. Meadows *et alia*, *The Limits to Growth*, Earth Island, London 1972.
8. "Limits to Misconception", *The Economist*, 11 March 1973.
9. H. S. D. Cole *et alia*, *Thinking About the Future*, Chatto and Windus, London 1973, p. 8.
10. Presidential Address to the Royal Economic Society, *Economic Journal*, Vol. 79 No. 316 December 1969, pp. 797–812.
11. Notably George Polanyi, *Short-Term Forecasting: A Case Study*, IEA, London 1973.
12. Herman Kahn, *On Thermonuclear War*, Princeton University Press, Princeton 1960. Chapter 10.
13. Robert Nisbet "Has Futurology a Future?" *Encounter*, Vol. XXXVII No. 5 November 1971, p. 21.
14. Henry Focillan, *The Year 1000*, Harper and Row, New York 1971, p. 65.
15. Perhaps significantly, the Second Report of the Club of Rome foreshortens its perspectives just a little. See Mihajlo Mesarovic and Eduard Pestel, *Mankind at the Turning Point*, E. P. Dutton & Co, New York 1974.

Part II

Economic and Social Stress: The Strategic Consequences

5

The Western Social Flux

(a) THE PERILS OF INFLATION AND RECESSION

As an old Oxford tag has it, Economics is one subject in which the examiners never have to set new questions because the answers change each year. At the present time, this gibe is peculiarly apposite because, against a background of "stagflation" within countries and pronounced instabilities in the trade between them, some of the most fundamental assumptions of the post-1945 economic debate are under urgent reconsideration.

The assumptions stemmed from the new approach to employment theory adopted by a coterie of radical economists in the aftermath of the great world slump of 1929 to 1933, a phase that had had especially horrendous implications in respect of world peace. It had undermined the forces of liberal democracy almost everywhere from Argentina to Spain, from Germany to Japan. It had enfeebled China and pre-occupied the United States. It had polarised British opinion between a Left waxing too Marxist to address itself properly to defence and a Right too obsessed with tax cuts to do so. Surely even the most cursory review of those years would be enough to convince anyone that, in the modern world, Economics must be an integral part of Grand Strategy.

At all events, although Michael Kalecki in Poland and Gunnar Myrdal in Sweden made noteworthy contributions to the post-1929 revolution in economic thought, the name of John Maynard Keynes in England is the one most widely identified with it. He converted himself to what we now know as Keynesianism in the mid-'thirties, and wrote and spoke extensively in this vein for the remaining decade of his life.

Not unnaturally, his emphases varied. But the gist of his argument was consistently as follows. In a given era of its economic history, a free society's net investment effort will appear as a rigid and quite simple function of its aggregate real income. And what this means, in practice, is that the volume of investment is always a determinant not only of future but of current income. This it is by virtue of a "multiplier effect"—i.e. any changes in the investment level will shift the general level of national economic activity in the same direction and by a preordained multiple. The lower this is allowed to fall, the more unemployment will result.

In the medium-term at any rate, the amount of investment will itself be regulated (at least in the private sector) by the prevailing rate of interest, the point here being that this is the measure of what investors have to pay to secure the requisite funds. Yet this rate of interest is, in its turn, a function of the supply of money; and this is something a modern government may aspire to control precisely, both through its influence over bank credit and by means of its own fiscal (i.e. budgetary) strategy. In particular, it can deliberately run a budget deficit, increasing expenditure (perhaps on public investment) whilst it holds down taxes and prints more money to cover the difference.

Fifteen to 20 years ago, Keynesianism was on the crest of a wave throughout the Western world. Even such Marxist analysts as the late John Strachey were conceding that its esoteric logic could be faultlessly applied to national economic systems.[1] In Washington, John Kennedy's "New Frontier" was soon to obey its injunctions with characteristic ebullience. Why then do commentators now feel so disabused of an economic theory that has, above all, steered us clear of any more Wall Street crashes à la 1929?

Inevitably, the explanation is severalfold. Though always most anxious to portray himself as a dynamic analyst, one liberated from the static formalism of his neo-classic predecessors, Keynes had only the vaguest notions about changes through time.[2] Nor did he address himself much to economic growth per se. Nor does expanding money supply look as efficacious as once it did as a means of inducing full employment. Between 1965 and 1974 the money supply in the United Kingdom nearly trebled; and so did unemployment!

Above all, Keynes was little concerned with fluctuations in price levels, an attitude interpreted by many of his disciples as positive endorsement of considerable and sustained rates of inflation.[3] Indeed, until perhaps four years ago, the hallmark of a progressive economist was widely taken to be that he was indulgent towards mild inflation. He was confident it could be kept mild. He welcomed the Keynesian implications for full employment. He noted how a gradual fall in money values necessarily involved a gradual redistribution of real income away from creditors and in favour of those indebted to them; and he saw much historical evidence of rents lagging behind general price levels. He spoke as if every creditor was a cadaverous Shylock and every debtor an aggrieved Antonio. Likewise, he talked as if every rentier was the rudest of robber barons. He also saw a moderately inflationary environment as the one most conducive to altering wage differentials and increasing tax burdens.

Today this sort of disquisition looks like the fading afterglow of the euphoric 1950s. The *via media* between the Scylla of hyper-inflation and the Charybdis of deflation-with-recession seems neither as broad nor as straight as once it did. For several reasons, moderate inflation may henceforward be alarmingly prone to slide into a headlong gallop at quite short notice. Sudden bottlenecks in the supply of oil or other key commodities may encourage governments hastily to generate more money, so as to enable themselves to cope without cutting back on the demand for other things. Meanwhile, wage claims and the like are made all the higher in anticipation of future price rises all round.

To which might be added the impact, actual and latent, of the accelerating revolution in the handling of money. My own suspicion is that professional economists have all along been inclined to underrate the rise in the velocity of monetary circulation discernible in some Western countries since 1939. At all events, this velocity may be the more prone to surge as and when, either by telephone or else through the insertion of a credit card in a computerised terminal, automatic data banks record most transactions. What makes this prospect rather threatening potentially is the inherent tendency of rapid inflation to reinforce itself just because it obliges people to regard money-in-hand as an eroding asset. Needless to say, for a given volume of money in all forms (coin, notes, demand deposits, and so on), the price level is a linear function of the velocity of circulation.

To Irving S. Friedman, professor-in-residence at the World Bank, "the fatal error in the thinking and policies of governments in the years following World War II" has been such indulgence towards lowish rates of inflation that expectations of persistent inflation have become ingrained everywhere.[4] He has stressed how readily anxiety, frustration and alienation can be brought on by chronic uncertainty and from "a deepening sense that one is running faster and faster only to find that one is going backward".

The socio-psychological traumas might, in the long run, prove the most paralysing of all politically, not least because chronic inflation is one form of malaise that the Communist world is relatively successful at containing.[5] But an especial adverse consequence could be one that does, in fact, lend itself to something like a standard Keynesian interpretation. It is that the flow of voluntary savings (corporate and maybe personal) will dry up because the interest rates preferred simply cannot keep abreast of diminishing money values and heightened risks. Accordingly, the equilibrium point between these savings and commercial investment sinks with debilitating consequences for the economy as a whole.

All of which leaves some cause for concern that an OECD forecast in the summer of 1976 said that, even if the world boom now slowly building up is managed aright, and is not disturbed by shock external events, the OECD area is likely still to be experiencing an annual monetary inflation of five per cent in 1979–80. Certainly, much above that figure would leave the countries in question uncomfortably vulnerable, in economic terms, to untoward occurrences: internal or external, economic or military or whatever.

This leads us on to the question of whether, in individual industrial nations and across the world at large, the aggregate level of economic activity remains liable to oscillations which are more or less rhythmic in nature and which may damage international security in manifold ways. Several distinct series have been perceived. One yields a low point every four years or so: 1949, 1954, 1958, 1961, 1967, 1970, 1975 in recent United States experience. Underneath there are said to be swings in building construction and kindred activities to be measured in terms of decades.

Thus half a century ago a Russian called N. D. Konratieff claimed to have identified cycles of some 50 or 60 years in length. Applying this model to British economic history, in particular, one finds low points in 1795, 1845, 1896, 1946 and 1996. Correspondingly, 1971 or thereabouts would be a high turning point.[6] Fortunately, this rather disconcerting interpretation has not, in fact, proved too effective a prognostic guide to date, the 1946 low apparently turning up in 1929.

Throughout this field there seems too little regularity to justify any predictive determinism. Obviously, wars can make a dramatic impact on economic trends. But attempts to demonstrate that their incidence is cyclical have not been at all successful. Then again, the very fact that, since 1945, the amplitude of the presumptively rhythmic shorter-term falls and rises in economic activity have been kept so much smaller than before does suggest that their duration, too, is susceptible to governmental modulation.

Nor should we underrate the propensity of the human mind to superimpose an orderly pattern on what it perceives but dimly. After all, Astronomy has long been a more exact science than Economics will ever be. Yet, from 1877 until 1925 or thereabouts, some leading astronomers were persuaded that the striations they discerned on Mars were a well-planned network of trans-planetary canals, the prime artefacts of a most orderly and advanced civilisation!

Besides, no cyclical representation of events can be predictively reliable unless its causation can be identified. In fact, economic historians very generally believe today that the supposed Konratieff swings owed much, if not all, to the sharp though largely fortuitous fluctuations in the discovery of new gold deposits in an age in which international payments were geared rigidly to the gold standard. Accordingly, they could only be a feature of the world which ended so cataclysmically in August 1914.

Meanwhile, most economists still agree that the first clue to the shorter-term pulsations is to be found in fluctuations in the level of new investment. And slowly but—it does seem—surely, a consensus has been emerging which accepts the interaction within each economy of internal and external causes: "endogenous" and "exogenous" factors, as the jargon usually has it. Among the endogenous are the monetary policies pursued by central banks and governments; alternating waves of optimism and pessimism among investors, entrepreneurs and civil servants; and the basic Keynesian interactions. Prominent among the exogenous are forceful confrontations between nation states.

Clearly, no tendency susceptible to so variegated an explanation could ever by projected into the future with a precision anything approaching what, say, an organic chemist or a nuclear physicist would regard as minimal. But to admit this cannot be to deny that the world economy will remain liable, through 1990 and well beyond, to recurrent perturbations quite sufficient to aggravate, in various ways, the international security situation.

Indeed, in the years ahead exogenous factors may occasionally have a disruptive effect considerably more severe than we had come to expect in the days before "Yom Kippur". Moreover, in an age of high expectations and growing international interdependence what might, by historical standards, be comparatively modest deteriorations in employment prospects and so forth may have more serious social and political repercussions than was once the case.

Yet, curious though this may sound against a background of concern for sustained economic growth, the last ten years have witnessed repeated flurries of interest in the deeper question of how much store we should lay upon continued growth in any case. Historically, of course, the anti-growth school has mainly been located on the political Right, where it has been closely associated with scepticism about human perfectibility—at any rate this side of the grave. Also with concern for such alternative priorities as stable currencies, national security, and minimal interference by governments.

Moreover, strong traces of this tradition persist, one example being Mr Enoch Powell's admonition to his fellow Britons that "an annual growth of productivity of even five per cent, if continued for a substantial period, could have equally or even more monstrous results" than a five or ten per cent inflation rate.[7] During the 1950s, however, the mainstream political Right in various countries—e.g. Australia, West Germany, Japan, the USA and the United Kingdom— came to endorse the "economic miracle" of the "affluent society" as a convincing riposte to Marxism.

Therefore, by the late 1960s, the centre of gravity of the limited or zero-growth philosophy had switched well to the Left of the political spectrum. There, two main objections to the materialistic view of progress were being adduced. One was that the orthodox "economic indicators" were no measure of the "quality of life". The other was that, in the final analysis, universal affluence would be physically impossible because of resource exhaustion and ecological disturbance. On both fronts, of course, the arguments advanced overlapped with those adduced by the counter-culture (see Chapter 1).

Presumably, few people in the West, professional economists or no, would unabashedly advocate the promotion of economic growth regardless of the social and political cost: forced savings, child labour, the use of a KGB to maintain industrial discipline and so on. Nor, on the other hand, could anybody seriously expect that the dynamic of economic expansion might be suddenly and abruptly curtailed. Thus far, however, this dialectic has usually been conducted as if there were, in fact, no middle way between maximal and zero.

Under these circumstances, those economists with anti-growth proclivities are prone to saddle themselves with a quite insupportable burden of proof. In consequence, they tend to appear as mere salon romantics, people not prepared to evaluate rigorously the practicality of their own aims and who would will the populace at large to accept an austerity their own life styles belie.

This is a pity because it is more than likely that, as we move towards and through 1990, the deliberate moderation of economic growth will take its place alongside the control of inflation as a key issue in academic studies and, not so long afterwards, in public policy.[8] If so, progress in each case will probably owe much to a new convergence between pure economics on the one hand and political sociology on the other: a revival, in a sense, of Political Economy.[9]

(b) THE AMBIGUITIES OF PROGRESS

Whenever we argue about the desirability or otherwise of economic growth, we are really exercising ourselves about three distinct themes. One is increasing material abundance. The second is the ever vaster networks of technologies and institutions that securing this abundance seems to require. The third is the pressure towards cultural homogenisation generated by both the first and the second.

To which one might object that, even if valid, this distinction is purely formal: these themes could never be separated. Maybe not. But neither are they entirely coincident. It could well be, for example, that the 1980s will experience slower and more erratic economic expansion. Even so, the impulses towards cultural change could the while remain as strong as ever. Innovations in pure and applied science (not least those in medicine) would alone be sufficient to ensure that.

In principle, the consequent broadening of horizons can be as favourable to liberal democracy as it is menacing to authoritarianism. The more motor-cars there are in service, the more freedom of travel matters. The more people understand, the more their freedom of expression matters. The more things change, the less secure is dogma.

All the same, there are no grounds for complacency overall. Thus there is a long intellectual tradition in which we are admonished that technocracy must ultimately prove inimical to the freedoms that liberal philosophers cherish. The apprehension of the young H. G.

Wells on this score was noted in Chapter 4.[10] Over half a century beforehand, in *The Communist Manifesto*, Marx and Engels were gleefully looking forward to the collapse of "bourgeois society" through a progressive polarisation of roles. Meanwhile, Alexis de Tocqueville (1805 to 1859), himself a scion of a shattered French aristocracy, was studying the American nation and his own, egged on by a passionate concern lest the priceless attribute of personal liberty was inexorably destined to erosion as the Western world evolved into huge political democracies characterised by a high degree of social uniformity.

De Tocqueville did not always distinguish himself by meticulousness of description or definition. Perhaps, too, he was unduly preoccupied with his own situation. Nevertheless, he survives as an influence not only because of his repeated flashes of stinging lucidity but also because of the laser-like accuracy of his intuitions. A particular instance of the latter is his prevision of an ultimate contest for world leadership between the United States and Russia. A more general proof is the extent to which he appears a harbinger of the theories of mass society which are a central feature of modern political sociology.

In essence, these theories apprehend that the century "of the common man" will prove in the end to have been that of the charismatic tyrant. Whilst increased industrialisation, bureaucratisation, mobility, mass communication and data dissemination may have led to an unwonted involvement of ordinary people both in material welfare and in the political process, they have tended also to undermine all the smaller or more local foci of loyalty, thereby leaving the way open for quite unprecedented concentrations of power and influence. Concurrently, a trend towards environmental decay accentuates the sense of being a cog in a machine.

In such a situation, more and more atomised individuals may perceive that their rosy expectations of "the good life" will never be realised, except in a decidedly uneven fashion. Hence they may lapse from consensus into disengagement, especially political disengagement. They may then, as Eric Fromm solemnly warned us in 1942, be open to seduction by the transitory yet potent appeal of authoritarianism—the sadistic vision of complete power over others coupled with the masochistic one of dissolving oneself in an overwhelmingly strong and pseudo-glorious collective identity. As experience has shown, it may require far less than a majority of individuals to be so converted to tip the balance of advantage in an open society under stress.

In Fromm's judgment, the dilemma can be traced right back—through both our social organisation and our psychological stereotypes—to the archetypal Renaissance figure, with all his new learning and enterprise. He was, says Fromm, a member of an emergent *haute bourgeoisie*, a dominator as well as an individualist. Harried and manipulated by him, the masses may actually have felt less secure inwardly than before. Yet so, through psychological isolation, did he himself.[11] In other words, we are deemed to be grappling with ambiguities inherent in nearly five centuries of post-Renaissance progress towards the widest possible horizons of knowledge. And, though this admonition is but an essentially intuitive perception of one strand of reality, we would do well not to brush it aside. Our liberal democracies pride themselves, above all else, on being the ultimate expression of the Renaissance spirit.

Fromm, like so many before and since, saw but this way out: do everything possible to ensure that every "individual actively participates in determining his life and that of society, and this not only by the formal act of voting but in his daily activity, in his work, and in his relations to others". Obviously, a prerequisite of this was a large measure of decentralisation, a movement some distance down the road towards what we have come to know as the "alternative society". Yet this had somehow to be reconciled with the incessant economic and technical pressures towards bureaucratic centralisation. Not an impossible task, Fromm thought, but undeniably a major one.[12]

Yes, indeed. Nor is the least of the conundra posed that of identifying, in a given situation, the form decentralisation should take. Nobody could claim, for instance, that the United Kingdom's record in this regard has lately been gratifying. Thus the considered view can not infrequently be heard that, by the time a massive reorganisation of local government had taken effect throughout Great Britain in 1974, the bulk of informed opinion was solidly against it! Nor has the vexed question of workers' participation in industrial decision-making been sorted out. Nor has a viable devolution plan for Ulster yet been devised. Nor do either Westminster or Whitehall approach Scottish and Welsh devolution with much confidence in a happy outcome (see Chapter 16).

Undoubtedly, the whole decentralisation debate has been much confounded these last ten years or so by an apparently vigorous resurgence, in many parts of the Western world, of self-awareness on the part of minority communities: Aboriginals, Afro-Americans, Amerindians, Basques, Bretons, Catalans, Corsicans, Quebecans and so on. Thus in Western Europe, where the communal pattern is at least roughly territorial, great concern is being shown to take due account of it by buttressing and multiplying the middle tiers of representative government.

Yet it is more than possible that, well before 1990, this revival will have burnt itself out, leaving behind aggravated cynicism plus a hotch-potch of new but already moribund elective bodies—too carefully tailored to adapt to more subtle purposes. Much of the justification for fearing this is the contradictory nature of the "local nationalism" trend. Usually, it seeks both grass-roots democracy and the consolidation of traditional cultures: two aims which by no means always coincide. It may also demand that central government exercises less control yet devotes more resources. It may insist on more equal treatment without being prepared to recognise that this perforce implies faster cultural convergence.

The contradictions that result from this are piquantly illustrated by the situation of what, after all, are among the more celebrated of Western Europe's minorities—the Basques. From time immemorial this society has been delineated by a language quite distinct from any other, a high degree of agricultural self-sufficiency, a conservative pride in political self-government, and an intense devotion to its highly puritanical branch of the Catholic Church.

Even in this epic case, however, the binding forces will surely weaken progressively, given the probable continuation in Madrid of a regime more sympathetic to the Basques as a people than Franco could ever have been. Already, two of the four Basque provinces in Spain have virtually detached themselves from the cause whilst, thanks to heavy immigration, not half the population of the other two speak Basque. Furthermore, even the true Basques dichotomize as between the militants and the moderate; and the former divide into the insurgents and the rest; and the insurgents are split between the radical nationalists and the social revolutionaries. One may surmise, too, that economic growth will continually erode the distinctive puritan ethic and aesthetics the Basques evolved historically.

Meanwhile, in the three French departments normally regarded as Basque, assimilation is visibly under way, aided by a steady brain-drain of young people to Paris and Toulouse. Agreed, some irridentism has lately been in evidence in this quarter too. But Paris is coping. On the one hand, it addresses itself to the genuine economic grievances this peripheral region has; and on the other, it nips violent extremism in the bud. Nor should we overlook the instructive contradiction that the activists resent the hot-house preservation of their culture for the benefit of the tourist trade.

Surely, too, all such irridentist resurgencies must either come soon to fruition or else fade away again. Twenty years hence, either a separate Basque state will have come into being (for the first time in recorded history, and astride the existing Franco-Spanish border) or else the Basque sense of exclusivity will be visibly on the wane. The latter outcome seems much more in line with general social evolution.

Nor is the outlook much, if any, better for separatists when they possess a potentially viable territorial base. Let us look, for instance, at Quebec where Les Felquists' urban guerrilla campaign in support of separation was launched in 1963 and followed by an upsurge of the Parti Quebecois (PQ)—the constitutional separatists. Though here as elsewhere, genuine economic grievances built up secessionist emotion, few analysts ever doubted that membership of the Canadian federation bestowed on Quebec some major economic advantages. A further complication was the substantial and swelling "immigrant" minority in Montreal and other Quebecan cities. Another was that the withdrawal of Quebec could hardly help but lead to the "balkanisation" of the whole of Eastern Canada, leaving each and every unit to come to terms with the United States as best it could. So maybe one should not really be surprised that the PQ had "amazingly little to say" about what might be deemed the all-important subject of the American connection.[13] Nor that it owed its success in the 1976 provincial elections to a calculated playing down of the separation issue in favour of more immediate "bread-and-butter" ones.

Presumably the communal revival will tend to continue longest in those situations where intermarriage with other groups has not yet become extensive. Quite possibly, too, it will be able to generate occasionally a bitter and unstable backlash against the 20th century, not to say the Renaissance, of the sort Ulster yet endures. But there can be little doubt either that sentiment of this essentially traditionalist kind cannot sustain itself indefinitely against the erosive forces of change. To think otherwise apropos anywhere in Western Europe or North America might be to engage in a most debilitating diversion.

Indeed, we would do well to assume that the more cosmopolitan forces of social or, if you like, cultural change will remain strong through the 1980s in various directions. One factor is simply the sheer fluidity of Western society as it now always is. Alvin Toffler advises us that, in the 12 months from April 1967, no fewer than 40,000,000 Americans changed their place of residence. In fashionable parts of West London, the annual turnover in this respect is likewise 20 per cent. Discussing the diminishing importance of place as a source of diversity, Toffler pointedly contrasts even the nomadism of the past with the social mobility of today. The nomad carried "his social setting with him and, as often as not, the physical structure that he called home".[14]

Then there is the prospect of further big advances in science; and, as regards society at large, these may be especially dramatic in Medicine, the reason being that some of the most seminal research in pure science these last few years has been in the realm of biology. Thus immunology seems on the threshold of great leaps forward. If so, transplant surgery will, and cancer treatment may, be prominent among the many branches of medicine to benefit. By 1990, too, anaesthetics should be able to keep many of the physically or mentally sick in a state of hibernation for weeks, if needs be. Maybe it will be possible directly to retard, at least on an experimental basis, the physiological processes of ageing. Almost certainly, some measure of pre-natal sex selection will be commonplace. Marked progress will also have been made with psychotropic drugs.[15] Nor is this list even intended to be comprehensive.

Alvin Toffler contends that "the most important disease of tomorrow" will, in fact, be a "future shock" induced by incessant innovation in almost all spheres of life.[16] The kernel of his argument is that, much as throughout history small societies have been bewildered and demoralised by abrupt contact with intrusive alien cultures, so our mass society will henceforward be ever more prone to disorientation and passivity as a result of technical and cultural change within itself.

Still, one does not have to wax as apocalpytic as this to see that the cumulative effect of advances as great as those just indicated for Medicine must be distracting to some extent. The ethical dilemmas they raise will reinforce the general climate of moral uncertainty. More concretely, they will consume a lot of time and energy that could otherwise be devoted to other aspects of policy, either internal or external. Neither the onward march of nuclear arms nor Soviet imperialism nor any other issue has aroused passions throughout Western Europe and North America these past several years at all comparable to those generated by abortion law reform.

However, whilst Medicine may have a pronounced effect on the atmosphere of a modern society, it does not alter its structural foundations in the way developments in engineering and electronics can. Here one calls most readily to mind the automation of specific mental and manual skills, a trend which is especially identified with the computer.

Many novelists and a few futurologists love to write as though the computer is destined to direct our lives within a generation and then for centuries, if not millennia, to come. Some foresee anguished public debates about "computer rights" and "computer participation", debates in which the computers themselves will earnestly take part. Rule either by computers outright or by coalitions in which computers hold most of the key posts are portrayed as the inevitable climax.

Before succumbing too meekly to such an onrush of speculation, however, it would be well to recall that, thus far, automation has been taking place in a much more leisurely fashion than many expected 15 to 20 years ago. After all, some of the biggest labour redundancies in recent years have been "the result of much more . . . old-fashioned influences: farm labourers have been put out of work by bigger tractors, miners by the cheapness of oil, and railwaymen by better roads".[17] Male employment levels have also been affected in some sectors by the rising employment of women.

In all probability, this will remain generally true in industry for a decade or so yet, whatever economic growth the advanced nations achieve or resolve to settle for. Thus one study envisages systems for computer-aided design and integrated production control being introduced into the manufacturing and chemical processing industries sometime during the 1980s; and until these foundations have been laid, the on-line control of machinery is likely to remain insufficiently attractive, at least as far as manufacturing is concerned.[18]

But in the meantime, both the white-collar professions and the domestic environment will continually be modified in all sorts of small, though cumulatively important, ways through the continual miniaturisation of the computer on an ever more cost-effective basis. Already a chip a fifth of an inch square may contain 20,000 printed transistor units and perhaps be as powerful as were the large computers of the first generation. A corollary is that general computer costs could conceivably fall by as much as 90 per cent between now and 1990, as civil and military research beneficently interact.[19]

Understandably enough, computer advances, at the micro- as well as at the macro-level, are easiest to make when the problems presented are patently numerate. Yet some quite promising experiments have reportedly been carried out with computers in what one might have regarded as the peculiarly human preserve of psychiatric diagnosis. Donald Michie, Professor of Machine Intelligence at the University of Edinburgh, has given the median date at which a computer psychiatrist is expected to enter general service as 2000 AD. For an automatic language translator, 1995 is cited.[20] Meanwhile, the electronic transmission of data from place to place will be progressively extended. Obviously, various devices, such as cable television, will figure prominently in this extension. Still, Peter Drucker probably weighed the situation well with his observation that "the computer is to the information industry roughly what the central power station was to the electrical industry".[21]

In communications in the more tangible sense, namely the transportation of materials and people, the trend towards larger scale operation (aided and abetted by more automatic control) has already gathered pace. Considerably higher voltages in grid lines should facilitate the longer distance transmission of electricity. By 1990, too, water supply grids extending across many hundreds of miles will be widely under construction in order to meet the relentlessly growing demand for this vital resource. The next generation of supersonic aircraft and jumbo-jets respectively will be considerably bigger than its predecessor. Driverless trains could well be commonplace by 1990. If the construction of supertankers has boomed again by 1985 (as probably it will have), some of the vessels then being laid down could represent yet another leap forward in displacement.

Any endeavour to assess the connotations for society of more automatic control by dint of electronics ought to take full cognisance of the evident truth that, whilst there may be a large debit account, there is also a large credit one. No evolution can be entirely negative if it leads to higher productivity. Nor if it diversifies consumer choice by facilitating short yet quite economic production runs of subtly different varieties of a given class of goods. Nor when it makes communication within established bureaucracies faster and more multilateral.

Nor, for that matter, when it enables certain utterly routine tasks to be dispensed with altogether, thereby releasing labour for what may be more rewarding assignments. By 1973 the percentage of the total labour force engaged in manufacturing had dropped to 23 per cent in the USA (as compared, for example, with 37 per cent in Britain); and it is likely to be close to ten per cent there by the turn of the century. Agreed that cannot be proof conclusive, since by no means all manufacturing jobs are tedious nor all the so-called tertiary or service ones exhilarating. Nevertheless, it clearly owes much to the truism that those tasks which are more individual (and so, broadly speaking, more satisfying) are usually hard to automate and are, in addition, liable to be in greater demand as incomes rise all round.

But against these beneficent aspects should be put contemporary warnings, notably from the Geneva headquarters of the General Agreement on Tariffs and Trade, that the world will find complete recovery to full employment harder after the recession of the middle 1970s, than it has done after similar trade cycles in this Keynesian era. One reason is said to be that a gradual reshaping of the industrial structure will make movement back into pre-recession occupations a less available option than before. In principle, such a tendency towards structural unemployment could be contained by retraining and by such other stratagems as shorter working hours and earlier retirement, always provided that private and public resources were able to cover the extra economic demands which more leisure habitually generates. In practice, we could be faced with a good deal of chronic redundancy, especially if automation takes place within a context of slow and unsteady economic growth.

Yet the employment index is only one facet of the challenge posed by automation. A too rapid rate of job obsolescence is psychologically upsetting even if it does not result in a total loss of work. After all, very many millions of men and women all down the ages have defined their own identity largely in terms of what they have taken to be the lasting worth of their particular occupations. Warning us of this, one American manpower economist has remarked how the airline profession of flight engineer emerged and then began to die within a span of but 15 years.

Closely related is a tendency for automation to make most jobs within a given industry more tedious and impersonal whilst it makes a minority more interesting and influential. Executive decision-making tends to get concentrated to a far greater extent than might be justified in terms of the spread of trained talent. By the same token, small groups of craft workers may get into a position to wield a quite disproportionate amount of industrial power.

Enough has perhaps been said to establish the proposition that, even apart from the disturbing effect exogenous factors (wars, embargoes, and the like) may have, the 1980s will generate considerable social strains within the advanced industrial democracies. And as soon as one considers how these strains might manifest themselves, one thinks again of the "youth revolt" of the 1960s, especially that within the universities.

However, anything like an exact replication of that episode is extremely unlikely. The first justification for saying this is the universal one that History can never repeat itself because the actors unfolding the present drama witnessed the denouement of the preceeding one. To it may be added two causes of moral turbulence which, by definition, cannot recur: the general introduction of the contraceptive pill and the war in Vietnam. A third consideration is that many of the university reforms demanded in the 1960s have been conceded, albeit with consequences less gloriously benign than their advocates anticipated. Lastly, no matter how much is said about the relevance of particular syllabi or whatever, it is becoming harder and harder plausibly to berate one's Dean of Faculty as the maladroit father-figure, the man personally responsible for a progressively increasing excess of labour supply over demand in those areas which command the status (and offer the challenges) young graduands have customarily been encouraged to look forward to.

A signal probability is that henceforward youthful dissent will normally peak less but taper off more gradually. In the salad-days of student life, a revolutionary spirit may become less endemic, and also more liable to a backlash from the "great silent majority" within its own peer group. During the subsequent five or ten years of life, on the other hand, it could become more evident than now, perhaps encouraged by a considerable deferment of the average age at which marital responsibilities are assumed.

In fact, something akin to this seems now to be happening to the "women's liberation" movement: as hard-core zealotry recedes, a more subtle influence diffuses. At the same time, signs can be discerned of a growing occupational militancy among young white-collar workers of both sexes.

Not that we should discuss white-collar and blue-collar alienation as if they are on two quite separate planes. For, in reality, this problem of graduate unemployment and underemployment may itself serve to stimulate an interplay between them. Even today, it is not unknown for New Left social scientists with middle-class backgrounds to enlist in industry at shop floor level, ready for shaping careers for themselves as organisers of disruption. Perhaps they are far-sighted, according to their lights. The least that must be acknowledged is that the New Left might find it considerably easier to exert some political pressure through industrial action than ever it would via the ballot box.

Another possible linkage is through the burgeoning, under the auspices of the New Left and the counter-culture, of iconoclastic tendencies in Education at secondary school level, these being reflected in mounting truancy and indiscipline among the pupils themselves. Under such circumstances, we could witness a strong resurgence of the scepticism about the relevance of prolonged formal schooling long endemic in working-class circles in many countries but largely held in abeyance since 1945. If so, the foundations would be laid for a "Why draft teenagers into high school?" movement sufficient to cheer the anti-Renaissance philistines of both extreme Left and extreme Right.

A related cause for anxiety must be the way a questioning of the nature of family life abruptly became much more prevalent throughout the West during the middle 1960s. Nor does one have to be blindly convinced that our grandparents had all the answers for all time to feel this anxiety on behalf of the generation coming to maturity in the 1980s and beyond. For every serious commentator on this matter of parenthood seems to accept two basic propositions. One is that this whole subject is still beset by imponderables. The other is that too rapid a change in social mores in any sphere precludes what might otherwise be satisfactory adjustments in neighbouring spheres.

This being so one cannot but remark on how, for example, the divorce rate in the United States doubled between 1967 and 1974, having remained extraordinarily steady throughout the previous 20 years. And, whilst varying interpretations may be placed on that particular indicator, nobody would deny that mounting evidence throughout American society of the ill-treatment or neglect of children is disturbing.[22] Similar observations can be made of other

Western countries, and the connotations for social and political stability cannot be good.

We almost certainly have to accept that the 1980s will be an era of economic and social change sufficiently sustained, complex and stressful to discomfort continually all interests and all shades of opinion. Also that many if not most of the open societies of the West—Britain, Japan, the United States, Scandinavia, the Old White Dominions—now stand more exposed to aggravating external factors than ever they felt themselves to be in their historical formative years. What we must never resign ourselves to, however, is repeated polarisations of attitudes into confrontational dialogues of the deaf: young versus old, Left versus Right, doves versus hawks, Church versus State, Black versus White. . . . These would lead not only to clumsy handling of the novel problems posed. They would also consume vast amounts of political energy best devoted to other matters, not least in external affairs. Above all, they would reduce the great silent majority in each country to bewilderment and then passivity, thereby leaving the polity in question wide open to violent subversion.

No assessment of the prospects for avoiding a migration to extremes would be complete without some reference to the mass media in general and television in particular. To my mind, an exceptionally succinct yet incisive assessment of the role of these great oligopolies was recently provided by the Chief Rabbi in Britain, Dr Immanuel Jakobovits,

> They have made an immense contribution to strengthening the social and moral conscience of Mankind. . . . For the first time in history, they have made people really care for, and become involved in, the sufferings of others thousands of miles away. . . . But these tremendous benefits have been secured at an unnecessarily high, perhaps sometimes excessive, cost. . . . It lies in the nature of our system of mass communications that by publicising the freak more than the common, the exceptional becomes the norm. . . . The media thus amplify dissension and muffle the voice of stability; they advertise lawlessness while reducing the appeal of decency and order. . . .[23]

David Holden, a reputable British journalist who has likewise addressed himself seriously to such matters, fears that the knowledge explosion of today can be just as conducive to myth-acceptance as the knowledge dearth of yesterday:

> The world gets divided into goody goodies and baddy baddies, like the cast of a second-rate Western. We're all expected to recognise, for

example, that South Africa is a baddy baddy country—and how comforting it is to be so sure of it. . . . We actually harden existing attitudes. It's as if in sheer self-defence we reach for stereotypes and predigested images to protect ourselves against the otherwise incomprehensible barrage of words and pictures.[24]

These strictures are ones that de Tocqueville would well have understood. They also coincide closely with the Fromm stereotype of the apotheosis of Renaissance Man. Unfortunately, there is only a sporadic public debate on these and related issues, largely because the mass media themselves tend to be more sensitive to criticism than they expect others to be.

No doubt their sensitivity mainly derives from apprehension lest the implications of criticism are total state control. Yet this association of ideas may not be entirely rational. To point out the less desirable consequences of canalising the flow of information through oligarchies can hardly be to demonstrate that monopoly would be superior.

Fortunately, however, this particular wheel may be going full circle by 1990. Already in some aspects of communication a strong swing back towards the multiplication of outlets and decentralisation has begun; and all the indications are that this will extend further across the board, not least into television. Moreover, this trend is not due solely or even primarily to the spread of affluence, education, and leisure. It owes most to the follow-through of the self-same technological revolution as induced the great concentration to start with. Among the most relevant manifestations of this follow-through are or will be these: offset printing, xerography, hand-held cine cameras, television by satellite and telecast newspapers.

Inevitably this transformation, too, will be unsettling in some ways. It is easy to imagine many intellectuals, for example, being more than a little worried by any suggestion that the book was an obsolescent art form! Even so, enormous scope will be afforded overall for the devolution of political and cultural activity, thereby consolidating liberal democracy around its grass-roots. By this is meant not the underwriting of such separatist proclivities as 600,000 Basques or 6,500,000 Quebecans then retain.

Rather it will be a matter of focusing on a multiple improvement in the "quality of life" at shop floor, urban precinct or village level. Such a benign reversion would be very much in line with some of the salient contemporary aspirations within the revolution of rising expectations: "consumerism", parent-teacher consultation, adult education, workers' participation, humanising the working environment and so on. At the same time, it might harness to the advantage of all parties the surpluses of idealistic talent now being generated by the almost constant expansion of full-time education, especially higher education.

All the same, this in itself will not enable us to avoid a major crisis in the 1980s over educational means and ends, the preparation for life and work of the young people who are any nation's prime guarantors of survival, in every sense. My recollection is that it was the late J. B. S. Haldane who said some 25 years ago that, by the turn of the century, the greatest public debates would be about educational philosophy. At all events, it was an extraordinarily prescient remark. For instance, the whole Western world cannot but be within a few years of a most searching reconsideration of the wisdom of consigning ever more teenage people to full degree courses at a time when the societies to which they must return are becoming far shorter of plumbers and electricians than ever they are of geographers or even electrical engineers. Contrariwise, access to higher education later in life stands almost everywhere in need of improvement. Then again, one does not have to endorse some of the more facile talk about Councils of the Future in the high schools and Chairs of Futurology in the universities to appreciate that, in all modern education, both techniques and syllabi need continual revision in anticipation of changing requirements. So may the premises on which they rest.

The big danger is that, fearful of depriving Education of its mystique, powerful influences will seek to defer or circumvent so general a reappraisal. But if so, they may precipitate, however inadvertently, a crisis throughout the open societies of the West perhaps as grave as defeat in several limited wars.

Still, the chances are that so apocalyptic an outcome will be avoided. Accordingly, we may expect educational expansion to proceed more or less smoothly. Between 1960 and 1970 the mean proportion of the Gross National Products of the developed world devoted to Education rose from 3·7 to 5·4 per cent; and a further rise to c. 7·5 in 1990 seems probable. But henceforward this trend is not likely to be justified by bold claims that big dividends readily accrue. Instead, the contention will be that preparation for membership of a modern society is a long and arduous slog, involving heavy outlays and oft-diminishing returns. In other words, a more austere climate of opinion will have replaced the heady optimism of the 1950 to 1965 era, when Education was veritably a secular religion with the universities as its cathedrals.

But there is one sector of civil affairs which had similarly major implications for social stability and in which sober reassessment has long since begun. This is, of course, urban expansion and renewal. How does one combine the functional advantages of the large scale with the human attractions of the small? How does one plan without stereotyping? Can an overview leave room for local initiatives?

One has only to recall how widespread was the cult of the high-rise blocks of flats two decades or so ago to recognise in all humility that the liberal democracies have not been conspicuously more successful in resolving these dilemmas than have the Marxist states. For these now generally discredited bases for family life were endorsed almost as glibly in North America, Western Europe and Scandinavia as in Eastern Europe and the Soviet Union. What makes this sorry truth the more germane is the prospect that (as will be shown in the next chapter) the urban problem is one the newly developing world will find looming ever larger. Therefore, it is likely to figure more and more prominently in the ideological struggle world-wide between open societies and closed.

Notes

1. John Strachey, *Contemporary Capitalism*, Victor Gollancz, London 1956. Chapter XIII.
2. See H. V. Hodson's "Re-Reading Keynes's General Theory: Still Relevant Today?" *Encounter*, April 1973.
3. John Hicks, *The Crisis in Keynesian Economics*, Basil Blackwell, Oxford 1974, p. 61.
4. *1974 Encyclopedia Britannica Book of the Year*, Encyclopedia Britannica, Chicago 1974, p. 19.
5. See Chapter 8.
6. See Peter Jay "Will Konratieff prove stronger than Keynes?" *The Times*, 24 December 1971.
7. *The Times*, 12 January 1973.
8. See Chapters 22 and 26.
9. In the 18th and 19th centuries, this term served to cover what we know as the discipline of Economics. In fact, it was couched thus to distinguish that relatively olympian subject from its more parochial cousins, "domestic economy" and "rural economy".

Just occasionally, and particularly in Scotland, it is accorded this pristine meaning still. In all probability, however, the majority of specialists would today take it to refer to attempts to bridge the gap which has yawned open between Economics and political studies.
10. H. G. Wells, *Anticipations* (1901) p. 146.

11. Eric Fromm, *The Fear of Freedom*, Kegan Paul, Trency, and Trubner, London 1942, p. 40.

12. Ibid., pp. 236–8.

13. Robert Gilpin, *Foreign Policy*, No. 70. Spring 1973, p. 124.

14. Alvin Toffler, *Future Shock*, Bodley Head, London 1970, p. 83.

15. See, for example, *Medicine in the 1990s, a technological forecast*, The Office of Health Economics, London 1969.

16. Toffler, op. cit., p. 13.

17. Michael Stewart, *Keynes and After*, Penguin, London 1972. Chapter 12.

18. See E. J. Fisher in Lord Avebury *et alia*, *Computers in the year 2000*, National Computing Centre, Manchester 1972. Chapter 11.

19. "The Thumbnail Brain", *The Economist*, 7 August 1976.

20. *The Times Higher Educational Supplement*, 8 June 1973.

21. Peter Drucker, *The Age of Discontinuity*, William Heinemann, London 1969. Chapter 2.

22. *The 1976 Britannica Book of the Year*, Encyclopedia Britannica, Chicago 1976, p. 166.

23. "Religion has a major role to play in leading civilisation away from the brink of disaster". *The Times*, 27 January 1975.

24. *The Listener*, 8 January 1970.

6

The Urban Implosion

That the incessant rise in the human population of this planet is sure to be one of the most powerful determinants of our future environment is something "every schoolboy" knows. What merits a deal more attention than it has yet received, on the other hand, is an accelerating tendency for the overall rise to find expression in urban increase. The implications, not least from the international security standpoint, appear awesome for the 1980s and beyond.

Let it be admitted straightway, however, that the subject is one which has attracted far more than its fair share of facile generalities. Large cities are not afflicted with social malaise as inescapably as the more shrill critics of this mode of existence would have themselves and the rest of us believe. Nor is the cause of definitive analysis and instructive prediction furthered by glib correlations (*pace* Lewis Mumford) between urban expansion and the pervasive cult of gigantism in technology and administration: "The swish and crackle of paper is the underlying sound of the metropolis".[1] Nor has the tension associated with city life always been uncreative. Nor must urban frustration invariably find release in the same set patterns of deliberate violence. For instance, though modern Tokyo is a vast and extremely congested conurbation, it has as yet been relatively free of such individualised crime as mugging and vandalism. Likewise, the recorded rate of murder and manslaughter in another East Asian centre, to wit Hong Kong, is as yet lower than its parlous circumstances might lead one to expect (see Chapter 15).

But the fact remains that the inadequacy and fragility of city life has been too prominent a theme in fiction and, latterly, in social science to be carelessly brushed aside. Nor should we be too quick to dismiss as pure convention a recurrent disposition, certainly in English literature, to look back to a supposedly idyllic rural-urban balance of a generation or two ago: George Orwell, Thomas Hardy, William Cobbett and Oliver Goldsmith being familiar exemplars. The general inference which could be drawn is that the really vexatious aspects of urbanisation stem less from its total extent at any given time than from the rate at which, and the manner in which, it is extending.

What makes this thought the more pertinent is the dramatic way the implosion of people into towns and cities will gather strength over the next two decades, very particularly in the newly developing world. One United Nations estimate of the number of urban dwellers in the more developed regions showed growth from 717 million in 1970 (66 per cent of their total population) to 864 in 1980 and 1021 (or 76 per cent) in 1990 AD. The corresponding figures for the newly developing lands are 635 million in 1970 (25 per cent of their total), 990 in 1980, and 1496 (or 36 per cent) by 1990.[2]

Moreover, this latter trend is bound to quicken all through the 1980s, about half the net gain being caused directly by migration from the countryside. In fact, parallel UN calculations show a transference from rural to urban environments within the newly developing countries alone of over 200 million in the coming decade as against a modest 90 million in the 1950s and only 25 million in the 1920s.

Unfortunately, such prognoses are rendered the more disturbing by the way the urban implosion tends to focus on capitals and other cities that are already large, the London metropolitan area lately being something of an exception. Thus by 1985 Greater Tokyo will have, on current showing, a population of 25,000,000. Among the other conurbations with 12 million or more will probably be Bombay, Buenos Aires, Calcutta, Los Angeles, Mexico City, New York, Osaka, Peking, São Paulo and Shanghai. So, decidedly exclusive though this category may be, the only major regions untouched by it are Australasia, Europe, the USSR and Africa. The London metropolis is predicted to lead the European league with 11 million, Moscow the Soviet with eight and Lagos the African with four.[3] Actually, the London figure was nearly 13 at its 1971 peak.

Already, as Ursula Hicks has so forcefully reminded us, big cities are in trouble the whole world over:

> The troubles seem to be particularly severe (if one can particularise) in Japan, India, and the USA; very likely also in China, but that is unknown territory. The worst difficulties occur in areas that have populations of one million or over, rising steadily with the size of the total population. . . . The resultant congestion breeds physical and psychological strain and disturbance. It increases health hazards for even the most fit. It becomes increasingly difficult to collect taxes from the residents and even more so from the army of commuters who daily surge into the city for work, but live outside its jurisdiction. Services in the city are deteriorating, especi-

ally education and public health. Law and order can no longer be taken for granted. In some areas crime is increasing in volume and severity in a quite alarming manner.

Thus it is, says Lady Hicks, that in the urban areas even of "some of the richest . . . countries, the standard of life is visibly going down-hill".[4]

One major complication, so far as the advanced countries are concerned is a shift of population (and, ahead of it, employment opportunities) from the big cities' centres to their newer suburbs: an explosion within the implosion. Thus the numbers inside what are now the limits of the Greater London Council have been falling continually from 9 million at the 1939 peak to a presumptive 6·5 million in 1981.

However, it is the newly developing countries that are experiencing the most blatant manifestations of urban malaise. Two familiar examples may perhaps be cited: Tehran and Calcutta. The haze of pollution that regularly envelops the former epitomises all too well what can happen when the prevailing economic philosophy is too completely *laissez-faire* apropos such matters. Likewise, undue indulgence towards land speculators has led to a hopelessly higgledy-piggledy pattern of new construction. The water supply is quite inadequate despite the presence, immediately to the north, of the majestic Elburz mountains with their heavy rain and snow falls. Instead of underground sewage there are cesspits and open drains, a situation made the more unpleasant by the uncontrolled flow of water from the Elburz. Both traffic regulation and public transport are notoriously chaotic.

What strikes one so forcefully about the Calcutta situation is the sheer pace of population increase. Forty to 50 years ago the popula-tion of Greater Calcutta was well under two million. By 1965 it was seven million; and no less than 57 per cent of the multi-member families had not more than one room to live in.[5] Yet the projection then being made for 2000 AD was of the order of 50 million. Long before the problem reached that pitch, however, some peculiarly nasty Malthusian checks would have been bound to come into play. Mani-festly, too, these would not have improved the prospects for parlia-mentary democracy and the rule of law throughout India as a whole.

Furthermore, urban stress is being seriously aggravated, in a lot of the newly developing countries, by a persisting shortage of administrative and planning expertise. But this in its turn has thus far been largely a reflection of desperate financial stringency. Municipal revenues for all purposes amounted to no more than $84,000,000 in Bombay in 1970 or barely $330 per head of that year's net gain in population. Even in Caracas, the capital of oil-rich Venezuela, municipal revenues totalled only $120,000,000 or little more than $1,000 per head of the population increase.

Given that a major part of all such revenues is perforce earmarked for the continuation of established services to the existing inhabitants, such general indications as we do have of the average capital cost of urban infrastructure by no means reassure. At 1972 price levels, the basic installation of piped water and sewerage typically costs $200 per new resident. So does the construction of standardised "low income" housing. Then another $100 or thereabouts should be allowed as an appropriate slice of investment in primary education. And to this aggregate of $500 must be added the large capitalisation programmes needed for public transport, health, police, fire protection, garbage collection and the like.[6] Small wonder that standards do appear to be widely in decline.

Not that we can rely on rising urban incomes automatically to ameliorate this syndrome, even assuming these rises do occur at all extensively. On the contrary, in the newly developing world as in the Atlantic area, the external diseconomies of scale inherent in city life tend to operate more strongly as consumer durables become more widespread. Almost always, in fact, the motor car rapidly emerges as a salient case in point. Every extra car is an unmitigated nuisance to all except the few who travel in it.

Nearly three-quarters of all the automobiles in Thailand are today to be found in Bangkok; and nearly three-fifths of those in Kenya in Nairobi. Brazil, with barely one car for every 60 people across the country as a whole, has one for every six in São Paulo.[7] Even in so underprivileged a metropolitan area as downtown Amman in Jordan, a veritable barrage of revving and honking nowadays constantly pierces the customary, and far more euphonious, background of confabulation. In this discordance can be seen an all too vivid portent of the impact which will be made by the severalfold increase in car ownership forecast to occur between now and the turn of the century in the newly developing world.

Nevertheless, various writers have rightly emphasised that a glamorous image of urban life has long been endemic in many cultures and that it still allures, especially in late adolescence or just beyond. The colour, diversity, tumult and relative absence of social constraints may all be compellingly attractive at this stage in life. No less evident, however, is the sensitivity of those either side of, say, the 16 to 23-year old age bracket to the filth, congestion and ugliness of the shanty town environments so grimly characteristic of, to use Barbara Ward's graphic phrase, "the cities that came too soon". In Francophone West Africa, the shanty districts are colloquially named after the surplus *bidons* or steel drums much used in their construction. For the *bidonvilles* of Dakar read the *bustees* of Calcutta or the *barriadas* of Lima or the *favellas* of Rio de Janiero.

Besides which, a decidedly negative inference may be drawn from the proposition that young people often leave for the cities simply because they are attracted by what they know of the life styles there. So may it from the way this urban drift is continually being accelerated by the increasing mechanisation of agriculture. This inference is that the prospects of employment in the urban areas are not usually weighed at all carefully and are, in fact, anything but assured. Various surveys of rates of urban unemployment conducted in what generally can be termed the boom era of the late 1960s show this kind of percentage spread: 3·4 in Bangkok and 4·6 in Tehran; 6·0 in urban Chile; 11·6 and 15·0 in the urban districts of the Philippines and Ceylon respectively; and 13·6 and 18·8 in Bogota and Caracas. Generally, too, the rates in the 15 to 25-year old bracket were something like twice the overall average.[8] Inevitably, this urban employment problem will grow more acute in the 1980s.

But this does not mean that we must totally resign ourselves, apropos 1990 or soon thereafter, to a *Nineteen Eighty-Four* norm of urban existence: an utterly uglified and soulless milieu in which a semblance of law and order is retained only by a comprehensive paraphernalia of repression. Calcutta, of all places, has lately given the lie to such profound and fatalistic pessimism. For in the early 1970s the whole situation there did improve markedly following the establishment, under very able leadership, of the Calcutta Metropolitan Development Corporation. Bolstered by an extra inflow of central government funds to the tune of £40,000,000 p.a., this body swiftly applied itself to such amenity improvements as the widespread replacement of the city's 120 miles of open sewers. Almost certainly this tangible reaffirmation of government commitment contributed significantly to the recorded decrease in "Maoist" attacks with bottle bombs and similar devices from 1,600 in 1971 to 570 in 1972.

Even so, it would be naive to imagine that the threat of urban terrorism might always be headed off by good works alone. Quite apart from anything else, the hard core terrorist outlook is characteristically too retrospective and far too paranoid to be thus persuaded. To which one should add that under way already is a general reversal of the swing away from the urban barricade to the rural ambush heralded by Mao Tse-tung and his colleagues in the hills of Kiangsi from 1927 onwards.

In his seminal study of mass urban unrest in "pre-industrial" France and England, George Rudé drew our attention to the critical part the loyalty of the security forces may play in the struggle waged by established authority to retain control.[9] He emphasised as well that this loyalty will largely be determined by the social and political situation overall. What modern practice and theory indicate, however, is that pinpoint actions by a small cellular network may be much more menacing than mass mobilisation to riot or to man barricades (see Chapter 12(b)). Some idea of just how disruptive a judicious mix of such stratagems might be in large conurbations, in particular, is afforded from time to time by strictly apolitical "acts of God". Single power failures have been known to switch off virtually all the air-conditioners or central heating units over very wide areas.

Still, in the final analysis, much will depend on how the population explosion overall develops between now and the turn of the century. The United Nations "medium projections" (i.e. ones based on moderate assumptions about fertility and mortality) have lately been giving world totals in millions as follows: 3,000 in 1960 rising to 4,025 in 1975 and 4,925 in 1985, then to 5,450 in 1990 and 6,500 at the turn of the century. Moreover, the proportion living in the newly developing territories have been expected to rise from 68 to 78 per cent within this overall time span.

Over the years the United Nations has been prone to underestimate rather than exaggerate the upward demographic trend. Nevertheless, the obstinately optimistic would probably draw succour from two tendencies in the current situation. One is a sudden falling off of birth rates in recent years in various advanced industrial nations, a trend that seems set to continue awhile (see Chapter 16(b)). The other is a progressive erosion of the religious taboos about artificial birth control as religious convictions either weaken or become less strictly sectarian. Presumably, this trend, which already is decades old, will continue through the 1980s.

Here the point of departure is that, historically speaking, practically all the major creeds have been at least somewhat hostile to artificial means of birth control. Fatalism and other worldliness have had much to do with it. So has a pro-natalist disposition arising from vigorous endorsement of the family nucleus and of the closely associated precept of male dominance. So, more basically, have the circumstances of penury and high mortality in which these several faiths arose in the first place.

Nevertheless, the consequent constraints have been visibly weakening over the last few decades. Thus *fatweh*—i.e. authoritative pronouncements by religious leaders—issued in Turkey in 1960, in Egypt in 1963, and Jordan in 1964 formally reaffirmed previous contentions that contraception was not necessarily in conflict with the precepts of Islam. Obversely, whilst Hinduism as a whole has no very explicit doctrine on this matter, the attitude of the late Mahatma Gandhi was both militantly overt and viciously bigoted. But it is reasonable to assume that the influence of some of his cruder arguments will steadily diminish as time goes by.

Alongside which one should set the active debate carried on within the Roman Catholic communities world-wide about the absolute stand taken by the Vatican not merely against abortion but against all forms of artificial birth control. Thus in episcopal conferences in at least a dozen countries strong reservations were expressed about *Humanae Vitae*, the Papal Encyclical of July 1968 on this subject. And this reaction can properly be regarded as part of a continuing evolution of thought and practice within the Catholic witness.

What does tend to get overlooked, on the other hand, is the way euphoria about demographic expansion is encouraged by certain of the secular credos of our time. Naturally the Marxist corpus of thought contains no doctrinal objection to family planning per se. Evidently, however, Lenin and others have felt that their declarations of faith in the forthcoming era of Communist abundance had to involve a blanket rejection of Malthusian scepticism. Also that this rejection required the adoption of a strongly pro-natalist posture. One legacy is to be seen in the prevarication so long evinced towards population control by Chairman Mao and his colleagues: the half-heartedness of the 1956 and 1962 essays in that direction and the consequent delay until 1969 of the introduction of a serious programme. In much the same vein was the curiously sympathetic reception accorded *Humanae Vitae* in Cuba and Albania.

Nor is the Kremlin much disposed to promote population control within the boundaries of the USSR. Wide open spaces, the propinquity of China, and an anticipated doubling of the number of old age pensioners during the last three decades of the century militate against this. So does the Soviet "conventional wisdom" that the USSR faces a chronic labour shortage: a belief which, it must be said, is not easy to relate to the persistently inefficient use of so much of its existing labour force.

Above all, an inhibiting anxiety is felt by the Great Russians (54 per cent of the total population in 1970) about the prospect of being overtaken arithmetically by other ethnic groups. The crux of this apprehension is that liberal attitudes towards such conjugal matters as contraception may gain sway more readily in, say, the fashionable suburbs of Moscow than in the towns and villages of Kirghizia. Therefore, it is most improbable that, in the 1980s, mainstream Soviet thinking on global demography will progress beyond the cant of treating it as a pseudo-problem, a mere facet of the "crisis of capitalism". Only Andrei Sakharov and some of his fellow dissidents can be expected to challenge what will otherwise be a decidedly negative contribution to an urgent world debate.

Unfortunately, too, concern with numerical ascendancy (either for totemic reasons or else as a source of voting power) serves to vitiate population control in other inter-communal situations around the world. Thus the fact that family planning has been, to all intents and purposes, a taboo subject in political and official circles in Kenya appears to derive, first and foremost, from the extremely delicate character of the multi-ethnic and multi-sectarian balance there. Likewise, one link in the chain of events which led to the civil war in Nigeria (1967–70) was a huge and deliberate overestimation by the Northern Region in the federal census of 1962 and by all regions in the repeat performance in 1963.

Then again, although in general Jordan has displayed an admirably constructive attitude to economic recovery since 1967 and although, too, family planning is already practised by a high proportion of the more educated people, there has been a manifest disinclination to encourage it officially. Whilst this may, in part, stem from a fear of precipitating a head-on clash with the Moslem Brotherhood and other conservative factions, it is also the product of a desire not to lose the numbers game with Israel.[10] Not so very different, one might add, is the way Gaullists attach almost as much importance to

France's demographic weighting within Western Europe as they do to its nuclear deterrent.

And to the above considerations must now be added a strong inclination throughout the newly developing world to dismiss talk by the advanced nations of the merits of smaller families as a neo-colonialist con-trick: commending as a solemn obligation for lesser mortals what they themselves are opting for as a matter of hedonistic preference. In short, a whole complex of political attitudes continue to militate strongly against birth rate reductions. So, in some territories, do such infrastructural weaknesses as a shortage of nurses and doctors. So, in many, do the broader connotations—cultural and administrative—of backwardness. In fact, in most of the countries in which family planning programmes have had a discernible effect on fertility (e.g. South Korea, Taiwan and Singapore) the birth rate had already started to fall in association with a steady improvement in living standards.

Yet none of these judgments provided the chief key to the Malthusian dynamic so far as the 1980s at least are concerned. Instead this lies in what the demographers know as the "pyramid" of age-distribution within a given society. In 1970, for instance, the proportion of the total population below the age of 15 averaged 40 per cent in Southern and Eastern Asia, 42 per cent in Latin America and no less than 44 per cent in Africa, as against norms of only 25 to 30 per cent in the demographically more stable societies of North America, Europe and the USSR. And, as a rule, one implication of any percentages in excess of 35 or so is that the next ten to 15 years are virtually certain to see a sharp rise in the rate at which new family units are created, a rise sufficiently marked to offset heavily any tendency for the number of births per family to diminish.

What is more, plenty of scope remains in certain regions for further dramatic falls in the death rate. Ominously enough, movement in this direction was arrested, in various parts of Southern Asia and Africa, in the hungry early 1970s.

Certainly, there is little enough sign at present of any overall abatement of population pressure across most of Afro-Asia and Latin America. Precious little indication, indeed, of much this side of 1990. Over the first half of this century the mean global rate of increase was 0·8 per cent per annum. In the 1950s there was a spurt to 1·8 per cent and, in the 1960s on to 2·0 per cent. Between mid-1972 and mid-1973 the world total, as estimated by the United Nations, rose by 78 million to 3,860 million. Over the next 12 months the rise was reckoned to be 72 million or 1·9 per cent; and this was with sharp falls in the natural increase under way in the Atlantic area and also East Asia, two zones that together embraced 40 per cent of Humanity. Among the territories that would double their population by 1995 at their 1973 growth rate were Algeria, Morocco and Rhodesia; Gaza, Iraq, Jordan, Pakistan and Syria; the Philippines and Thailand; the Bahamas, Honduras, Mexico and El Salvador; Colombia, Ecuador, Paraguay, Surinam and Venezuela. Metaphorically, that list alone could be termed a disconcertingly far-flung empire of Malthusianism.

In all fairness one should, by way of conclusion, enter a caveat. It is that we have gained to date only a limited amount of experience in projecting urban increase on the global plane within the given context of population growth as a whole. Moreover, what we do have does seem to confirm that urban trends may be more sensitive than are the overall ones to such variables as the present decline of birth-rates in the West and the Far East. Even when the most generous allowance is made for this penumbra of uncertainty, however, there cannot be much doubt that ill-prepared urban increase will be an increasingly serious source of instability throughout the newly developing world as the 1980s progress. Some of the consequences for international security are considered elsewhere in this study.

Notes

1. Lewis Mumford, *The City in History*, Pelican, London 1961, p. 622.
2. Population Studies No. 49. *The World Population Situation in 1970*, UN Department of Economic and Social Affairs, New York 1971. Chapter 6. A more recent, though less far-ranging, UN survey shows a two to three per cent decrease in the projected level for 1980 in the more developed countries and a similar increase in the less advanced.
3. *New Patterns of Urbanisation*, International Union of Local Authorities, The Hague 1975, Table 2 and 3.
4. Ursula K. Hicks, *The Large City: A World Problem*, Macmillan, London 1974, p. 3.
5. Nirmal Kumar Bose, "A Premature Metropolis", *The Scientific American*, Vol. 213, No. 3, September 1965, pp. 91–102.
6. *Urbanisation*, World Bank, Washington 1972, p. 19.
7. "You're never too poor to have a traffic problem", *The Economist*, 22 September 1973.
8. Richard Jolly *et alia*, *Third World Employment*, Penguin, Harmondsworth 1973. Chapter 2, Table 2.
9. George Rudé, *The Crowd in History*, John Wiley, New York & London 1964, p. 266.
10. See the author's "After the Showdown: Jordan is on the Move", *The New Middle East*, No. 48. September 1972, pp. 20–4.

7

The Pressure on World Resources

Not infrequently, discussion of the world resource outlook revolves around the assumption that the most critical bottlenecks will perforce occur in what are termed "the non-renewable" products—e.g. oil and, some recycling of scrap excepted, the metals. Yet this assumption is one which not only lacks theoretical justification but also accords less than perfectly with our current experience. As much can be seen by reference to the situation in marine fisheries plus whaling. Suddenly, it is dawning on us that, in this respect as in others, the notion of the "indivisible world ocean" as a "great universal common", on which all people may garner what they will, is fast becoming obsolete, a trend that could have evident and unhelpful connotations for international law and world peace well before 1990.

Yearly estimates of the world catch of fish rose from 25,900,000 tons in 1953 to 48,400,000 tons in 1963 and to 69,700,000 tons (i.e. forty pounds for every living person) in 1971. However, by this last date proof enough of overfishing (which only a decade or two before had largely been confined to the North Sea and certain inshore locations) was coming in from many parts of the Atlantic, the Pacific and even the Indian Ocean; and the following year total world output was actually to fall by six per cent. Nor did any appreciable recovery take place in 1973.

One sector in which the sequence of rise and fall was extraordinarily dramatic was the production of anchoveta off the coast of Peru, largely for conversion into fishmeal. Between 1956 and 1970 this rose from virtually nothing to over 12,000,000 tons annually. Yet within three years the yield was back to well under 3,000,000 tons, thanks to a slackening of the nutritious Peruvian cold current and drastic overfishing. How complete and sustained will be the recuperation since observed in these waters, time alone will prove.

Just how disturbing the overall picture looks can be illustrated by the fact that, in Japan and many other countries in the Far East or

4*   93

sub-Saharan Africa, about a half of the animal protein consumed comes from fish. Still, much consideration has been given in recent years to the possibility of hunting for fish more widely and deeply and, in due course, of multiplying catches severalfold through fish-farming, this being done in fresh water as well as salt.

Meanwhile, the more radical commentators talk freely of extensively harvesting other forms of life in the sea food chain—e.g. plankton and seaweed. Nor do they do so without reason. After all, a widely accepted figure for the continuous creation of organic matter in the world's seas and oceans is *c.* 130 billion tons a year or over half a ton a week for every man, woman and child on Earth.[1]

Even for the more exotic ideas, there are firm historical precedents. In Aztec Mexico, vegetables were grown in gardens floating on fresh water whilst loaves were made from algae reared in fresh water lakes. Fish-farming in ponds and tanks has been practised in China for a good four thousand years and in Europe for two. Today work on hatching and maybe rearing various species of fish continues on a modest scale in many places around the world.

But the very fact that such activities have this impressive historical and geographical spread, and yet are still no more than ancillary, reflects the persistence of serious constraints on their development, constraints which probably preclude their making a substantial contribution for another decade at the very least. Furthermore, whilst some of the negative factors at work are cultural or political in nature, the most serious are severely practical. Phytoplankton are in such dilute suspension that, in order to harvest just one ton of them, it would usually be necessary to process about a million tons of ocean by some manner of means! Then again, even in favourable locations fish-farming in inshore waters poses major problems of environmental control; and the solutions to these problems will usually require not only much capital but also far more experimental data than we yet possess.

A dearth of the sort of knowledge needed to plan systematically the hunting or farming of fish and other marine animals is, in fact, one of the legacies of the customary view of the sea as common domain, a sphere to which all have access but for which none bear specific responsibility. Another is the continued use of the seas as a dumping ground, a practice rendered the more immediately damaging by a high proportion of Mankind's fin-fish supplies (plus, of course, all its saltwater shellfish) being found in the relatively shallow waters of the continental shelf. Already pollution by Man is having a decidedly deleterious effect on several of the more enclosed seas—e.g. the Caspian and the Mediterranean.

What is more, such attempts as have been made at the multilateral regulation of marine harvests have been less than brilliantly successful. Thus the present altercations about fishing quotas off Western Europe's coast are not exactly edifying. Nor did the establishment of the International Commission for the North-West Atlantic Fisheries in 1949 end the undue exploitation of those important waters.

Still less could anybody claim that the creation the previous year of the International Commission on Whaling ushered in a new era of good husbandry in the sector in question: the narrow chauvinism evinced by the USSR and Japan precludes that even now. Nobody would ever guess on the current showing that, ever since the dramatic whaling boom experienced during the Antarctic summer of 1930–31, solemn warnings have repeatedly been given by experts that the celebrated whaling industry in those waters was slowly but surely destroying itself much as its counterpart in the North Polar seas had done. Nor that between 1964 and 1971 the world output of whale and sperm oil fell by almost exactly half.

When social and political considerations are blended with technical, the impression left is that we will be lucky indeed to sustain the harvest from the sea at its present level through 1990. In any case, this marine produce can only alleviate significantly the world shortage of fats, protein and certain vitamins: it can have little bearing on the carbohydrate balance. For these several reasons, the decisive campaign in the battle against starvation will perforce be that waged on land.

Assessments of the prospects for world agriculture are characterised by a starker contrast between the pessimists and the optimists than is apparent in regard to fisheries. Also by pronounced fluctuations in the public fortunes of the two schools of thought. What is little in doubt, at any rate, is the drama of the situation.

In 1969, several years of work on the newly developing lands within the Food and Agriculture Organisation (FAO) of the UN came to fruition with the publication of an Indicative World Plan for Agricultural Development (IWP). Allowance was made for an anticipated population increase between 1962 and 1985 of 75 to 80 per cent as well as for eliminating the malnutrition from which some 15 per cent of the population of Afro-Asia and Latin America was reckoned to be suffering.

A need to accommodate a substantial general increase within these regions in spending power per head was also taken into account.

Duly, the aggregate rise in the volume of food required by the newly developing part of the world over the 23 year span in question was calculated to be no less than 142 per cent—i.e. 3·9 per cent per annum as against the 2·8 per cent p.a. actually registered there in the decade, 1955–65. True, the FAO described the IWP as provisional. Agreed, too, that some believe the FAO does tend to over-estimate minimal calorific intakes, a disposition which could derive from a reluctance on the part of experts to make proper allowance for differences in average weight, climatic background and whatever other factors may be thought by the naive or malevolent to confirm ethnic stereotypes. Added to which are the difficulties involved in measuring median food intakes to within about 10 per cent.

Nevertheless, it was clear that hunger, actual or prospective, posed a global challenge of very considerable magnitude. Before the IWP was published, indeed, some well-informed observers had resigned themselves to this challenge being insurmountable, to an extensive Malthusian catastrophe being not only unavoidable but also rather imminent. Herein lay, of course, the genesis of the notion (referred to in Chapter 2) that "triage" was the only answer to the famine destined to stalk the Earth by 1975.

The immediate cause for concern was that, in 1965 and again in 1966, harvests had been so poor in many areas—mainly as a result of rainfall deficiency—that food output per head in Africa, South and East Asia, and Latin America was little, if any, higher than the average for the late 1930s. But then, in 1967, aggregate crop yields in these lands rose no less than six per cent.

This rather remarkable recovery owed something to higher prices and better weather and also to the maintenance of a general improvement in methods. In addition, however, severalfold increases in output per acre were locally registered in various countries (notably India and Pakistan) by the use—in conjunction with intensive irrigation and lavish applications of fertiliser and pesticides—of new "dwarf" strains of wheat, rice and maize. By virtue of having short but stiff stalks, these could absorb in solution a great deal of nutrient without growing too high and collapsing. Their advent was the result of over

20 years of concentrated research, principally under the auspices of the Rockefeller Foundation.

Even when due note had been taken of such contributory factors as climatic fluctuation and expanding acreages, the UN index of food production per capita for "the developing market economies" soon bespoke the onset of this "Green Revolution". From a value of 100 in the averaged base years of 1961–65, it dropped to 97 in 1966 only to rise to 102 by 1970. Hence all the sanguine talk heard at that time of such rosy prospects as the Indian subcontinent's finally becoming self-sufficient in grainstuff from 1975 onwards.

Yet now the outlook is being adjudged less cheerful again, the energy crisis being one shadow across the future. Admittedly, of the 17,000,000 tons of oil India, for instance, was importing by 1973 only one million was diesel destined for consumption in agricultural work.[2] In other words, annual usage for this purpose was not yet one gallon per cultivated acre as against dozens of gallons in the advanced nations; and similar ratios obtain apropos artificial fertiliser, another range of commodities which have become much more expensive in the wake of the energy crisis. However, these contrasts should be seen, first and foremost, as an indication of how heavily an increase in farm yields in countries like India will depend on a big expansion of hydrocarbon imports. The Green Revolution is nothing if not capital-intensive; and that most certainly means energy-intensive as well. So what about the resultant strain on the balance of payments?

Another spectre which has lately appeared at the intended feast is what some apprehend may prove to be a sustained and radical change in the global climate, a change which, irrespective of its character, will be much for the worse if it occurs too fast to allow adjustments to be made. At the heart of this problem lies the question of whether the atmosphere of the Earth (or at least of the Northern Hemisphere) might not be steadily cooling. Between 1880 and 1940 the mean temperature of the Northern Hemisphere did, in fact, rise $c.$ 0·8°C. But in the subsequent three decades nearly half this gain was lost. Thus examination of the mean sea temperatures recorded by Ocean Weather Ships on North Atlantic stations in the 1950s and 1960s reveals a general downward trend which, though variable over time and between locations, was frequently pronounced.[3] Then again, in England at least, the awesome Western European winter of 1962–63 was quite the worst since 1740, whilst the 1947 one had been the severest for more than a century. Meanwhile, the North polar ice was visibly increasing. Furthermore, extrapolation from the analysis of ice cores in Greenland and tree rings in Lapland portend a good half century of colder weather than at present.[4]

Now even on this comparatively simple matter of alterations in the global temperature there can be, and are, contending schools of thought. Some would insist, for example, that such techniques as ice core analysis are altogether too crude to be used for prediction a mere decade or two ahead. More importantly, a recent study in the Meterological Office does suggest that since 1970 the downward drift of mean temperature has been arrested, at any rate in the higher latitudes where it had mainly been concentrated. Correspondingly, there has been a marked reduction in the land snow cover (except for an area north of the Himalayas) and in sea ice.[5] In March 1976 there were 1,400,000 more square kilometres of open water between South Greenland and Novaya Zemlya than seven years previously.

On the other hand, under ten per cent of the past several hundred thousand years have experienced climates cooler than those to which we have become accustomed. What is more, during the geological era in question, major turning points from warmer to cooler conditions have characteristically occurred at intervals of something like 30,000 years; and, on that basis, the next is already overdue. Once again, we are faced with the crudity inherent in applying so sweeping an overview to a decade or so. Nor can we extrapolate with any great confidence the chaotic shorter term patterns. On balance, however, the evidence does suggest that the period 1977–90 will be no warmer than the decade 1965–75; and that seems to have been the coolest such interval across the Northern Hemisphere for a good half century.[6]

Naturally, a general cooling down often has a direct agricultural effect, shorter growing seasons and so on. Nevertheless, some experts would attach more importance to what they see as the broad concomitants of this trend. They would say that it is associated with big alterations in the whole planetary wind system. For one thing, the successive belts of climate (which are basically aligned latitudinally) are gradually being pushed equatorwards, an oft-cited example being the way the Sahara has been slowly swinging south as rainfall averages rise around the Mediterranean and fall around an axis through Dakar and Lake Chad. For another, the atmospheric circulation as a whole is weakening, one manifestation in southern England being a decrease in the mean annual number of westerly-type days from 110 around 1925 to 75 around 1968. As a result, rain-bearing winds from the sea carry less readily into continental interiors; and this in its turn means that, so far as the world's land masses are concerned, coastal regions exposed to the prevailing air current tend to get wetter (because the moist air lingers) whilst the drier areas (most notably, the continental interiors) correspondingly get even drier. Needless to say, neither tendency is good news for farmers.[7]

Another correlation perceived is that, in the absence of a sufficiently strong general circulation to iron out incipient aberrations, random and freakish climatic patterns become more frequent. By this argument, the succession of exceptionally mild winters North-West Europe has lately enjoyed can be made to co-exist happily, at least on first examination, with the more fundamental cooling of the atmosphere referred to above. In like manner, the great Western European droughts of 1975 and 1976 can plausibly be squared with the mean changes in rainfall patterns world-wide. The same goes for the failures of India's monsoon in 1965, 1966 and 1972 and for the sundry climatic perversities that have plagued Bangladesh.

Yet once again some acute difficulties present themselves. Most basic is the sheer complexity of the global "weather machine". Thus the interiors of the USSR and the USA have evident geophysical similarities. Even so, the former remained comparatively moist during what were for the latter the "dust bowl" years of the 1930s. We tend also to think of the North and South polar regions as subject to similar mechanisms. But in the first few decades of this century, when the ice fields in the former zone were visibly receding, the latter were, if anything, tending to increase. Similarly, our admittedly patchy Southern Hemisphere data base currently affords little indication of the Northern trends of general cooling and an expansion of the polar vortex.[8] What is more, parameters that do correlate well in one decade, either regionally or globally, often utterly fail to do so in the next.

Nor is the situation helped in any wise by the plain fact that the cousinly sciences of climatology and meteorology have not been vanguard ones for very long. Deficiencies in the joint data base have often been serious, especially in the days before satellite reconnaissance. Sophisticated macro-analyses of the patchy yet voluminous material being made available have had to wait upon, among other things, very high performance computers. Moreover, extraordinary though it might sound, it is not hard to discern—even in meteorology —a bias against predictive investigation as opposed to what are seen as purer forms of research. Hardly surprising then that specialists are still unable to identify with any confidence the critical variables, Man-induced or otherwise, in the natural sequence of weather and climate. This is why some do, indeed, feel able to explain the alarming Western European droughts of 1975 and 1976 in terms of the "freak" hypothesis whilst others can go on quite the opposite tack and say that the median axis of the Azores high pressure belt is once again swinging northwards.

The fact remains, however, that, by 1975, the incidence of climatic aberrations did seem disconcertingly high in many territories both sides of the equator.[9] Nor could this state of affairs be accounted for at all convincingly in terms of sunspot cycles or other such transient factors. In the light of this and of the other considerations here adduced, it would be only common prudence to assume that such occurrences will remain relatively frequent through the 1980s with adverse implications for agriculture, not least the Green Revolution.

Even in the halcyon days of 1969–70, however, the Green Revolution was not immune from criticism. As market prices showed, the new strains of rice and some of the high yield wheats were widely regarded as inferior in taste and consistency. Concern was also expressed lest the monolithic imposition of a mere handful of newly standard varieties might aggravate the epidemic risk. In principle, the obvious answer is repeatedly to cross these "miracle grains" with their local cousins. In practice, lack of knowledge and time might preclude this, as witness the susceptibility to infection of Indonesia's rice crop in 1974.

But what has occasioned most anxiety is the Green Revolution's social impact. Through being applicable, first and foremost, to the best-watered regions, it has been liable to accentuate regional imbalances, at any rate within large countries. Then again, the big demands it makes on capital and raw materials tend to favour the richer peasants and the large landowners as against the poorer peasants, tenant or otherwise. To grasp fully the social and political traumas this effect could induce, one docs best to recall again just how backward, in terms of capital and inputs, agriculture thus far remains across so much of the newly developing world. In 1969 Fritz Baade wrote of several hundred million families across the world at large using no tool except a hoe or little wooden plough.[10]

Linked to this is the question of whether, being capital intensive, the Green Revolution will undermine the rural labour market and so make the urban implosion even faster. Mercifully, the first signs have not been too discouraging on this score. Thus in Northern India, West Pakistan and other regions where the "miracle grains" caught on quickly, the net demand for labour rose considerably as entrepreneurs showed remarkable adaptability in the local development of the engineering industries needed to service the Green Revolution. All the same, it would not be very surprising if, as time goes by, the paramount trend became instead the investment by the farmers of their newly accumulated wealth in labour-saving machinery.

Certainly, fear of an acceleration in this manner of the drift from the land has made many governments understandably chary of the Green Revolution as a whole. No doubt this is why even in Southern Asia, which is generally taken as a spearhead region in this regard, barely a tenth of the total grain acreage was involved by the start of this decade.

Since then the impact has been either masked or curtailed by the other factors alluded to above. Suffice to note that, in 1975 (itself a year of recovery), the per capita food production in the developing market economies was almost exactly the same as for the 1961–65 base line. Even in absolute terms, the advance registered over the dozen or so years in question was but 35 per cent or $c.$ 2·5 per cent per annum. This was too far short of the IWP to be excused in terms of any tendency for that projection to overstate the rising need. Indeed, it even seems uncomfortably far below the actual achievement between 1955 and 1965.

Taking the world as a whole then, one great question is whether food production in the 1980s can be much expanded by pushing out the frontiers of cultivation as per the reclamation done in this generation by the Dutch in the Zuider Zee and the Israelis in the Negev. Inspiring though such particular examples are, however, scepticism may still be justified apropos the overall prospect. A generation ago future-oriented publicists were urging the application to arid margins the world over of the methods pioneered in and near the American "dust bowls" by Franklin Roosevelt's Soil Conservation Service: shelter-belts, strip cropping and the like.[11] Yet even now the great agents of erosion, wind and also water, cause millions of acres to be "abandoned each year in the poor countries, forcing rural people into already over-crowded cities".[12] Nor is dry farming assisted by either the Green Revolution as presently defined or, of course, climatic vagaries.

Then again, some people who should know better haver about the opportunities that ostensibly exist for feeding extra people by clearing vast stretches of rain forest from Amazonia and elsewhere.[13] Yet, whilst to traverse by air a pristine jungle canopy is certainly to imbibe a breathtaking impression of fecundity, the real agricultural potential does not match up. For the lateritic soils which extend in depth across these regions have structures that are not well suited to shallow rooted vegetation and are, in addition, prone to erode rapidly when laid bare to the elements. Besides, extensive deforestation could have ramifying effects on the ecosphere as a whole, a point especially germane to West Africa in view of what some believe to be a continuing southward creep of the Sahara.

One striking feature of the agricultural scene as compared with pre-World War II days is the relatively large increase in yield generally to be discerned in Western Europe and North America, at least when measured per head of population. Undoubtedly, too, there are districts within most of the countries that impinge on the North Atlantic basin in which substantial scope for further advance remains. In fact, in the decade 1963 to 1973, total food production rose by 23 per cent throughout this region, only five percentage points less than in the developing market economies of Afro-Asia and Latin America. Meanwhile, the food output of the centrally planned economies of Eastern Europe and the USSR reportedly rose by 53 per cent despite all the travails of Soviet farming.[14]

Nevertheless, it does now appear that to increase further the material inputs in the agricultural sectors of the advanced nations could be to invite, in many situations, steadily diminishing marginal returns. Already, indeed, evidence has accumulated on some lands of how each successive increment of fertiliser does less to stimulate output and more to pollute the natural drainage. Meanwhile, anxiety has burgeoned, not least in Britain, about the effects on the topsoil of "industrial farming" and the monocultural crop pattern that is its normal concomitant. Assuredly, biological research will go on making an impact, continually ameliorating the bad aspects of modern practice and accentuating the good. Even so, the course is at present set for a progressive retardation of agricultural advance more or less throughout the Atlantic Alliance through 1990, a persistent drift of labour elsewhere usually being a contributory factor. It is a judgment which reinforces the impression that, during the 1980s, the world's farms will recurrently fail to produce the total volume of food the world's population needs, a prospect which augers ill not only for international trade but also for international security.

Moreover, this whole subject is complicated further by a general insistence on the part of the experts that the most serious dietary deficiency may often be not in aggregate bulk or in cumulative calorie yield but in the weight and character of the intake of pure protein. Also by an equally general admission that our knowledge as to human requirements of these body-building materials is even less exact than it is in respect of the prime energy yielding foodstuffs. For instance, whilst few specialists would dispute that animal protein can be more beneficial than plant, there is quite a wide range of opinion as to what quantities should minimally be involved.

One thing is clear. This is that the global spread of protein consumption is wide and getting wider. New Zealanders are said to eat 103 grammes a day, 74 of these being animal. For the Japanese the figures given are 67 and 18; and for India 48 and eight, the latter no doubt being very unevenly distributed.[15] Probably the adult minimum should be at least 50, a fair proportion of it animal. There are 454 grammes to a pound.

A worthwhile boost to the protein diets of the world's poor could, in principle, be achieved forthwith by cutting that of the sizeable minority of the human race which eats a good deal more than it needs or maybe than is good for it. Closely related to this notional possibility is that of by-passing certain side-channels in the flow of protein production: eleven tons of fishmeal fed to chicken, for example, yield but one ton of food for human consumption.

Given the realities of the fragmented world we live in, however, the best hope of sharply augmenting, over the next few years, the supplies reaching newly developing communities probably lies in raising the protein content of standard grains by genetic improvement. Experiments indicate that 100 per cent gains through controlled mutation are within the existing state of the art and so might soon be applied in various parts of the world.

Furthermore, it is protein supply which is likely to benefit most from the more exotic forms of food production being introduced or evolved in the advanced countries. Thus already soya beans are in the forefront of a vigorous drive to manufacture from crops analogues of meat, milk and cheese. Soya has a 40 per cent protein content as against the ten in wheat and 20 in beef whilst it is also rich in fat. And to transmute it into the desired "textured vegetable proteins" industrially is much more efficient quantitatively than using an animal as a converter. Qualitatively, too, the results achieved to date are generally encouraging although the amino acid balance tends to remain vegetable rather than animal.

So it would seem that the potential does here exist for providing a substantial part of the 100,000,000 tons of solid protein which, even on the extremely naive assumption of an equitable distribution, is the absolute minimum the world's population will need to consume directly in, let us say, 1985. How fully this potential will be exploited, by then or subsequently, is another question. One restraining factor may be that, for many years past, some two-thirds of the world's output of soya protein has come from the United States, a state of affairs that does make the extensive world trade in this commodity appear disconcertingly liable to disruption, especially in the aftermath of the ban on soya bean exports Washington temporarily imposed in 1973. The portents are, however, that the development of new strains of soya will permit a wider geographical diffusion. Meanwhile, its native East Asia may come to figure more prominently. At all events, the amount of pure protein harvested in the form of soya content rose from $c.$ 16,000,000 tons annually in 1966 to $c.$ 26,000,000 in 1973; and, on an exponential extrapolation, that could mean $c.$ 60,000,000 tons per annum by the late 1980s. By then, too, other plants (e.g. rapeseed) will be drawn upon.

In the meantime, production processes which are synthetic in a more fundamental sense have got under way in various locations in an endeavour to provide fats, vitamins, amino acids, protein and yeasts considered fit for livestock, at any rate, to eat. Thus one major breakthrough came as early as 1959 when researchers at British Petroleum's French subsidiary discovered—more or less by chance—that, under the right conditions, certain micro-organisms could grow very quickly on some fractions of crude oil, thereby constituting a rich source of protein. True, the economics of petro-basing have become less attractive in the interim. Nevertheless, the medium-term prospects for animal feed thence look good, though it remains doubtful whether—this side of 1985, at least—products of this kind will much be made available for the kitchen table.

Hydroponics (i.e. the growth of plants without soil) is not expected to make a significant impact on the global food balance, protein or otherwise, during this century. The problem here is that, until such time as energy becomes really cheap again, the higher yields per acre will be negatived by exorbitant costs. Still, great store never was set by this possibility.

So, as regards the world protein balance, there is this to be said by way of summation. Thanks largely to social and cultural maldistribution, chronic deficiencies, especially of animal protein, at present seem more widespread in this sector than apropos foodstuffs in general. In particular, the Indian subcontinent is estimated to have embraced 19 per cent of the world's population in 1973 yet produced barely one per cent of its meat supply and not four per cent of its fish.[16] On the other hand, it is entirely conceivable technologically that, by the late 1980s, the various protein gaps will be closing more rapidly than will some of the other shortfalls in world food supply.

(b) THE CRITICAL MARGINS: THE METALS

Alas, the outlook seems a good deal harder to determine with tolerable exactness where the metals are concerned. Certainly, lay circles everywhere are unaccustomed to digesting synoptic assessments of the availability of metalliferous ores which are at all comparable with those put out on the food balance by specialised institutions or individual experts.

For one thing, though the production potential in the latter case is pretty much a function of the Earth's surface features, in the former it emphatically is not. In numerous mines of various kinds, faces one or two thousand feet below the surface are worked, whilst in the central Rand gold has been mined at depths exceeding two miles for many years past. Furthermore, everybody who has ever considered the matter is aware how much the calculated reserves of all metals would be increased if only the respective ores could be recovered from locations much further inside an Earth's crust which is, it should be remembered, between 25 and 40 miles thick.

An added complication is that its unique combination of physical and chemical properties may make any particular metal a special case in the way no foodstuff ever is. Commercially speaking, nothing can quite match chromium for resistance to atmospheric corrosion, platinum for a variety of catalytic actions or tungsten as a hardening ingredient in steel. No perfect substitute exists for copper in many of the more intricate electrical fittings. Mercury's low melting point gives it a unique value in certain contexts. What is more, the metals as a genre have, in their varying degrees, a range of attributes neither wood nor plastics nor anything else can match: ductility, malleability, thermal and electrical conductivity, and so forth.

In the absence of any very coherent overview, both the pessimists and the optimists are left plenty of free rein. The kernel of the former's argument lies in the ineluctable reality that the world's known reserves of various important metals will, even at their present consumption rates, be exhausted in the not very distant future; and if roughly exponential rates of expansion are maintained, at still closer points in time.[17] Thus it does appear that the copper deposits discovered to date, and workable under present conditions, would be gone by 2010 on a linear projection and 1995 on an exponential one. For some other metals, the respective total exhaustion dates are, on these illustrative calculations, approximately as follows: manganese, 2160 and 2020; nickel, 2100 and 2010; molybdenum, 2070 and 2000; lead, tin and zinc, 1995 and 1990 in each case; and mercury, 1984 either way.[18] These terminal years have been derived from certain well-known across-the-board forecasts; and, wherever the sources in question have proved to be considerably at variance, precedence has been accorded the most sanguine.[19] Needless to say, too, production could never go on rising right up to the notional end date. Inevitably it would start to tail off many years before.

The first thing to notice, however, is the omission from this particular list of several metals which are of great utility and of which Nature seems to proffer an almost inexhaustible supply: aluminium, chromium, iron, magnesium, silicon, ... Thus whereas about 510 million tons of pig-iron and associated ferro-alloys were produced world-wide in 1974, it is now realised that Australia alone has several tens of billions of tons of mineable iron waiting in the ground.

Allowance must also be made for the plain fact that mining firms usually have little incentive or inclination to prospect more than a decade or two ahead of immediate need, and often prefer to keep their own counsel about exactly what they have found as yet. This consideration largely explains why, for instance, known copper reserves have expanded from 100 to 300 million tons since 1945, even though 93 million tons have been mined in the meantime.[20] Presumably, too, this is why *The Limits to Growth* gave aluminium reserves a life expectancy of barely thirty years on an exponential curve!

To which consideration may be added the general trend—itself the product not only of rising demand but also of improving technique—towards the exploitation of ores of progressively lower grades. Here again copper can serve as a salient example. At the start of the twentieth century, smelters did not, as a rule, process cupriferous ores of below five per cent copper content. By 1940, one per cent was normally deemed tolerable. Fifteen years later ores with 0·5 per cent or thereabouts were not infrequently being worked. Now the threshold is often lower still.

On the other hand, quite a number of metallic ores do not characteristically display so long drawn out a gradation in richness as the cupriferous ones tend to. Among them are those which contain cobalt, gold, lead, manganese, mercury, nickel, tungsten and zinc respectively. Besides which, the exploitation of low grade deposits may depend on forms of open-cast mining that are environmentally deleterious.[21]

Then there is the question of how much further exploration may postpone the days of reckoning. The Western Australian iron ore fields are one example of huge mineral deposits that were unsuspected as late as 1960. The bauxite reserves of Brazil and the cupriferous rocks of Papua–New Guinea are two more cases in point. A fourth is Australia's very substantial concentrations of nickel ore, production from which rose from almost nothing before 1967 to 36,000 tons (over a twentieth of the world's total) in 1973.

In the Australian context, such discoveries were facilitated by a boosting of the estimated annual expenditure on mineral exploration from five million Australian dollars in 1958 to 40 million a decade later. Yet a great deal of prospecting still remains to be done there. So does it in the vast shield areas of Canada, Siberia, Africa and Brazil. Likewise in such countries as China, Indonesia and Argentina. Over much of the newly developing world, indeed, basic geological mapping is far from complete. Meanwhile, even in the British Isles, which one might think had long since had a surfeit of geological exploration, several score localities are currently being surveyed for fresh mineral finds.

All the same, few people believe that, within established technology, Britain any longer harbours dramatic possibilities for the exploitation of truly virgin deposits. And, even on the global plane, the argument about new frontiers is becoming decidedly double-edged. Granted, a sustained reconnaissance-in-force across previously remote regions can open up entirely new mineralogical vistas, as was, in fact, well demonstrated by Soviet scientists during the first Five

Year Plan (1928–33). Furthermore, such novel or fast-evolving techniques as reconnaissance from Space and the use of seismic or electromagnetic sensors for exploration in depth can enable these dividends to be realised more swiftly than ever before. Yet the corollary must surely be that the frontiers will close all the more quickly and so perhaps take us completely unawares.

What is more, if exponential growth rates in supply have to be assumed, even a severalfold increase in known or assumed reserves may not be of very great avail. Let us hypothesise, for example, about a mineral X of which there are 30 years' reserves at the current rate of consumption. Let us assume, too, that the rate of consumption is, in fact, doubling every 15 years. Then the predicted exhaustion date becomes just under 20 years away. But what if the estimated reserves were multiplied by, let us say, a factor of five which represents, after all, a fairly generous allowance for new discoveries and the like? Then we find that, thanks to the sustained acceleration in consumption, the exhaustion date is postponed only another 20 years or so.

Arguably, however, this inexorable calculus may be offset in significant measure by an empirically-based thesis, developed through analysis at the University of Pennsylvania. What this says is that, as advanced industrial society moves into a phase in which the service trades figure progressively more strongly in economic growth, the use of some key raw materials becomes less intensive overall. Thus, whereas the United States economy consumed 157 thousand tons of crude steel per billion dollars of gross domestic product between 1951 and 1955, this had fallen to 136 by 1966–69. It is reckoned that (at constant prices) the figure for the year 2000 could be as low as eighty-five.

Still, a certain scepticism is justified on this score. Even in regard to the United States, it is not difficult to identify a whole variety of basic materials (ranging from smelted copper to hydrochloric acid), the consumption of which has actually been increasing faster percentagewise than has that of all goods and services. Moreover, when the world as a whole is considered, the output and consumption of minerals (other than the fuels) seem to have been expanding very much in line with economic activity *in toto*. According to the United Nations estimates, both grew by 64 per cent in the decade, 1960–70.[22] Therefore, it would be most unwise to look for any levelling off in demand due to economic evolution such as might be sufficient to lessen overall the pressure on mineral resources.

Nor should we forget that, over the years, the tendency has been to underestimate the growth in demand for key minerals. As much can be seen by comparing forecasts made by the Paley Commission on behalf of the United States government in 1952 for 1975 with the consumption recorded in 1969—six years before the chosen deadline. In the case of lead and also of tin the 1969 figure was five per cent higher. With copper it was 40 per cent, zinc 50 per cent and steel nearly 60 per cent.[23] The astonishing magnitude of the Japanese "economic miracle" should probably be a key part of an explanation.

What needs be borne in mind, too, is that any endeavour to respond to rising expectations by boosting the living standards of the newly developing world to anything remotely approaching North Atlantic levels would place a great extra strain on mineral supplies. Thus the inhabitants of the United States number less than six per cent of the world's total and yet consume between 30 and 45 per cent of all the aluminium, copper, molybdenum, nickel and platinum produced. Even in respect of iron, that most ubiquitous of metals, the American requirement was nearly 30 per cent.

All of which encourages speculation about revolutionary methods of metallic mineral recovery. One approach which commends itself, at least on first examination, is to take ordinary rock or maybe soil and break it down physically and chemically, relying on bulk handling and heavy energy inputs to offset what may often be a very low proportion of the required end product, say one part of usable metal per thousand parts of granite or whatever. But, other considerations apart, there is here a special problem of waste disposal because to granulate solid rock is to increase its volume by between 20 and 40 per cent.

About a hundred years ago, scientists became aware that rather mysterious "manganese nodules" were scattered extensively across the ocean floor. Some 20 years ago, a more widespread interest developed in the possibility of dredging these up, on a commercial basis, from the depths of two miles or more at which they usually occur. Since their distribution is markedly irregular, calculations of their aggregate weight remain inexact. However, one authority believes it could amount to a trillion tons under the Pacific alone.[24]

Though the chemical composition of these nodules also varies widely, a quite typical balance includes 10 to 30 per cent manganese and similarly iron plus around one per cent cobalt, copper and nickel respectively. On the basis of these figures the Pacific deposits alone might, in principle, meet 1976 levels of world demand for cobalt, manganese and nickel for tens of thousands of years together with both copper and iron for several centuries. Large quantities of aluminium, lead and magnesium seem also to be located in this source zone. In addition, the red clays that often line the sea bed in deep waters may eventually be worth mining too.

However, it is doubtful whether the relevant technologies could possibly be developed sufficiently fast to allow any exploitation of deep ocean deposits to become routine is less than 20 years. Nor can we assume that human factors would allow progress to be even that rapid. For one thing, innovations as revolutionary as this do have a tendency to get themselves typecast as goals so remote and elevated that only eccentrics feel any impulse actually to move towards them. Therefore, it does seem that (offshore oil apart) mining the sea-bed will impact on the world scene by 1990 only in the teleological sense that coming events cast their shadows before.

Almost certainly, the same applies to the direct extraction from sea water of such metals as molybdenum, sulphur, tin and uranium. Admittedly, substantial quantities of salt, bromine and magnesium have been obtained in this way for some time past. But, with the other products cited, the throughputs of sea water needed are likely long to remain unacceptably large.

Therefore, it does seem that, come the late 1980s, the relative prices of certain metals will be tending to rise quite steeply as the physical impediments to keeping supply abreast of demand are reinforced by deliberate policies of conservation on the part of producers, either for straight strategic reasons or else in anticipation of price rises to come. Which particular metal markets will experience the resultant strains most acutely must be a matter for specialised prediction. Suffice now to plead that more studies along such lines be initiated urgently.

The same could go, too, for the closely related issue of commercially-viable substitution. Here two rather contrary axioms are set in apposition. One is the uniqueness of each metal individually, and of all metals collectively, alluded to above. The other is the option theoretical economists delight to throw into high, albeit ethereal, relief with their hypothetical "indifference curve" maps, depicting the relative preferences for any two goods at varying purchasing powers and comparative prices. Armed with these models, they are most reluctant to accept that the peculiar merits of chromium, tungsten and so on could ever be such as to rule out substitution in some form, either direct or indirect.

Nor can it be denied that they draw some support from recent history as well as from their own esoteric geometry. Only 30 years ago, it would have seemed extraordinarily difficult to replace tungsten in the cathodes—i.e. negative electrodes—of vacuum valves. In the interval, however, not only have several tolerable alternatives to expensive tungsten been brought into service in electrodes, but the entire situation has been transformed by the wholesale replacement of valves themselves with solid-state transistors using silicon, one of the substances of which we could never run short. Meanwhile, molybdenum has proved just as suitable an ingredient as tungsten in a wide range of hard steel applications.

So should we now be too concerned about the prospect of molybdenum, in its turn, becoming ever more scarce? Might we prove well able to rely on it less to alloy steel and, for that matter, as a catalytic base in industrial chemistry?

As regards the bulk-usage metals, the superabundance of both iron and aluminium potentially affords much scope for redesign and substitution. Thus reports speak of work at the University of Tel Aviv which could lead to vastly improved protection of a variety of metal surfaces by electroplating them with aluminium at an acceptable cost.[25] Meanwhile, plastics continue to displace metals in such configurations as ball-bearings and instrument cases, though it has to be admitted that attempts to match some peculiarly metallic properties (meaning, in particular, electrical conductivity) have thus far met with little success.

All the same, anything like a crash programme for extensive substitution would ineluctably involve rising costs and reduced efficiencies; and this is tantamount to saying that more energy would be demanded per unit of output. By the same token, the extraction of minerals from locations that are less accessible or in which they occur in lower concentration is bound to require more (often, indeed, a good deal more) energy. Probably, it would be fair to say that, to at least as great an extent as with the production of foodstuffs, the final breakthrough to abundance in mineral supply will wait upon the advent of a new era of cheap energy. But can that occur this century?

(c) The Energy Prospect

Estimated world production of energy, expressed in billions of tons of coal equivalent, rose from 4·3 in 1960 to 8·0 in the crisis year of 1973. In other words, it had been expanding almost as fast as the total output of goods and services.

Comparing the several major regions, no very clear pattern of differential growth emerged. What must be said, however, is that the consumption gap between rich nations and poor generally remained even more pronounced than the disparity in average living standards. Incredible though it may sound, per capita energy consumption in the United States was reckoned to be over 400 times that in Bangladesh.[26]

In calorific terms, a ton of coal corresponds to 0·65 tons of diesel fuel or 2,500 kilowatt-hours of electricity. From the latter equation, one may calculate that, if all the energy the world used in 1973 had taken the form of electricity, it would have amounted to 20,000 billion (if you like, 20 trillion) kilowatt-hours (kwh).

What makes this calculation of some practical consequence is an already established tendency for electricity to grow in importance, relative as well as absolute, as an intermediate energy form. Thus, between 1960 and 1973, the production of it roughly trebled to become 6,000 billion kwh or about 30 per cent of the aggregate energy output. On this showing, nearly half the 17·5 or so billion tons of coal equivalent the world might be expected to use in 1990 could take this form. Furthermore, every improvement in the efficiency with which the standard fuel sources are converted to electrical power will steepen even this projection. Not that any such improvements are likely to be big in the time-span we are looking at.

All in all, it is a prospect that widens the scope for substitution of oil through the steady introduction of nuclear power and a modest revival of coal; and, of course, an economic or strategic need for such substitution will, in its turn, sustain or even accelerate the swing towards electricity. There may well, for instance, be a renewed emphasis on electrified rail transport. What can virtually be ruled out for this side of 1990, however, is the regular use of the battery-driven car.

Perhaps, too, this last judgment may serve to underline a more basic reality. It is that electricity is no elixir which can enable us to duck the crucial question of whether the world's oil supplies can possibly last sufficiently long to permit a manifold, but not too traumatic, adjustment to their eventual exhaustion. World consumption of petroleum was nearly 2,800 million tons in 1973, and had lately been increasing at about seven to eight per cent per annum. As regards the proportions of total energy requirements met from this source, these were put at 25 per cent in 1972 in the Sino-Soviet zone, 45 per cent in the United States, 65 per cent in Western Europe (80 per cent in coal-starved Italy), and c. 75 per cent in both Japan and Latin America.[27]

By that year Japan was quite the biggest oil importer, topping the 200 million ton mark, in fact. But Britain, France, West Germany and Italy took between 100 and 120 million tons apiece. Meanwhile, the United States was rapidly overhauling all four of them. Furthermore, in each of these cases save the last, reliance on North Africa and the Middle East was of the order of 90 per cent. Indeed, about 40 per cent of the total world output was coming from that broad band of territories.

Were prices to remain tolerably steady, the world demand for petroleum would probably rise by around five to six per cent a year between 1977 and 1990; and five would closely correspond, of course, to a doubling of the annual output over the period in question. What this general inference means in terms of the international flow to the OECD countries, in particular, does depend considerably on exactly what assumptions are made about the economies of the member states. Will their economic growth rate average out at, say, 4·0 per cent a year or will it be 4·5 per cent? And might not such marginal differences be very important in this context? Then again, how vigorously and successfully will the states concerned pursue oil conservation policies? Needless to say, projected oil imports are going to be especially sensitive to the precise circumstances and objectives of those countries (e.g. the United States and, in the 1980s, the United Kingdom) in which they do not constitute a dominant fraction of total oil consumption.

Grappling with these imponderables, the International Energy Agency has lately made these forecasts. The United States will import nearly 400 million tons in 1980 and between 215 and 550 million tons in 1985. The EEC will import 450 million tons in 1980 (i.e. a quarter less than in 1974) and much the same in 1985. The Pacific members of OECD, principally Japan, will import over 350 million tons in 1980 and between 450 and 590 million tons in 1985. Actually, all these figures are rounded conversions of estimates originally made in millions of barrels per day.[28]

Not surprisingly, the debate about how long a petroleum famine may be staved off, plus the collateral one about how readily dependence on the Middle East might be reduced, resemble in outline those about the long-term availability of certain metallic ores. Nevertheless, the differences are significant. Most metals occur in the extremely old rocks of the several continental shield areas—e.g. the Canadian Shield and those fragments of ancient Gondwanaland which now comprise much of Brazil, sub-Saharan Africa, India and Australia. On the other hand, the oil deposits were mainly laid down beneath the warm coastal waters of a few score million years ago, and have always accumulated within suitable formations of permeable sediment.

In many places, thick sedimentary deposits stretch beyond the present shore-lines and so across the continental shelf. Usually, the resultant strata contain few concentrations of solid material then worth recovering. Quite often, however, they prove to be submarine reservoirs for large hydrocarbon deposits which, being either gaseous or liquid, may be extracted with cost penalties that are not intolerable. Seventeen per cent of the world's oil output was offshore in 1970; and, a decade hence, the figure could well be 40, particularly if the China Seas and the Soviet Arctic have as much potential as some believe.

Thus far, extraction operations have been confined to the shelves proper—i.e. to depths not in excess of 600 feet. But there may be great scope for further development in the relatively steep slopes through which the shelf regions phase into the deep ocean floor. Already, exploratory drillings have passed the 2,000-foot submarine contour.

Nor should we discount the possibility of fresh discoveries on land of large reserves, mineable so long as all extra costs can be passed on to the consumers. New Guinea, Siberia and the Orinoco valley spring readily to mind in this connection. Nor should we forget the scope which exists for increasing, again at a price, the proportion of each deposit actually extracted.

Against all this, must be set the now visible waning of long-standing producing fields in, for instance, various parts of the United States and the Maracaibo region of Venezuela. Thus by the end of 1975 Venezuelan output was but 40 per cent the 1970 mean, though it is only fair to add that this was partly due to a deliberate policy of conservation with an eye to benefiting from, and perhaps helping to force, renewed price rises.

Not long ago, Sir Kingsley Dunham, a most eminent authority on such matters, cited, as a median gauge of expert opinion, the figure of 305 billion for the number of tons of crude still left in the Earth in what one may term conventional deposits, either on land or offshore; and he reckoned that this would represent just 33 years' consumption on a basis of sustained exponential growth.[29] Near the upper end of the informed estimates is the 600 billion tons or thereabouts considered probable by Peter Odell, Professor of Economic Geography at Erasmus University in Rotterdam. Near the lower end is the 250 billion lately subscribed to by Mr H. R. Warman, the exploration manager of British Petroleum.

At the impressionistic level at which a layman has to make his appreciation, there are two related and disturbing peculiarities about the current situation. One is that the rate at which new strikes are made has been diminishing since 1965. The other is that global estimates of the kind just quoted have also been levelling off, in general, since around that date.[30] All things considered, it would seem extremely likely that the world output of petroleum from conventional sources, both on land and in tidewater, will pass its peak sometime between 1985 and the turn of the century. Even if the latter date proves to be the actual one, the rate of expansion would probably be retarding markedly by the end of the 1980s. Rising extraction costs in marginal areas would certainly be one reason. Deliberate conservation by the major exporting states could well be another.

In the meantime, we shall have to live with the added complication of gross imbalances in the distribution of the reserves in question. Let us take, for example, the world proven reserves as published at the close of 1974. Out of the total figure of 98 billion tons, 23 per cent was in Saudi Arabia, and another 39 per cent elsewhere in the Middle East and North Africa. About 16 per cent was in the Sino-Soviet zone and 12 per cent in the Western Hemisphere. Of the remaining 10 per cent, barely a third was in Europe.[31]

Given this unsatisfactory situation and outlook, more radical responses to the oil shortage are being evoked. Among them is the working of tar sands—i.e. hydrocarbon deposits that are a good deal more viscous than is the average fraction of crude petroleum and which must therefore be extracted and processed in special ways. Quite substantial tar sand reserves do exist in Venezuela and, it is thought, Colombia, whilst significant ones occur in Utah and various parts of the Eastern Hemisphere. Far and away the biggest known, however, are those in the Athabasca basin in Alberta: some 30 billion tons of heavy oil equivalent, albeit at varying depths.

Though initial exploitation proceeds, it does so haltingly. Thus, the physical environment in the Athabasca, being decidedly adverse at all times, occasions considerable extra cost. So does an ecological requirement to redeposit carefully the washed sand—no less than 15 tons of it for every ton of oil. Four years ago, the National Petroleum Council of the United States forecast a maximal yield from Athabasca in 1985 of something approaching a 100 million tons.[32] Probably, this prognosis still holds pretty good.

Usually "oil shales" are discussed alongside tar sands as sources which might, and probably will, be utilised henceforward in less of a piecemeal fashion than they have been historically (e.g. in East Scotland from 1848 to 1962). The term is one which embraces a range of materials that contain organic matter eligible for separation into oil, gas and carbonaceous residue.

The shale deposits in Colorado, Wyoming and Utah are often credited with 300 billion tons of mineable oil and those in Brazil with over 100. It is said, too, various other parts of the world probably contain together at least as much again.

It is doubtful, however, whether more than a quarter of the grand total has a concentration of more than ten Imperial gallons of oil per long ton of shale—i.e. about one part in 27 by weight. Yet, at so low a concentration, the cost of the energy input alone may approach the value of the oil extracted, at any rate with established technology. Related to which are the awesome problems posed, mechanically as well as environmentally, by trying to handle so much Earth material in what may be quite restricted areas.

All the same, headway is apparently being made (e.g. in the USA and the USSR) with the use of retorting *in situ* to limit or eliminate the need for rock removal. Furthermore, the US National Petroleum Council report just quoted considered that the main Colorado field could be induced to yield about 50 million tons annually by 1985.[33] So if the price of crude petroleum does stay high, oil from shale could be making a minor but not negligible contribution to the world oil budget by 1990.

In the meantime, the situation is being eased somewhat by increasing reliance on the assortment of gaseous hydrocarbons collectively known as "natural gas". Between 1945 and 1972 world production rose from 120 to 1,000 million tons oil equivalent per annum; and, by

1985, it is expected to be near the 2,000 million mark. Already, indeed, this form of fuel satisfies about 33 per cent of the energy needs of the United States, 25 per cent of the Soviet Union's and 12 per cent of Western Europe's. The geographical distribution of the world's natural gas reserves seem rather wider than those of crude petroleum though the actual locations are similar and, not infrequently, identical.

Admittedly, data on the total extent of these reserves of gas tends to be even more patchy and tentative than that for their liquid counterparts. Granted that it may be a minimal figure in every sense, however, the 1972 calculation was c. 100 billion tons oil equivalent. A fifth of this was in North America, nearly a tenth in Western Europe, and rather over 35 per cent in the Soviet bloc. In this case, too, some of the most promising possibilities for exploration are offshore—e.g. in the Gulf of Thailand and within the confines of the Indonesian archipelago.

But, as regards usage, a major caveat has to be entered. It is that transportation and storage still pose serious economic problems, notwithstanding some important recent advances in handling techniques—e.g. large diameter pipelines and refrigerated tanks underground. This being so, we are only likely to see full and proper utilisation of the vast volumes of natural gas available in the Middle East, in particular, when that region has appropriately developed large petrochemical complexes.

What then of coal, the original hydrocarbon of the Industrial Revolution? During the fuel crisis induced by the bitter European winter of 1946–47, it was confidently proclaimed that no European coal miner need fear for a job for the rest of the century. Yet, in the course of the next two decades, coal was displaced by oil so extensively that it came widely to be assumed that, in the 1980s, the only production of this fossil fuel continuing in Europe would be the quality coking coals of Durham and the Ruhr. But now the outlook for coal seems better than for some time past, and this not only in Europe. As coal-fired power stations were being commissioned anew in the United States in 1974, the first "Project Independence" studies envisaged production being more than doubled to 1,200 million tons by 1985, and then boosted to perhaps 4,000 million by the turn of the century. Today about 775 million is more often quoted as the target tonnage for the first of these dates, environmentalist anxieties about open-cast mining being a major influence behind this reining back.

5

World production of coal in 1974 was just over 2,275 million tons, a very modest increase of 15 per cent as compared with the annual mean for the middle 1960s. Yet estimates made during a 1968 World Power Conference Survey put total coal reserves at roughly 6,650 billion tons. In this compilation a distinction was drawn between seams which had been measured, more or less directly, and those which had merely been inferred. All seams less than a foot or so thick and more than 4,000 or so feet below the surface were automatically excluded from either category.

What the survey showed beyond doubt was the paramountcy of the Soviet Union. Its reserves were believed to exceed 4,100 billion tons, though as much as 96 per cent of this total was inferred. In the USA there were thought to be a good 1,100 billion, 93 per cent inferred. Apparently China, too, has over a trillion tons in the ground.

The two other big pivots in the geopolitical power balance—the Common Market and Japan—are far less well endowed. Nevertheless, Britain (the strongest EEC member in this respect) was credited with over 15 billion and Japan with nearly 20; and even these comparatively diminutive aggregates would allow current production to be maintained for several generations in the former case and several centuries in the latter.[34]

Throughout the world, however, even those coal seams actually being worked vary markedly apropos the ease with which this is being done. Thus geological superiority (shallower and thicker seams, and so on) go far to explain the fivefold superiority of the American mining industry over the British in output per manshift. In fact, a fairly large proportion of the global reserves could never be extracted with profit in the context of present technologies and current market prices. Besides, both environmental and social considerations will always militate against a dramatic revival of coal. So may the fact that a new deep-shaft mine takes between five and ten years to bring to full operation whilst even open-cast workings take several.

A tantalising set of problems on the technological front concerns the improved utilisation of coal, particularly beguiling possibilities being its use as a raw material in the manufacture of Synthetic Natural Gas (SNG) and also synthetic petroleum. The former technique is unlikely to become important between now and 1990. The latter has already assumed some importance on strategic grounds alone. Substantial quantities were produced in Nazi Germany during

World War II. For some time past, a quarter of a million tons have been coming each year from a plant at Sasalburg in the Orange Free State. In 1981 a second installation will go on stream in the Evander-Trichardt district of the eastern Transvaal; and this should boost the national oil sufficiency of South Africa from 15 to 35 per cent.

Reports from there lately stress that, thanks to economic change and technical advance, oil-from-coal is getting much less uncompetitive commercially. Even so, the break-even point is unlikely to arrive for quite a few years—assuming, indeed, it does arrive at all. To date, the coal thus expended has generally exceeded the oil manufactured by a factor of at least five; and to reduce the ratio even to three will be hard going. One particular difficulty is the need to supply a lot of extra hydrogen, coal being very deficient in this highly combustible element.

A few words on lignite may be appropriate, seeing that this "brown coal" stands in a relationship to coal proper curiously similar to that between natural gas and crude oil. Frequently these geologically immature deposits occur in great thickness and with little overburden. Accordingly, they tend to be extracted in massive open-cast operations with all that this entails for good and ill. Here again one constraint is that the hydrocarbon in question is too bulky to transport far.

Nevertheless, the global production of lignite is running at some 800 million tons, nearly half of this being from the two Germanies. Reserves are believed to exceed 2,000 billion tons world-wide.

If lignite is one long-established energy source that will remain useful but never become decisive, Hydro-Electric Power (HEP) is another, its ecological attractions notwithstanding. Certainly, HEP capacity has tended to expand in the more highly developed economies much more slowly of late than has that for electrical generation as a whole. At present, it provides but a fiftieth of the world's output of electricity. Theoretically, its contribution could be multiplied six or seven times. However, a variety of constraints seem to preclude this consummation. Usually the low return on fixed capital is prominent among them.

Nor does tidal power hold out any real promise of making the force of gravity do Man's work for him. In fact, it is considerably more capital-intensive even than HEP and far more restricted apropos suitable sites. Similarly, the world potential for mobilising geothermal energy is but a trivial several thousand megawatts, at any rate until the state of this art has developed sufficiently to exploit certain very deep-seated "heat-traps".

However, some have been disposed to attach overriding importance to the fact that the rate at which energy falls upon the Earth direct from the Sun is of the order of ten thousand times the power output obtained, through Man's ingenuity, from terrestrial sources. Also, that this same ingenuity has already led to thousands of domestic-scale solar heaters being installed on a more-or-less commercial basis, notably in Australia, Israel, Japan, the USSR and the USA.

But despite decades of decidedly *avant-garde* technological specu-lation, the enthusiasts have failed to come up with any solutions for harnessing this source which are eligible for mass application. Like its first cousin, wind-power, it is hamstrung by extreme variability and by the harnessing process being low-intensity and low-tempera-ture. Accordingly, disproportionately heavy capital outlays mean that the forecast cost is always exorbitantly high in relation to that anticipated for alternative energy sources. Furthermore, a sheer shortage of space for deployment would often circumscribe pro-grammes. So would the persisting failure to find a satisfactory means of storing the energy flux received. Therefore, it is hardly surprising that systematic studies of solar power have regularly been inclined to defer its serious impact until sometime in the period, 1990–2020.

The upshot is that Mankind would stand no chance at all of achieving the extra eight or nine billion tons of coal-equivalent it is likely to need for its energy budget by 1990 without the due applica-tion of nuclear fission. Between 1963 and 1973 the total electrical capacity installed in the USA rose from 229,000 megawatts to 458,000 whilst the nuclear fraction thereof rose from an almost miniscule 750 to a much more significant 21,000. For the nine members of the enlarged EEC, the aggregate figures were 140,000 and 257,000 respectively: the nuclear 1,500 and 12,400.

Because of the direct and grave connotations for international security indicated in Chapter 9, the world growth in installed nuclear capacity recorded during the last decade and in this one is outlined in Chapter 10. From those power reactors came, in 1973, some 180 billion kilowatt-hours of electricity.[35] This was equivalent to rather less than one per cent of the recorded world output of energy in all forms. What it also represented was an average utilisation of these reactors of barely half their full power output; and that is a lower fraction than might have been expected in the light of what one is often told about the base-load role of nuclear electricity.

An indicative energy projection completed by the OECD in 1974 included a basic programme for the introduction into its zone of nuclear capacity. This envisaged about 200,000 megawatts being installed by 1980 and 980,000 by 1990. An accelerated programme could yield, it was then thought, 240,000 megawatts by 1980 and as much as 1,370,000 by 1990.

The close to exponential expansion of nuclear reactor capacity foreseen in this post-Yom Kippur assessment would enable the world to avoid the most obvious and dire of economic catastrophes: a yawning energy gap inducing a cost-push inflation so febrile as to culminate in a precipitate collapse of effective demand. For, even assuming the persistence of a relatively low utilisation rate, the lesser of the capacities thus envisaged for 1990 would be sufficient to cover about a fifth of the expansion in energy demand to be expected in the interim. Probably, too, a good three-fifths could be met by incremental oil and natural gas production, whilst coal might be counted on to produce a substantial part of the final fifth: a fine balance but a viable one.

Apparently, however, the OECD experts have since come to feel that even the basic projection will not be at all easy to realise, 325,000 MW being their current forecast for 1985. For one thing, the constant price cost of a thousand megawatt plant of the Light Water Reactor variety is now reckoned of the order of a billion dollars. This means that reaching the 1990 level quoted above would require the investment of a good trillion dollars between now and then; and this is a calculation which ignores not only monetary inflation but also the need to invest for further expansion after 1990.

The trouble, in all facets of the resource debate, is that the applied scientists who supply most of the fundamental physical data are prone to underestimate how difficult some adjustments are to make in terms of the adaptation of human institutions. The world economy is not a pudding basin, wherein sundry ingredients may be freely stirred to obtain a judicious mix. Rather it is a Heath Robinson edifice of pressure points and linkages: a piecemeal improvisation that is liable to reverberate alarmingly if any part of it is disturbed.

Certainly, one senses that, as a community, nuclear scientists and engineers wax too dismissive about the financial stresses that may be occasioned by the expenditure of a trillion dollars even over 13 years.

Mobilising such vast amounts of capital would, in fact, recurrently impose a heavy strain on either government budgets or stock markets or both. Meanwhile, the large transfers of resources between states that would also be involved could seriously imbalance the always fragile structure of international payments. After all, a trillion dollars is the current United States national income for nearly a year. Alternatively, it can be matched with American manufacturing output for three or four years at current rates or defence expenditure for 12. Then again, it equals the present level of world trade sustained for about two years or of development aid flow for roughly a quarter of a century.

To the capitalisation problem must be added that of management. Nine years may elapse between the decision to build a reactor and its being commissioned, a time-lag sufficient to make it very difficult to forecast future needs within the rather narrow margins required. Moreover, some nuclear programmes have lagged badly in the past because of persisting inefficiencies in reactor operation. Now the zeal of some environmentalist pressure groups is tending to slow them down.

All the same, the prospect may still be that the 1974 basic target for 1990 could almost be realised. But even this consummation would not *ipso facto* usher in some kind of golden age. We must never lose sight of the truism that the international security implications of this nuclear revolution are all too uncomfortably akin to the sowing of dragons' teeth (see Chapter 9). Nor dare we discount in this context the adverse impact that other geopolitical factors may make on world economic change.

Besides, there would be little chance of nuclear fission power setting in train a return to an era of cheap energy, however smoothly its introduction went. Some allowance should probably be made for further rises (in real terms) in the predicted construction cost of the average reactor. Almost certainly, allowance must be made for a substantial increase over time in nuclear fuel costs. Therefore, the most that the advent of this nuclear age is likely to achieve is a holding of energy costs tolerably close to their post-1973 relative levels.[36] It will do this not only by limiting the margins of surplus profit the oil producers will be able to secure even whilst engaged in free selling. Also, it will diminish any inclination on their part to hoard their oil reserves in anticipation of future price rises.

Obviously this effect will be valuable, maybe absolutely vital. But it cannot negate the ineluctable prospect that the energy situation will recurrently aggravate the multiple strains the world economic order will, in any case, be subject to in the 'eighties.

Notes

1. N. W. Pirie, *Food Resources, Conventional and Novel*, Penguin, London 1969, p. 134.
2. R. M. Honavar in *Third World*, April/May 1974, Vol. 3, No. 7, pp. 8–9.
3. A. H. Perry, "The Downward Trend of Air and Sea Surface Temperatures over the North Atlantic", *Weather* December 1974, Vol. 29, No. 12, pp. 451–5.
4. Nigel Calder, *The Weather Machine*, BBC Publications, London 1974, p. 12.
5. D. J. Pointing, *Meteorological Office Research Paper*, No. 35, 1976.
6. See the 1976 Symons Memorial Lecture by B. J. Mason, *The Quarterly Journal of the Royal Meteorological Society*, Vol. 102, No. 433, July 1976, pp. 473–98.
7. H. H. Lamb "Whither Climate Now?" *Nature*, Vol. 244, No. 5416, 17 August 1973, pp. 395–7.
8. K. E. Trenberth, *Q. J. Roy. Met. Soc.*, Vol. 102, No. 431, January 1976, pp. 65–75.
9. H. H. Lamb and Hans Morth, "A Climate of Extremes", *Development Forum*, Vol. IV, No. 5, June 1976, p. 5.
10. Robert Jungk and Johan Galtung (Ed), *Mankind in Year 2000*, Allen & Unwin, London 1970, p. 154.
11. E.g. Ritchie Calder, *Men Against the Desert*, George Allen and Unwin, London 1951.
12. Lester R. Brown, *World Without Borders*, Random House New York 1972, p. 99.
13. E.g. John Maddox, *The Doomsday Syndrome*, Macmillan, London 1972, p. 69.
14. *1974 Statistical Yearbook*, United Nations, New York 1975, Table 6.
15. Keith Reid *et alia*, *Man, Nature, and Ecology*, Aldus Books, London 1974, p. 367.
16. *1974 Statistical Yearbook*, op. cit., Tables 18, 46 and 80.
17. An exponential change of, say, ten per cent per annum in the rate of any input or output would cause it to double in just over seven years.
18. World output of mercury was virtually the same in 1973 as in 1964. This was partly due to environmentalist objections to its use.
19. E.g. "Blueprint for Survival", *The Ecologist*, Vol. 2, No. 1 ,January 1972, Figure 2, and *The Limits to Growth*, Table 2.
20. Professor Wilfred Beckerman, *The New Statesman and Nation*, 19 October 1973.
21. See the 19th Graham Clark Lecture by Sir Kingsley Dunham, Council for Engineering Institutions, London 1974, pp. 8–10.
22. *1974 Statistical Yearbook*, op. cit., Tables 5 and 8.
23. Kenneth Warren, *Mineral Resources*, Penguin, London 1973, Table 33.
24. E. L. LaQue "Deep ocean mining: prospects and anticipated short-term benefits" in Elaine H. Burnell and Piers von Simson (Ed.), *Pacem in Maribus 1*, Vol. 4, Royal University of Malta Press, Valletta, 1971, pp. 43–55.
25. E.g. Nicholas Valery, "Aluminium declares war on corrosion", *The New Scientist*, 26 December 1974.
26. *1974 Statistical Yearbook*, op. cit., Table 142.
27. *The Economist*, 3 November 1973.
28. The standard conversion factor for crude oil is that a million barrels per day equals 50,000,000 tons a year.

29. *Illustrated London News*, Vol. 262, No. 6911, June 1974, pp. 55–61.
30. Gerald Foley, *The Energy Question*, Penguin, Harmondsworth 1976, Table 23.
31. *Oil and Gas Journal*, 30 December 1974.
32. *The United States Energy Outlook*, The National Petroleum Council, Washington 1972. Chapter 8.
33. Ibid, Table 126.
34. *1972 Statistical Yearbook*, United Nations, New York 1973, Table 52.
35. *1974 Statistical Yearbook*, op. cit., Table 144.
36. See *The Scientific American*, Vol. 234, No. 1, January 1976, p. 25.

8

The Working of the World Economy

To be blunt, one major reason for wanting to control inflation better must perforce be the comparative success of the Communist states in this regard. Whilst no official indices are published in the Chinese People's Republic, prices seem to have risen hardly at all during its first quarter of a century, in almost bizarre contrast with the closing years of Kuomintang rule. In the USSR, the official retail index rose from 100 to 139 between 1940 and 1960 but has scarcely altered since.

However, this Soviet plateau of prices is to some extent a mirage. Not so long ago, for example, "a new brand of vodka appeared, ostensibly of better quality and at a much higher price, while the cheaper variety has become hard to find".[1] What is more, prices for the fruit, vegetables and so on in the free peasant markets frequently run 40 to 60 per cent ahead of the official pegged prices. Then again, excess demand is constantly causing not only prolonged scarcities of staple commodities but also its *alter ego*, a flourishing black market at substantially inflated prices. Recent emigrants to Israel have put the size of this *sub silentio* sector of the economy at anything between a tenth and a half the licit part.

Making due allowance for all such factors, Western analysts adjudge the true Soviet inflation rate to have averaged two to four per cent over the past few years and to be liable to worsen a bit in the immediate future as wages drift accelerates and as private savings are offloaded. Furthermore the record of the East European states (even excepting Yugoslavia) is manifestly less impressive, partly because of their proportionately greater involvement in trade with the wider world. Thus the annual rate in Poland and Hungary has lately been running at a good ten per cent. Perhaps it is pertinent to recall, too, that Allende's Chile did very badly in this regard.

Even so, this record is sufficiently enviable to underline the need to continue the essays in the central direction of wages and prices (often underscored with statutory power) which have been embarked on widely in the West during this crisis-ridden decade. Not that it has proved at all easy to reconcile such close yet Olympian monitoring with the maintenance of free market operations and, indeed, a free society. As one might expect, such policies are more likely to curb an inflationary trend which is only moderate to start with. By the same token, they are more likely to be effective in the shorter-term. Besides which, the decisions required are often plumb in the middle of the ensnared and peculiarly ill-charted march-lands between economics and politics.

Still, the question of how best to use economic regulation to curb resource, monetary and—in the final analysis—political instabilities is by no means entirely internal to Western democracies. It is encountered, too, on the world plane. And it is, in fact, a problem with which the post-war world has come to terms conspicuously well in one major respect: the lowering of tariff barriers, this largely under the auspices of the General Agreement on Tariffs and Trade. Thus in 1974 the average tariff on all goods entering the United States was seven per cent as against 18 per cent in 1934. That of the EEC was six and of the more protectionist Japan just under ten. What is more, pressures to "export unemployment" by raising duties have been contained commendably well throughout the world recession, 1974–76.

Nevertheless, complacency on this score would be unjustified because demands from the newly developing world for further liberalisation apropos trade in manufactured goods, in particular, are already audible and liable to become much more so. For one thing, certain of the smaller newly developing states, notably several on the strategically-sensitive maritime periphery of East Asia, have geared their social stability to very high economic growth rates which, in their turn, rely on the rapid expansion of manufacturing, this largely for export. Thus between 1970 and 1973 alone the manufacturing sector grew 65 per cent in Singapore and 79 per cent in South Korea.

By 1973, the OECD area was, in fact, receiving c. 7·5 billion dollars worth of industrial goods from the newly developing world, most of this being from the type of economy just identified. Historically, cheap textiles have led the field. But today such knowledge-intensive products as high quality textiles, precision instruments and electronic apparatus are assuming importance in such pace-making locations as Hong Kong and Singapore.

Meanwhile, the manufacture of motor vehicles is one quite heavy industry which has started to relocate itself as education spreads and the urban implosion gathers pace. Among the countries said now to be producing at least 1,000 a month are Argentina, Brazil, India, Mexico, Spain and Yugoslavia. To them may be added ten more emergent economies which are assembling at least 1,000 a month: Algeria, Chile, Colombia, Iran, South Korea, Morocco, Peru, the Philippines, Portugal and Venezuela. At the same time, Japan has started to emerge as something of a pioneer in the building of mineral processing plants in the country from whence comes the ore: a steel mill in Brazil, a copper smelter in Zambia and so on.

Better access all round to Western markets is, of course, a prime aim of the poorer member countries in the United Nations Conference on Trade and Development, a forum established by the General Assembly in 1964 and most in evidence since in its quadrennial plenary sessions. At the third of these, in Santiago in 1972, there was an alarmingly sharp dichotomy on many issues between Group B—i.e. the West—and the "Group of 77"—i.e. the newly developing states. Wide-ranging commodity agreements was one policy aim of the latter that, whilst it did get some backing from the ever *étatist* French, encountered much strong opposition elsewhere in the West, particularly Federal Germany and the United States.

Nevertheless, one of the few tangible results of Santiago was the setting in train of negotiations which led to the conclusion of a cocoa commodity agreement later that year. Since such agreements were already in operation for coffee, olive oil, sugar, tin and wheat, it could be said that a quarter of the exports (other than fuel) from the newly developing countries to the advanced ones were thus being regulated, however erratically or light-of-rein.

To these arrangements could be added a number—e.g. for hard fibres, jute and tea—which, though not internationally binding, enabled both importing and exporting countries to exchange views in order to promote market stability. Then there were various agreements which were quite formal but which were also comparatively limited in their geographical scope. These had long figured prominently, for example, in the world sugar trade.

Between Santiago and the next plenary session in Nairobi in the summer of 1976, new alignments could be discerned in two salient respects. One took the form of a divergence between the oil-producers and the rest in the wake of the big oil price increases of 1973–74.

Thus the special session on raw materials and development held by the UN General Assembly in the spring of 1974 was apparently bedevilled by behind-the-scenes wrangles along these lines within the Group of 77. One bone of contention has been the almost total failure of the members of the Organisation of Petrol Exporting Countries (OPEC) to make any concessionary price arrangements for their less privileged colleagues.

Meanwhile, governmental thinking in the United States has been coming round to what may roughly be termed a compromise position on consumer-producer co-operation. At Nairobi, Dr Kissinger proposed the creation of an international resources bank designed to deploy through bond issues about a billion dollars of private capital. This deployment would primarily be intended to develop mineral resources faster but part could be used to help extend the pattern of commodity agreements. He further made it clear that the Americans are now persuaded that, in principle, buffer stocks are a suitable technique for price stabilisation; and that they are prepared as well to talk definitively about individual commodity accords. Presumably, Mr Vance will maintain this pitch.

As Nairobi also demonstrated, however, we are still a long way from a genuine meeting of minds about a "new economic order" as between the West and the newly developing world as a whole. Partly this is because of the post-colonial suspicion widely felt by the latter towards the former. When the West makes technical assessments of schemes, these are judged to have political undertones. When it calls for international programmes for environmental protection it is deemed indifferent to the economic imperatives of the poor. When it would establish heavy industries in the poorer lands, it is accused of trying to "export pollution". It is against this background that President Boumedienne of Algeria laid such stress on economic sovereignty in his keynote speech to the 1974 special session.

Fair though it may be to characterise this pervasive suspicion as "post-colonial", it would be unwise to infer that it will steadily wane with the passage of time. Such euphoric optimism can easily be gainsaid by reference to one recent effusion alone: that of concern with the actual and prospective roles of the large and ramifying multinational corporations.

In motivational terms, this concern owes much to New Left neo-Marxism. However, it draws most of its ammunition from two interrelated tendencies. The one is the spread of foreign investment, in such newly developing regions as Latin America, into manufacturing and related sectors, as opposed to the extractive industries and public utilities to which it was largely confined historically.[2] The other is a perceived trend towards the ever-greater prominence of a shrinking number of giant firms, this concentration presumptively being the consequence of horizontal and vertical amalgamations. "Horizontal" means of similar firms in quite different industries and "vertical" of firms at successive stages in the same productive chain.

Anxiety has been aggravated by a number of well-authenticated instances of political manipulation by certain of these firms. Nevertheless, the relative extent of this may be nothing like as great as the neo-Marxists are keen to infer. Although we live in an age of leaked information, no general *exposé* is ever effected in the vast majority of cases. Nobody could plausibly argue, for example, that the Middle East policy of the United States has been shaped over the years more by a craven deference to the oil producers' lobby than by a heartfelt sympathy for Israel. Manifestly, oil was only a very ancillary consideration until the Yom Kippur war; and even then the voice attended to above all others was that not of some latter-day Rockefeller but of Sheikh Yamani of Saudi Arabia. From which only this conclusion can be drawn: either the oil firms are a sight less self-seeking than the New Left might encourage us to believe or less influential or both.

Another objection often levelled is that some of the biggest multinationals are, in reality, insufficiently "multi-national" in the organisation and composition of their top management. Furthermore, some weight is lent to this contention by the fact that a good two-thirds of the hundred largest multinationals originated in the United States.

However, the merger boom that developed in Western Europe, and especially in France and Britain, in the 1960s could prove the herald of a larger and more distinctive European presence on the international plane, always assuming the enlarged EEC acts as a base for this more than as a magnet for foreign business zeal. The commercial rise of Japan may enable it, too, to generate more in the way of multinational enterprise, as witness the formation through merger in 1970 of the massive Nippon Steel Corporation. In 1964 the 200 largest non-American corporations registered sales equivalent to but 45 per cent of those achieved by their United States counterparts. Ten years later the corresponding percentage was 80.[3]

Yet this essentially mechanistic forecast, based on the managerial economies of scale accruing from the communications revolution, could well be overriden in the newly developing world by a "self-defeating prophecy" effect. In other words, the Marxist critique of the multinational ascendancy will have gained such influence, at least in a bowdlerised form, as to reverse the trend it deplores. In fact, a reaction akin to this seems to have set in already with the all-important international oil trade. Little more than a decade ago, there were fewer than a dozen companies and kindred institutions which really mattered at the international level. Today the total exceeds one hundred and fifty.[4]

Nevertheless, further big amalgamations across national boundaries can be expected in the OECD area, not least in the automobile and chemical industries. Moreover, a rising tide of Western European and (albeit to a much lesser extent) Japanese investment in the United States suggests that often the centres of the ramifying matrices will be non-American. Paradoxical though it may sound, however, increasing agitation against such firms in the newly developing lands could actually strengthen the hand of the Americans there as against their OECD colleagues. This is because the American philosophy of big business management, set by firms like Du Pont a good half century ago, is relatively favourable to the delegation of executive responsibility to the heads of geographical and functional divisions.

But, irrespective of how the pattern evolves or how subject it becomes to international codes of conduct, the West has a right—nay, a bounden duty—to insist that, in certain important respects, the intrusion of the multinationals has definitely been benign. Such evidence as there is does not suggest that the average profit margins on investment by American firms in less developed regions has been unduly high of late, especially in relation to the high risks and the practice of re-investment.[5] Then again, Lester Brown reckons that most of the several billion dollars' worth of technical equipment the USA alone exports each year is transferred within corporations.[6] Transfers of entrepreneurial skills and ethos may be no less important, although they are not susceptible to even approximate quantification.

Such collateral factors apart, the net transfer to the newly developing world of private investment capital, via multinationals or otherwise, is tantamount to the gratuitous sacrifice of extensive opportunities for extra production and fuller employment at home, the flow in question being a good ten billion dollars in 1973. Contrariwise, it could be said that a recipient country may not benefit proportionately because this investment tends to be distributed inappropriately. But the same charge has been levied in some quarters against governmental aid. Besides which, it may be inconsistent to protest against both this and the diversification trend alluded to above.

Accordingly, the inclusion of incremental private investment in the calculations of total aid flows done by such bodies as the Development Assistance Committee of OECD may not be as palpably dishonest as is sometimes suggested on the Left.[7] Likewise, it is hard to treat as anything other than quasi-Marxist extravaganza the contention that any "socialist aid programme" must give general recognition to a developmental need simply to expropriate foreign assets and, indeed, "seek to help in meeting the technical and financial problems which may arise".[8]

No doubt expropriations will be, in some sense or other, inevitable from time to time; and they may well on occasions approximate to a kind of rough justice. But that is no reason for their being given blanket endorsement in advance by those in positions of influence. The years ahead will see quite enough disorder as it is.

All the same, the record of the OECD zone apropos aid of every sort is not yet one to celebrate uproariously. Notwithstanding what has just been said, it is a shade disturbing to find that, in the years leading up to the 1973 climacteric, the percentage of aid emanating from official sources was tending to go down. And inexcusable on any grounds, save mounting world-weariness, was the relationship between the international target for total aid flow set for the first UN Development Decade (1961–70) and what, in fact, materialised. For this target was one per cent of its Gross National Product from each aid-giving country, whereas the percentage registered fell from 0·95 in 1961 to 0·74 in 1970, recovering only to 0·78 in 1972. True, even this trend represented a flow increase of over 30 per cent in absolute terms during these years but that was scarcely enough to match population growth.[9]

When official assistance alone is considered, the percentage of GNP thus transferred fell across the OECD zone as a whole, from 0·44 in 1965 to 0·33 in 1974 and 0·35 in 1975, this last coming to rather over 13·5 billion dollars (at current prices) and equivalent to just half the stipulated official target for GNP percentage.

A countervailing theme was the big expansion in total aid from OPEC: to nearly seven billion dollars in 1974 to be more precise, though a goodly percentage of this went to the Arab "confrontation" states. Less dramatic but not inconsequential had been a counter-trend among the smaller OECD states: Canada up from 0·19 to 0·56 between 1965 and 1975; Denmark from 0·13 to 0·57; the Netherlands from 0·36 to 0·74; Norway from 0·16 to 0·65; and Sweden from 0·19 to 0·82.[10] It was as though an awareness of belonging to a single global village was overriding, slowly but surely, a sense of being too small to exercise any kind of leverage in the league of national power and influence: the OECD mean for total aid was 1·05 in 1975.

Here could be seen some grist for Gunnar Myrdal's contention that the best way to get a democracy to sustain a substantial aid programme these days is to appeal not to some narrow and trite interpretation of national self-interest but to a sense of universal obligation.[11] Even so, the real-world options are not (and are most unlikely to become) anything like as simple as that. No doubt over the years too much has been said—or hinted at—to the effect that aid is the continuation of geopolitics by other means. This is why, for example, Vietnam got rather more economic aid from the United States between 1948 and 1970 than India did. But this would be no justification for reacting to the other extreme and absolutely dismissing geopolitics as either unconvincing or downright irrelevant.

A straight comparison may suffice. Jordan and Paraguay each number about two-and-a-half million people. Yet the proposition that it was no more important to preserve the stability of King Hussein's regime than that of General Stroessner is one that would never be endorsed by any responsible commentator.

Yet, when all the travails and imperfections of the West's aid programmes have been admitted, one bitter-sweet consolation remains. This is that the record of the Soviet bloc is less admirable on just about every count. The bloc members refused to accept the one per cent target as something applicable to themselves. As a very general rule, their aid has taken the form of loans closely tied to exports from the respective donor countries, a disposition which has often been rendered most tedious by vagaries of quality and delivery.

Thanks to a big increase in disbursements by the USSR itself, the annual outflow more than trebled between 1970 and 1973. Even so, the total recorded was barely two billion dollars in the latter year.

What is more, the orientation has been markedly geopolitical. Thus of total outgoings of around 15 billion dollars between 1954 and 1973, Egypt and India received over two billion apiece, and Afghanistan, Algeria, Chile, Indonesia, Iran, Iraq and perhaps Pakistan at least half a billion.[12] No attempt has been made by the United Nations to monitor the large subventions to Cuba.

What we do need to guard against, however, is a tendency to concentrate overmuch on these specific economic linkages between nations as against the monetary milieu within which they develop. To take a rough analogy with the wool trade (one of the earliest to become intra-regional in many parts of the world), we worry too much about the mechanics of warp and weft and too little about the quality of the skein. If the flags of authoritarianism, Red or anything else, do fly over Oslo and Tokyo, London and Washington in the year 2000, a collapse of the international monetary system will most likely be partly, if not largely, responsible.

The proximate cause of our latent weaknesses in this sphere can be traced to the way the "post-war era", as mapped out at Bretton Woods in 1944, came traumatically to an end between 1967 and 1971. In outline, its point of departure was as follows. Thanks to their respective roles in the promotion of wartime victory and post-war recovery, the United States and Britain would be running very considerable deficits abroad, these always being represented by other countries' holdings of dollars and sterling respectively. Accordingly, it seemed sensible to accept formally that dollars and, on a smaller scale, sterling had come to be looked on as international reserve currencies. What this involved was a general understanding that they could be used alongside gold and some other relatively minor assets to finance multilateral world trade.

This formula required the acceptance, especially by London and Washington, of three specific conditions. One was that the two countries must always be prepared to pay gold on request in exchange for dollars or sterling. The others that all international exchange rates should be rigidly tied, at any given time, to the dollar and hence gold; and that they should never be altered except as a last alternative to savage deflation or some equally mortifying crisis reaction. To regulate and lubricate the whole system, the International Monetary Fund was set up.

For more than 20 years, the Bretton Woods solution worked remarkably smoothly, little disruption being occasioned by a sterling devaluation in 1949. However, with a second such devaluation in November 1967, the sequence of events became convulsive. In the spring of 1968, a series of rushes on the American gold stocks induced a separation of the official and private prices. Over the next three years several major currencies were either revalued or allowed to float. Then, in August 1971, President Nixon suddenly brought matters to a head, principally by suspending the convertibility of the dollar.

The denouement came that December when a meeting between Presidents Nixon and Pompidou was closely succeeded by a fore-gathering in the Smithsonian Institution in Washington of representatives of the "Group of Ten"—i.e. ten of the non-Communist world's leading trading and banking nations. The chief outcome was an upvaluing of gold in relation to the dollar. Moreover, the limits within which exchange rates could freely fluctuate around the given norm was widened appreciably: to 2·25 per cent as opposed to one per cent theretofore.

What had begun in 1967, in fact, was the eruptive release of latent strains emanating from a variety of causes. A major one was the way in which the international reserves of the United States (meaning, above all, the stocks of gold at Fort Knox etc.) had been declining absolutely and, worse still, in relation to other countries' liquid holdings of dollars. To be precise, the official ratio of reserves over liabilities had fallen continually from 2·73 in 1951 to 0·45 in 1967; and it was to slide to 0·15 by the end of 1975.

Anxiety was compounded by a fundamental alteration in the character of the American deficit that had, in fact, been discernible by the end of the 1950s. No longer could it simply be ascribed to an essentially voluntaristic outflow of aid and long-term investment so large as to more or less negate a vast and constant surplus of imports over exports. Instead, that surplus was eroding. Duly, in 1971, the annual balance of trade actually turned negative (for the first time since 1893) and did so to the tune of two billion dollars; and the next year this gap was destined to treble. Meanwhile, devaluation had not secured a British "economic miracle".

Yet still both countries were hamstrung considerably by the Bretton Woods obligation to avoid devaluation if humanly possible. For it left them with no options in normal circumstances other than deflation (with all its adverse implications for employment and economic growth) or else deep and arbitrary cuts in overseas aid and investment. Hardly surprisingly, each was coming to feel that the peculiarly worrisome burdens they incurred through financing world trade outweighed the attractions thereof: the prerogative of seigniorage together with the capital charges which thereby accrued plus, if you like, some measure of prestige. Ironically enough, these feelings were obliquely reinforced by a waxing French resentment at what Paris continued to insist was the inordinately privileged position of the Anglo-Saxon currencies.

A closely related cause for concern was that, whereas world trade had risen in value *c.* 150 per cent during the 1960s, total world liquidity had increased little more than 50 per cent in spite of the mounting dollar deficits. Manifestly, the constricted supply of gold was considerably to blame, this metal constituting over 60 per cent of all international liquidity at the start of the decade and a good 40 per cent at its close.

One remedy that then commended itself strongly to France, to say nothing of the USSR and South Africa, was to create much extra liquidity at a stroke by doubling or trebling the official price of gold. But in most other circles an alternative approach had been mooted for years, one which did not redound first and foremost to the benefit of Moscow and Pretoria. Though the USSR did not release production figures, it was known to be a major gold producer, morbid credit being especially due to the Kolyma section of the "Gulag Archipelago". And, of the rest of the world's output in 1973, three-quarters came from South Africa.

What this alternative approach consisted of was the introduction into world trade of fiat money—i.e. a medium of payment backed not by gold or some other time-honoured token of worth but just by the formal endorsement of intergovernmental authority. Indeed, an initial move in this direction had already been made with the launching, in the immediate aftermath of the 1968 gold crisis, of Special Drawing Rights (SDRs). These units of "paper gold" are created under the auspices of the International Monetary Fund (IMF) and distributed to members through their IMF quotas. By 1971 SDRs had added three or four per cent to overall liquidity (see below).

Had the Smithsonian agreement not been arrived at, the whole non-Communist world would have been teetering on the very edge of a slide back into fissiparous protectionism. All the same, Professor Karl Schiller, then the Federal German Minister of Economics, spoke for a broad spectrum of informed opinion when he cautioned against anyone regarding this accord as anything more than a fragile cease-fire. Effectively this cease-fire had collapsed by the time of the IMF annual meeting held in Nairobi in September 1973. A second devaluation of the dollar that spring had capped a whole succession of freer floatings of other currencies.

At this Nairobi conference, general agreement was reached that the SDR should gradually become the main reserve asset in a system to be based on stable though adjustable par values. Yet wide differences of opinion persisted on how these principles might best be applied. Therefore the Board of Governors set 31 July 1974 as a deadline for the working out of basic guidelines whilst recognising that the process of institutional adaptation would perforce take a while longer.

But in the interval the Yom Kippur war was to set in train dramatic alterations in the world monetary order, the redistribution of foreign exchange reserves being perhaps the most critical. According to one authoritative estimate, the oil exporting countries moved from a collective surplus on current account of 3·5 billion dollars in 1973 to 68 billion in 1974 and 42 in 1975. The rest of the newly developing world went from a deficit of seven billion in 1973 to one of 28 in 1974 and 29·5 in 1975. The Soviet bloc shifted from a marginal deficit in 1973 to one of several billion in 1975. The OECD zone gyrated from a 3·3 billion surplus in 1973 to a deficit of 34·5 in 1974 and six in 1975.[13] The 1976 balance may not be very different from the 1975 except that much of the OECD zone has been sliding back into deeper deficit as it spearheads the modest world boom of the late 1970s.

One regrettable carry-over into this new situation is a heavy debt burden for the non-OPEC developing countries. At the end of the 1960s the Commission on International Development set up by the World Bank under the chairmanship of Lester Pearson reported that, in the official aid sector at least, debt servicing and repayment would be exceeding new disbursements by 1977, if present trends continued. Since then, inflation will have eroded considerably the real weight of some of the monetary obligations in question. On the other hand, the large balance of payments deficits incurred since 1973 have necessitated heavy emergency borrowings from both official and private institutions. Therefore, whilst this problem of indebtedness looks as serious and chronic as ever, its general profile cannot really be predicted at this point in time. An added complication is that nearly half the newly developing world's deficit on current account in 1975 (and over half the $63 billion it collectively owed foreign banks at that year's end) was run up by seven of its more dynamic national economies: Argentina, Brazil, Mexico, Peru, the Philippines, South Korea and Taiwan!

Another sphere that has become disconcertingly chaotic is that of exchange-rate relationships. Thanks to more or less surreptitious countervailing purchases or sales by central banks, the exchange rates have not, in fact, floated freely these last several years. Even so, many of the alterations have been quite considerable, a prime example being the depreciation of sterling from 2·61 dollars to the pound in late 1971 to 1·68 at the time of writing. Indeed, many economists conclude that the way the world has slid into this "managed float" strategy has been unfortunate. Uncertainties have been compounded and control over domestic inflation vitiated. In consequence, speculative movements in currency have increased when in theory they should have diminished. At the same time, differences in national performance have been accentuated. What is more, these negative effects have, it has been said, been aggravated by "a marked decline in the international consultation characteristic of the Bretton Woods system, each country now determining its own exchange rate policy presumably in line with what it sees as the national interest"[14].

Meanwhile, the international liquidity situation has worsened again. At the end of 1970 total world reserves stood at just under 94 billion dollars or 33·2 per cent of the money value of world exports for that year. Five years later these reserves were rated at nearly 225 billion dollars but that percentage had dropped to 28·3.

Furthermore, the composition of the reserves had altered remarkably. Gold had fallen from 39·8 to 18·5 per cent. Yet SDRs had only risen from 3·3 to 4·5, not enough to offset a decline from 8·2 to 6·1 in the special disbursements made by the IMF to countries in exceptional short- to medium-term difficulties. Sterling fell from 6·1 to 4·1 this perhaps heralding a final phasing out of the reserve currency role, a prospect now universally welcome in Britain. Against all of which could be set increased reliance on other currencies. Needless to say, the dollar remained quite the most important, its percentage increasing from 25·4 to 33·6.

In the late 1960s extreme dependence in this sphere on the American dollar came to be regarded as risky because it was feared that a developing United States trading deficit (plus the declining ratio of gold reserves to dollar liabilities) could one day cause a catastrophic run on the dollar. Today the chief danger may be the opposite of this. It may be that by the 1980s the United States will be running surpluses on current account consistently enough to make extra dollars unduly hard to come by (see the next chapter). If so, the overstretch of world reserves will tend to get worse and worse.

Furthermore, even if there were no such underlying trend, the extremely erratic character of the United States balance of payments position, as measured year by year, would be bound to cause complications. Thus between 1972 and 1975 the average swing on current account from one year to the next was almost ten billion dollars. Then again, in the crisis year of 1971 there had been an outward surge of very short-term capital assets to the tune of 20 billion or thereabouts.

To cap everything, there is the on-going problem of the accumulation of reserves by the members of OPEC. Even before "Yom Kippur" this prospect was causing some concern. In its immediate aftermath, the kind of forecast being made was of 600 billion dollars (at roughly constant money values) by 1980 and further big increases beyond that. By the middle of 1975, however, a peak of 200 to 300 billion around 1980 was more generally being envisaged.[15] The reason was that the states in question had proved more willing and able than had been anticipated to "recycle" revenues through economic development, foreign investment and defence expansion, the fall in the OPEC surplus between 1974 and 1975 noted above being largely an expression of this. By the spring of 1976, indeed, Iran was running into a balance of payments deficit overall.

All the same, the signs still are that a peak of something like 200 billion dollars (at early 1975 money values) will be collectively achieved by the OPEC states within five to ten years, aided by a renewed expansion of the current account surplus in the immediate future. And anything approaching that holding of liquid assets by this small and comparatively closely-knit group of states would be a latent source of major instability in the world economic and strategic scene, not least because of the possibility of much of it suddenly being deployed to stockpile scarce commodities. For instance, 200 billion dollars would cover the total world output of uranium oxide for over 500 years at 1973 price and production levels. This is a figurative comparison but not an entirely inapt one.

Notes

1. Alec Nove, "How the Russians Balance Their Books to Disguise the Effects of Inflation", *The Times*, 30 October 1974.
2. See, for example, Osvaldo Sunkel, "Big Business and 'Dependencia'", *Foreign Affairs*, Vol. 50, No. 3, April 1972, pp. 517–31.
3. *The Financial Times*, 6 September 1976.
4. Peter Odell, *Oil and World Power: Background to the Oil Crisis*, Penguin, Harmondsworth 1975, p. 165.
5. Roger Elgin, "Are the Multinationals really such Monsters?" *The Sunday Times*, 25 March 1973.
6. Lester Brown, *World Without Borders*, Random House, New York 1972, p. 220.
7. E.g. Gunnar Myrdal, *The Challenge of World Poverty*, Allen Lane, London 1970. Chapter 10.
8. Judith Hart, *Aid and Liberation*, Victor Gollancz, London 1973, p. 256.
9. *The Flow of Resources to Developing Countries*, OECD, Paris 1973, pp. 3–8.
10. *The Economist*, 10 July 1976.
11. Gunnar Myrdal, *Against the Stream*, Macmillan, London 1974, p. 49.
12. *1974 Statistical Yearbook*, United Nations, New York 1975, Table 201.
13. *The 1976 Britannica Book of the Year*, Encyclopedia Britannica, Chicago 1976, p. 297.
14. L. W. Ross, "Flexible Exchange Rates", *The Yearbook of World Affairs 1976*, Stevens & Sons, London 1976, pp. 258–72. But for a more sympathetic (and highly authoritative) appreciation see Professor Richard Cooper, "Five years since Smithsonian", *The Economist*, 18 December 1976.
15. See "Out of the Fire", *An Economist Survey*, May 1975, p. 27.

9

The Implications for Security

A fear now endemic throughout the West is that henceforward all those national societies which are heavily dependent on commodity imports will recurrently be knocked off their pedestals of stability by sharp rises in world commodity prices, these being effected in each case by the collusory action of a limited number of primary producers.

Britain's experience in the aftermath of "Yom Kippur" is instructive in this respect. In analysing it, the best point of departure may be its terms of trade—i.e. the price of its exports divided by the price of its imports, each being calculated against the same base year (1970 in this instance). In fact, Britain's terms of trade fell from 93 in the second quarter of 1973 to an average of 75 in 1974 though in 1975 it was to recover to 80.

About a quarter of Britain's total national income is regularly derived from imports. Therefore a deterioration of approximately 15 per cent in the power of exports to purchase these imports was equivalent, more or less, to a quarter of the country's income costing 15 per cent more to obtain than it had previously done. In other words, an expansion of national output of about four per cent would be required to offset this; and, on the British showing of the previous several years, such a diversion would be tantamount to zero growth for 18 months—an inference that, even taken at face value, could have quite serious implications for a political democracy habituated to rising expectations and continuous innovation.

Now it would be fair to say that, since Britain's growth has long been below par, 18 months for Britain might mean only eight to 12 months for others. But what also is true is that all the countries concerned are rendered considerably more vulnerable than such simple arithmetic suggests by the general failure to regulate money supply properly, either internally or internationally. At this early stage, a definitive assessment of the world recession ushered in by "Yom Kippur" is not possible. However, we do know that by the beginning of 1976 the industrial production of the leading OECD members was anything between 10 and 30 per cent below at what should have been on a projection of the secular trend.

Of course, the economic part of the explanation for the abruptness of the post-"Yom Kippur" shock over oil prices was that, for more than a decade past, these prices had been held too low in relation to the long-term supply prospects. Correspondingly, the leading oil importers had waxed euphoric about increasing their own dependence on this energy source. Part of the legacy was the absence of any systematic dialogue between them and the exporters.

Since 1973 two approaches to the establishment of such a dialogue have been adopted. In 1974, the United States launched the International Energy Agency (IEA), its purpose being to enable a wide grouping of consumer nations to harmonise policies on energy conservation and self-reliance and hence to confront OPEC eyeball-to-eyeball if needs be. The following year the French launched a series of multinational meetings on the principle of an equilateral triangle: the oil consumers; the oil exporters; and other newly developing countries. Out of this initiative has come the Conference on International Economic Cooperation (CIEC) plus its four commissions. As the name CIEC implies, the terms of reference extend well beyond oil supplies.

Even on best case assumptions, it is likely to take eight to ten years satisfactorily to merge these avenues of advance with each other and with such further ones as the UN Conference on Trade and Development (UNCTAD). After all, it took a good dozen years for OPEC to become really effective, even though all its members were—so to speak—the same side of the counter.

Besides which, a bend sinister extends across this whole escutcheon. It is the possibility that oil embargoes will again be used for political ends, most probably apropos the Middle East or Southern Africa. Such concern was felt about the way this weapon was deployed after the outbreak of "Yom Kippur" that Henry Kissinger was among those who warned that military force might be used against militant oil producers were an embargo by them ever to precipitate the "gravest emergency", meaning "some actual strangulation of the industrialised world". As it was, the Israelis were robbed of a crushing victory over the Egyptian Third Army near Suez because of the global threat posed by an Arab oil blockade applied more full-bloodedly than ever before.

Given this precedent, it is extremely likely that an outright denial of oil would, in fact, be resorted to afresh were an Arab army again being so badly worsted by the Israelis as to raise to fever pitch a pan-Arab sense of outrage and alarm. Indeed, you could say that its essential function in conflict is to serve as a strategic deterrent against such an eventuality once more coming to pass.

Short of so apocalyptic a scenario, however, strong inhibitions would be felt throughout the Arab world against waging economic warfare on the West in quite this manner, irrespective of a counter-vailing military threat. One constraint is the clumsy magnitude of the stratagem in question. It seems about as appropriate to the attempted modification in detail of Israeli policy, say, in East Jerusalem (or, for that matter, South African in Namibia) as would a hydrogen bomb in a cod war. For one thing, the issues at stake are too localised and intricate to lend themselves to pressure transmitted over great distances and through intermediate links. For another, men like the present rulers of Saudi Arabia would not want to risk the Communisation of the West in the aftermath of an economic collapse induced by oil starvation. In the final analysis, they are not afraid they might lose: they are afraid they might win.

On the other hand, an extra dimension is now being introduced into this situation by those mounting Arab currency reserves, a high proportion of which are being held in banks in the West. Clearly, major movements of them between the various financial centres could be very destabilising. Granted, these assets might in principle be frozen. But this response might be hard to evoke satisfactorily in practice, even assuming a high degree of policy co-ordination between the leading Western states. Nor would the difficulties be just technical. In prospect, such a reaction could induce the Arabs to diversify into gold and sundry commodities or, at any rate, to shift their money away from those they saw as the chief instigators of any freeze. So might it in retrospect.

Conceivably, these monetary holdings will come to be manipulated for political ends in a fashion that is too subtle to lend itself to drastic reprisal but which is menacing none the less. By the same token, any increases in posted oil prices might come to have a stronger political motivation than now. In other words, instead of a dialogue whereby political negotiations consolidated the economic links, one would have a dialectic in which the economic links served to highlight political differences. Not that this has happened yet. On the contrary, Saudi Arabia, though still quite militant on the Arab–Israel dispute as such, has stuck out for moderate oil prices these last two years or more. But we might do well not to take too casually Sheikh Yamani's warnings that this posture remains conditional on progress in the said dispute.

At all events, the tendencies in respect of other primary products are not yet as threatening as with oil. As one special study of this whole question notes apropos bauxite (the chief aluminium ore) and copper:

> The more ready supply of substitutes, the availability of scrap, the greater geographical dispersion of reserves, the differing population and financial characteristics of producer nations, and the lack of a strong political focus all argue against an OPEC-type situation developing. . . .[1]

As was noted in Chapter 7(b), however, copper is a metal which will come into short supply sooner rather than later. This being so, the formation, in 1967, of the *Conseil Intergouvernemental des Pays Exportateurs de Cuivre* (CIPEC) was an event of potential strategic significance. CIPEC comprises Chile, Peru, Zaïre and Zambia and accounts for 70 per cent of the copper exports of the non-Communist world. Moreover, copper provides well over half the export earnings of Chile, Zaïre and Zambia respectively.

In 1972, CIPEC adopted a militant stance in support of Allende's arbitrary acceleration of the nationalisation of Chile's copper mines, although (or perhaps because) the world copper market was currently depressed. The year after, faced with the closure by Ian Smith's illegal regime in Rhodesia of its frontier with Zambia, CIPEC formulated a collective strategy for combatting such acts of "economic aggression".

That CIPEC is not yet able to influence prices as effectively as OPEC now can, is shown by the way in which, in about nine months from May 1974 world copper prices fell by well over 50 per cent, reaching their lowest levels (in real terms) since the 1950s, and undercutting production costs extensively. Yet even this sorry pass may have so depressed development investment as to put CIPEC in a stronger bargaining position, or at any rate a tougher frame of mind, in several years' time. A lot may depend on the future of the exporter–importer dialogue initiated in the spring of 1976 against a background of price-recovery.

What then of bauxite, bearing in mind what also was said in Chapter 7(b) about aluminium prospectively being in eternal supply?

Though Australia alone now produces over 20 per cent of the world output (as against two per cent only 12 years ago), about 40 per cent of the total still comes from four much less developed countries: Jamaica, Guyana, Surinam and Guinea. In March 1974, an International Bauxite Association (IBA) was formed at a meeting in Conakry which was attended by Guinea itself, those Western Hemisphere producers, Sierra Leone, Yugoslavia and Australia. The immediate aim was to ensure that a higher proportion of the bauxite processing is done in each country of origin.

On the face of it, this bauxite oligopoly does not appear to have a potential strength comparable, in the medium-term, to CIPEC, to say nothing of OPEC. However, quite a lot may depend on such variables as these: changing notions about fair returns in the light of the very high energy consumption during processing; the extent to which aluminium is stockpiled; the extent to which its scrap is recycled; the effect on development investment of the 1975 slump in demand; and the political balance in Australia.

Thus, the geostrategic significance, between now and 1990, of the world mineral trade is even harder to assess with any precision than is the long-term availability, on the global plane, of these minerals. Decisions apropos investment policy and so on may modulate considerably the underlying supply and demand trends. Marked shifts in the ideological alignment of major producers may have profound effects, as witness the fact that two-thirds of the world's tin is mined in South-East Asia and that a half of the non-Communist output of unrefined chromium comes from South Africa and Rhodesia. The overall political background will also be a major determinant of any given situation.

Still, this much can be said. As 1990 approaches, the world prices of various key commodities, at least in the minerals category, will tend more and more to reflect the overall political relations between the newly developing countries and the West. Nevertheless, total embargoes on the movement of one or several major products to the West are unlikely except in one of two circumstances. The first, as suggested already, is something like another Six Day War or Third Army *débâcle* in the Middle East. The second, a more general one, is a resurgence of Communist expansionism that was utterly uninhibited and which had already made substantial headway. In this latter connection, it is important to remember that this form of confrontation would correspond rather closely to two classical Marxian concepts: economic determinism and the dialectical interplay of thesis and antithesis. To all of which one might add that one particular country does stand in some danger of eventually being subject to a broad range of interlocking material embargoes and related economic sanctions. This country is South Africa.

Another sphere in which economic development seems bound to make an increasing impact on strategy is the sea. The connecting link is how in several sectors (fishing; mineral exploitation; transit; pollution control) the pressure on the "great universal common"— *alias* the "indivisible world ocean"—is growing to such an extent as to require standards of management superior to anything heretofore. Meanwhile, a conviction is growing that the only way to ensure such management is to divide major sea areas. Sometimes, as with fishing limits in the EEC and pollution in the Mediterranean, some attempt is made to run the resultant sectors regionally. But the dominant inclination of world opinion is towards ever wider single-state control.

The view that the parcellation will continue beyond the present round could gain some support from simple extrapolation. At the first United Nations Conference on the Law of the Sea (held in Geneva in 1958), much debate turned on whether territorial waters should everywhere be extended outwards from a three-mile limit to twelve. But when the third such conference opened in Caracas, the capital of Venezuela, in 1974, the vast majority of the 149 states represented endorsed a 12-mile limit. Nor had they left themselves much choice. By that time, about half had unilaterally advanced beyond the customary three miles. Ten years previously, only 15 had staked such claims.

A major complication is that even a general limit of 12 miles would constitute a *prima facie* threat to the open waters status of no fewer than 116 straits, among them Dover, Bab el Mandeb, Hormuz and Malacca. At Caracas this problem was by no means resolved despite both the Superpowers being keen to keep passage through these narrow fairways as free juridically as possible.

Another issue left over from Caracas (and being considered at follow-up sessions held in other places) is the exact character of an "economic zone" which, it is now generally accepted, should extend to 200 miles offshore. Part of the problem is whether the ownership of, let us say, one small islet entitles a state to claim certain exclusive rights over some 125,000 square miles of surrounding sea, an interpretation which would result in zonal claims automatically extending across nearly a third of the world's ocean surface.

Then there is the question of what exclusive rights over the economic zone should be conferred on a riparian state. Britain is among those who have deplored African and Latin American demands that these rights be made tantamount, more or less, to full jurisdiction whilst the USSR has occasionally urged that some special allowance be made for distant water fishing fleets. Hopefully, a new convention intended to resolve all these difficulties will be adopted in 1978. But Iceland, the USSR and several newly developing states have already extended their economic limits unilaterally, whilst the United States and the EEC are among those expected to do so during 1977.

It could be said that there is enough political momentum here to keep the process of parcellation going, irrespective of any objective necessity. Be that as it may, one particularly urgent and compelling argument does present itself the whole time. It is the way the increasing demands being made on the world's fishing ground have effectively been turning them from a renewable resource into a finite and hence contentious one. After all, the world's fishing fleets have grown by 54 per cent to just over 8,000,000 tons since 1969, whereas the catch has risen only 11 per cent in this interval. The Soviet fleet is now three million tons, over half this tonnage being in ships over 10,000 tons. The Japanese is a million tons whilst the combined EEC fleets are of the same order. This is the law of diminishing returns with a vengeance.

Meanwhile, the role of the sea as the prime medium for the transit of goods and services becomes ever more conspicuous. Between 1965 and 1975 the world's mercantile marine doubled to 320 million gross register tons, a good 40 per cent of it being oil tanker. So, even if we predicate some reduction below exponential growth from now on, a figure around 700 million gross register tons is arrived at for 1990.

Technically, this should present no insuperable hurdles. For instance, the incidence of collisions at sea has lately been tending to fall, except in particular areas—e.g. the Malacca Straits.[2] But what such a projection does do is throw into high relief the sheer scale of the global economic mechanism at the end of the twentieth century and the closeness with which it is interlocked. With some justice, economic historians stress how a dynamic global economy was woven together, under British leadership, in the century after Waterloo. Yet the fact remains that the world's merchant shipping tonnage in 1913 was barely one eighteenth of that just hypothesised for 1990.

But this is not to say that we should endorse fashionably utopian talk about "a world with no frontiers". By that we might mean a world in which nations get so intertwined, economically and culturally, that they can no longer draw up battle lines against each other. And we might cite Canada and the United States or France and Germany as culminations of this process. However, enough has been said above to demonstrate that nationalism is still as liable to shape economics as is economics to dissolve nationalism. Nor should we forget that, throughout the middle of the 19th century, the great Manchester school of liberalism set great store by ever wider and freer trade as the pathway to universal peace; and we all know how brutally their hopes were dashed at Tannenburg, Mons and the Marne.

Even on the more neutral interpretation of closer intermeshing for good or ill, the "world with no frontiers" scenario is only unevenly applicable. Thus in the early 1970s about an eighth of the national income of the world's market economies was derived from imports. But the size and resource balance of the United States is such that the fraction was only an eighteenth in its case. What is more, much the same applied to the biggest of the centrally planned economies—that of the USSR.

A similar impression is gleaned from a look at the particular question of trade with the newly developing world. In 1973 the EEC imported over 34 billion dollars worth of goods from what the United Nations identifies as "developing market economies", whilst Japan took nearly fifteen. Meanwhile, the USA took a relatively modest 21 billion, and the USSR a meagre 2·5.[3]

Undoubtedly, some disadvantages are inherent in a high degree of self-sufficiency. Though the flag no longer tends to follow trade, some increments in political and cultural influence still may. But this must surely be far more than outweighed by the diminished vulnerability to having one's economy blown off course by untoward political events. At all events, the rather special position each Superpower finds itself in is worthy of further examination.

A starting point might be the hypothesis that both will gradually get more integrated into the world trading pattern as their domestic supplies of various raw materials either dwindle or fail to keep pace with rising demand. Also by virtue of the general tendency for advanced industrial economies to trade with one another progressively more in order to realise, through intra-national specialisation, the advantages of large-scale enterprise.

Moreover, this does appear to be happening. Allowance has to be made for the fact that the import statistics supplied by the USSR to the United Nations seem not to reflect fully the big, albeit rather surreptitious, grain purchases from the United States in the early 1970s. When this is done, it looks as if the fraction of total world imports taken by the USSR expanded somewhat in the period 1963 to 1973. Certainly, this was true of the United States.

Since then, of course, all concerned have had to come to terms with what looks like a chronic oil crisis. What this means for the USSR has been hard for the experts to divine, partly because of the crudity and paucity of the information available on the current situation and partly because of the variables involved. Still, we are officially advised that Soviet crude oil production was 430 million tons in 1973—i.e. it had just about caught up the USA's whereas only a dozen years before it had lagged by half.

Duly, Professor Peter Odell, sanguine as ever about the global oil boom, foresees an extension of Soviet oil exports into "many parts of the world over the next decade".[4] Contrariwise, Mr Rockingham Gill believes that, throughout the early 1980s, the USSR will be faced (like its East European partners) with a mounting oil deficit.[5]

Perhaps both will be proved nearly right in that the actual balance will be marginal and dependent on several variables. Among these are the interlinked questions of how fast the Russians can close the technology gap in this particular sphere, and how willing and able they will be to enlist Western help (especially Japanese) in so doing. Then again, energy substitution looks easier, from the supply side, than it does in some other countries, principally because of an abundance of coal and natural gas. Furthermore, this situation is helped on the demand side by the limited recourse to private motoring, this being one form of oil consumption in which it is exceptionally difficult (both technically and politically) to substitute alternative energy sources. Even come 1980, the USSR is unlikely to be expending annually on private cars more than a twentieth of the 300 million tons the USA does now. For one thing, its cars tend to be smaller, the "top brass" limousines excepted.

So it seems sensible to anticipate that, in the 1980s, the Soviet Union will be able to dovetail its oil production and consumption quite exactly, hence balancing substantial imports with substantial exports. Presumably, however, Eastern Europe's situation will be very different. Having risen from 50 to 100 million tons since 1970, its oil deficit may more or less double again by 1990. On the other hand, a significant fraction of this region's requirements should soon be coming from the Middle East, thereby depriving the USSR of some incremental geostrategic leverage but diminishing *pari passu* its economic responsibility.

We should assume, too, that, notwithstanding inefficient management and low sector morale as well as the overhanging menace of climatic vicissitudes, even Soviet grain harvests will continue to stagger upwards, albeit in the most giddy fits and starts. Perhaps, indeed, variegated inputs of Western technology will assist in this regard. Meanwhile, the shortfalls will mainly affect livestock feed rather than direct human consumption.

Whilst Moscow's official statements on grain output per year are not entirely reliable, they may be sufficiently so to bear out this broad inference. The annual average for 1956–62, as calculated from the official returns, was 126 million metric tons. Whereas, in 1966, a crop of 171 was still rated bumper, in 1972 what was said to be just a few million tons less was adjudged a bad shortfall, necessitating the importation of over twenty million tons. For bounteous 1973 the gross figure published was 225 million though 1974 and 1975 dropped to 195 and 140 respectively. Yet even the last-mentioned figure represents about four pounds per person per day. Therefore the decision to import similarly large amounts again that year only had to be taken to preclude too abnormal a slaughter of livestock. Besides which, the 225 mark was hit again in 1976.

Accordingly, it is likely that by the middle 1980s the USSR will be effectively self-sufficient in grainstuffs. Nor should we exaggerate the efficacy in the interim of any endeavour to utilise a recurrent grain dependence to promote political accomodations. The dependence will not be that absolute. Therefore, if any economic leverage can be exercised these next ten years, it is perhaps more likely to arise out of tens of billions of dollars of international debt the USSR appears to be running up.

Yet even in this sector several considerations militate against such a strategy. One is the sheer technical complexity of debt negotiations and the tendency to handle them through specialist channels. Another is the discordance of any such tactics not only with the

6

current mood of the West but also with its long-standing economic philosophy: with, if you like, the liberality of its political economy. The third is that a Soviet Union that was really on the warpath, if only metaphorically, might resort to the orthodox Marxian tactic of debt renunciation. Alternatively, it may either avoid or cover debt accumulation by extensive gold sales. In 1973, for instance, a need to offset grain purchases coupled with the incentive of a temporary gold boom induced these Soviet gold sales to peak at an annual total of 275 tons. This figure, which is thought close to the USSR's own production level, met about a fifth of the world's demand for new gold that particular year.

For its part, the United States will manifestly share, at least in large measure, the acute vulnerability of the Western world as a whole to either a physical interruption of oil supplies or else deliberate manipulation of the foreign exchanges. In more normal circumstances, however, it can be expected to enjoy a strong trading position through the middle 1980s, at any rate in relation to the Soviet bloc and to its own leading allies.

The justification for saying this is chiefly that the extra oil import bill it will be paying by then should be roughly counter-balanced by a quite dramatic trade expansion in three or four different directions. In all probability, the bill in question will amount to several tens of billions of dollars a year, at present-day money values. On the other hand, incremental earnings of the order of ten billion dollars are likely to accrue from increased grain exports (see Chapter 23). A similar windfall could also accrue from the export of civil nuclear facilities. Likewise, from a boost in the export of other high technology products, notably in the fields of electronics and aeronautics. As of 1976, it has three times as many computers installed as does the rest of OECD.

To which one might add that the United States will also be comparatively strongly placed apropos its degree of self-sufficiency in many raw materials. Thus estimates made by the United States Bureau of Mines in 1973 (and geared to 1971 pricings) suggest that, making due allowance for rising demand, the known reserves of copper will last through the year 2000 whilst those of, for instance, lead, zinc and molybdenum should suffice well into the next century.[6]

On the other hand, it is possible that, even though the exotic technologies may thrive, American manufacturing in general may lose some of its competitive cutting-edge, due to such factors as rising labour costs and the diffusion of vaguely "anti-growth" attitudes. Yet, all things considered, there is little likelihood that the trade balance will be consistently and massively adverse. Besides, such trade deficits as may temporarily occur may be largely offset by capital inflows from OPEC and elsewhere.

A priori, one could say that the relative prospective strength of the American economy could, if indeed borne out by events, dangerously accentuate the asymmetries within the Atlantic Alliance. Yet this may not be so. For one thing, the great majority of Americans have realised ever since 1940 that their own nationhood would be traumatised unbearably if such great centres of Western thought and culture as Athens, Heidelberg, Oxford, Paris and Rome lost their freedom once and for all. For another, a United States not distraught by involuntary and continual drains on the dollar might be more sympathetic towards the evolution of a European technological community, not least in the weapons sphere. In the event, however, the swings of relative fortune from one year to the next may complicate things unduly. Even between 1972 and 1975, the American balance of trade with the "Europe of the Nine" swung from a one billion dollar annual deficit to a six billion dollar surplus.

Still, not a few commentators would now argue—and with good reason—that all the above considerations are utterly overshadowed by one linkage between economics and strategy which imminently poses a threat to peace and freedom world-wide and which is quite unique in scale and character. It is the threatened proliferation of fission warhead deterrent forces as a result of the cumulative and virtually world-wide dissemination of stockpiles of a fissile isotope known as Plutonium 239, this in its turn being a consequence of the progressive extension of civil nuclear power.

By definition, an element—e.g. oxygen, copper, uranium, plutonium—is a substance so basic that it cannot be further separated out by chemical means. Nevertheless, all elements are composed of what generally are, in nature, invariable proportions of several isotopes—substances which may behave identically chemically but which do have subtly different atomic structures and therefore weights. Thus the atomic structure of Uranium 235 (one of the three isotopes of the element in question) is such as to render it considerably fissile and therefore peculiarly suitable for either slow-motion or explosive nuclear chain reactions. Usually, the uranium used in even a slow-motion reaction has been "enriched" beforehand—i.e. the proportion of U235 has been increased by one of two or three exotic physical techniques, each of which exploits the marginal differences in atomic weights between the three uranium isotopes (see Chapter 10). Needless to say, uranium supplied to one country by another for use inside a reactor (industrial or research) will never be enriched by the former to the extent required to make a nuclear bomb (c. 85 per cent U235); and, thus far at least, only about half-a-dozen countries the world over have uranium enrichment facilities.

So the rub vis-à-vis the years immediately ahead lies chiefly in this. Whenever rods of uranium are consumed in a reactor, many of the particles liberated by the disintegration of U235 nuclei will move fast enough to enter those of the much more stable—and in nature much more preponderate—U238 isotope, thereby at once releasing more heat and transmuting this U238 into the artificial element plutonium, including the all-too-suitably fissile Pu239. Subsequently, the plutonium can be separated from all the other elements and compounds in the reactor residue by means which may not be simple but which are at least chemical.

What is more, all the recent evidence shatters one early hope of those concerned to see nuclear proliferation checked. This was that the Pu239 would regularly be so contaminated by other isotopes of the same metal (notably the phenomenally toxic and excessively fissile Plutonium 240) as to be ineligible for use as a core substance in fission warheads. Admittedly, if a power reactor is run for the absolute duration of one set of uranium rods (perhaps two to three years at peak intensity), this plutonium by-product may include 15 to 25 per cent Pu240 and other contaminants. If, on the other hand, these fuel rods are withdrawn after, say, only 12 months the deleterious fraction will be considerably lower. Nor does there now appear to be any incontrovertible reason why a nuclear warhead should not consist of only 75 to 85 per cent Pu239. Much will depend on the specific design.

To make a plutonium bomb of much the same strength as the 20 kiloton one dropped over Nagasaki in 1945 would require six to eight kilogrammes of this metal. And this quantity would normally be produced in the course of a year's continuous and high-intensity operation by a reactor with a thermal rating of between 25 and 30 megawatts. As a general rule, the thermal rating of a power reactor is a little more than three times its electrical rating.

One might have assumed that, even though it depends on chemistry rather than sub-nuclear physics, the process of extracting plutonium or anything else from reactor residue would be too difficult a technological challenge for many of the prospective nuclear powers to surmount. After all, much of the material in question will be extremely radioactive; and it will be so toxic that the ingestion of a 100,000th of a gramme may kill. The fact remains, however, that a good half-a-dozen of these countries already possess reprocessing plants; and that is without taking account of the European Nuclear Energy Agency facility at Mol in Belgium, opened in 1966 but currently closed down. Among the countries in question are Czechoslovakia, Federal Germany, India, Japan and Spain.

Whilst these plants are mainly concerned at present with the recovery of unused uranium, most of them could quite readily be reoriented to plutonium if required. A typical installation cost is $20,000,000; and the throughputs are of the order of several hundred kilogrammes a year.

So what we could face is a most alarming follow-through of the cataclysmic alteration military science underwent in 1945. For thousands of years before, firepower had been so scarce a resource that the supreme test of generalship lay in conserving it for application at the crucial time and place. Suddenly, it promised to become so abundant that it would be madness ever to release more than the tiniest fraction of the total quantity available to Man. Moreover, this decidedly morbid promise was to be heavily underscored in the early 1950s with the advent of the hydrogen or thermonuclear bomb—a device reliant on a nuclear fusion reaction and hence able to effect explosions any distance up the megaton scale.[7]

Notes

1. Philip Connelly and Robert Perlman, *The Politics of Scarcity*, Oxford University Press, London 1975, p. 140.
2. See A. N. Crockcroft, "Statistics of Collisions at Sea", *The Journal of Navigation*, Vol. 29 No. 3, July 1976, pp. 215–25.
3. The estimates in these two paragraphs are chiefly derived from *1974 Statistical Yearbook*, United Nations, New York 1975, Tables 149 and 184.
4. Peter Odell, *Oil and World Power*, Penguin, Harmondsworth 1975, p. 64.
5. R. Rockingham Gill "Soviet Oil in the 1980s: Shortage or Surplus?" *RUSI Journal*, Vol. 121 No. 2, June 1976, pp. 73–77.
6. Connelly and Perlman op. cit., Appendix B.
7. A megaton is an explosive yield equivalent to a million tons of TNT, whereas a kiloton corresponds to 1,000 tons.

Part III

The Military Factors

10

The Nuclear Balance

By the early 1960s, estimates of the thermonuclear stockpiles of each of the Superpowers were running into scores of thousands of megatons.[1] Contrariwise, the British and French deterrents will together amount to a mere 250 megatons or thereabouts through 1980. Probably much the same will still hold good for China even though, by 1980, its nuclear stockpile is likely to be expanding a good deal more rapidly than heretofore. At present, it is thought to comprise some two to three hundred fusion and fission warheads.[2]

Yet it could well be that the huge differentials hereby indicated between the Superpowers and the other three members of the nuclear (and thermonuclear) club owe much to the formers' respective stockpiles being vastly superfluous to strict operational requirements. After all, authoritative estimates show but six million tons of high explosive to have been released by all the combatants everywhere throughout World War II. Nor should we forget that this ordnance was free from the fall-out and peculiarly lethal heat flash associated with nuclear weapons.

Not that anybody imagines that trite arithmetic comparisons of this sort could ever give anything like a complete and entirely accurate impression of any balance of nuclear power. For one thing, it is usually the number, quality and variety of the delivery systems (offensive and also defensive) that determines the character of the strategic nuclear balance. Thus at the time of the 1962 Cuban crisis the Soviet Union lay very exposed to pre-emptive disablement, principally because its own deterrent then basically consisted of a mere 75 Intercontinental Ballistic Missiles (ICBMs) of the cumbersome liquid-fuelled variety. A remarkably close parallel to this situation (which does much to explain both the origin of the Cuban crisis and its satisfactory resolution)[3] is to be found in the size and configuration of China's strategic deterrent. Accordingly, this will probably remain uncomfortably exposed to a disarming first strike from the USSR or, for that matter, the USA until the late 1980s. By that time China should have in excess of 500 land-based strategic missiles, many of them of the compact and fast-reacting solid-fuelled kind. China may also have some submarine-borne missiles with ranges of the order of 500 miles.

By the same token, however, both Moscow and Washington today seem set to maintain indefinitely an "assured second strike". In other words, their respective strategic forces can henceforward be counted on always to inflict totally "unacceptable damage" on any adversary even after enduring a full-scale surprise attack themselves. It is a circumstance so novel, and so consequential to Humanity at large, as effectively to constitute a technical revolution within the technical revolution.

Here the most fundamental consideration is what is meant by "unacceptable damage". As the modern deterrence debate got under way in the United States 20 years ago, a broad consensus seemed to emerge that if, say, its 75 largest cities were smashed by thermonuclear explosions the whole national life of either Superpower would effectively be destroyed; and arbitrary though such estimates were, they did bear some relation to the spatial distribution of the Soviet and American populations as well as to other economic and social parameters.

But from now on, to preclude such retaliatory damage by the respective ICBM echelons alone, an attrition well in excess of 95 per cent would have to be achieved almost instantly against them! Besides which, the great majority of analysts would now acknowledge that quite the most stable element in each Superpower's second strike is not the ICBM echelons at all but the flotillas of Fleet Ballistic Missile (FBM) submarines. Already each has well over 650 strategic missiles with ranges at least 1,750 miles installed in such boats. Now the USSR is commissioning a modified D-class, every member of which will be able to fire 16 missiles a good 5,000 miles. Moreover, the United States will be deploying from 1978 the massive Trident class with 24 missiles apiece; and each of these weapons will reportedly carry up to 17 MIRV[4] warheads. So what chance will there be henceforward of a crippling first-strike against the FBM force of either Superpower? Could such powers of retaliation ever be pre-empted?

Many references can be found in the specialist press to the modest progress made since 1945 in regard to acoustic scanning, this having been the only method of detecting totally submerged vessels available in World War II. As often as not, however, the discussion at least implicitly involves a straight comparison with the state of Anti-

Submarine Warfare (ASW) towards the end of the Battle of the Atlantic, whereas the setting for a nuclear exchange would be much more conducive to the triumph of the submarines. For one thing, an FBM is not concerned, as were the U-Boats, with closing to action with enemy vessels, surface or otherwise. On the contrary, it has a duty to elude them, in which aim it is assisted by the special attributes it derives from nuclear-propulsion and the novel hull designs associated with this. Thus it may travel deeply submerged (and either very fast or very quietly) for maybe two months on end, perhaps under the fringes of polar ice-caps or in other awkward locations.

We must always bear in mind, in any case, that even in May 1943— a month of decisive victory for the Allied escort forces on North Atlantic stations—the average attrition of U-Boats at sea was a bare 1·0 per cent per day. Yet a pre-emptive first strike against what would be a well-dispersed FBM force would probably have to achieve something very close to 100 per cent success in under half an hour. Stated in these terms, the stipulated requirement is too far fetched to merit further discussion, certainly for the Superpower FBMs and prospectively (see Chapter 24) for the European as well.[5]

Nor do the more exotic approaches to this problem hold out any real hope of the requisite breakthrough. Objections that are very similar to, though even more serious than, those against the use of sound energy for submarine surveillance can be levelled against any application of electromagnetic waves to this end. Nor ought we to pay much heed to claims that infra-red sensors mounted in unmanned orbiting satellites may detect the small and highly localised rise in the temperature of the sea surface that may be induced by the rapid passage of a nuclear-driven submarine perhaps one or two hundred feet below. What if such a boat is travelling only very slowly or is down at, say, 300 fathoms? Suppose it does glide beneath an ice-sheet? What if a heavy sea is running? How might positive identification be effected? How quickly could analysts obtain and interpret the data gleaned? Surely, neither laser scanners in sea water nor other sensors in Earth orbit are going to make possible the huge leap forward required.

And for any who remain unconvinced on this score, there is always the prospect of the mobile ICBM. As early as 1961 much effort was put into a scheme to fit up 100 US railroad cars with perhaps 500 Minutemen. It was found, however, that the reliability of the missiles was reduced unacceptably, that the unit cost would be up to three times greater, and that the reaction time would be extended to 15 minutes. For these and other reasons the project was cancelled though, of course, it could always be revived in some form. In fact, the SSX-16, a missile with a range of 5,000 miles that is now being tested in the USSR, is understood to be land-mobile. True, the United States has officially queried whether systems so elusive are compatible with the Strategic Arms Limitation Talks (SALT). However, its own development of small but long-range and deadly accurate cruise missiles is undermining this objection.

Finally, there is the question of whether a more extended deployment of Anti-Ballistic Missiles might disturb the Superpower nuclear balance in the 1980s. The 1972 SALT agreement consisted of two parts: an interim agreement curbing the deployment of the main offensive missiles and a treaty delimiting sharply the deployment of Anti-Ballistic Missiles (ABMs). To be precise, the latter allowed each Superpower to possess two ABM screens, each to be comprised of not more than 100 static ABM launchers and the associated radars. One of these screens could be for the defence of the national capital, whilst the other could cover an ICBM field. And, in fact, in 1974 an additional protocol obliged the two signatories to settle for either rather than both.

The genesis of this dichotomy had been that the respective ABM networks already under preparation were geared to different premises. Thus under the Safeguard modification (announced by Richard Nixon in 1969) of the USA's original ABM programme, the main emphasis had been switched from the "thin-screen" defence of American cities against the relatively moderate and uncomplicated attack of which China was deemed capable by the late 1970s. Henceforward the prime aim was to be the point defence of hardened ICBM sites against a heavy and sophisticated pre-emptive onslaught of the sort it was feared the USSR—and it alone—might be in a position to launch within the decade ahead.

Meanwhile, although the Soviet installations of ABMs had proceeded only slowly since its inception in 1966, it had already become clear that the Kremlin was concerned merely to minimise the effects of a rocket strike against large and vulnerable civilian objectives, foremost among them Moscow. Characteristically enough, no direct mention was ever made of Peking in this context. But, given the relevant aspects of the technical balance, this aspiration would have made no sense at all except against the putative Chinese threat.

Though the ABM treaty was to "be of unlimited duration", it was subject to review every five years. That the 1977–78 review will lead to any serious erosion of the original concept mercifully seems most improbable. What cannot be entirely discounted, is the possibility that the 1982–83 one will do so, thanks to the way the Chinese strategic build-up is reawakening the traditional Soviet obsession with total defence. The word "obsession" is chosen advisedly. Nobody familiar with, let us say, the effort still being put into the anti-aircraft defence of the USSR (in this, the age in which the ICBM and FBM have come fully into their own) could fail to discern behind it a large measure of phobic irrationality: 550,000 men in a separate command, operating 5,000 radars and 2,500 interceptor aircraft and *c*. 5,000 Surface-to-Air Missile (SAM) launchers!

Nevertheless the odds are probably stacked heavily against renewed ABM expansion in 1983 or thereafter. Even suppose it did take place, it would be extremely unlikely to destroy the nuclear deadlock between the Superpowers either by 1990 or subsequently. The reasons for saying this are manifold. Chief among them is that, by definition, an Anti-Ballistic Missile is ineffectual against a tiny, contour-hugging cruise missile. Another is that, even as things stand, the scenario in question is one in which the inestimable advantages of tactical surprise, in terms of technique as well as timing, would rest very heavily with the offence. One has only to think of the innumerable combinations of multiple warheads and decoy devices the United States, in particular, is known to have at its disposal already. Nor should one forget that it has arrived in this position at but a sliver of the cost either it or the USSR would incur in providing themselves with a nationwide ABM coverage of matching quality and density.[6]

But to argue that the Superpower nuclear stalemate is inherently extremely stable is not *ipso facto* to prove that the Strategic Arms Limitation Talks have been irrelevant throughout. To codify and institutionalise a situation may be to preserve it the more felicitously, whilst affording those concerned valuable experience in negotiations of this rather esoteric kind. Verification, too, may provide instructive experience—by no means all of it reassuring, to judge from the evidence to date. Furthermore, some have attached importance to "linkage" politics: the notion that a good Moscow–Washington dialogue within SALT may be conducive to one on the Lebanon, Namibia or wherever. Certainly to be in the United States as SALT got under way in the autumn of 1969 was to be made aware of great expectations of this sort in respect of South-East Asia and the Middle East.

All the same, it might be a mistake to see in the progress of SALT, actual or prospective, a *sine qua non* for what is fast becoming a desperate struggle to curb the spread of nuclear weapons throughout the world as a whole. In sadder earnest, one is driven towards a similarly open verdict, albeit on rather different grounds, apropos the Non-Proliferation Treaty of 1968. Under this NPT signatories pledge themselves to halt the spread of fully independent nuclear deterrents and, more specifically, the non-nuclear nations agree to accept inspection "in accordance with the statute of the International Atomic Energy Agency and the Agency's safeguards system" (Article III).

Part of the trouble is quite simply that many of the most relevant countries have still to adhere to the NPT. Algeria, Argentina, Brazil, Chile, China, Cuba, France, India, Israel, North Korea, Pakistan, Saudi Arabia, South Africa, Spain and Vietnam are among those who have not even signed. Colombia, Egypt, Indonesia, Kuwait, Switzerland and Turkey are the main ones that have signed but not as yet ratified. Judging by the general rates of accession these last five years, this situation is unlikely to improve much through 1980.

Besides, the NPT does not bind irrevocably—even notionally—those who do accede to it. Any party can withdraw at no more than three months' notice should it decide "that extraordinary events related to the subject matter of this Treaty have jeopardised the supreme interests of its Country" (Article X). What is more, resentment against what many in the non-nuclear world have seen as the unacceptably discriminatory character of non-proliferation per se led to the treaty being formally wedded to the old utopian vision of complete nuclear disarmament: the implication being that, if this aim were not fruitfully pursued, some of the NPT's non-nuclear signatories might not feel so committed to it. Thus the preamble commits all signatories to work towards the utter "liquidation of all" military nuclear stockpiles whilst Article VIII stipulates that, five years after the treaty came into force in 1970, a conference should convene at Geneva "with a view to assuring that the purposes of the Preamble and the provisions of the Treaty are being realised". Further such conferences may be called at five yearly intervals if a majority of the signatory states so determine.

In May 1975, the first review conference duly took place. It did so against a background of general acceptance, either eager or reluctant, of the proposition that nuclear reactor capacity must be expanded rapidly in order to close the energy gap. Only limited and tentative progress was made in tightening international safeguards, promoting national measures to ensure the physical security of nuclear materials and facilities, and studying the peaceful applications of nuclear explosions. But it has been agreed that the second such conference shall be held in 1980.

Just how efficacious the NPT's spindly structure might, in fact, become is best assessed in relation to the growing scale and complexity of the proliferation threat. Needless to say, the "enrichment" of natural uranium is a basic routine in this regard. By "enrichment" is here meant increasing the proportion of the very fissile isotope, Uranium 235, so as either to permit, for industrial purposes, a slow-motion chain reaction or—by enriching the sample to 90 per cent or thereabouts—to facilitate an instant and hence explosive release. The solution resorted to in turn by the five established nuclear powers— the USA, the USSR, Britain, China and France—was "gaseous diffusion", a method which involves exploiting the subtle differences in mass between the atoms of the respective uranium isotopes by passing the gasified metal through thousands of micropore membranes.

Very generally, however, expert opinion in the rest of the world has already written off gaseous diffusion as impractical. Whilst this is partly on account of the extraordinarily esoteric technology required, it is also because the process can only operate at anything like its optimum pro rata efficiency in a plant which has cost one or two billion dollars to build and regularly consumes over 1,000 megawatts of electricity. Thirty-five years ago the directors of the Manhattan Project did consider relying instead on the centrifuge method—i.e. spinning gasified uranium so fast that the heavier atoms are thrown outwards.

Not that this very elementary principle is at all easy to apply. For one thing, each rotor must revolve something like 1,000 times a second, thereby achieving supersonic speeds around its own periphery. Nevertheless some marked improvements in centrifuge technology were registered in Europe during the late 1960s; and these led to an agreement being signed in 1970 between Britain, Federal Germany and the Netherlands for the joint production for industrial use of enriched uranium. That same year South Africa reported that it, too, had now perfected a technique for enriching uranium on a modest scale basis.

Probably this is centrifuge though it may be yet another method, one first conceived in West Germany and known as jet nozzle. Technically, this may be simpler than centrifuge in that separation within the gas stream is obtained by deflection off a curved wall. But it is understood to make heavier demands on electricity. Brazil has lately acquired a jet nozzle facility, this being part of the nuclear contract with the Federal Republic referred to in Chapter 25.

At all events, the current prognosis for the centrifuge is that plants consuming perhaps 30 megawatts of electricity apiece can be made commercially competitive with gaseous diffusion models, notwithstanding rather higher capital costs per unit of output. Apparently, too, the centrifuge is the only method of enrichment which permits a rapid and easy switch from the gain of a few per cent usually required for nuclear reactors to the 85 per cent or so needed for nuclear warheads.

Therefore, it does seem that the centrifuge is quite the best answer for a medium industrial nation seeking an independent and maybe clandestine source of enriched uranium. No doubt *ad hoc* initiatives will continue to be taken, not least by the United States, to limit the spread of the relevant arts. Yet, in the absence of a hard-and-fast international compact, it is quite conceivable that a dozen or so countries will be competent in this field by 1990.

Uranium 235 is the most suitable fissile material to use in the first attempts, always fraught with difficulty in any case, to trigger a fusion explosion—i.e. make a hydrogen or thermonuclear bomb. For a number of reasons, however, it is doubtful whether any more states will even seek thermonuclear status this side of 1990. This being so, our most immediate concern should be the proliferation of fission warfare deterrents as a more or less direct consequence of the cumulative and virtually world-wide dissemination of stockpiles of Plutonium 239 through civil nuclear programmes.

Working to the reasonable formula of a production of nine equivalent warheads from the regular operation over one year of 100 megawatts of electrical capacity (MWe), one comes up with some positively alarming figures for 1980, to say nothing of 1990. Thus the rise in total capacity installed world-wide is estimated as follows: 3,300 MWe in 1963; 19,000 in 1970; 46,000 in 1973; 105,000 in 1976;

and 220,000 in 1980. Nor should anyone dismiss this last figure as futurological speculation. Of the 345 power reactors expected to be in service on this date, all but 23 were reported under construction at the close of 1975.

Among the countries classified as "non-nuclear" in military terms yet possessed of at least 100 MWe of industrial nuclear power in 1975 were these: Argentina, Belgium, Bulgaria, Canada, Czechoslovakia, West and East Germany, India, Italy, Japan, the Netherlands, Pakistan, Spain, Sweden and Switzerland. By 1980 additions to this list are expected as follows: Austria, Brazil, Finland, Hungary, Iran, South Korea, Mexico, Romania, Taiwan and Yugoslavia. So by then, too, the total electrical megawattage controlled by all the non-nuclear states will amount to just 40 per cent of the total cited above.[7]

To complicate matters further, there is every indication that, by the mid-1980s, a substantial and ever-expanding fraction of the world's rapidly increasing reactor capacity will consist of "fast breeder" installations. What happens in this type of reactor is that a chain reaction sustained within a charge of Plutonium 239 gives rise to enough surplus neutrons to bombard extensively a charge of natural uranium present; and these neutrons are moving sufficiently fast to disintegrate the nuclei of Uranium 238—the comparatively stable isotope that, in fact, constitutes over 99 per cent of natural uranium—thereby not only augmenting considerably the heat emission but also transmuting this U238 into almost pure Pu 239. Therefore, if the reaction is sustained for perhaps several years, the total amount of plutonium available at the end will be anything up to twice what was there to start with!

These breeder reactors have been subject to their fair share of developmental snags, notably in relation to the alarmingly high temperatures which build up in their cores. Nevertheless, models with capacities well in excess of 200 MWe "went critical" in the USSR, France and Britain in the early 1970s, whilst several in the 300–600 MWe range are under construction. About ten countries already have fast breeder programmes.

Besides, the energy-producing installations are by no means the only factor in this balance. To them must be added the research reactors. Some 374 were reckoned to be distributed around 46 countries in 1975; and by 1980 there should be 391 in 51 countries, the five extra members of this league being Bangladesh, Cuba, Libya, Malaysia and Peru.[8]

Quite the most important, from the strategic standpoint, is the natural uranium facility built with French patronage (and without a safeguards agreement) at Dimona in Israel between 1957 and 1964. For this is rated at 24 thermal megawatts and so adjudged able to produce virtually every year enough Pu 239 to make a Nagasaki bomb. Yet even, let us say, the relatively tiny Soviet-built research reactor the Yugoslavs have operated since 1959 may yield sufficient for two such warheads every decade.

So what can be done to arrest what looks like a relentless and gargantuan sowing of nuclear dragon's teeth? Some still see the best hope in limiting the spread of the reprocessing plants by means of which usable Plutonium 239 can be recovered from the reactors. A case in point was a speech by Henry Kissinger to the United Nations in September 1975. In this he described the "spread under national control of reprocessing facilities" as the "greatest single danger of unrestrained nuclear proliferation". Accordingly, he strongly backed the creation of "multinational nuclear fuel cycle centres", a possibility that the NPT review conference had considered—albeit only cursorily—five months before.

Hard though it undoubtedly would be at this late hour so to regulate the extension of plutonium separation and uranium enrichment facilities, any multilateral control over the production of natural uranium seems much more impractical. Working to a break-even production cost of ten dollars a pound, the United Nations in 1970 estimated world reserves of uranium oxide (which is about 85 per cent uranium) at 760,000 metric tons—i.e. 35 years of output at the current rates. Three countries were known to have over 175,000 apiece: Canada, South Africa and the United States. Others with 9,000 tons or more included Argentina, Australia, the Central African Republic, France, Gabon, Niger, Portugal and Spain. Among those with at least 1,000 tons were Brazil, Italy, Japan, Mexico, Turkey and Yugoslavia.

True, the International Atomic Energy Agency (IAEA) was then calculating that the world's known reserves would need to grow to two or three times the figure just cited in the course of 15 years. But against this could be set the fact that many countries, notably those behind the Iron and Bamboo Curtains, did not report. Also, the usual tendency for any mineral shortage to push up the world price and so make what are now sub-marginal deposits worth mining.

Ultimately, too, a large extra dimension could be introduced into the world situation by thorium. For when the nuclei of this metal are bombarded by fast neutrons within a breeder reactor, it is transmuted to U233, another highly fissile isotope but one which is little in evidence in natural uranium. Already thorium deposits well in excess of a million tons have been identified. Countries with over 40,000 tons apiece include—in descending order—Canada, India, Brazil, South Africa, Australia and the United States.[9]

There can be little doubt that the diffused accumulation of plutonium, in particular, is easily the most important strand in the web of international security hazards that threatens to enmesh Mankind. This being so, it is curious the extent to which—over these last few years—the environmental objectors to nuclear power have ignored this dimension, concentrating instead on such ecologica aspects as the risk of a reactor accident or the difficulties occasioned by the disposal of waste plutonium, given that it will retain a quarter of its radioactivity after 50,000 years.

Though the record in Russia and China is a matter of conjecture, it is probable that the total number of deaths caused by nuclear accidents does not yet exceed a score world-wide. Theoretically several thousand, or even several tens of thousands, might die if a larger power reactor were to go so badly out of control that its nuclear charge melted. Yet macabre though such an eventuality would be, it would not begin to approach in frightfulness even a regional nuclear war. Nor does the leakage of waste plutonium present quite so overhanging a menace.

We should not forget either that, even in countries which may pride themselves on technological sophistication, the possibility of significant amounts of plutonium surreptitiously falling into terrorist hands cannot be entirely excluded. Nor that internal disorder could lead to the illicit expropriation of nuclear facilities, especially in the "soft states" of the newly developing world. What might happen to the many hundreds of warheads it might then have amassed, if China were to experience in, say, 1985 something akin to a Cultural Revolution?

Notes

1. E.g. Dr Linus Pauling as quoted in *The New York Herald Tribune*, 13 September 1963.
2. *The Military Balance, 1975/6*, IISS, London 1976, p. 49.
3. See the author's "Towards the Superpower Deadlock", *The World Today*, Vol. 22 No. 9, September 1966, pp. 366–74.

4. Multiple Independently-Targettable Re-entry Vehicles: a missile so equipped is able to strike simultaneously and very accurately at several different targets, scores of miles apart.

5. For a fuller discussion of the ASW problem, as appertaining to the British Polaris force, see the author's *British Arms and Strategy, 1970–80*, RUSI, London 1969. Chapter 4.

6. For the classic riposte to the ABM lobby see Richard Garwin and Hans Bethe, *The Scientific American*, Vol. 218 No. 3, March 1968, pp. 21–31.

7. See *SIPRI Yearbook 1976*, Almqvist and Wiksell, Stockholm 1976, Table 1B. 4.

8. Ibid, Table 1B. 5.

9. *United States Mineral Resources: Geological Survey Professional Paper 820*, US Government Printing Office, Washington 1973, Table 94.

11

Air and Naval Power

(a) TACTICAL AVIATION: A CRISIS OF ADJUSTMENT

If a special case can be made for bracketing air and naval power together, it is chiefly that their offensive application is less liable to be constrained by the ambient environment than is that of land power. Relatively weak armies resting on the defensive have from time immemorial turned landscape features to good effect. Then again, guerrilla movements have often used physical and human geography to turn the tables on security forces far better placed in terms of manpower or technology. In aerial or maritime conflict, on the other hand, it has customarily been much easier to exploit rapidly an initial advantage in either mass or quality.

Currently, this point is especially pertinent as regards quality. This is because of the dramatic advances the next 15 years seem destined to witness in the sphere of military electronics. Ability to operate with adequate strength on a higher frequency might, in principle, be taken as the acid test of superiority in this field. In practice, however, the diversity of electronic equipment and tactics is already far too great for so neat a comparison to be drawn.

All the same, there can be no doubt that, in the years ahead, electronic supremacy will often be a crucial factor, particularly in respect of air warfare. Probably, it would be fair to say that, during the Battle of Britain, to be half a generation ahead electronically was tantamount to a 50 per cent numerical advantage. In air combat in 1980 the equivalent percentage might exceed five hundred. One ominous corollary is that this is a field in which espionage could yield exceptionally high dividends, just as it did in nuclear research in the 1940s. Much the same might apply to ill-judged trade agreements.

If the great strides made in electronics these past few years by Soviet forces in Central Europe are anything to go by, the pace and importance of electronic innovation in the 1980s threatens—in some aspects of military science—to benefit the Soviet Union as against the United States. Obversely, it will be conducive to the United States maintaining its lead in military technology over Western Europe, if only because of the superior facilities for field testing the former can be expected to enjoy for both spatial and political reasons. At the same time, it will help to preserve a technology gap between the advanced industrial nations as a whole and the newly developing ones.

On the other hand, it would be prudent not to make too much of this last point. Granted that the limited acquisition of one or two prestigious weapons systems is no guarantee of all-round competence in the esoteric arts of modern war, one dare not discount too much the world-wide diffusion of modern strike-fighters and the like. Thus the countries outside NATO with some variant of the Phantom in service include El Salvador, Honduras, Iran, Israel, Japan, South Korea and Spain. Among those outside the Warsaw Pact with the Mig-21 (the Phantom's Soviet counterpart) are Afghanistan, Algeria, Bangladesh, China, Cuba, Egypt, Finland, India, Indonesia, Iraq, North Korea, Somalia, the Sudan, Syria, Uganda, Vietnam and Yugoslavia. Correspondingly, at least one member of France's remarkable Mirage series has been procured by Abu Dhabi, Argentina, Australia, Brazil, Colombia, Egypt, Israel, Kuwait, Libya, Pakistan, Peru, South Africa, Spain, Switzerland and Venezuela.[1]

Unfortunately, the efficacy of tactical aircraft through 1985 cannot be predicted with much precision for several interrelated reasons. Some of the main categories of weapons and support systems involved are relatively new and therefore have great development potential left in them. Furthermore, much of this is in specific electronic applications that are always heavily shrouded in secrecy and which would, in any case, be very difficult for laymen to comprehend. Experience does suggest, too, that the cost-effectiveness of particular weapons in this sphere, can be acutely sensitive to marginal changes in the performance of either themselves or their antidotes.

By much the same token, the relationship between stipulated tasks and required force levels is more difficult for the non-specialist, or indeed the expert, to gauge in the air than on land or even at sea; and this last problem is, it seems to me, seriously compounded by a propensity on the part of war historians to treat the sky as though it were a background factor in recent campaigns, prominent yet still not integral. Were H. G. Wells alive today he would find the science of air warfare far more complex, and hence even harder to evaluate, than it was (see Chapter 4) in his own times!

Nevertheless, one underlying trend now suggests itself, not least via a comparison of the Arab–Israel war of 1973 with that of 1967. It is for tactical aircraft to become progressively more vulnerable and so less effective when used offensively in "sophisticated" though non-nuclear environments. Moreover, the signs are that this trend will be maintained at least through 1985 as air defence networks get ever more refined and diversified, both electronically and in other respects.

At the lower end of the scale of weight and of complexity are such man-held missile launchers as the British Blowpipe and the Soviet SAM-7. Already these pose a formidable threat, under clear weather conditions, to helicopters and other relatively slow-moving machines. Meanwhile, the easier reconciliation of compactness and efficiency in those more elaborate surface-to-air missiles normally deployed in batteries is being facilitated by continual innovation in computers and in radar. A major example is a ramifying application by the Atlantic Alliance and, in its wake, by the USSR of Continuous Wave radar—i.e. the kind which exploits what is known as the "doppler effect" in order to pick out aircraft or missiles travelling close to the Earth's surface.

Evidently, still faster and lower flight could help intruding aircraft to counter some of these trends. However, severe dilemmas are always posed by a combination of really low altitude—i.e. 50 to 300 feet—and high subsonic or supersonic speed. Close contour-flying over terrain which is at all irregular will depend on elaborate electronic aids and maybe, too, such special airframe features as variable-sweep wings. Nor will the incorporation of such remedies by any means ensure the elimination of serious buffeting.

Suppose it did, a fundamental geometrical difficulty would remain: a low altitude drastically curtails horizons and—even worse—dramatically increases the angular velocity, as perceived by a fast-flying pilot, of the ground beneath. As a result, targets of opportunity become hard to spot at all, whilst even pre-located ones may prove difficult to attack with enough precision. To all of which one must add that, whilst flying very low and fast may ensure tolerable immunity from ground-based weapons, it may sometimes afford a less foolproof guarantee against interception from above, another tactic that is deriving some benefit from technological advance. Hence the recent debate within NATO about AWACS.[2]

Still, this does not mean that manned aircraft are about to lose completely their role in offensive action. One obvious counterpoint to make is that the sudden and mass use of aircraft may achieve a saturation effect. Another is that, in many situations, the restricted horizons argument can be inverted with a vengeance. Let us take, for example, the situation of a country like Egypt. Providing enough surface-to-air missiles and so on adequately to screen the Suez Canal approaches against low-level intrusion is manifestly within its considerable military means. Affording such protection to the whole of its national territory might be a very different proposition, Soviet essays in that direction notwithstanding.

Besides, even strike aircraft obliged to fly uncomfortably fast and low can avail themselves of the new area weapons that may collectively be effective against a wide variety of pre-located targets, airfields being prominent among them. Napalm is the most familiar of these weapons. Now clusters of bomblets or minelets are coming into vogue. Canisters which, on impact, scatter thousands of steel pellets across hundreds of yards are also among these grim possibilities.

An alternative approach is to exploit the potentialities inherent in radar or televisual guidance to aim an air-to-surface cruise missile precisely at a target from somewhere outside the effective reach of the local defensive weapons. Judged overall, this solution is likely to be especially successful against ships at sea, the point being that these tend to constitute discrete and brittle targets and may often, too, lack a concentrated and in-depth air defence environment. Nevertheless, a whole variety of land targets from key bridges to master radars have become susceptible.

Then there is the possibility of Electronic Counter-Measures (ECM), a response of which we have over 30 years' experience but which continues to evolve rapidly. Certainly, it showed its worth abundantly during the air campaign against North Vietnam. Thus the United States Navy concluded that, without ECM, the air offensive it waged between 1965 and 1972 would have incurred five times as many losses. Apparently, too, the United States Air Force reached a similar verdict about the Linebacker operations its B-52 squadrons launched against Hanoi and its environs towards the end of 1972.[3]

Yet several caveats about ECM must here be entered. The first is that, so far as set-piece warfare between major adversaries is concerned, there is now a very high premium on achieving a good measure of success if not immediately then during the first few days or even hours of fighting. But throughout such an initial phase, most if not all of those concerned will be totally devoid of combat experience, a circumstance that will usually incommode those in the air more than it does their adversaries on the ground. And to this human factor one must add an ineluctable technological tendency. It is for counter-measures to lag significantly behind the means of surveillance and acquisition.

Another consideration is that over certain hostile environments in the 1980s (East Germany being, for NATO, the salient example) the sheer density and diversity of the defensive systems may make ECM difficult. Nor should we forget that the restoration of effective air dominance eventually brought about by the Israelis on the Suez front during the Yom Kippur war owed much to an intrusion by their ground forces into a key SAM-6 line.

Some truly remarkable warplanes will grace the inventories of the world's more advanced air forces in the 1980s. Perhaps the most versatile will be the Multi-Role Combat Aircraft (MRCA), now at the prototype testing stage of its development by Britain, Germany and Italy. Among the most specialised will be the Fairchild A-10, which also exists already in the form of several prototypes. It is claimed that a single such aircraft might destroy dozens of enemy tanks in the course of one shallow dive.

Even so, the indications are that, during the decade in question, manned aeroplanes will rarely come to operate in the unilateral manner they normally did in the past. Instead, they will be nodal elements in a complex mix of systems, a state of affairs that will obtain both in close-support and in the deeper strikes. Some of the far-ranging implications of this conclusion are considered in the next chapter.

(b) THE ACCELERATING NAVAL REVOLUTION

An urgent need in naval strategy is identification of the cardinal themes. Among them may be a trend whereby land-based power progressively extends its influence over adjacent waters. The air-launched cruise missile mentioned above is one manifestation of this. Another is the surface-to-surface missile, cruise or ballistic: perhaps with either a manned aircraft or a reconnaissance satellite playing a key role in directing it onto target. Granted, ships at sea can always avail themselves of electronic camouflage in the form of decoys or other ECM stratagems. Even so, they are likely to remain consider-ably more susceptible to long-range yet pin-point missile attacks than are the vast majority of targets ashore.

There can be little doubt that, during the 1980s, great developmental opportunities along these lines will present themselves. Thus a B-1 strategic bomber fitted with a Harpoon anti-shipping cruise missile could make its presence felt, in nuclear or non-nuclear terms, several thousand miles away from its land bases and at but a few hours' notice. Furthermore, surface-to-surface missiles could steadily displace tactical aircraft as the prime instruments of shore-to-ship engagement within a few hundred miles of any coastline.

To date, however, such possibilities are largely hypothetical. Powerful influences within Strategic Air Command resist the idea of the exotic B-1s being geared in any wise to piecemeal local actions, much as Curtis Le May was reluctant to countenance his B-52 force having an auxiliary and non-nuclear role, such as that they eventually assumed in Indo-China. Moreover, Sweden, which happens to have a strong tradition of coast artillery, seems the only country currently much interested in covering its seaward approaches with missiles emplaced ashore; and its Rb-08 missile has the comparatively modest range of 135 miles.

But against these instances of tardy advance can be set another category of weapon that now figures prominently in the plans of various navies, not least some of the smaller ones. This is, of course, the Fast Patrol Boat (FPB) of a few hundred tons displacement and able to launch in quick succession several surface-to-surface missiles, each with an explosive force perhaps equivalent to that of an eight-inch shell. The sinking of the Israeli destroyer *Eilat* in October 1967 was the first use in earnest of this weapons system. The outstanding performance of Israel's new FPB force during the Yom Kippur war confirmed its potency. Among future FPB types will be some of hydrofoil design. An early example is the Hu Chwan vessels China has supplied to Romania.

Since FPBs rarely operate more than two or three hundred miles from an established naval base, they can fairly be interpreted strategically as another extension into coastal waters of the military power of littoral states. This, coupled with their low unit costs, means that they will lend considerable physical support to the parcellation of the High Seas which is apparently under way.

It can plausibly be argued, too, that hunter-killer or attack submarines (i.e. the kinds primarily designed for limited or non-nuclear war service) may also be of particular benefit to local navies even though such vessels may not operate to their best advantage in the more shallow inshore waters. The point is that even a single submarine may be able to harass an approaching naval task force in a way a single frigate or cruiser could never match. Accordingly, a submarine squadron may be highly effective as a local and non-nuclear *force de dissuasion*.

This being so, the proliferation of submarines in regions well beyond the confines of NATO and the Warsaw Pact is a trend of considerable moment. Already 80 are distributed among the following 15 countries: Argentina, Australia, Brazil, Chile, Egypt, India, Indonesia, Israel, Japan, North Korea, Pakistan, Peru, South Africa, Taiwan and Venezuela. Ecuador, Iran and Yugoslavia will shortly be acquiring such vessels. Indeed, the planned Iranian outlay is reportedly to the tune of £450,000,000;[4] and that could well mean dozens of boats in service in the late 1980s.

What none of these navies even hopes to have, on the other hand, are submarines possessed of the advantages that stem from nuclear propulsion and the hull designs associated with it: the quantum jump in underwater speed and manoeuvrability plus an enormous extension of range and endurance. Some 40 of the attack submarines the USSR has in service are nuclear-driven as against 12 some 13 years ago. In the United States Navy the corresponding increase has been from 20 to 65 and in Britain's Royal Navy from one to nine. In 1973 France announced plans for its first such boat, the SNA 72; and this is intended to displace, when surfaced, only 2,500 tons.

Considering nearly all the nuclear-driven submarines completed to date have a standard displacement in the 3,500 to 8,000 ton range, this looks like a departure the other navies just mentioned might (and quite possibly will) emulate with advantage. Evidently, smaller craft could be rather less expensive and a good deal more agile.

So, as and when they are generally introduced, the age of the nuclear submarine will have dawned as resplendently as did that of steam or of the breech-loader. Moderate numbers of reasonably sized vessels with the superior sea-going qualities listed above (and benefiting, too, from a steady progress in offensive armament) could well pose a deadly threat to even the best-protected ocean lanes. Needless to say, too, all the general arguments cited in Chapter 10 in connection with the Fleet Ballistic Missile (FBM) boats apply here as well, save the FBM's legitimate interest in avoiding tactical engagements in all circumstances. In any event, the SNA 72 will be a much more formidable instrument of war than were, say, the U-Boats of Types VII and IX in 1943. By 1990 the total number of nuclear-driven submarines of all kinds afloat may well be around the 400 mark.

So far as Anti-Submarine Warfare is concerned, the probability is strong that a balanced mix of airborne, surface and submarine systems will still be needed. But this balance may be struck differently as the 1980s progress. For one thing, the frigate or destroyer may come to play a less prominent part. Even with a helicopter borne, a frigate will never find it easy to react to a submarine that may readily travel at 35 knots and a depth of 2,000 feet. Nor are the prospects facing it improved by the likelihood that the practice of closely escorting merchantmen grouped in convoys may henceforward be unfeasible in most situations. To which one might add that the general purpose role of the frigate may be becoming less viable or relevant in many situations.

Given that what is required, above all, is a vessel that can outpace the submarine over long distances, many analysts set great store by the hovercraft as an ASW spearhead in the medium term. Riding on an air cushion the way a hovercraft normally does may be bad for fuel consumption. But it does secure speeds of 70–100 knots and seems, in addition, good for sonar reception. Several years ago the United States Navy began to promote actively the development of 2,000-ton Surface Effect Ships: air cushion vehicles adapted to the use of water propulsion, either screws or jets. The first of these vessels, which will include ASW among their combat tasks, should commence experimental sea trials in 1981.

What may be worthy of considerations, however, is whether the development of the hovercraft in the ASW field should not be paralleled by the redevelopment of land-based but long-range maritime patrol aircraft: the modern equivalents of the Catalinas and Sunderlands and so on of World War II. Perhaps it is pertinent to note that the number of these famous flying boats constructed was 3,400 and 740 respectively. Also that alongside them flew the planes borne by dozens of small escort carriers plus many hundreds of other land-based aircraft geared to the anti-submarine task: Hudsons, Liberators, Wellingtons. . . . Compare that with the 350 or so Atlantiques, Nimrods and Orions in service with Atlantic Alliance countries at the present time. Whatever allowance is made for changed circumstances (and by no means all the changes are reassuring), the contrast between yesterday and today suggests that this facet of the anti-submarine panoply has been gravely neglected.

True, that is no justification for now neglecting the hovercraft in order to correct a prior aberration. Nevertheless, the case for a dual approach can be made, at least *prima facie*. The main strands in it would be as follows. A Long-Range Maritime Patrol (LRMP) aircraft may cost an order of magnitude less to build than would a 2,000-ton ASW hovercraft. Furthermore, the former would have obvious advantages apropos the surveillance of large surface areas. The problem of acoustic search for submerged submarines is so subtle that it may be most desirable to continue to develop the sonobuoys LRMPs employ alongside the dipping sonars which hovercraft and other surface craft possess. Last though perhaps not least, there is the fact that LRMPs are generally operated by air arms rather than navies. Its significance lies in the likelihood that, in the 1980s, manpower may become somewhat more freely available for LRMPs than for hovercraft on the single service basis. This would be thanks to a diminution in the close-support and strike roles of tactical air power.

What can be anticipated, in any case, is a gradual extension of organic naval aviation into the Vertical/Short Take-off and Landing (V/STOL) monoplane configuration, this being at the expense of the ship-borne helicopter and also of the standard carrier-borne monoplane. The biggest objection to the former is its limited operational radii; and to the latter a dependence on mother ships of anything between 25,000 and 75,000 tons displacement.

Not that V/STOL is, even conceptually, the complete answer to anything. Nor are any of the technological paths to its realisation free from serious impediments. Nevertheless, those navies in which the planners already are seriously interested in, if not committed to, this solution include "the British, French, Spanish, Italian, Indian, Brazilian, Australian and—most notably—Russian": plus, of course, the American.[5] Among the ships being designed with this form of sea control principally in mind are the three 20,000-ton anti-submarine cruisers Britain is building. At the other end of this particular spectrum is the possibility of increasing the number of positions at sea where V/STOL machines might alight (and perhaps refuel) during extended sorties. Reinforcing the flat weatherdecks of container ships might be one answer. Then again, both the speed of hovercraft and their characteristic profiles could make them useful auxiliaries in the handling of V/STOL.

In 1971 or thereabouts the Soviet Union laid down the founding member of the Kiev class, 40,000-ton carriers intended to carry a mix of rotorcraft and V/STOL monoplanes. Now the third is on the Black Sea stocks. Conceivably, the Red Navy will henceforward focus its ship-borne aviation on vessels of this size, perhaps ten being commissioned by 1990. No less plausible, however, is the notion that, having started with the commissioning (in 1967 and 1969 respectively) of the 15,000-ton helicopter carriers *Moskva* and *Leningrad*, the USSR will soon continue this progression by building large fleet carriers—i.e. vessels of 60,000 tons or more, especially if it seems able to stretch still further the Montreux Convention apropos transit of the Turkish Straits.

In the face of either prospect, one is sorely tempted to say that Western navies must continue to operate fleet carriers too. But it is important to remember just how conservative about military doctrine and technology the Russians frequently are. To emulate them may often be to breed white elephants.

What our judgment about the future should hinge on is the perceived interaction between three concurrent technical trends. One is the gradually diminishing effectiveness of manned aircraft (carrier-borne as well as other) used overland for close support or deep strike. Another is the increasing vulnerability of surface ships to missile attack, probably with manned aircraft in an auxiliary role. A third is the mounting threat posed to most such vessels by submarines.

The need for submarine evasion is one axiom which might also be accorded more prominence in the anxious debate that continually goes on, in the United States at any rate, about how fast and how far to convert the surface fleet to nuclear propulsion. At present the United States Navy has nuclear main engines in two aircraft carriers and several smaller warships.

The big attraction of nuclear propulsion as applied to, let us say, a guided missile destroyer is that (since fuel consumption is negligible) the ship's cruising speed and maximum speed are effectively the same—i.e. 35–40 knot range above which the frictional resistance created by surface wave motion becomes intolerably large. One tactical advantage which accrues is that, when travelling at 25 to 30 knots or more, no ship is at all easy for a submerged submarine to track. This is because the noise the latter generates around itself at such speeds impairs its own acoustic reception.

Agreed, the converse may be no less true. However, this does not alter the fact that, if his main propulsion unit is nuclear, the combat options open to any commander are thereby increased. So, too, is his strategic mobility.

What then of the battle on and above the surface, chiefly with missiles and aircraft? Undoubtedly the ability of the USA and maybe, by 1990, the USSR to mass a plurality of carriers and guided missile ships could count for much in some situations. Yet even this stratagem is likely to lose its efficacy as time goes by. Not only will all surface craft become individually more vulnerable, relative to the corresponding objectives ashore. In addition, the complex mix of weapons and tactics we can expect in such environments in the 1980s is liable to be hard to integrate in the maritime environment. Furthermore an added need for dispersal tactics is prone to make inconveniently large the amount of sea space a sizeable and well-balanced task force will require to deploy in. After all, even these days one composed of two or three attack carriers, 15 to 20 cruisers and destroyers, and other supporting vessels typically extends over a box some 200 miles square when deployed for action. Moreover, it is desirable to leave one or two hundred miles more between the task force perimeter and a hostile coastline and also to have several hundreds of miles extending in other directions to allow for tactical manoeuvre.

The conclusion which emerges is that, come 1990, even the Superpowers will be finding it increasingly difficult to use naval strike power cost-effectively against land forces. Correspondingly, large-scale but non-nuclear amphibious operations against well-defended coastlines are becoming less and less easy to execute. One threat to them is that posed by ultra-sophisticated sea-mines, such as those laid in 1972 in the Hanoi–Haiphong fairways or the Captor mine-cum-torpedo the United States Navy has evolved. Even during the American tactical landing at Wonsan in North Korea in the autumn of 1950, 50,000 men in 250 ships had to stand off for eight days whilst 3,000 acoustic, magnetic, pressure and hybrid mines were cleared from the harbour.

True, the mine and other fixed obstacles may be at least partially circumvented by greater reliance on helicopters and hovercraft. However, the problem does not end there. In modern times major amphibious landings have very generally relied on total control of the sea and also on overwhelming air support, two conditions that are all too liable to remain unfulfilled henceforward. Besides which, on not a few occasions the operations in question look, in retrospect, decidedly hazardous. Douglas MacArthur's remark about the brilliantly decisive landing which he effected at Inchon shortly before Wonsan comes readily to mind: "It was a 5,000 to 1 gamble". Even if this verdict then owed something to hyperbole, it might not in a similar situation in 1985.

So just about all the relevant lines of argument do point to a two-fold conclusion. Those forms of armed strength which are essentially land-based or littoral will, other things being equal, find their influence gradually extending further across the High Seas. Obversely, sea power will find it ever harder, in the limited war context, to influence events ashore.

Thinking of the Churchillian metaphor of the Whale and the Elephant, one might infer a resultant shift in operational advantage from the West to the Soviet bloc. In the present world situation, however, the opposite is *a priori* the case, simply because the Western Alliance collectively possesses a far longer ice-free coastline than do its main adversaries. But what also follows is that, provided they are abreast of modern naval technology, small states will find it easier than heretofore to exercise hegemony over adjacent waters. To that extent the accelerating revolution in naval science seems destined to facilitate the jurisdictional fragmentation of the world's seas and oceans.

Notes

1. To which one might add that an ability to manufacture high-performance military aircraft may once again have started slowly to proliferate among nations, thereby reversing a trend towards international concentration observable in the previous two or three decades. Among the countries that have lately proved both able and eager to design and fabricate, on something like an autonomous basis, their own transonic or supersonic warplanes are India, Israel, Japan, Romania and Yugoslavia.
2. AWACS stands for Airborne Warning And Control System.
3. Edgar Ulsamer "Tac Air—History's Most Potent Fighting Machine", *Air Force Magazine*, Vol. 59 No. 2, February 1976, pp. 23–6.
4. *Jane's Fighting Ships 1975–6*, Macdonald & Co. London 1975, p. 99.
5. G. G. O'Rourke "Why V/STOL?", *United States Naval Institute Proceedings*, Vol. 102 No. 1/875, January 1976, pp. 40–5.

12

Non-Nuclear Conflict On Land

Defence studies is not a discipline renowned for semantic exactitude. We say "intercontinental" when we really mean "inter-
hemispherical". The exact interpretation of such basic terms as
"strategic" and "tactical" depends very much on the context. Even
apparently explicit words and phrases like "regular" or "terrorist" or
"urban insurgency" or "indirect approach" or "forward strategy"
can have varying connotations. Chemical devices as a genre have
frequently been bracketed with nuclear and bacteriological as "*the*
weapons of *mass* destruction". Indeed, the word "chemical" itself is
thereby employed in a somewhat esoteric sense.

Yet no other term used in this field even begins to match in constrictive inappropriateness "conventional" war, forces, weapons and
so on. The genesis of this malapropism lay, of course, in a desire to
find an adjective able to embrace the notion of set-piece but non-
nuclear conflicts between regular (as opposed to guerrilla) forces.
Yet, in practice, we often speak of, let us say, "conventional forces"
when referring to elements that are, in reality, relevant to nuclear
conflict as well as to non-nuclear, either in the sense that they could
actually release nuclear warheads themselves or because they could
have other roles germane to a nuclear environment.

However, the most serious objection to the term "conventional"
is that it conjures up images of warfare 1945-style. Yet the truth of the
matter is that, come 1985 or thereabouts, the pattern of non-nuclear
conflict to be prepared for in such theatres as Central Europe will
bear no more resemblance to the Battle of the Ardennes than did that
to the Battle of the Marne. Great advantage will rest with the side
that has comprehended most quickly and synoptically just how
unconventional military science has become across virtually the whole
spectrum of tactics and technology.

Multifarious though the changes will be, most are likely to point
towards a much greater reliance than heretofore on indirect fire, most

particularly by surface-to-surface weapons. Admittedly, to equate this with a resurgence of artillery, as the title of this section implicitly does, is to invite the rebuke that one is being malaproprian oneself. After all, a traditionalist might insist that artillery means guns and not missiles. Then again, on the great majority of occasions, historically speaking, artillery batteries have engaged in direct fire: the targets have been visible to the gunners.

All the same, neither objection would be easy to sustain in the light of evolving practice. The distinction between guns and missile-launchers is being blurred by several contemporary developments. Among them will be the fitting to shells of rocket-boosters and terminal guidance. Relevant, too, is the capacity of both shells and missiles to benefit from the new cluster technologies (the bomblets and the minelets) already mentioned in connection with air-delivered ordnance. Then as regards indirect fire, all that need be said is that it is overwhelmingly the manner in which the artillery arm (and, to all intents and purposes, that alone) has engaged its adversaries throughout the 20th century.

The argument that artillery thus defined is about to wax very strong is an ambidextrous one. On the one hand, its sundry manifestations will together figure prominently in the complex mix of systems that can be expected to displace tactical aviation, pure and simple, in the close-support, interdiction and reconnaissance roles. On the other, the use of the battle-tank as a means of affording the infantry continual backing with direct fire is liable to be circumscribed increasingly.

Tanks have always laboured under serious handicaps as the mailed horses of modern war. They are rather clumsy and very conspicuous; and they tend to be partially blind and virtually deaf. Hitherto these weaknesses have been offset by their high degree of immunity to a variety of weapons, especially man-portable ones.

However, this comparative immunity is now being seriously eroded in several ways, not least through the advent of the guided missile and other new devices. Moreover, the anti-tank guided missile is still, in contrast to the tank itself, at a youthful stage of its generic evolution. Therefore, it should retain a greater potential for further development than does tank armament and armour; and a case in point is the beam-riding technique some members of the next generation will employ. The overall impact may well be to induce at least part of any tank force in the 1980s to rely more on indirect fire, thence becoming more akin in configuration and deployment to the self-propelled artillery gun.

In a quite different category, yet with a comparable significance, are the new anti-tank mines or minelets. An example is West Germany's Pandora. Being literally as compact as a clenched fist, it may withstand even nuclear blasts; and it can be scattered in large numbers from aircraft or perhaps by means of shells and rockets, the purpose being to immobilise advancing armour. Herein may lie, in fact, a potent application of the tactical helicopter.

But what may warrant more scepticism than it sometimes receives is the expectation that the tactical helicopter can prove the chief means of filling the gap which seems bound to be created by a gradual diminution in the use of monoplanes for close support. This expectation rests, first and foremost, on the belief that by "nap-of-the-earth" flying up to, though not beyond, the Forward Edge of the Battle Area (FEBA), well-armed and armoured helicopters can repeatedly engage advancing infantry and tank columns without enduring undue wastage themselves.

Yet whether they could, as a general rule, be cost-effective in this context must be doubted. Making helicopters robust enough long to withstand fire from automatic cannon and the like is difficult, not to say impossible. Any major ground battle on, for example, the North European plain might soon become so confused that no FEBA as such could any longer be delineated. Properly equipped ground troops might often be as effective (tactical minelaying excepted) in occasioning attrition and delay.

For deeper penetration, Remotely Piloted Vehicles are holding out great promise for area reconnaissance, target designation and electronic warfare, this mainly by virtue of their general compactness and moderate cost. They may be either ground-launched or air-launched, the former perhaps being subject to control from the air. Assuredly, too, satellites in orbit will have a substantial contribution to make to tactical reconnaissance as well as strategic.

Correspondingly, the deeper strike tasks will eventually be taken over, in considerable measure, by cruise missiles. Recourse to them is being rendered attractive by advances in turbo-jet technology and by the progressive miniaturisation and general refinement of inertial guidance and other electronic aids. The cruise missiles of the 1980s will be tolerably cheap and compact; and they will be able to approach their targets quite fast and low. But their supreme attribute is that, when surface launched, they can be pre-programmed to retain a high accuracy over an extended range. Here again is a veritable revolution in warfare: no longer must precision be an inverse function of distance.

Among the broader inferences to be drawn from these and other innovations is that it will be far more difficult for the attacking side to secure a decisive air superiority over and beyond the battlefield after the manner of the Luftwaffe in the blitzkrieg era or as the Israelis did even more dramatically in 1967. Air combat *en masse* appears to be a thing of the past. No less pertinent in the light of our recent experience, almost all the more novel systems will be far less vulnerable to instant immobilisation than piloted monoplanes only able to fly from and to long concrete runways. Obviously this is true of Surface-to-Air Missile launchers; and of RPVs and cruise missiles; and of V/STOL monoplanes and helicopters. To which one might add that, notwithstanding a continuing need for runways, most military airfields in Central Europe and the Middle East, at any rate, now have much better protection (both active and passive) than did the Arab ones in 1967.

Few analysts would dispute that tanks and tactical aircraft have nearly always played a decisive part in the mechanised offensives that have succeeded the murderously costly infantry and (in 1914) cavalry onslaughts all too indelibly associated with the Western Front of six decades ago. This being so, it is tempting to conclude that a simultaneous waning of each of these weapon categories must favour a renewed ascendancy of the Defence, even in open terrain.

To which one might add that, whilst he himself might not have endorsed this particular line of argument, that renowned harbinger of mechanised warfare, the late Sir Basil Liddell-Hart, was firmly persuaded that, ever since the Napoleonic Wars, ". . . the Defence has been gaining a growing material ascendancy of the Offence".[1] This he ascribed to a steady reduction in the number of troops required to hold a mile of front in battle, thanks to continual improvements in firepower, mobility and communications. He dismissed the manifest supremacy of the Attack in 1940 as an aberration due to the neglect of certain elementary principles by the defending commanders.

However, military affairs are too complex and incommensurate to lend themselves to deductions quite so neat. Changes in regard to such matters as the ratio of troops to linear space ought, even if verifiable, to be taken merely as guidelines to the tactical situation and not as determinants of it. A major cause of the final collapse of the feudal system in Europe was the destruction with gunpowder of baronial ramparts. In several of the big offensives on the Western Front in 1914–18 the aggregate casualty list could be split remarkably equally into the attackers and the defenders; and this was basically because the havoc wreaked by the machine-gun against men advancing in the open was offset by that wreaked by shells and mortar bombs against men dug in. In short, in each of these eras the progress of artillery was decidedly to the disadvantage of the Defence.

So might it be in the years ahead. For one thing, the new varieties of ordnance might cause such wear-and-tear (psychological as well as material) in forward units under bombardment that heavy and sustained reinforcement and replacement would be imperative. In other words, added demands might be made on manpower which could prove acutely embarrassing to the Defence, at least on the normal assumption that this will start the weaker numerically. Furthermore, this effect may be aggravated by the ever-improving aids to combat by night as well as day.

Nor should we forget that, even if technological evolution might be expected, in principle, to favour the Defence, this affords no guarantee that it will actually do so in specific situations. Let us consider, for example, the problem the NATO brigades and divisions in Germany face. Since the frontages they have to cover tend to be unusually wide, they have to resort to an exceptionally mobile form of defence.

Yet this is a pattern of warfare in which heavy reliance is placed on the launching of counter-attacks as well as on fighting from unprepared positions. In consequence it would be bound, almost by definition, to be peculiarly susceptible to the extra demands on infantry manpower in the new technological environment anticipated above.

To which complication must be added another that may also be especially apposite to Central Europe. This is that, as what we have so frequently been pleased to term "conventional war" comes to appear more and more unconventional, certain protagonists may start to feel less constrained than heretofore by the taboos against recourse to chemical and low-yield nuclear weapons. Some may no longer accept that, whilst canisters of napalm or steel pellets are legitimate anti-personnel weapons, non-lethal gases are not. Nor may they be persuaded that the very precise delivery of, say, a single nuclear warhead with a yield which might be barely a hundredth that of the Hiroshima or Nagasaki bombs (see below) automatically presages the end of the world.

Nuclear warheads remain, in fact, the crux of this matter. For we can still assume that, if chemical weapons (non-lethal or otherwise) are ever introduced into limited war at all, this will be because they have deliberately been chosen as an alternative to crossing the nuclear threshold. Therefore, the whole notion of qualitative escalation hinges on where this threshold will henceforward lie.

In May 1974 the director of the Arms Control and Disarmament Agency in Washington averred that the United States has "no intention to move in a direction that could blur the distinction between nuclear and conventional arms".[2] But as much as 15 years ago the American forces in Europe had installed in certain air-to-air missiles, and briefly in Davy Crockett mortars, nuclear warheads in the 250 to 500-ton range; and since then further miniaturisation has been achieved.

Suffice to note that a nuclear charge equivalent to, say, 300 tons might not make a significantly more awesome material impact than, let us say, one of the ten-ton "block-buster" bombs dropped over the Third Reich. According to the cube law, the former would have a lethal radius of destruction against a given target barely three times greater. If set to burst above the ground, its fall-out would be utterly negligible. True, the initial flash could constitute a singularly macabre menace but not through cloud or haze.

In the 1980s the United States and its allies will require tactical nuclear doctrines that are able to take due account of these realities without being hopelessly subordinated to them. What also will be needful is that these doctrines take some note of the views on tactical nuclear release espoused by the USSR and its allies. Deterrence rests, in part, on a kind of dialogue.

Obviously, we have no means of telling at this point precisely what Soviet tactical nuclear doctrine will be in 1985 or 1990. What we can confidently assume, however, is that it will continue to be informed by the Clausewitzian notion that warfare between mass armies is inherently too rough and clumsy to lend itself to precise direction. After all, Clausewitz came from the same Hegelian background as Marx himself. Lenin made detailed notes on him and occasionally referred to them. Tolstoy, a near contemporary of Clausewitz, fully shared what one may identify as his characteristically continentalist distrust of the whole idea of exact command and control. Therefore, whilst the Soviet general staff and its acolytes are very likely to try and preserve a distinction between non-nuclear and nuclear war (and also between regional and global nuclear war), they are almost certain never to evince much interest in attempts to graduate very subtly the process of nuclear escalation.[3]

To which one must add that several reasons can be adduced for apprehending that sudden and massive pre-emptive action may come to play a much larger part in Soviet military doctrine and contingency planning in the 1980s than it has done in the recent past: a shift of emphasis that would, after all, accord with much of the technological evolution examined above. In essence, the concept of the dialectic borrowed from Hegel by Marx is that, at a certain stage in any gradation, a quantitative change may become a qualitative one; and this could be interpreted to mean that, at some point in the deepening world crisis, the time will be ripe for revolutionary upheaval. Lately, too, the authoritative warnings of Alexander Solzhenitsyn have been along similar lines.

Furthermore, certain aspects of Soviet military theory and practice do lend weight more directly to this sombre conclusion. In 1961 Marshal Malinovsky, the then Defence Minister, explicitly reintroduced into the Soviet strategic nuclear debate the option of preemption. Admittedly, this was probably to offset the growing vulnerability to a Total Counterforce strike by the USA of what was then a weak and unsophisticated Soviet deterrent. But this does not exclude the possibility of the option in question being taken up, in some other manner, in changed circumstances.

Then again, John Erickson has recently advised us that the terms *podavlenie* (neutralisation) and *porazhenie* (annihilation) are now "assuming the form of pre-emption" within the context of the shock conventional breakthrough by Soviet troops.[4] Pertinent, too, is the opportunity for pre-emptive attack at sea inherent in the regular and close shadowing of Western naval forces. To all of which one could add that the anti-satellite devices the USSR has under development could conceivably be used to degrade the Space-borne early warning network (see the next chapter).

Arguably, there are quite enough pointers here to a real possibility of instant and massive attack by the Warsaw Pact at some stage—a possibility conceptually in line with Korea in 1950, Czechoslovakia in 1968 and the Middle East in 1973. But a more concrete evaluation of this apparent threat should perhaps wait upon a synoptic assessment of the global prospect—i.e. be deferred until Chapter 24.

(b) THE MENACE OF INSURGENCY

Underlying everything that has just been said is a conviction that the evolving techniques of limited warfare of the Korean or "Yom Kippur" kind attract as yet too little open discussion. But this is a charge nobody could level in regard to insurgency war! On the contrary, as we turn to consider the prospects for containing the global insurgency threat in the 1980s, we find ourselves enveloped by a veritable plethora of studies of past guerrilla wars and the theories appertaining to them.

One reason why so much attention is paid to this pattern of conflict lies in the extent to which it plays on the raw nerves of the Western liberal conscience. Thus the discordance between his earlier insistence that the end cannot justify the means and his endorsement of the Irgun Z'vai Leumi terrorists in Palestine in the 1940s has exposed no less a figure than Arthur Koestler to attack from more than one quarter.[5]

The basic realities would appear to be these. Guerrilla movements always place considerable reliance on calculated terror, not least against the people they purport to be liberating. So it was, for example, that the EOKA gangs in Cyprus in the 1950s killed many more of their fellow Greeks than they did British soldiers.

Then again, most such movements are prone to oversimplify or falsify wildly, as witness the waves of British jet fighters shot down by Radio Biafra. Likewise, most have little compunction about frontier violations and other breaches of international law or local undertakings, as the Viet Cong and their North Vietnamese allies so amply demonstrated. As a general rule, too, the insurgent leaders themselves are—one might say have to be—exceptionally intolerant fanatics. Small wonder that the regimes they create, as and when victory is attained, are usually extreme examples of total political mobilisation under the auspices of a revolutionary ideology.

Yet all this notwithstanding, it would seem that virtually every liberal intellectual in the West is well-disposed towards at least some insurgencies. Indeed, the sardonic might be tempted to take that as a definition of liberal intellectualism. So what are to be the criteria for discrimination?

Occasionally it is suggested that if a revolution has made headway, it must have been justified to start with. However, all recent experience refutes this Hobbesian logic. Instead it indicates that the most crucial factors in success are not the intrinsic merits of the insurgents' cause but the geographical environment and whether or not there is sufficient access to arms supplies from without.

Apropos the geographical environment per se, the chief question to ask is whether it is accessible to the various forms of mechanised mobility normally possessed by security forces these days. Undoubtedly, certain types of terrain do become much easier to traverse as roads are macadamised and as helicopters become more widely available. Nevertheless, forest in general—and tropical rain forest in particular—will always favour guerrilla bands considerably. The jungle could never be neutral.

As regards arms supplies, the Gaza Strip and Johannesburg are obvious examples of localities that would be much more explosive than, in fact, they are but for extremely efficient surveillance of illicit weapons movements by zealous security forces. Much the same may also be true of parts of the USSR and, indeed, sundry other territories. Contrariwise, there are quite a few more—e.g. Ethiopia, the Lebanon, Mexico, the Philippines, Saudi Arabia, the United States and Yugoslavia—where it is customary for a high proportion of all adult males to sport at least one gun for hunting or self-defence. Thus hundreds of thousands were handed in during the arms amnesty announced by President Marcos of the Philippines in 1972. Nor should we forget that in Ulster, for example, home-made bombs weighing hundreds of pounds have been detonated in earnest.

All the same, no internal supply is likely to yield a flow of weaponry, spare parts and—above all—ammunition comparable in quantity or pattern with what may accrue from infiltration across a friendly border. A classic illustration was afforded by the Communist insurgency in Greece between 1946 and 1949. Two years after its onset, 20,000 rebels were holding their own countryside against royalist forces ten times as numerous. They were doing so by virtue of the firm backing of depots and sanctuaries in Albania, Bulgaria and Yugoslavia—three countries that supported the uprising from the outset in spite of marked equivocation on the part of the USSR. But then came Moscow's dramatic break with Belgrade, partly over the Greek question, and its concurrent curbing of Sofia. Some 12 months later Marshal Tito inclining now towards the West forbade the Greek

7*

rebels to deploy on Yugoslav territory; and shortly afterwards their rebellion collapsed completely.

The same cause-and-effect relationship can be seen in the singular significance for the recent Indo-China war of the Ho Chi Minh trail down through Laos and into the Central Highlands of South Vietnam. Admittedly until late in 1964, at any rate, only a very minor fraction of the men and materials reaching the Viet Cong came down this network of pathways; and many of the men in question were, in fact, returnees as opposed to first-time infiltrators. However, the nub of this argument does not lie in rough-and-ready essays at volumetric comparison. Rather it is to be found in the entry via this route of specific items of military paraphernalia, quite modest in total amount yet of critical importance to that escalation of armed violence needed by the Viet Cong in order to rend asunder the social fabric of South Vietnam. An intimidated or disaffected hamlet in the Mekong delta might give rice to Communist guerrillas. It was unlikely to yield up wireless codes or recoilless rifles; and any weapons it did hand over would be liable thereafter to lack a regular supply of appropriate ammunition.

Well before the death of John Kennedy in November 1963, active consideration was being given to the possibility of using specialist ground troops to sever the Ho Chi Minh trail, thereby preventing its Pandora's boxes from being opened within the South.[6] Had this been done as soon as, and explicitly because, Hanoi had broken the 1962 Geneva agreement on Laotian neutrality, so watertight a political justification could have been advanced that the double standards of morality often employed in such matters would have been hard to adopt in any quarter.

Moreover, a relatively narrow frontal zone in Southern Laos would have been a sight easier to screen than the length and breadth of South Vietnam. Hence it would have required far fewer troops and would have involved far less collateral suffering to civilian populations or ecological damage. It would have been more directly relevant, and less counter-productive psychologically, than the years of bombing of North Vietnam (plus Laos and Cambodia) which eventually came in its stead. Above all, a firm military shield would have been created behind which the South Vietnamese would have had a chance to push through—no doubt, after much prodding—stabilising economic, social and administrative reforms.

One general inference to be drawn is that the Communist triumph in Indo-China no more confirms that insurgency is the irresistible tide of the future than did certain successes between 1939 and 1941 prove the blitzkrieg to be forever invincible. A better guide to a true perspective is Britain's uniquely varied and far-flung experience this last quarter of a century.

By 1954 or thereabouts the back had been broken of the insurgency that had begun in Malaya in 1948. About the same time the Mau Mau uprising within the Kikuyu tribe in Kenya was crushed. EOKA in Cyprus did not achieve union with Greece. On the contrary, the island gained its independence under special terms mainly designed to protect Turkish Cypriot interests and to provide for a continuing British presence, political as well as military. Meanwhile, Saudi indirect aggression against Inner Oman was successfully contained with the aid of light British detachments.

When Her Majesty's Forces pulled out of South Arabia in 1967, the successor regime in Aden was not (as had been feared) the Cairo-backed Front for the Liberation of the Occupied South Yemen. Instead, it was the more authentically indigenous National Liberation Front. Nor had Indonesia's combination of direct and indirect aggression destroyed Malaysia. Nor did a concurrent bombing campaign in Hong Kong lead anywhere. Nor has the IRA come to power in Ulster. And now the rebellion in the Dhofari province of Oman is fading fast away. In short, every counter-insurgency campaign that the United Kingdom has been engaged in since the late 1940s has been at least partially successful.

Still, it is not without significance that most of these campaigns were mainly rural. For there are one or two particular reasons for believing that the global prospects for armed revolution in the countryside are steadily receding, that—if you like—the Maoist wave of the future is prematurely breaking. Almost all the large-scale rural or predominantly rural insurgencies which flourished awhile in the wake of World War II—e.g. China, Indo-China, Malaya, Philippines, Poland, the Ukraine and belatedly Algeria—did so in territories which had been fought over in the course of that conflict.

Nor is this mere coincidence. The traumas of occupation and liberation were radicalising in various ways. Resistance cadres were formed and acquired caches of arms from both friend and foe.The departure of the Axis powers left, however transitorily, a political and administrative vacuum.

But circumstances such as these are unlikely to be replicated unless and until we slide into a Limited World War (see Chapter 21) so widespread, savage and prolonged as to resemble the two great struggles which dominated the first half of this century. What is more, the social and economic balance may not, in many areas, evolve in such a way as to favour these uprisings. As Eric Wolf has pointed out, it is the middle-rank peasant proprietor rather than the landless labourer who is most likely to spearhead whatever revolt there may be. The former has sufficient at stake not to be apathetic towards adverse change. In addition, he is more exposed to radicalising influences from the developing proletariat in the towns.[7] But it is this middle peasantry which is most prominent among the groups that stand to gain most from the Green Revolution which has been advancing, whether smoothly or not, in many agricultural areas.

However, the obverse side of this coin is that, in certain regions at least, the incidence of urban insurrection could escalate seriously. As was noted earlier, various insurgent groups have started to reverse a trend away from the urban barricade to the rural ambush that had been dominant in guerrilla warfare ever since Mao Tse-Tung and his colleagues in the Kiangsi hills after 1927 transformed the Chinese Communist Party into a movement able to "use the villages to encircle the towns"; and, even though this reversal has yet to achieve any very dramatic success, its inception is ominous enough. Thus in the early 1960s Venezuela all but proved a prototype for successful urban insurgency in Latin America. Moreover, this is a continent to which that insurrectionary strategy could prove well-suited. This is because the proportion of urban dwellers has remained relatively high, whereas the rural density of population is usually below the optimum for coordinated dissidence. (See Chapter 18.)

The guerrilla campaigns waged in South Arabia in the years leading up to the British departure were largely concentrated in Aden and the townships immediately around. Virtually the only exception was the sporadic violence in the Radfan, a district abreast the main route through to the Yemen and one in which tribal society had long been fissiparous. Then, but two months after the last British troops had carefully executed their tactical withdrawal from Aden and its environs, urban insurgency took another leap forward with the 1968 Tet offensive in Vietnam: a sensational, even though militarily ill-starred, attempt to take the war into the towns in order to inhibit the full use of the heavy firepower at the disposal of government and allied forces. Two years later the Maoists in India were to switch their main effort to the great wen known as Calcutta. Meanwhile, the Palestinian fedayeen made Amman the prime centre of their defiance of the Jordan Arab Army, a tactic that might have worked had those adopting it been a shade less complacent.[8] More recently, Beirut has been the chief battleground in the protracted Lebanese strife.

Now we would do well to face the probability that gradually urban insurgent leaders will emerge with a firmer grasp of both tactics and strategy than some of those alluded to above. In his tract, *Minimanual of the Urban Guerrilla*, Carlos Marighella—the Brazilian terrorist leader killed in a gun battle with São Paulo police in 1969—examines a whole series of tactical options: assaults, raids, strikes, the occupation of factories, kidnapping, sabotage, propaganda, raising false alarms, and turning mass demonstrations into violent confrontations through the use of snipers and bombers.[9]

Manifestly some of the cities that are coming too soon in the newly developing world might lend themselves only too well to such rich admixtures of violent and non-violent stratagems, the former calling for much less in the way of military paraphernalia than would normally be requisite in a rural setting. What is more, we dare no longer assume that the cities of the developed world stand aloof from this menace. The recent history of the Black ghettos of the United States and the Catholic ghettos of Ulster is proof enough of that.

Notes

1. "The Ratio of Troops to Space", *RUSI Journal*, Vol. CV No. 618, May 1960, pp. 201–12.
2. *The New York Times*, 24 May 1974.
3. For a fuller discussion of this aspect of Russian military culture see the author's *European Security, 1972–80*, RUSI, London 1972, pp. 58–9.
4. *RUSI Journal*, Vol. 121 No. 2, June 1976, p. 49.
5. E.g. John Atkins, *Arthur Koestler*, Neville Spearman, London 1956. Chapter 23.
6. John R. Bottinger (Ed), *Vietnam and American Foreign Policy*, D. C. Heath & Co, Boston 1968, pp. 26–7.
7. Eric R. Wolf, *Peasant Wars of the Twentieth Century*, Faber and Faber, London 1971, p. 292.
8. See the author's "The Jordanian Civil War", *The Military Review*, Vol. LI No. 9, September 1971, pp. 38–48.
9. Robert Moss, "Urban Guerrilla Warfare", *Adelphi Paper* No. 79, The International Institute for Strategic Studies, London 1972, Appendix.

13

The Future of Intelligence

Recourse to clandestine intelligence services as a means not just of surveillance but of covert intervention is a practice that is loaded with emotive and vexatious questions so far as the open societies of the West are concerned. For one thing, these societies are considerably vulnerable to such operations themselves, as witness the thousands of Communist agents acknowledged to be at large in the German Federal Republic alone. For another, the privy use of any arm of government is directly in conflict with the precept of democratic control. Indeed, it may even result in policy discordances within the government machine itself. One case in point is the way in which, during the early months of the Nigerian civil war, French intelligence agents supported "Biafra" even though the *Quai d'Orsay* still spoke in favour of federal Nigeria.

Unfortunately, the languid euphoria commonly evinced over international security matters these last few years has led to a general evasion of the very real dilemmas here presented. In their place have come glib assertions that intelligence operations may as well be laid bare because they are consistently ineffectual anyway. A full decade ago Mr Malcolm Muggeridge (drawing a bit too heavily on his own wartime experience) was airily advising us that most espionage organisations are "as easy to penetrate as a cooperative store" and that all of them "know more about other intelligence services than they do about anything else".[1] Soon it became fashionable to argue that purely mechanical methods of surveillance—meaning, in particular, reconnaissance from Space—had rendered the James Bonds of real life positively antediluvian. Now a desire to destroy the CIA so obsesses many people, especially within the United States itself, as to unhinge completely their capacity for balanced judgment on this score. Thus in their sustained polemic against the agency, Victor Marchetti and John D. Marks cavalierly comment that, ever since the Bay of Pigs *débâcle* of 1961, it "has lost many more battles than it has won, even by its own standards. Furthermore, the very fact that the United States operates an active CIA around the world has done incalculable harm to the nation's international position".[2]

Perforce both halves of this statement carry weight at a point in time when, in the USA in particular, many seem no longer to accept that to have eaten the government's salt places them under a certain obligation to confidentiality. For no less than 14 years, Mr Marchetti was himself a CIA official whilst Mr Marks has been a career diplomat. Were the contradiction less blatant, it would be dismissed as incredible.

However, as and when we enter again an era which is less amorphous ethically, we may have to subject intelligence work to sterner tests of principle for the very reason that its efficacy will be less in doubt. What must also be said is that a whole variety of current tendencies point towards both espionage and covert intervention looming a good deal larger, in their shadowy ways, in the world of the 1980s and beyond; and that, if the Western democracies do not take some cognisance of this prospect, they will merely give the totalitarians a free run in what could prove a very decisive sphere. Thus the growing sensitivity of military balances to their electronic dimension means that enormous dividends can accrue from prior knowledge of the enemy's operating frequencies, ECM tactics and the like; and much the same applies, though perhaps a shade less forcefully, to the mounting concern with logistic resupply. Then again, what does now appear to be (see Chapter 1) an increasing ruthlessness in the conduct of international conflict might place an added premium on forewarning of adversary intentions.

Rising economic and social tension would also favour intelligence operations, not least those of an interventionary kind. Urban insurgencies or *coups d'état* may readily be fostered by the *sub rosa* introduction into metropolitan areas or elsewhere of modest quantities of small arms and explosives. The worsening corruption of many newly developing regimes will afford innumerable opportunities for interventionary intrigues of this and other kinds. So will the sheer physical difficulties of border control they often face. So, too, will the persistence of communal and other cleavages within the body politic. So perhaps will their tendency to adopt political ideologies that are sufficiently ambidextrous, abstract and incoherent to lend themselves to starkly varying interpretations by contending factions.

One is reminded of how, before and during World War II, the Abwehr, as the military intelligence service of the Third Reich was known, deftly spread dissent in advance of invasion among such minorities as the Croats, Flemings and Ukrainians. Likewise, over the past quarter of a century, the CIA has instigated or supported the overthrow of governments in regions as far apart as Indo-China, the Persian Gulf and Latin America. In addition, it appears to have been responsible for many minor actions either against or on behalf of incumbent regimes or else to give general support to the ideological battle against Muscovite Communism and its presumed affiliates.

Moreover, we have to reckon with the probability (examined more closely in the next chapter) that the deepening internal contradictions of the Soviet Union will induce it to become more belligerent in the 1980s. If so, it will assuredly be tempted to employ the KGB more aggressively as an instrument of indirect aggression.

What also is likely is that this temptation will, on balance, be increased by the way political terrorism has, like syndicated crime, been internationalised. Groups conspire in Sydney with their thoughts on Zagreb. Guerrillas are trained in China for action in Rhodesia. Lethal letter bombs may be dispatched world-wide. Nuclear or biological bombs could conceivably be smuggled as well. Evidence has accumulated these last few years of functional links between, for example, the Baader-Meinhof revolutionary group in West Germany, the Black Panthers in the USA, the Popular Front for the Liberation of Palestine, the Red Army in Japan and the Turkish People's Liberation Army. True, Moscow dislikes the New Left ideology that nearly all such groups broadly espouse. Nor could it ever discount the risk of the terrorist virus spreading into the Soviet bloc. All the same, it might be justified in entertaining some confidence that, in the short-term at any rate, the USSR itself is less vulnerable to disruptive pressures than are either the "open societies" of the West or the "soft states" of Afro-Asia and Latin America.

Therefore, we must not at this juncture allow the intense glare of adverse publicity to which the CIA's record now stands exposed to blind us to the machinations its Soviet counterpart is known to have conducted already. The KGB was instrumental in the fore-closure of Dubček's "Prague Spring" and must have been privy to the remarkable *volte-face* by Lin Piao, formerly Chairman Mao's successor-designate, which culminated in his ill-fated dash to Soviet territory in 1971. As early as 1948 the Yugoslavs flatly condemned Soviet intelligence (the MGB as it then was) for recruiting and other machinations within their borders whilst several years ago evidence emerged of KGB overtures to Croatian *emigrés* in Munich and elsewhere. The obverse side of this latter coin is the kidnapping or murder, all too well authenticated in at least a few cases, of *emigrés* to the West from the Ukraine and other parts of the USSR.[3] A parallel with the Stalinist assassination of Trotsky in exile readily suggests itself.

It does seem, too, that the KGB can take, at least obliquely, much macabre credit for the violent deaths of 1,690 people in Ulster these last seven years. In October 1971, the Dutch authorities intercepted a cargo of Czech arms being flown out to the IRA "Provisionals", the less Leftist yet more violent wing of the main insurgency. Thirteen months later the Provisionals started to use Soviet RPG-7 rocket launchers. In March 1973, the Irish navy took off a ship five tons of Soviet arms and munitions dispatched via El Fatah.

Then there is the question of whether, as has been surmised,[4] "darker and less controllable" hands than the Foreign Ministry in Moscow play a special part in Soviet policy towards the Middle East. Certainly, the way the USSR set up the 1967 war by disseminating false intelligence points to active KGB involvement. So does the dichotomy between the consistent Soviet support, at a formal diplomatic level, for the continuation of a state of Israel and the hardly less constant flow of arms from the Soviet bloc to the Palestinian guerrilla organisations, all of which have very consistently made the destruction of the Zionist state their explicit war aim.

Nor should we ignore the smaller straws in the wind. Sometimes these reveal much about the general drift of the Soviet system in the intelligence sphere as in others. Thus in 1973 Palestinian guerrillas boarded in Czechoslovakia a train carrying Soviet Jews to Israel. Subsequently they seized several hostages.

Surely nobody could imagine that this would have been possible without KGB connivance. Nor that two Black September agents could have approached Andrei Sakharov in Moscow to warn him against adopting a pro-Israeli stance unless they, too, were in cahoots with the KGB.[5] Suffice to add that many Western analysts are convinced that, in Soviet embassies around the world at large, a majority of the staff are intelligence personnel; and that the KGB also operates chains of cells independently of the diplomatic corps. Evidently it has the resources swiftly to go over to a much more determined offensive should the time ever be ripe. Were it to do this, Yugoslavia and China would probably be among the prime targets.

Though today only the KGB and the CIA run intelligence networks with a truly global spread, various countries have secret services which are quite active and far-flung. Among them are Britain, Cuba, Egypt, France and Israel, as well as Yugoslavia and certain other East European states.

Obviously, the tinder-box that is the modern Middle East is especially rich in opportunities for the surreptitious exercise of influence by governments indigenous to the region and also some outside it. A well-recognised instance, in 1966, was the removal with British connivance of Sheikh Shakbut bin Sultan, the somewhat besotted ruler of Abu Dhabi. Sadly but ineluctably, his traditional bedouin prejudices against banking houses and the like simply did not gel with the "black gold" the new oil-wells were effusing: "When I was just a poor desert sheikh, nobody gave a fig for me. Now that I am oil-rich, nobody will leave me alone."

Against which may be cited an apparent example of intelligence networks deliberately withholding from an established regime knowledge essential to its own survival. Others might concur with the view that "Britain and America made a costly mistake in not forewarning King Idris of Libya against the coup in 1969 which saddled the comity of nations with Colonel Gadafi, world-wide terrorist paymaster and organiser".[6]

Needless to say, too, Israel is a central figure in the modern intelligence drama as in various others. Plenty of hard evidence exists to indicate Israeli military assistance, via pre-Amin Uganda, to the late rebellion in the Southern Sudan.[7] Nor should making allowance for Baghdad's paranoia about the "Zionist octopus" cause us to lose sight of the possibility that there may have been substance behind its assertions that the most recent Kurdish rebellion enjoyed extensive Israeli help.

Many people would insist, of course, that the Arab regimes in confrontation with Israel have been fair game in this regard. Even if this point were conceded unconditionally, however, the question of Israeli espionage and the like further afield would remain. At the time of the abduction of Adolf Eichmann in 1960 Mrs Golda Meir, then the Foreign Minister of Israel, said that "my government sincerely believes that this isolated violation of Argentine law must be seen in the light of the exceptional and unique character of the crimes attributed to Eichmann".[8]

Alas, the apologia looks decidedly dated. A wave of covert counter-terrorist terrorism was launched by Tel Aviv across Western Europe in the wake of the Munich massacre in 1972. Three years previously, Israeli agents, acting in defiance of a French arms embargo, had stolen blueprints of the Mirage III fighter and then, on Christmas Day, wafted five gunboats out of Cherbourg harbour. To *The Guardian* newspaper, their subsequent passage to Haifa ranked "for daring with the voyages of John Paul Jones".[9]

Instinctively, one is drawn towards this endorsement. Even so, this, the arch-champion of the great Mancunian traditions of constitutional liberalism, might have been less laudatory in the light of all that has been learnt in the few intervening years concerning the fragility of open societies in the face of those who take the law into their own hands for reasons of political commitment. In the long-run, undercover action of this sort by one parliamentary democracy against another can bring comfort only to the Tripolis and Moscows of this world.

To my mind, this maxim was underscored by a report published early in 1973 in a British newspaper well-disposed to Israel and with a good reputation for factual reliability in such matters. For this firmly averred that, official disclaimers notwithstanding, Israeli small arms had been dispatched to George Grivas's subversive organisation in Cyprus.[10]

No doubt any such departure was regarded by those concerned as a natural extension of an established struggle against Arab guerrilla groups on the island. Also as a counterweight to the close links the Makarios administration had with Arab governments. All the same, Israel never stood to gain overall from the reduction of its only non-Arab neighbour to a state of chaos and misery. Nor should a social democracy have truck with the likes of the late General Grivas, an archetypal exemplar of authoritarian reaction if ever there was one. Similar reservations have lately been widely expressed about Israel's running arms supplies to the Christian Rightists in the Lebanon.

But to examine thus the Israeli record, as we understand it, is to highlight the very real agonies of choice that may repeatedly be faced, in the 1980s and beyond, by parliamentary democracies at bay. Tel Aviv's recourse to clandestine intervention cannot fairly be adjudged all that immoderate, bearing in mind the way manifold opportunities have presented themselves against the background of a continuing state of belligerency. Nor would anybody with a regard for humanitarian precepts feel inclined to condemn the rescue of innocent hostages from Entebbe, a commando sortie which evidently had certain analogies with the less colourful (or, at any rate, less visible) operations here being considered.

Even so, this strategy of covert action has involved a selection of priorities that by no means everybody would endorse. A premium has been placed on immediate advantage; and this has probably been measured too strictly in accordance with single state interests as opposed to those of the broad comity of democratic nations. Furthermore, this selection has taken place behind closed doors; and the fact that this has been unavoidable for the most elementary tactical reasons still does not make it accord with the ground rules of parliamentary democracy.

Yet to imagine that the answer, in Israel or the United States or any other Western state, lies in wilfully crippling the intelligence arm is to evince the most horrendous complacency about the situation of the democracies in the decade or two immediately ahead. What is needed instead is a series of guidelines for intelligence work intended to reconcile as far as possible the conflicts of aim thereby occasioned (see Chapter 24).

Added weight is lent to this conclusion by the continuing usefulness of networks of intelligence agents in their more basic and freely acknowledged role of secretly obtaining information. Again the Middle East conflict serves as an instructive case-study. Over the years, Israelis have fed back whole mines of relevant information from Arab corridors of power; and, despite the way Egypt and Syria kept their joint plan for "Yom Kippur" secret, they can be assumed to pick up a fair amount even now. By the same token, for the Atlantic Alliance to forgo intelligence gathering in Eastern Europe would be gratuitous folly. All else apart, one of the constraints against pre-emptive military action by the Warsaw Pact may be that the NATO countries might obtain prior knowledge.

More particularly, on-the-ground surveillance is as necessary as ever, for the Superpowers as well as other states, for some very elementary reasons. Satellites in orbit cannot peer through solid structures. Nor can they penetrate the minds of men. Nor may they be immune to deception by camouflage or the use of dummy objects or false signals. All this is why, for instance, quite wide differences of opinion have persisted within the United States intelligence community as to the aggregate weight of the Soviet defence effort.

Having conceded this, however, one is still bound to conclude that automatic reconnaissance from Space does provide many of the more factual aspects of intelligence with a comprehensiveness and exactitude quite without precedent. And what makes this innovation all the harder to come to terms with is the prospect that, even allowing for a rudimentary effort on the part of the Chinese, the Soviet-American duopoly in this field will continue virtually unbroken, at least through 1985. Ever since 1961, in fact, the United States Air Force (USAF) has been conducting optical surveillance by means of unmanned satellites orbiting several miles up whilst the Soviets have been doing likewise since 1963. Within several years of its first application, the state of this complex art was such that the cameras borne could regularly pick out such features as aircraft on runways or vehicles on roads and even elicit a modicum of specific information about them.

Furthermore the detail thus recorded optically was being supplemented by that from other kinds of sensors. Ultra-violet and infrared may respectively be especially effective in detecting nuclear explosions and lowish intensity sources of heat. Radar sets are sometimes installed. So, too, are wirelesses able to record quite low-power radio-transmissions from at or near ground level, at any rate in the VHF and UHF bands.

In fact, a mix of sensory devices is carried by some of the satellites the United States Air Force now operates. Among them are the 12-ton Big Birds designed for the extremely detailed inspection of preselected areas. Such evidence as we have suggests that Soviet technology continues to lag behind American in some relevant respects. But the gap is only of the general order of two or three years.

One worrying prospect is that the continuous collection by these "spies-in-Space" of vast masses of detailed information from all over the world (and appertaining to a very wide range of sensitive subjects) seems bound to generate cumulative resentment as awareness of it becomes more widespread. After all, we live in a world in which literally dozens of states remain almost obsessively concerned with their national privacy and do so for reasons which extend far beyond the confines of military security as such. Furthermore, though the global relay by satellite of television programmes will not be a prerogative confined to the Superpowers, its advent will make more people conscious of the general potentialities of Space as a medium for data reception and transmission.

So what should any United States administration, in particular, do with all the information it will be amassing by means of Space reconnaissance? Always to release to all and sundry only carefully selected and diluted portions of it—e.g. to support world resource studies or to justify changes in national defence postures—would be to leave itself open repeatedly to charges of news manipulation. But then to disseminate more detailed material beyond the official domain on a selective and presumably non-attributable basis could be to appear guilty of a new form of bureaucratic patronage. Yet to make more or less everything freely available to all comers might be to stir up far more dangerous antagonisms.

The confused way Washington responded to the first Israeli protests against Egyptian missile movements in violation of the "standstill" agreement along the Suez Canal in 1970 can be seen as an ominous precursor of the agonies of choice which may not infrequently be posed over the course of the next decade or so. Moreover, in this sphere, as in others, the esoteric trends have to be set within the general probability that the 1980s will witness a less relaxed world scene than that we have lately known. And if this deterioration were very marked, it could even be that the anti-satellite satellites the USSR has experimented with (1967–71 and again since 1975) would at some stage be used in earnest.

The mere fact that Outer Space is supposed to be an international domain, just as the High Seas have customarily been, does not preclude this eventuality. On the contrary, some might even be persuaded that this status, plus its essentially unpeopled situation, rendered it eminently suitable for presumptively harmless tournaments.

Notes

1. Malcolm Muggeridge, *Tread Softly for You Tread on My Jokes*, Collins Clear-Type Press, London 1966, p. 215.
2. Victor Marchetti and John D. Marks, *The CIA and the Cult of Intelligence*, Jonathan Cape, London 1974, p. 373.
3. Robert Conquest, *The Soviet Police System*, The Bodley Head, London 1968, p. 92.
4. George F. Kennan, *Encounter*, February 1971, p. 54.
5. *The Daily Telegraph*, 22 October 1973.
6. R. H. C. Steed, *The Daily Telegraph*, 12 December 1974.
7. E.g. *Arab Report and Record 1970*, p. 154.
8. Marie Syrkin (Ed), *Golda Meir Speaks Out*, Weidenfeld and Nicolson, London 1973, p. 127.
9. Editorial, *The Guardian*, 30 December 1969.
10. John Bulloch, *The Sunday Telegraph*, 4 February 1973.

Part IV

Regional Perspectives

14

The Approaching Soviet Crisis

At no time in the last half century has the Soviet Union been discounted more heavily than it is today by the great bulk of Leftist opinion, even Marxist opinion, in the West. The reasons are various. Lately Cuba and now China have seemed plausible as alternative foci for those who yearn for a radical nostrum to endorse. Respect for Soviet technology is at a low ebb. The titanic struggle of Solzhenitsyn has obliged all but the most obdurate to acknowledge, at least *en passant*, that the affirmation of individual rights is just as indivisible as peace itself. The defiant heroism of so many Soviet Jews has finally exploded attempts to pass off anti-Semitism in the USSR as but a small and shrinking residue from Czarist days—one which, at whatever point in time, was significant yesterday but is not today.[1] And these are only the most conspicuous of the causes of disenchantment.

Not that we can assume that the strident Russophilia, well-laced with doublethink and strong-arm fantasies,[2] that became so prevalent among the Western intelligentsia in the 1930s could not revive in the 1980s. Were violent crime, drug addiction, Watergates, graduate unemployment and all the other emergent or persistent ills of affluent Western society to become much more serious, the blemishes on the Kremlin's escutcheon would be less remarked. So might they if, as is quite possible, Soviet science and technology enjoy a modest rejuvenation. So would they if, by fair means or foul, the Sino-Soviet split were repaired and if, either by relatively fair means or else by more foul ones, communist movements gained control of further territories.

So might they, too, if a general world crisis developed that seemed to approximate, no matter how crudely, to the Marxist scenario for capitalist collapse. For one thing, the neo-Marxist school of thought that became fashionable in many Western universities as the 1960s wore on (and which yet retains no small part of the influence then won) has often proved exasperatingly prone to isolate its profound distaste for the Kremlin from the rest of its world view. Sometimes the USSR is simply ignored. At other times, there is a blatant failure to draw even the most obvious general inferences from the strictures delivered against this, the original Marxist-Leninist state.

The following is a striking example, taken from the peak year of campus unrest, of just how far this fractional distillation of thought may be carried. The Cohn-Bendit brothers sought instantly to set the turbulent events of May 1968 in France in a broader perspective of time and space. In the course of this endeavour, they rallied round the banner that the fiery Polish Jewish Marxist, Rosa Luxembourg, had raised early in the wake of the Bolshevik revolution of 1917:

> No matter what Trotskyist historiographers may tell us today, it was not in 1927 nor in 1923 nor even in 1920, but in 1918 and under the personal leadership of Trotsky and Lenin that the social revolution became perverted—a fact Trotsky could never understand—simply because he was one of its prime architects.[3]

Now it might be thought that a Russian revolution, which had gone off the straight-and-narrow at the very outset and yet rumbled on regardless for a full half century, must *ipso facto* have become a decided menace, certainly enough so to justify elaborate collective security arrangements on the part of the West. However, in that same summer of 1968, some 25 New Left admirers of the Cohn-Bendits in Britain published their collective interpretation of the contemporary world scene. In the chapter on "America and Europe" since 1945, there is not the slightest reference to the overhanging might of the USSR as the prime reason why the New World had felt obliged once more to come and redress the balance of the Old. Likewise, the USSR might not even exist so far as the chapter on "The New Imperialism" is concerned, the Polaris missile solemnly being depicted as a means of retaining dominion over the newly developing states of Afro-Asia and Latin America.[4] World historical perspectives can, it seems, be extremely asymmetrical.

What makes such lacunae even more disturbing than they might otherwise be is the sheer bureaucratic power of the Soviet military-cum-heavy industrial complex and the uncompromising manner with which this power is exercised. Thus the standard period of military conscription is two full years during which each draftee is subject to highly intensive training schedules, a markedly hierarchical chain of command, an elaborate code of etiquette, a draconian code of discipline, a pervasive web of political informers, and quite heavy political indoctrination. Prior to call-up he will probably have carried out a good deal of part-time training, this being arranged through the massive DOSAAF organisation and in the high schools.[5] After release, he remains subject to recall for many months of refresher training spread over many years although it does seem that, in practice, he is likely to complete only a very minor fraction of the total liability.

Two factors militate against the resultant juggernaut posing as big a menace as one might expect from its size and geographical disposition. An inadequate Soviet regard for the precept of comparative cost-effectiveness is one and the realities of nuclear deterrence the other. Nevertheless the USSR will continue to possess a formidable capability for offensive action in several spheres. Notwithstanding all we have heard in a contrary sense, the USSR poses a formidable military threat to China at several levels.[6] The USSR retains, too, an awesome capacity for quasi-imperial intervention in Eastern Europe. And were the Warsaw Pact as a whole to launch a major non-nuclear attack on any part of NATO Europe tomorrow, the defending alliance would be obliged to resort to tactical nuclear weapons within several days at the most.

Nor should we forget that, during the early 1970s, the fractional edge NATO enjoys over the Warsaw Pact in declared defence expenditures shrank appreciably.[7] Yet NATO depends on this putative lead not only to offset its much higher pay and welfare costs (plus undeclared outlays on the other side) but also to cope with the sundry difficulties that geography presents. So were this differential movement to persist, the nuclear Rubicon might become avoidable, anywhere in the European theatre, only for the first few hours of any major conflict. Choices that might be less immediate yet hardly less agonising could be posed as the Red Navy consolidates its ability to contest control of pretty well any part of the "indivisible world ocean", the arena that matters so much more to the maritime nations of the West than ever it does to the USSR.

So does this mean that the Soviet Union is locked in the grip of its military men? Certainly, the military played a big part in the rise of Khrushchev in 1955–57, whilst their studied indifference to the pressures building against him was one factor in his downfall in 1964.[8] Apparently, too, the swing to a more narrow authoritarianism during the ensuing year or two gained extra impetus from well-orchestrated military pressures.[9]

Since then the interplay between soldiers and politicians has not been easy to discern, the signs being scanty and various. Thus in 1967 an attempt was made to break all precedent by appointing a civilian as Minister of Defence: the man proposed being, in fact, Dimitri Ustinov, a leading arms magnate since Stalingrad days. This move proved abortive. On the other hand, in 1969 the military parade customary in Red Square on May Day was cancelled, apparently to intimate that the generals would not be allowed to obstruct Mr Brezhnev's strategy of *détente*.

Still, the crux of the matter may be that, since Mr Khrushchev's departure, the party leadership has never split into two distinct and evenly balanced factions, thereby giving the general staff scope for active arbitration. Also that there is now a more stable consensus than ever before between the party as a whole and the officer corps as a whole on the need to preserve throughout the Motherland the traditional ethos of martial puritanism. The fact that the vast majority of Soviet officers of field rank and above are party members underwrites this consensus. The advancement of the late Marshal Grechko, then the Minister of Defence, to the Politburo in 1973 capped it rather dramatically. Previously, Soviet spokesmen had always been pleased to cite as proof of civilian control the invariable exclusion of the senior soldier from this supreme organ of government. Contrariwise, Dimitri Ustinov did succeed Andrei Grechko as Minister of Defence in 1976.

What then are the implications for the post-Brezhnev era? As a basis for answering this question, one should perhaps start from the tolerably safe assumption that the first phase in this era will be one of collective leadership by the septuagenarians who flank Mr Brezhnev today. After this interregnum, which may last three or four years, the succession is likely to pass to men of about 50, men whose formative years bestrode the climax of the Great Patriotic War. These men are likely to have relatively advanced ideas on scientific management. However, they are unlikely much to espouse liberalisation in any broader sense. Even were they inclined to do so, their tough-minded peers in the officer corps might curb them.

Just how discordant this peculiarly rigid brand of authoritarian conservatism is with the tenets of the Western world at large can be gauged by reference to all the standard tests of liberal democracy: freedom of speech and of access to information; electoral choice; the right to strike; and so on. But perhaps the morbidity with which this whole business is suffused is exemplified best by official reactions to three themes which are plumb central to contemporary social change:

travel, youthful dissent and women's liberation. Thus one unsavoury aspect of the bureaucratic impediments to travel is the absurdly high cost of the kind of passport required to visit a non-Communist country and the cumbersome, secretive and protracted vetting procedures involved. Another is the neo-Czarist requirement to carry an internal passport for travel within the USSR.

Nay, it can hardly be said that a polity has shaken off entirely the long shadow of agrarian serfdom when late in 1974 its rulers can decree in all seriousness that, whilst permits for specific journeys will still be required as a general rule, collective farmers over the age of 16 shall soon enjoy the automatic entitlement to internal passports long accorded their urban compatriots. Nor does it require much psychological insight to perceive a connection, in terms of official attitudes of mind, between these archaic restrictions and the appalling quality of Soviet roads, the frequently rigid zoning of residential areas on an occupational basis, the incessant falsification of maps, and all sorts of obstacles to ready access to officials and the like.

To get some measure of the on-going attitude of the Kremlin towards the aspirations of modern youth, it is instructive to turn again to the climacteric year of 1968. In an address to 6,000 Komsomols in the Kremlin Palace of Congresses that October, Leonid Brezhnev warned against self-professed "friends of the youth" who seek "to draw into their nets the unstable and immature elements, to lull their class and revolutionary vigilance with false bourgeois-liberal arguments, to appeal to nationalist sentiment, and to find renegades who long for a life of ease". Later on, a full page article in the pro-Establishment *Literaturnaya Gazeta* castigated the "pure anarchism" of Herbert Marcuse as an opportunistic blend of Trotskyism, Maoism and social democracy designed "to integrate the working class movement into the capitalist system". To clinch this indictment it admonished its readers thus, "Today it is known that Marcuse really worked in the Office of Strategic Services, which was later transformed into the CIA".[10]

Female emancipation, as it was then called, used regularly to be cited by Stalin's admirers abroad as one of his most positive achievements. Yet even in this area the record looks uneven as the 60th anniversary of the Russian revolution approaches. Agreed, women have gained a remarkable measure of access to virtually all the most interesting and prestigious professions. Thus one in three of the engineers and the lawyers and three in four of the family doctors are female in the USSR today. Among several items on the debit side, however, is the almost total exclusion of women from top-level political participation. Thus in 1957 Mrs Ekaterina Furtseva, who from 1960 was Minister of Culture, became the only woman member of the Politburo there has ever been. Alas, at the time of her death in 1974 she was in serious trouble for allegedly misappropriating state funds to refurbish her private *dacha*.

A good deal less subtle, however, is the bias evinced by officialdom and the established media against the dissident intellectuals. Whilst the overt rebels are still a very tiny minority, they are also a coherent and resolute one. What is more, they are backed by a ramified underground press, the thousands of *samizdat* (literally, "published by yourself") on contentious political, social or religious topics that circulate internally on a wide scale and—in hundreds of cases—reach the West. One early indication of the resurgence of repression post-Khrushchev came in a 1966 amendment to the criminal code. This made any denigration of Soviet government and society punishable by up to three years in prison.

But let us not forget how oscillatory the Khrushchev regime was on such matters, however benign it may look by comparison with what came before and after. In 1960 Anatoly Marchenko, a 22-year-old shift worker on a Siberian building site, began a six year term in prisons and labour camps. In a subsequent *samizdat* entitled *My Testimony*, he told how many of his fellows, reacting against their maltreatment, tattooed their faces with such bitter jibes as "Khrushchev's Slave", "KGB", "Lenin was a Butcher". He also affirmed that political prisoners got beaten more savagely and fed worse than ordinary criminals.[11] Inevitably, such episodes reinforce doubts as to whether any post-Brezhnev liberalisation will be either profound or sustained.

What then are the potentialities of this internal protest movement? Obviously it has never yet invoked anything approaching a groundswell of popular endorsement among the Great Russian masses, people who are not only tightly controlled but also imbued with an anti-intellectual propensity that is closely bound up with traditional xenophobia. Nor have the dissident leaders yet formulated what could properly be described as an alternative political programme. In the main, they have simply talked rather defensively about a need to keep to the spirit of the revolution and the letter of the constitution, trust the man-in-the-street, preserve common decency and the like.

Nevertheless, it did seem six or seven years ago as if the movement was gaining ground fast, among the more encouraging aspects being the involvement with it of some prominent members of the scientific community and of the prestigious literary journal, *Novy Mir*. Gradually, however, the forces of repression intensified their counter-pressure. Early in 1973 the International Committee for the Defence of Human Rights in the Soviet Union put the prison population of that country at 1,200,000, many thousands of them serving terms for political offences. An even more sinister stratagem was the incarceration of hundreds—maybe thousands—of dissenters in mental homes after the fashion of Stalin and certain Czars. Among the better-known cases has been Major-General Pyotr Grigorenko, former Professor of Cybernetics at the Frunze Military Academy.

But a hard-core of protest has survived, partly through the bold exploitation of such opportunities for closer rapport with the liberal West as have been generated by the atmosphere of *détente*. In the spring of 1975, the authorities felt impelled to launch a savage though inconclusive campaign against the tiny Soviet branch of Amnesty International. A year later, the radical activists established a special committee to monitor the USSR's observance of those aspects of the 1975 Helsinki agreements which appertain directly to individual freedom and political communication.

Perhaps the greatest source of strength to the radicals, in the longer-term, is their large measure of identification with the resurgence of political consciousness among the national minorities of the Soviet Union. In the vanguard of this renaissance, partly because of the special enthusiasm it engenders in the West, is the Jewish community of around two million people, a quarter of whom live in Moscow itself. Uniquely among the USSR's national minorities this last half century, it has been denied even notional self-determination in education and other matters, except within the hollow mockery of an autonomous region established at Birobidzhan on the Manchurian border in 1927. One result has been a decline from 70 to 17 per cent between 1926 and 1970 of those giving Yiddish as their mother tongue. The number of synagogues now open is about 50 as against 450 in 1956 and 3,000 in 1917.

True, Russian Jews today enter the professions on a scale quite unknown in Czarist times. On the other hand, the strong anti-Semitic impulses endemic in this political and social culture are often fostered or condoned by the regime. Examples include the way anti-

Jewish ruffians marred the World Student Games in Moscow in 1973, and the disproportionate number of Jews executed for "economic crimes" even in the comparatively liberal early 1960s.[12] Likewise, official attitudes towards emigration to Israel have been very arbitrary and volatile.

Petitions alleging religious persecution and bearing the names of 17,000 Roman Catholics were sent to the United Nations and to Leonid Brezhnev from Lithuania in March 1972. Two months later, thousands of Lithuanian youth rioted in Kaunas in sympathy with a political protester who had burned himself to death, only to have his body spirited away by the KGB. That August, the Crimean Tartars started a fresh campaign to regain their old homeland by sending to Brezhnev a petition with 20,000 signatures on it. Some months previously, another community with strong links with Turkey—namely, the Meskhetians—had forcefully reasserted themselves. Perennially, both the Ukraine and Georgia are major foci of strain, as witness the bombing campaign in the latter in May 1976. Nor should we assume that Central Asia as a whole will forever be quiescent.[13] In fact, ethnic identities will generally remain much more distinct and coherent through 1990 and throughout the USSR than they will for similar minorities in the countries around the North Atlantic.

In an endeavour to preclude such centripetal tendencies interacting with the new expectations aroused by an intrusive technocratic culture, the Brezhnev regime has been considerably inclined to promote pan-Soviet chauvinism and underpin it by further Russification through propaganda, language training and outright settlement.[14]

Even apart from the evident risk of a direct backlash from the national minorities, however, this strategy is fraught with hazards. One is that men and women of the hue of Solzhenitsyn will gradually turn the Russian Orthodox Church into a vehicle of protest and change, this notwithstanding its tradition of pliancy and currently moribund condition.

For a good dozen years before and then again after World War II, a cardinal theme of Soviet propaganda was that a radical regrouping of the USSR's resources into larger units, operating within a Marxist-Leninist master plan, would lead to dramatic economic progress, not only throughout industry but also in agriculture. Waves of pioneer settlements in the tundra in the 1930s and in the semi-arid "virgin lands" of Central Asia in the 1950s were said to bespeak a vision unique to Soviet Man. Large dams and extensive canals, endless belts of new forest, rural electrification, collective farms and tractor stations were made the symbols of a revolution throughout the Soviet countryside. An afterglow of this multiple vision may perhaps be discerned in the somewhat immoderate enthusiasm Moscow currently evinces towards Peaceful Nuclear Explosions (PNE); and in plans to redirect the big Siberian rivers.

In the light of all this, it is ironic that, in 1972, the international market in grain was severely disrupted by the surreptitious import by the USSR of over 20,000,000 tons of American grain; also that, in 1975, she again imported a large quantity, some 25,000,000 tons to be more exact. Still, it can be said in mitigation that, in reality, centralised planning is never easy to apply to agriculture. After all, this does so much depend on local and contingent factors, the most obvious being weather. Besides which, the alterations presumptively taking place in the world's climate are always liable to hit Soviet farming especially hard. And river diversion is a hazardous remedy.

All the same, it is far from clear that any very special benefits have accrued from this planning philosophy anywhere in the Soviet economy. Not that anybody denies that today, as indeed quite often in Czarist times, the best scientists in the land are right in the forefront of fundamental discovery: sub-nuclear physics and radar astronomy being impressive examples. No one doubts either that Soviet governments are capable of single-minded concentration of the sort that may eliminate, within specific sectors of applied science, the "technology gaps" between their country and the leading Western nations. Defence at present affords some disturbing examples.

At the same time, however, the overall spread of consumer goods lags remarkably, not only in display and design but also in quality. Similarly, the reliability of machinery in general and vehicles in particular tends to be poor and their repair facilities grossly inadequate. In addition, an awareness is belatedly burgeoning within the USSR itself that the ecological damage caused by economic activity has been far more widespread than might have been expected, given the ideological renunciation of "capitalist jungles" and in view, too, of the relatively low output of goods and services per unit area.[15] Herein lies a major reason for the sorry condition of the Caspian.

Nor is it just ecology that is now under review. In the wake of a disappointing performance, more or less across the board, of the

8

1971–75 plan, the overall prospects for economic growth are being reappraised. Thus the aggregate growth rate envisaged under the 1976–80 plan is a modest four per cent per annum as against an average achievement of six per cent during the early 1960s.

Absolutely central to an understanding of the USSR's patchy performance in the more exotic forms of technology is its leeway in respect of computers. In terms both of numbers and of quality it has trailed well behind the EEC and Japan and far behind the USA. At the start of this decade the number in use was reckoned to be less than a tenth of the American total whilst the qualitative lag was anything between five and 12 years. Until the beginning of 1976, indeed, the annual depreciation allowance for computers was a mere two per cent. In other words, the solemn expectation was that each machine would last half a century!

The signs are, however, that what the Russians extol as their "Scientific and Technical Revolution" will gather some pace over the next decade. For one thing, they are gradually attuning themselves to successive imports of Western know-how; and computers, cars and trucks, special steels, oil and natural gas, and animal husbandry are among the areas which have been (or soon will be) benefiting. Now the depreciation rate for computers is a much more trendy ten per cent. Thanks to the completion of the huge Fiat works, the output of cars rose from 530,000 in 1971 to 1,200,000 in 1975; and it should be a 100,000 more in 1980.

Some of the directly strategic results to be expected from Soviet technological advance are examined elsewhere in this study.[16] Suffice now to consider the implications for the USSR's internal development and the effect this, in its turn, may have on its external posture. This subject is one with a long pedigree. Immediately after the death of Stalin, there was a great upsurge of talk about a spontaneous and sustained "convergence" of political attitudes between the USSR and the advanced industrial nations of the West, this allegedly being an irrefragable concomitant to broadly similar patterns of economic and social change. As Maurice Duverger euphorically opined, "only one thing seems certain, the convergence of the evolutions of East and West towards democratic socialism".[17]

Well in the forefront of this school of thought was the late Isaac Deutscher, another Polish Jewish Marxist. Writing in *The Times* barely 18 months after Stalin's death, he applauded the "restless and dangerous heart-searching" being carried out by "the whole" of the

Soviet intelligentsia. He exuded confidence that the imperatives of a modernising technocracy made the pressures towards freedom of thought and expression irresistible in the long run, "The aircraft designers must be let out of the prisons, literally and metaphorically, if Russian aircraft design is to meet the demands which the international armament race, to mention only this, makes on it".[18] No matter that only the previous decade, German designers, labouring under the shadow of the Gestapo, had notched up some very impressive achievements in aeronautics and rocketry.

Over 20 years later the prognosis is manifestly less cheerful. By the standard tests of liberal democracy alluded to above, the progress registered in the interval has, in fact, been nil or negligible. About all that can be said is that, starting with the execution of Beria late in 1953, the ambit of what we now know as the KGB was curtailed by about half. This amelioration has not been unimportant. But it was not fundamental and has not been carried forward.

Clearly the "convergence" enthusiasts were altogether too glib. They assumed that the process they foresaw would be a steady one, a kind of inevitable broadening down of freedom from precedent to precedent. Probably, too, some of them (Deutscher included) paid too much attention to the progressive alterations in production technique associated with economic growth as opposed to the consequential changes in consumption patterns.

However, they were surely sound in their intuition that economic advance must present a basic challenge to the existing order in such a land as the USSR. More affluent life styles are very prone to lead on to what we would recognise as Western political aspirations. Obviously if somebody has acquired a motor car or even a camera, he is bound to be more interested than heretofore in freedom to travel. Then again, a town-dweller is likely to expect to be able to voice his opinions on a much wider range of issues than is a peasant in a remote village; and between 1968 and 1974 alone, the recorded percentage of urban dwellers within the Soviet Union rose from 55·1 to 60·1.[19]

To my mind, the rub is that greater freedom of expression for all Soviet citizens might allow the germination of secessionist movements which ultimately could split the USSR asunder. Suppose a free political debate were to break out and ramify on such matters as the devolution of decision-making from Moscow, the decollectivisation (partial or total) of agriculture, the toleration of religious belief and observance, the burden of defence expenditure, the price mechanism or the individual and the law. Soon there would be a strong differentiation of attitude along nationality lines, most of the national minorities taking the more liberal line most of the time.

What is more, some of the most restive minorities would be ones concentrated in sizeable and well-defined territories just inside the western and southern borders. Accordingly, they would be quite well-placed to secede (as formally the Soviet constitution allows them to) were the situation to become ripe. In the meantime, they may orchestrate their several protests increasingly, the Ukraine being a natural dais for this purpose.

In short, whilst the Kremlin cannot afford not to liberalise its regime, it cannot afford to either. In a reference to the nationality question in 1968, Zbigniew Brzezinski regretted what he saw as "the inclination of many western scholars of Soviet affairs to minimise what I fear may be a very explosive issue in the Soviet polity".[20] As 1990 draws near, events may well vindicate his concern.

Notes

1. For a brilliant critique of Alexander Werth for repeatedly indulging in delayed *exposé* on this score see the letter by Leopold Labedz in *The New Statesman*, 13 October 1967.
2. See George Watson "Were the Intellectuals duped?", *Encounter*, Vol. XLI No. 6, December 1973, pp. 20–30.
3. Gabriel and Daniel Cohn-Bendit, *Obsolete Communism, the Left-Wing Alternative*, Penguin, London, 1968, p. 244.
4. Raymond Williams (Ed), *May Day Manifesto 1968*, Penguin, London, 1968, Chapters 16 and 18.
5. DOSAAF: The Voluntary Society for Cooperation with the Army, Aviation and Fleet.
6. See the author's "The Myth of an Asian Diversion", *RUSI Journal*, Vol. 118 No. 3, September 1973, pp. 48–51.
7. *SIPRI Yearbook 1976*, Almquist and Wiksell, Stockholm, 1976, Table 6A, 1.
8. C. A. Linden, *Khrushchev and the Soviet Leadership 1957–64*, John Hopkins, Washington, 1966, p. 205.
9. Roman Kilkowicz "General and Politicians: Uneasy Truce", *Problems of Communism*, Vol. XVII, 3, May–June 1968, pp. 71–76.
10. *The Times*, 19 December 1968.
11. Anatoly Marchenko (Translated by Michael Scammell), *My Testimony*, Pall Mall Press, London, 1969.
12. Robert Conquest, *The Listener*, Vol. 85 No. 2181, 14 January 1971, p. 53.
13. George Schopflin "Nascent Islam threatens Cohesion of Communist Empire", *The New Middle East*, No. 44, May 1972, pp. 23–6.
14. Wolfgang Leonhard "The Domestic Politics of the New Soviet Foreign Policy", *Foreign Affairs*, Vol. 52 No. 1, October 1973, pp. 59–74.

15. Margaret Miller "Environmental Crisis: the Soviet View", *The World Today*, Vol. 29 No. 8, August 1973, pp. 352–62 and John M. Kramer, "Prices and the Conservation of Natural Resources in the Soviet Union", *Soviet Studies*, Vol. XXIV, January 1973, pp. 368–74.
16. Chapters 9, 15 and 21.
17. Quoted in Alfred G. Meyer, "Theories of Convergence" in Chalmers Johnson (Ed), *Change in Communist Systems*, Stanford University Press, Stanford 1970, pp. 313–41.
18. Isaac Deutscher, *Heretics and Renegades*, Hamish Hamilton, London 1955. p. 215.
19. *The 1974 Demographic Yearbook*, United Nations, New York 1975, p. 148.
20. *Problems of Communism*, Vol. XVII No. 3, May–June 1968, p. 47.

15

The Manifold Duality

Perhaps the most radical adjustment in the world balance that the early years of the nuclear era experienced was the replacement of the multipolar structures which had usually obtained in the previous few centuries by one heavily dominated by two Superpowers, each appearing more or less equal to the other and head and shoulders above their nearest rival. Arguably, the struggle England or Britain continually waged with France between 1668 and 1815 was a precursor of this situation though the comparison is vitiated by the role played then by Austria and other states as autonomous and important balancing factors. Otherwise, to find a close parallel in the mainstream of European history you have to go back to Rome and Carthage or to Athens and Sparta.

Just what the 1980s may hold for this bipolarity would be anything but easy to summarise. For whilst additional centres of national power have been steadily emerging—especially in Europe and the Far East—they have been doing so at a time when the key criteria of power have become more confused and contingent than ever before. Hopefully, the European Common Market is evolving towards a quite novel form of confederal nexus, one that may make it equivalent to, if not higher than, a superstate in some ways albeit a good deal less coherent in others. Similarly, across the world at large trans-national links, both institutional and cultural, seem to be growing in importance even though some countries—most notably the USSR—seem both anxious and able to insulate themselves from this trend to a considerable extent. A further complication is the grave economic threat posed to Mankind as a whole by the energy crisis and recurrent shortages of other materials. The patterns of conflict in a world running short of copper would probably be very different from, and maybe a good deal more savage than, anything any of us have experienced or can readily envisage. To cap all, there is the persisting uncertainty as to what exactly we mean by nuclear sufficiency.

Probably, the truth of the matter is that it is no longer helpful to enquire whether the global balance is going to remain effectively bipolar or whether it will gradually acquire a multipolar matrix. The question is one which begs too many others and, in so doing, threatens to canalise our thought in a manner inappropriate to so fluid and intricate a situation. What we can say with confidence, however, is that what the International Institute for Strategic Studies (as it is now known) once graphically described as the Adversary Partnership between Washington and Moscow will continue to be a distinct and important factor in world affairs. Also that the attention accorded it by specialists and others is liable to be the greater on account of the way it corresponds to a dualism that is embedded in many facets of human perception throughout all cultures: good and evil, Yin and Yang, night and day, hot and cold, man and woman, war and peace, Sun and Moon, the Eastern and Western Hemispheres. . . .

· Accordingly this special relationship is bound to remain the subject of continual reassessment world-wide. Quite possibly it will not henceforward be sufficiently well defined fully to merit the title, Adversary Partnership. At all events, we are on safe ground if we employ the looser term, Manifold Duality.[1]

Faith that the current phase of *détente* between the Superpowers will continue indefinitely (and more or less unequivocally) is sustained by a widespread impression that it is quite unprecedented within the nuclear era: that between the collapse of the Axis powers in 1945 and the resolution of the Cuban crisis in 1962 the Washington–Moscow interaction was but one of mutual and uncompromising hostility. Yet this impression is ill-founded. Its decisive lead in nuclear development notwithstanding, the United States response to Soviet expansionism was restrained, not to say casual, until the summer of 1946. For instance, White House hostility to Britain's intervention in Greece late in 1944 was a good deal more vocal than it had been to the USSR's calculated betrayal of the Polish Home Army during the Warsaw Rising that August.

In addition, those rendered soporific by the notion that the current era of diminished tension is utterly novel would do well to study the period 1954–56. For every bit as much optimism was then evinced about the impending and conclusive termination of the Cold War. The death of Stalin was regarded as auspicious, particularly since it was soon followed by negotiated settlements of the wars in Korea and Indo-China. The decidedly amicable "summit" conference held in Geneva in July 1955 was judged by many to underpin the new mood. So had been the conference of 29 Afro-Asian states (China, India and

Japan among them) which had taken place that April at Bandung in Indonesia.

As we all know to our chagrin, however, resurgent tension in Eastern Europe and the Middle East soon put paid to the "Geneva Spirit". And by the time of the Sino-Indian border clash in 1959, there was not much left of the "Bandung Spirit" either.

Nevertheless, there has at least been one singular feature of the recent return to *détente* politics. Indubitably verbal exchanges between the Superpowers have been more consistently couth of late than was customary, say, 25 years ago and along with this comparative civility have come several fresh attitudes and perceptions. Nor will there be much dispute that some of these have been beneficent: the reduced emphasis on ideology for its own sake; a readiness to engage regularly in dialogue, at least about immediate anxieties and short-term intentions; an acceptance that defence and arms control may be the two sides of the same coin; and an incipient awareness of the action—reaction phenomenon whereby extreme hawkishness by one side tends to thrive on extreme hawkishness by the other and vice versa. It is to be hoped that, as and when *détente* ebbs again, these new habits of thought and demeanour will not be washed away entirely.

Granted all this, it behoves us still to remember that strong undercurrents of hostility have persisted throughout, especially from the direction of Moscow. Let us recall, for example, the circumstances under which Communist military pressure built up again in South Vietnam during the first half of 1974, in blatant disregard of the cease-fire agreement secured by Henry Kissinger early in 1973. By that time the Communists had massed over 500 Soviet-made tanks in South Vietnam although, thanks to the swing of opinion on Capitol Hill, its opponents were even being denied essential logistic support. Furthermore, the People's Army and Viet Cong had been able to improve vastly their own supply arrangements in theatre and had covered their main deployment areas with a formidable shield of Soviet-made anti-aircraft guns.[2] Needless to say, this, too, was in flagrant violation of the Paris Agreements, Article 7 in particular.

Likewise, whilst the authorities in Moscow (plus or minus the KGB) may well have had grave reservations about the Arab offensive against Israel in 1973, both they and the Americans had massive arms lifts under way to their respective clients only a matter of days after battle commenced. Furthermore Soviet spokesmen had actively been advocating, via radio broadcasts and other channels, recourse by the Arabs to their oil weapon.

Nor should we ever forget that the present phase in Washington-Moscow political relations has evolved concurrently with the advent of a very stable strategic nuclear stalemate between them. Today received opinion has it that this state of affairs is unambiguously satisfactory, productive of confidence on both sides and thereby conducive to a steady broadening of dialogue and *détente*. However, only 15 years or so ago, the expectation was widespread among analysts that the apparently imminent disappearance of the United States margin of strategic nuclear superiority would encourage the Russians to wax more daring in regard to local probing actions.

Thus General Maxwell Taylor wrote in 1959 that, in the years ahead, the Russians, blessed with what he foresaw as an actual superiority in missiles, "may be expected to press harder than ever before, counting on submissiveness arising from our consciousness of weakness".[3] Around that time, too, Sir Basil Liddell-Hart was similarly warning that "Nuclear nullity", as he called it, "inherently favours and fosters a renewal of non-nuclear aggressive activity".[4] The impression made on him by the reasoning of these two scholarly, and by no means illiberal, students of strategy was a mainspring for President Kennedy's drive to build up American and allied local war capability.

Maybe the real prospect before us is a decidedly double-edged one. Perhaps in what will, to all intents and purposes, be an era of Superpower nuclear parity the USSR will both "talk softly and carry a big stick". When in exile in London during World War II, Charles de Gaulle was wont to advise his Anglo-Saxon colleagues: "I am too weak to compromise". But the incumbents of the Kremlin in 1980 and beyond will have no military reasons to cling to any such taboos. Therefore they may prove ever more willing to sustain a dialogue with the United States, in particular, on arms control and sundry other issues. Yet concurrently they may grow more willing or even eager to brandish their military wherewithal from time to time. Clearly, the probability of this *a priori* reasoning in the field of geostrategy being borne out by events is considerably increased by the way in which (as argued in the last chapter) the deepening contradictions in the body politic of the USSR point towards the same conclusion.

When trying to predict more definitively what the Manifold Duality will mean for the world of the 1980s, it is tempting to keep in the mind's eye the dumb-bell model of an essentially rigid and bipolar framework, each end of which is more or less a mirror image of the other. After all, each Superpower continues to be more self-sufficient economically than are most of the more advanced states, not least as regards energy supplies. Likewise each has an exotic technology base that by general world standards is exceptionally highly developed, whatever doubts or shortcomings may currently beset it. Oceanography and the control of nuclear fusion are spheres of research in which their mutual lead may well increase through 1990, in the former case through a broad spread of empirical investigation and in the latter through a concentrated attack on the fundamental difficulties presented. Furthermore, manned space flight is a field in which their technological supremacy is likely to be absolute into the next century, unless at some stage either or both of them do evince a strong political resolve to share their skills and opportunities with the scientists of other nations (see Chapter 26).

Last but by no means least come the distinctive military attributes the USA and the USSR possess. Their degree of nuclear overkill and capacity for global surveillance have already been mentioned. What also promises to set them apart from now on is their ability to conduct major military or naval interventions almost anywhere in the world.

Even on the quite different plane of political culture, there are certain affinities between these two great nations which add up to a kind of exclusivity. Both are federal or multicommunal. Customarily, each has regarded itself as less ridden by class distinctions and by imperialistic aspirations than it understands other advanced states to be. Nostalgia for the simple folk ways of their rural past has often loomed strong in both cases. Yet so, too, has a disposition to think big in technology and government interlaced with a dynamic belief in ever-expanding wealth and hence contentment. Arguably, this pristine faith in growth and progress has owed quite a lot to a long experience of seemingly limitless extension across wide-open spaces.

What is more, both the Soviet Union and the United States have lately been experiencing a serious internal crisis: dissent has been more widespread and strident and established authority more plagued with self-doubt.[5] And weight is added to these developments by the fact that, in both these polities, the pressures towards endorsement of whatever happens to be the dominant set of opinions have been noticeably stronger historically than they have in, say, Britain.

Yet it is at this very point that this dumb-bell model breaks down completely. For one thing, the contrast in political style and ethos between the USSR and the USA remains profound in spite of occasional lapses into a militant intolerance by such elements in American public life as the late Joseph McCarthy and various of Richard Nixon's close associates. For another, the two nation states here considered are reacting in diametrically contrasting ways to their not dissimilar inner traumas.

This differential movement, which merits more attention than it normally receives, was well epitomised a few years back by a distinguished correspondent of *Le Monde*. He observed that the Soviet Union "has tended to ignore or hush up its problems, and concentrate on building its armed might and extending its influence", whereas the United States "has been seeking to reduce its commitments abroad so as to concentrate on domestic tasks".[6]

Of late, a number of analysts[7] have made appreciative reference to a synoptic review of United States history since 1776 conducted over 20 years ago by Frank Klingberg, then a professor at the University of California. He concluded that the record could be divided quite sharply into alternating phases of extroversion and introversion, the former being characterised by "expansion and the extension of influence" and the latter being the times of "consolidation and preparation—*plateaux* preceding the *mountain climbs* ahead". Thus he calculated that, all in all, the extrovert periods had witnessed 124 annexations and armed expeditions by the USA as against a mere 12 in the introvert.

He found that, whilst the mean duration of the introvert phases was 21 years, the extrovert lasted six years longer, maybe because they were usually associated with more dynamic leadership. Cautiously he inferred that the extrovert phase which began in 1940 might give way in the course of the late 1960s to one of retraction. During the onset of this, "It is quite possible that the major problem . . . will carry heavy moral implications. . . . The aspirations of the people of Asia and Africa could well furnish the chief cause, along with repercussions from America's own racial problem". His inclination was to explain all these more or less rhythmic swings in terms of the alternating interaction of successive generations.

There are conceptual difficulties about the Klingberg thesis, a critical one being precisely what "introvert" and "extrovert" mean as applied to the age of the "moving frontier". Nevertheless one cannot but remark how the first signs of a retrenchment are to be seen in

1967, exactly on schedule on a straight extrapolation of the median Klingberg cycle and in circumstances closely akin to his surmise. The most notable specific instances were the USA's refusal to become immersed in the conflicts in Nigeria and the Congo or over Egypt's precipitate closure of the Straits of Tiran. Meanwhile, criticism of the Vietnam War was starting to ramify visibly.

So must we wait until 1988 or thereabouts for the next surge of the USA towards globalism? Certainly one does not have to be a slavish devotee of Klingberg to realise that the current withdrawal phase may not yet have reached its nadir. Inevitably one hazard is the presence in the White House, sooner or later, of someone more susceptible to the sundry retrenchment pressures than the Nixon-Kissinger and Ford-Kissinger axes proved. Another possibility which cannot be ignored entirely is a more vigorous resurgence of economic autarkism as a result either of liquidity troubles, or else of commercial competition (at least in certain sectors) from the East Asian rim or Western Europe, or else of deepening despair about the prospects for a new economic order across the world. A third is a catastrophic political crisis in the United Nations or within the Atlantic Alliance, the Middle East being the most likely apple of discord in each case. A fourth is a continued and pronounced decline in internal social cohesion leading to an illiberal "America Firstism".

In many respects, however, the American scene has looked far sunnier through its Bicentenary than many would have thought possible five or ten years ago. The urban "ghettos" are quiet and so are the campuses whilst even the hard drugs cult makes much less of a morbid impact than once it did. Nevertheless, some of the yardsticks of alienation continue to indicate a general worsening of the social situation.

Chief among these is the rising incidence of crime. Extrapolation on the basis of the rather erratic statistical fluctuations of the last few years would, of course, be far from easy. But if instead you project exponentially the 1960–69 decennial increase, which was well over twofold, you could approach as early as 1990 a stage where rational public attitudes—not only towards race or law and order but to other political matters as well—would be nigh impossible to sustain. Let us look, for example, at the recorded annual rate of murder and manslaughter per 100,000. In 1972 this was 19·1 in New York and 8·6 in San Francisco as against, for instance, a mere 2·82 in crowded Hong Kong and 1·53 in care-worn London. Obviously the

USA must curb its own crime wave if it is to sustain its crucial contribution to the survival of peace and freedom elsewhere.

Yet behind all these particular considerations lies an imperative need to come to terms with the grim traumas of Watergate and Vietnam. Thus one of the more valid lessons to draw from Watergate may be that the United States should move closer to a British-style system of strong Cabinet government. As one of the vanguard members of Kennedy's "New Frontier" put it well before the Watergate crisis broke, whilst augmented prestige and authority for the Cabinet-level officers would naturally reinforce the Presidency as a whole, it could "also reduce the need and the temptation for sudden interventions by the President as an individual".[8] Obversely, if the Presidency had rather more discretionary power in certain fields, the impulses towards ersatz Caesarism might sometimes be weaker. Presumably, too, the resolution of America's social problems requires an augmentation, at least in certain respects, of the power of the federal executive.

But in place of a sober reassessment along these or any other lines, what we have lately witnessed has partaken more of an inchoate reaction against Washington and everything it is deemed to stand for. In terms of philosophical content, this reaction has been a mere mish-mash of attitudes that, on any deeper analysis, would prove hopelessly discordant: bicentennial nostalgia, New Left communitarianism, the "Pacific Firstism" discussed below, the cult of the sun-belt, Dixiecrat defensiveness. . . . Unfortunately this surge has been reinforced by many of the liberal intelligentsia, the very people who were the most committed ideologically to Kennedy's "New Frontier" and Roosevelt's "New Deal".

More disturbing, however, have been the gyrations of these "New Frontiersmen" over Indo-China. In the speech he was to have delivered in Dallas the day he was murdered, John Kennedy conceded that assistance to nations on the periphery of the Communist world "can be painful, risky, and costly—as is true in South-East Asia today. But we dare not weary of the task. . . . A successful Communist breakthrough in these areas, necessitating direct United States intervention, would cost us several times as much as our entire foreign aid programme—and might cost us heavily in American lives as well". He went on to list the "nine key countries" that currently were "confronted directly or indirectly with the threat of Communist aggression". Among them were "free China, Korea, and Vietnam".[9]

Nor was the subsequent revaluation of the war at all rapid. True, it does seem that, as early as 1963, Robert Kennedy was becoming identified as a dovish sceptic apropos Vietnam.[10] Nevertheless, as late as 1967, he deplored a tendency to romanticise "kindly Uncle Ho" and reminded all and sundry that surrender to the North Vietnamese regime "is now impossible", if only because tens of thousands of individual Vietnamese "have staked their lives and fortunes on our presence". He advocated instead a carefully nego- tiated compromise culminating in truly free elections throughout South Vietnam.[11] From all this one might fairly have concluded that nobody could ever have engaged in root-and-branch condemnation of the Kissinger-Nixon strategy on Indo-China from within the confines of the Kennedy tradition.

Yet in February 1971 the Democrats in the Senate voted by no less a majority than 31 to nine for a unilateral and complete withdrawal from Indo-China by the end of 1972, Senator Mansfield duly per- suading himself that this would "strengthen the hand of the President" in his quest. Likewise, the pitch adopted by George McGovern throughout the 1972 Presidential was utterly capitula- tionist. Even so, he himself was prepared to harness to the full the residual charisma of the New Frontier by selecting Sargant Shriver to be the Eagleton replacement as Vice-Presidential nominee and enlisting Edward Kennedy as a principal campaign speaker.

No doubt some erstwhile members of the New Frontier would seek to explain this glaring contradiction in terms of their dawning realisation that there was no point in trying to defend the South Vietnamese since they had proved unwilling to defend themselves. Alas, the observed facts did not fit this interpretation at all well. In the course of this long conflict the Army of Vietnam endured con- siderably more fatalities than did its several allies from overseas combined. In at least three of the years in question—1965, 1968 and 1972—it was badly unnerved by the fury of a Communist offensive, only to recover its poise and fight back hard and successfully. No mass defections ever occurred from it at all comparable to those the Kuomintang army suffered during its last year on the Chinese main- land. Resistance by militia in isolated hamlets was not seldom just as resolute than that by elite units in the field. Though uncertain as to what they might be fighting for, many of those concerned knew full well what they were fighting against.

Nor is South-East Asia the only region in respect of which

American liberalism has lately seemed too prone to vacillation and inconsistency. Taken together, Europe and the Mediterranean constitute another. Thus in October 1973, Senator Edward Kennedy sent a message to the Ankara meeting of the North Atlantic Assembly urging an early reduction of American force levels in the European theatre and airily averring that, "What the Russians are doing in the Middle East should not destroy our confidence that we can move beyond the Cold War in Europe".[12] Several days later he was in Brussels praising President Nixon for initiating a general war alert because of the Yom Kippur crisis.

Hubert Humphrey has also been guilty of dichotomised thinking in recent years apropos his assessment of the Soviet threat in Europe and the Middle East respectively. So again has Edward Kennedy in his differential reaction to insurgent terrorism by the Palestinian extremists on the one hand and the IRA on the other.[13] Nor are these by any means the only examples that could readily be adduced of this kind of bifurcation.

Throughout this century the liberal wing of American politics (mainly located in the Democratic Party) has been the vanguard of its country's international involvement, most notably in its trans-Atlantic dimension. This being so, one is bound to doubt whether the current phase of retraction can be reversed until American liberalism has redefined its world view in terms that are not only internally consistent but also germane to the uniquely grave and manifold challenges Western democracy is likely to face in the 1980s.

What this redefinition may involve, however, is a synthesis with the "Pacific First" wing of American conservatism, especially as regards relations with China and also Japan. Even in the depths of inter-war isolationism the USA remained considerably interested in the fortunes of the Caribbean and the Pacific. Correspondingly, as the Cold War was reaching its climax in the early 1950s, such influential figures from the Middle and Far West as ex-President Hoover and Senators Dirksen, Knowland and Taft waxed indignant at what they saw as the creeping control of their Republican party and of their country by the Atlantic littoral—meaning, in particular, the liberal Ivy League colleges and Wall Street. However, their resentment at this found expression not so much in domestic "bread-and-butter" issues as in ideological and international ones. They placed more emphasis than did the mainstream Democrats and the Eastern Republicans on the need to combat the Communist threat from within; and also on the deterrent and punitive potentialities of air and seapower. They placed less on the need to keep wars limited or on the value of multilateral alliances and, more specifically, the commitment of more American combat troops to NATO Europe. Duly, Douglas MacArthur became their paradigm. And the Southern Democrats willingly gave them ear.

Ronald Reagan's recent concern with the future of the Panama Canal is a classic manifestation of this tradition. The steady shift in the demographic balance of the United States towards the south and west may be sufficient to augment its national influence between now and 1990.

In a sense, John Kennedy sought to create such a synthesis by strengthening the American military presence in both Europe and Asia in order to contain what was then regarded as (or at any rate treated as) the monolithic Sino-Soviet bloc. Yet Richard Nixon was to trump this by his personal *détente* with Chairman Mao; and Mr Nixon, with his political base in Orange County in Southern California, was an archetypal "Pacific Firster". But now the ball lies at the feet of Jimmy Carter; and his ability to play it could be enhanced by his own curiously liberal-cum-conservative political stance.

Another trend that has been closely associated (emotionally if not logically) with the "Come Home America" syndrome is a decreased effort apropos pure and applied scientific research. During FY 1976, aggregate spending by the United States on research and development will amount to 38 billion dollars; and of this 21 billion will be federal, about half of this second figure being earmarked for the Department of Defense. Impressive though this performance still looks, however, the total outlay is slightly lower than in 1967 and represents a fall as a percentage of GNP from 3·0 to 2·2. Furthermore, a decrease in funding for advanced education is likely to mean that, come 1985, the number of Ph.D graduands in such fields as physics and mathematics will be some 60 per cent fewer than now.[14]

However, when assessing the exact implications of such changes (plus the collateral ones on the Soviet side) for the shifting balance between American and Soviet technology, one needs to proceed with caution. This whole subject is not one about which we have a good track record of prediction. In 1945 the official American expectation was that the Russians would take not four years to produce a nuclear bomb but anything from 15 to 40, the explanation being found in the essentially crude and illiberal character of the

Soviet system. Then, during the 1950s, informed opinion throughout the West drastically reacted against this euphoria. Easily the largest contributory factor was the launching of Sputnik though subsidiary ones included various aeronautical developments and the launching, in 1959, of the world's first nuclear-driven surface ship. Typically, the inference drawn was that further dramatic breakthroughs, nuclear-driven aircraft or whatever, would result from the concentrated technological thrust made possible by the USSR's centralised system of government and by the uniquely high prestige accorded applied science by her propaganda machine.

But by the early 1970s, the failure of these dire predictions to be borne out by events had persuaded many observers in Washington and elsewhere to go back on the other tack: to insist that this "technology gap" would not only continue but actually widen through 1980 and beyond. They began to ask how a society could possibly succeed in high technology when its run-of-the-mill goods and services were so consistently tawdry.

So now it behoves us not to lurch once again to extremes and conclude that, by 1990, Soviet technologists will be 12 feet tall when, in fact, they may barely be seven. For one thing, one of the most intractable aspects of lag may be entrepreneurial, an insufficient flair for integrating diverse tasks to one exotic end—e.g. a cruise missile or a fusion reactor. The elitist concentration of talent in "scientific cities" may not be a complete answer to this nagging Soviet problem.

Conversely, however, we should not underestimate the geopolitical implications of even modest swings in technological and managerial advantage, especially in the military sphere. What has thus far been a persistent Soviet shortfall in aircraft design has been discussed by this author before; and has been adduced by him as a basic explanation of the most satisfactory outcome of successive air battles over Korea, the Formosan Straits, North Vietnam, the Sinai Desert and the Golan Heights.[15] Suffice to observe that, if the encounters had gone the other way in any of these areas, the contemporary world situation might have looked a lot more disagreeable to the West than, in fact, it does.

Notes

1. For a fuller discussion of background considerations, see the author's "The Manifold Duality: A Study of Soviet–American Relations", in *RUSI and Brassey's Defence Yearbook 1974*, Brassey's, London 1974, pp. 55–70.

2. *The Times*, 9 August 1974.

3. Maxwell D. Taylor, *The Uncertain Trumpet*, Stevens and Co. London 1959, p. 136.

4. B. H. Liddell-Hart, *Deterrent or Defence*, Stevens and Co., London 1960, p. 43.

5. For a lively and, indeed, disconcerting exploration of this theme see Peter Wiles "The Declining Self-Confidence of the Super-Powers", *International Affairs*, Vol. 47 No. 2, April 1971, pp. 289–301.

6. Michel Tatu, *The Guardian and Le Monde Weekly*. 28 August 1971.

7. E.g. Zbigniew Brzezinski "U.S. Foreign Policy: The Search for Focus", *Foreign Affairs*, Vol. 51 No. 4, July 1973, pp. 708–27.

8. McGeorge Bundy, *The Strength of Government*, The Harvard University Press, Cambridge 1968, pp. 55–6.

9. William F. Kaufman, *The McNamara Strategy*, Harper and Row, New York 1964, pp. 316–17.

10. David Halberstam, *The Best and the Brightest*, Barrie and Jenkins, London 1972, pp. 273–5.

11. Robert E. Kennedy, *To Seek A Newer World*, Doubleday and Co., New York 1967, pp. 169–221.

12. *The Daily Telegraph*, 23 October 1973.

13. E.g. "Ulster is an International Issue", *Foreign Policy*, No. 11. Summer 1973, pp. 57–71.

14. *The Economist*, 5 June 1976.

15. E.g. *European Security, 1972–80*, RUSI, London 1972, p. 74.

16

The European Balance

(a) EASTERN EUROPE: AN ARRESTED REFORMATION?

Hopefully, Ignazio Silone's quip to Palmiro Togliatti that the last war will be fought between the Communists and the ex-Communists will never come true on the world stage. Nevertheless, it may prove peculiarly apposite to the Soviet bloc in Eastern Europe in the 1980s and beyond.

Underlying all the separatist influences at work is a veritable patchwork of cultures and historical associations. As much can immediately be seen in the profound dissimilarity between the East Germans and the Poles, the two nations astride the highly strategic corridor known as the North European plain. Thus the East German regime bears many hallmarks of its Lutheran—not to say Prussian—heritage, whereas Roman Catholicism remains the bedrock of a deep sense of nationhood in a Poland tempered by centuries of strife against Russians or Germans or both.

During its brief history Czechoslovakia, too, has had to endure onslaughts from each of these directions in turn. However, it has lacked the kind of homogeneity which has enabled Poland to resist them with fervour. In this weakness is to be seen some part of the successive explanations for the tragic climaxes of 1938, 1948 and 1968.

The pattern in what used to be called the Balkans is even more diverse, the biggest single cleavage being one which can be traced back to the partition of the Roman Empire in 395 AD. In modern times, the resultant dichotomy has appeared as the basically Catholic territories of Hungary, Croatia and Slovenia against the districts to their south and east: the latter are largely Eastern Orthodox in some shape or form, although other faiths—notably Islam—have prevailed in particular localities.

Here, as in the USSR, communal identities—be their roots religious, linguistic or what—remain today much less corroded by economic and cultural evolution than is very generally the case west of the Iron

231

Curtain. But such corrosion, along with other shifts in social and political perception, will inexorably continue, thanks not least to the urbanization consequent upon rapid industrialisation. Thus by 1973 Romania had fixed a target for steel output of 20,000,000 tons in 1990. In other words, it was aiming to produce then three-quarters as much as Britain, a highly industrialised country with three times the population of Romania, had achieved in 1973.

One respect in which the Eastern European countries are already far ahead of the Soviet Union is in the diffusion of the youth revolt, at any rate in its less directly political aspects. Thus Bulgaria has always been regarded as having peculiarly strong pan-Slav affinities with Moscow. Yet three years ago the Prosecutor-General in Sofia felt obliged to publish an article warning Bulgarian youth against an infectious disrespect for society's norms as expressed through "perverted tastes . . . abnormal and trite Western fashions . . . long hair, disfiguring beards, and extremely short skirts". Satire is one of the easier ways in which these counter-cultural upwellings can be canalised into political protest.

In the light of which one may surmise that, in the period under review, the Soviet Union will become ever more preoccupied with its mirror image of the "domino theory". By this is meant its anxiety lest liberalising influences from the West spread through, say, Czechoslovakia to Poland, then on into Lithuania and so into Mother Russia. All the talk about the "limited sovereignty" of the "Socialist Commonwealth" adduced to justify the invasion of Czechoslovakia in 1968 was, in effect, a strident reaffirmation of the notion of falling dominoes; and this, one may note, at the very time when such thinking was being scornfully rejected throughout the West in respect of South-East Asia.

Obviously, one counter to this threat still at the USSR's disposal is open military intervention, perhaps followed—as it was in Hungary and Czechoslovakia—by the reintroduction of a Soviet garrison. Another is clandestine intelligence operations. A third is a progressive tightening of the multinational military integration achieved through the Warsaw Pact.

The extraordinary extent to which both the political and the military command structures of this alliance have been integrated and are Soviet-dominated has frequently been remarked.[1] Suffice now to emphasise that there are certain major categories of weapons system which none of the other member states has ever possessed: strategic missiles and bombers; missile-firing and nuclear-driven submarines; cruisers and helicopter carriers. Nor should we disregard a long-standing Soviet disinclination to position any nuclear warheads with the armed services of other members, even though these retain many units suitable for tactical nuclear delivery. In all probability, too, their stocks of chemical weapons are either small or non-existent.

No doubt in the 1980s this two-tier relationship will be blurred by a vigorous re-equipment programme at all levels in response to continuous, and indeed accelerating, innovation in weapons technology. However, it is improbable that it will substantially be modified in respect of any of the particulars just mentioned. On the contrary, at least the longer-range cruise missiles are likely to be added to the categories which are kept exclusively a Soviet preserve.

Then there is the Council for Mutual Economic Assistance (COMECON), founded in 1949 as the Soviet bloc's answer to Marshall Aid and OEEC. For its first few years, it served virtually as a cloak for the Stalinist pattern of direct and quasi-colonial relationships between the smaller countries and Mother Russia. But Khrushchev loosened these bilateral bonds and sought to promote instead full regional integration under the control of supranational institutions. Thanks largely to Romanian hostility, his endeavour failed.

After the crisis in Czechoslovakia in 1968, however, another big drive was launched to intermesh the "Socialist Commonwealth" members more completely in economic terms and to realise, as part and parcel of the same process, useful economies of scale. Thus an elaborate programme adopted in principle in 1971 envisaged extensive functional integration, especially in advanced technology fields, by 1986–91.

This drive has been a partial success. Even Romania joined the COMECON investment bank that came into operation at the beginning of 1971; and within two years this bank had sponsored 26 major projects in six countries. But since 1973 the USSR's main concern has been the promotion of a common energy policy—i.e. inducing the smaller COMECON countries to rely on the USSR for oil, thereby confirming a dependence in military strategic terms and generating an ever-growing need for roubles to pay for this now costly product. Quite possibly, this policy thrust will be relaxed somewhat in the 1980s, as the oil shipments involved become more burdensome. But at present all these states save Romania get at least

75 per cent of their oil imports from the USSR. Romania gets nil from that quarter.[2]

Were this complicated matrix of quasi-imperial Soviet control gradually to be dismantled, the several countries of Eastern Europe could conceivably evolve towards some quite agreeable patterns of social democratic pluralism. But the domino theory apart, one reason why this stipulation is unlikely to be met for some time yet is to be found in an equivocal attitude towards Soviet suzerainty on the part of the national Communist leaders. However constrictive they themselves may find it, they are not unaware of its potential value as a means of shoring up their own position against popular unrest.

The career of Wladyslaw Gomulka bears out this point all too well. His rehabilitation in 1956, in defiance of Soviet pressure, had seemed to usher in an era in which Polish Marxism would prove more authentic and hence more virile. A "concordat" was signed with the Catholic Church. The secret police was chastened. Most arable land was returned to private hands.

Twelve years later it became clear that this "national road to communism" was failing to keep abreast of rising and diversifying expectations. Gomulka's attempt to justify participation in the invasion of Czechoslovakia as "a patriotic, nationalist and internationalist duty" must be seen against the background of extensive student riots in his own country, riots met by thousands of arrests and call-up notices. Two years later he fell as a direct result of several days of bloody conflict between workers and troops in the Baltic ports.

Not that the ambivalence here being identified is confined to the local political leaderships alone. Apparently, close links have long obtained between the indigenous secret police forces and the KGB.[3] By the same token, one must assume that there are quite a few Lin Piaos (see Chapters 13 and 21) in the officer corps of the several Eastern European armies. Unfortunately, though much academic research has been done in the West on civil–military relations in the USSR and also in China, hardly any has yet been done on those in the Eastern European members of the Warsaw Pact.

Granted that every Communist country, like every other one, is *sui generis* to quite an extent, there is none which serves better than does Yugoslavia as a measure of how readily, in the absence of Soviet interference, Eastern Europe as a whole might progress towards the social democratic pluralism alluded to above. This is because, ever since her expulsion from the Soviet bloc in 1948, Belgrade has been confusedly searching for a *via media* (in internal affairs no less than external) between the relatively capitalistic West and Muscovite centralism. A fundamental law passed as early as 1950 laid down that each industrial enterprise should be managed through a Works Council elected by all the employees therein. Soon afterwards, a good 80 per cent of all arable land was decollectivised. Reforms passed in 1953 and 1963 confirmed the federal character of the constitution: it was to be the only federal one in Eastern Europe until the 1969 changes in Czechoslovakia.

In due course, too, market forces were given freer play in the Yugoslav domestic economy and emigration made easy. Several billion dollars of Western aid were accepted in the 1950s and 1960s; and now there is some commercial investment by the West in Yugoslavia and *vice versa*. Indicative of the prevailing ethos, too, is the maintenance of a modicum of press freedom, this in spite of a recent reaction towards illiberalism.

Needless to say, one fount of the recurrent illiberalism lies in the misgivings President Tito himself entertains about the cohesion of this federation after his demise. Several years ago, a 23-man Presidential Council was brought into being, its composition being based—first and foremost—on the principle of geographical balance; and Josip Tito then agreed to stay in power until 1976 (i.e. his 85th year) to give this "collective Presidency" a chance to take root.

However, constitutional amendments enacted in 1974 reduced the membership of the Council to nine. Meanwhile, the Communist Party gained considerable extra leverage within the machinery of government. In other words, the Yugoslav ship of state was on a centralist tack once more.

Nor could anybody claim that all aspects of Yugoslavia's economic performance boded well for Belgrade's essay in devolutionary Marxism. Even as far back as 1971 the annual inflation rate exceeded 15 per cent whilst early in 1975 it was 30 per cent. Repeated trade deficits and excess labour supply (500,000 unemployed in 1975) have been contained only by heavy emigration (900,000 at the 1974 peak).

Inevitably, the country's unsatisfactory economic performance at once exposes and accentuates the shortcomings of the self-management movement in industry. True, this concept continues to enjoy firm official backing, as witness the recent division of such large and multifarious concerns as the Split shipyard into more specific working groups, each with a fair measure of autonomy over its own account-ing and production planning. All the same, the fruits of the movement to date are sufficiently mixed overall to warrant scepticism about its long-term value from either the economic or the social standpoint.[4] As regards the latter, one study of a range of enterprises with *c.* 150,000 councillors between them found that, whereas in 1960 some 76 per cent were semi-skilled or unskilled, by 1970 the percentage had dropped to 50. Suffice to reflect that to visit Yugoslavia today is by no means to be persuaded that the problem of alienation at work has been wafted away from there.

Meanwhile, the tensions between the individual states and the federal government persist, not least because they are rooted in the stark facts of differential development. As one moves south across and beyond the dividing line of 395 AD mentioned above, one descends a steep economic gradient. Kosovo's average living standard is less than a quarter of Slovenia's.

Among some of the less well-placed minorities, such as the 1,500,000 Albanian "Shiptars" in Kosovo and districts nearby, separatist sentiments linger yet. However, these are of less moment than the resentment Slovenia and more especially Croatia feel at being made to support, through federal fiscal policies and the pooling of foreign earnings, their poorer neighbours. Moreover, their adverse feelings have been exacerbated by the steady growth of the old Serbian capital of Belgrade and a not unrelated preponderance of Serbians in such federal services as the diplomatic corps and the army general staff.

In the Croat case, terrorism by militants was posing an active security threat by the early 1970s. Accordingly, Croatia was the first state to be focused on in a big purge of separatist elements which began in December 1971. A follow-up campaign continued through 1975 in various parts of Yugoslavia and against "cominformists, neo-stalinists, bureaucratic-etatists, unitarists, Rankovicites, irreden-tists, nationalists of all hues and reactionary clergy". As in the USSR, the dilemmas posed by multi-communalism make the authorities all the more sensitive about individual dissent. Thus in October 1976 a district judge was found guilty of publishing anony-mously and abroad an article backing assertions about massacres of Slovene militia by Tito's partisans at the end of World War II. He was sentenced to five years in jail.

Agreed that East Germany, Poland, Hungary and Bulgaria have no such problem of communalism to contend with. Agreed, too, that none of us feels as sure as once he did about the preconditions for an open but stable society anywhere. Even so, the experience of a non-aligned Yugoslavia across nearly three decades does suggest strongly that the right balance will only be struck in Eastern Europe by the regimes becoming much more Western in character and purpose than either the USSR or their own ruling oligarchies can be expected to allow this side of 1990. And if this inference be correct, it can only mean that Eastern Europe will get more and more tense as the 1980s progress; and that cannot but complicate the security problem for Western Europe, if only by virtue of the anomalous situations of Yugoslavia and West Berlin.

(b) WESTERN EUROPE: A NEW RENAISSANCE?

Bearing in mind Napoleon's contention that the moral is to the physical as three is to one, it could be claimed that the challenge of European defence is not predominantly military in any esoteric sense. Instead it could fairly be regarded as, first and foremost, an acid test of whether the Western world has the solidarity needed to deter aggression. Will individual nations remain resolved to defend their own territory and liberty? Can this resolve be satisfactorily subsumed by a higher loyalty, European or Atlanticist? If the answers to these questions be affirmative, then surely—one might argue—a NATO alliance of over 550 million people enjoying, in 1974, an income of 2,750 billion dollars (i.e. 33 times the United States defence budget for that year) will have no problem.

Yet the distinction between the basic will and its technical application is not as easy to preserve as that. Those same idiosyncrasies of history and geography as give to the Atlantic community (and especially its European wing) both the strengths and the weaknesses of social pluralism help make the defence task analytically complex. Indeed, the very reason why the test here referred to is an acid one is that the interplay of geography and psychology renders the nature of a critical threat utterly imponderable. How much territory would an aggressor want to acquire in Central Europe in order to gain some kind of moral ascendancy? Could it ever be worth his while to seize and retain just a few square miles of territory? Or would he always be obliged to capture a major city plus much surrounding countryside?

Or would a dramatic raid by land or air, after the manner of the Israelis, be his best option?[5]

The nub of the dilemmas thus posed is that even an action which had but a trivial effect on the military balance of power within the region might still be of great propaganda value. Contrariwise, it might not.

Nor is the penumbra of uncertainty in any wise reduced by the USSR's perennial concern with the European theatre of operations, a concern that has not infrequently exceeded the bounds of needful prudence.[6] Nor by the lack of a clear-cut divide, geostrategically speaking, between Western Europe and a hardly less diverse (and much more traumatised) Eastern Europe. The West's commitment to lend military assistance to Yugoslavia is characterised by a studied ambiguity uncomfortably reminiscent of that evident in the United States guarantee to South Korea before June 1950. Meanwhile, West Berlin's tactical vulnerability is paralleled by its socio-economic weakness: an ageing population, low investment, heavy subsidisation and urban congestion. What is more, illicit interference with its access routes still takes place from time to time. We shall be lucky if we get through 1990 without another military crisis being focused on West Berlin, thereby necessitating countervailing action elsewhere.

To such persistent problems can be added certain burgeoning ones. Among them is nuclear control in the broadest sense. The old fear was that, were NATO to fade away, West Germany would join with others in the attempted creation of a grand European nuclear deterrent. The corresponding fear for the 1980s ought to be that, in the given eventuality, a good half dozen European states would opt individually for simple deterrents of the "bee-sting" or reflex retaliation kind. By so doing, they might set in motion a whole train of nuclear proliferation into the Middle East and beyond.

Grossly unsatisfactory though such an outcome would be for all the parties concerned, it might appear a sight less so than either attempting to counter Soviet nuclear warheads with machine-gun fire or else abandoning all pretensions of defence. Sweden is as good a test case as any. My own impression when discussing these matters in Stockholm late in 1974 was that the notion of going nuclear in the military sense had been pushed far to one side by the overwhelming majority of politicians and officials. Yet the analysis by Major-General Sköld quoted in a different context in Chapter 3 highlights, if only obliquely, some of the grave contradictions in the present posture, contradictions that could not be contained except within the continental context of a NATO-Warsaw Pact equilibrium of terror.

Thus, although it is acknowledged on all sides that Sweden has "no possibilities" of surviving assault with a large number of nuclear bombs, importance is still attached to her being able to ride out a small number.[7] Later on, the prospective appearance of much lower yield nuclear weapons able to be directed with high precision is alluded to: "Such a development would indisputably change the situation also of Sweden. The debate on nuclear weapons of the 1950s would have renewed relevance".[8]

About nuclear control within the Atlantic Alliance, only this much must now be said. The deterrent case for bilateral nuclear coordination between Britain and France and within an alliance matrix rests as it was,[9] save that, as the 1980s progress, the ramification of cruise missile technology may make French expertise in the means of strategic delivery less exclusive than it currently appears. Meanwhile, the tactical strains imposed on NATO by the impending end of "conventional war" may militate strongly in favour of a "lowering of the threshold" at which battle zone nuclear weapons may be employed. But this does not mean that the principle of tight central, and ultimately political, control of these devices is automatically undermined thereby. All will depend on collateral changes in the size and shape of this nuclear panoply.

Towards the other end of the scale of in-theatre violence lies another matter unduly neglected by NATO planners. It is the growing urbanization of Western Europe, a state of affairs which could favour the Defence but which is likely, above all, to favour whichever side has taken most account of it. A 1973 extrapolation suggested that the aggregate urban population of France, West Germany and Italy, which was an estimated 82,000,000 in 1968, would double between then and the year 2000.[10] Correspondingly, one can infer from a Hudson Institute study of the tactical implications of "urban sprawl" that if, in 1990, a double envelopment had forced what we currently know as Northern Army Group back onto, say, a Bremerhaven–Hanover–Aachen axis, the war a battalion commander fights would then become very predominantly for urban precincts.[11]

Urbanization is, of course, largely a function of general economic and social evolution. And, in this connection, one should note that its momentum may be moderated in Europe as elsewhere by one of the more dramatic of the contemporary changes throughout the Western world: a widespread and sustained fall in the birth rate. This has manifold implications, civilian as well as military, for Western Europe in particular. Therefore, it is worth dwelling on awhile at this point.

The interconnecting causes seem chiefly to be the advance of contraceptive knowledge, women's liberation, deferment of marriage and what the West Germans call *konsumterror*—the pressure to spend more on consumer durables, holidays in the sun etc. Now it is true that, historically, demographic adjustments in advanced societies have proved peculiarly hard to predict, as witness the misplaced British conviction in the 1930s and 1940s that our population faced imminent decline.[12] Yet one is bound to say, too, that the present trend does convey an impression of relentlessness. From a near post-war peak of *c.* 1,050,000 in 1964, the United Kingdom figure for live births recorded annually fell to *c.* 850,000 in 1972 and just below 700,000 in 1975.

One thing this development will, or at any rate should, do is to choke off any lingering disposition in continental Western Europe to revert to all-professional services *à la* Britain, Canada and the United States. The narrower the numerical base of the age-group concerned, the more likely it is that, in the continental environment, an equilibrium between manpower availability and manpower requirements will be struck by short-period conscription as opposed to volunteer service.

What it ought not to be allowed to do is justify the wholesale displacement of NATO's present philosophy by one of territorial defence in depth by lightly-armed militia—maybe female as well as male. Granted, militia could make a valuable contribution to the defence of West Germany, its urban areas included. Quite legitimately, too, there has been pressure over the years (not least from across the Atlantic) for a fuller use in field formations of mobilisable reservists. Nor has this plea necessarily been rendered otiose by the impending acceleration in the evolution of the equipment and tactics of major units.

Even so, territorial defence in great depth represents, in fact, an exceptionally uneconomic use of available manpower. Furthermore, it is almost irrelevant to some of the more subtle stratagems an enemy might employ. So is it to the problem of how to induce Italy and prospectively Spain to make a contribution to the central front in Germany. To which one must add that it would always be terribly difficult, not to say thoroughly invidious, to prepare hedonistic, fluid and open societies for a phenomenon as bitterly all-devouring as partisan warfare. Nor would militia defence be much help on Western Europe's ever more vital and ever more vulnerable maritime flanks.

One of several respects in which the emergent military technologies pose acute problems for NATO Europe is arms standardisation. Over the last five years or so, an awareness has spread rapidly that, as a rule, the strongest argument in favour of this goal is not the sharing of development costs but operational compatibility. And with this awareness has come a stronger resolve to do something about it. However, there is now a serious danger that commonality will be sought on the basis of undue technological conservatism, since the strains in any case inherent in multinational negotiation may thereby be moderated. Moreover, this danger is aggravated by the prior need to accommodate long-standing national differences over tactical doctrine. A well-known example is a persistent predilection on the part of the Royal Air Force for deep strike and on the part of the Bundeswehr for close air support. Also the wider reliance of insular Britain on air and naval power plus its related preference for volunteer armed forces.[13]

Furthermore, such divergences in tactical perspective are only part and parcel of a whole variety of contrasts in national interests and attitudes, contrasts that by 1990 will be diminished but by no means to vanishing point. One cause of Italy's social malaise is a persisting tradition of "city-state" localism. Likewise, one factor behind its having an unduly low profile in intra-European politics may be a preference on the part of its nationals for quiet diplomacy within such multinational bureaucracies as those of NATO and the EEC. An analogy with the papal legates of the Middle Ages springs readily to mind.

But in civil affairs, too, the United Kingdom stands out as a country possessed of exceptionally pronounced singularities. One external aspect is the now little-acclaimed special relationship with the United States. For all the talk about 1776, 1944 and a common language, this nexus has lately been largely a function of workaday diplomacy. In a whole range of situations around the world— Gibraltar, Malta, Cyprus, Jordan, the Gulf, the Indian Ocean, Malaysia, Hong Kong, Rhodesia, Nigeria ... —British and American officials have had more business to do together than either has with any other member of the Atlantic Alliance. This was less true in 1976 than in 1966. But it does not follow that it will be absolutely untrue come 1986.

Internally, the United Kingdom has become very much a test case of the staying power or otherwise of devolutionary pressures. Currently, legislation is being promoted on the assumption that political nationalism in Scotland, in particular, is no mere transient protest against the tendencies of the age but a culmination of them. Yet although the population of Scotland is barely five million, the two-way migration across the border with England runs at a rate of a million a year. Surely you cannot have that degree of miscibility without a progressive erosion of the separate Scottish and, of course, English identities through intermarriage and in countless other ways.

In this case as elsewhere, language is one of the best indices of cultural convergence. Thus whilst between 1961 and 1971 there was a marginal increase in Gaelic-speaking across Scotland as a whole, there was an ominous decline in the heartland of that language, north and west from the Grampian mountains. Meanwhile, the local dialects of English fade slowly but remorselessly both sides of the River Tweed.

So, too, with Wales. Here, or at any rate in the old Celtic strongholds in and around Snowdonia, great importance has been attached to the linguistic dimension, the Welsh Language Society having 4,000 members. Even so, the proportion of the 2,725,000 people in the Principality able to speak Welsh was given as only 21 per cent in the 1971 census as compared with 26 in the 1961 and 50 at the turn of the century. So by 1990 it may not exceed 10.

The key to buttressing parliamentary democracy in Britain does not lie in the proliferation of devolutionary machinery that may not meet grass-roots resentment against "big government" and which may, in fact, make the executive arms less responsive by dividing responsibilities in too ambiguous a fashion. Instead it lies in bringing social aims and economic prowess more into line with each other by effecting throughout Britain a managerial revolution that touches everything from the trade unions and the large corporations to Whitehall and the learned institutes.

The plain truth is that thus far Britain has adjusted too easily to the end of Western Europe's role as the omphalos of the world. It was the only European participant in World War II not to know the misery of occupation. It disengaged from the largest empire ever made with an all too consummate ease. Accordingly, it waxed too complacent. As late as 1962 a Reith Lecturer opined that "Britain is well-placed to give a lead to other countries" in virtuous humility because "we have succeeded in accepting the loss of a great deal of our former power and influence without losing our self-respect".[14] Today we wonder whether humility is such a perfect virtue when it seems to be so closely associated with economic enfeeblement.

Not even such apprehensive assessors of Britain's immediate prospects as Professor Milton Friedman exclude the possibility of a mild "economic miracle" over the next ten years, this being based on infrastructural changes plus the North Sea hydrocarbons and being, one might add, especially liable to benefit Scotland. But what needs be borne in mind, is that Britain as a whole has already fallen too far behind its European peers to avoid further slippage even if it does attain similar growth rates percentagewise. Thus in 1974 Britain's Gross National Product was barely two-thirds that of France and less than half Federal Germany's. So its contribution to the reborn Europe will be more as an enduring bastion of liberal democracy than as an industrial power house.

Almost up to the present day the extra-European roles of Britain and France have tended to abrade each other, tangentially at any rate. Taking the broad view, however, some strategic involvement outside Europe remains one of several key features Britain and France share with each other but not with any of their neighbours. Nuclear status and permanent membership of the UN Security Council are two more. A fourth is a long experience of national statehood. So it is not very surprising that Paris and London are, along with Copenhagen and Dublin, the main foci of the burgeoning resistance to the unification of Western Europe being pushed beyond a loosely confederal stage at any time in the foreseeable future.

Where Britain and France may eventually find themselves on the opposite sides of a fence is over whether EEC's full membership should be further enlarged to include, as is postulated, Greece by 1980; Spain, Portugal and maybe Norway by 1990; and Turkey by 1995. The present Labour government in London is supporting the Greek application as proffering, in its opinion, a valuable contribution to the building of "a new and wider Europe". In doing so, it is upholding a fairly strong British predilection in favour of a European confederation that is extensive rather than one which is closely knit.

This predilection can be directly traced back to the late 1950s, to the attempt by the Macmillan administration to promote a large European Free Trade Area as an alternative to the EEC. In a looser sense, it represents the continuation of a traditional awareness of the strategic significance of the flanks of Europe, a tradition built by Churchill, Nelson, Wellington, Marlborough and—if you like— Cromwell.

Being themselves set firmly in the centre of the European constellation, France and Germany have not infrequently adopted a different standpoint. The late Chancellor Adenauer and his successor, Dr Kiesinger, were among those who have warned against the EEC growing so large as to be at best unwieldy and at worst amorphous; and President de Gaulle was, on sundry occasions, most explicit about this danger. Likewise, in July 1969, President Pompidou pointedly observed at a press conference that Britain's joining the EEC "could not but mean the membership of a number of other countries" and therefore "raises difficult questions and involves profound changes for the Community"; and seven months later he firmly and publicly reiterated the point whilst in the United States.

True, the deliberations of the EEC summit at The Hague that December confirmed that the four accessions then envisaged would not automatically be precluded by anxiety on this score. Yet the point as stated is fair and accordingly merits more attention, especially in Whitehall and Westminster, than it has received. One has lately been fortified in this view by certain unofficial but authoritative reactions in London.[15] Also by the reservations expressed by the Irish government and within the EEC Commission about the early accession of Greece. Also by a growing awareness of how much stress would be generated either by accommodating Greece without Turkey or else by accommodating a Turkey that today ranks as a newly developing state and which has become much more footloose in foreign policy this last dozen years or so.[16]

As things stand, the EEC looks a tolerably symmetrical polygon. Each of its four largest nations has a population of between 50 and 65 million whilst the other five muster 32. At the centre lies France, a country which can not only boast a dynamic economy and (despite some dilution by anglophone cosmopolitanism) a richly autonomous culture but which is also possessed of large, well-balanced and future-oriented armed forces. Traditionally, its large Communist Party has been more Muscovite than has Italy's, as witness its decidedly low-key criticism of the invasion of Czechoslovakia. But this adverse factor seems at least offset by the political Centre and Right having greater inner strength in Paris than in Rome.

On the other hand, even the existing EEC is beset by serious problems of institutional compatibility, problems that should have first claim on its political energies. First of all, there is the European Parliament to build up. After which, attention ought urgently to be directed to the Community's functional links with other multinational bodies: OECD, NATO, the Council of Europe, Western European Union—to say nothing of COMECON, the IAEA and the UN.

Certainly, the multiple dovetailing required will not be effortless. For one thing, the distinction between consultative institutions and executive ones is easier to draw in text-books than to preserve in practice. For another, sharp differences in priority on this score already exist within the Atlantic Alliance, whilst others are liable to emerge. Suppose, for example, a scheme was launched to form within NATO a Western European Command geographically coincident with EEC. In some capitals, including Paris and London, it might be almost automatically assumed that its commander-in-chief would himself be a Western European. Yet in others, notably Bonn and Washington, it might seem imperative (for nuclear reasons) that the incumbent be American. Meanwhile, some might be asking whether Ireland could stay inside the EEC yet outside NATO. Likewise others might wonder whether a Spain in NATO but maybe not in EEC could be called on to dispatch a division or two to the Central Front in Germany.

Presumably, unravelling this tangle of loose ends would a be little less irksome all round if, in cultural and leisure pursuits, there was a greater sense of European togetherness. Thus in the academic world, and especially the social sciences, Western European perspectives might be more purposively cultivated in order to offset certain biases—e.g. the cult of behaviourism—which some of us see as too deeply ingrained between Berkeley and Boston. At all events, the groundwork for a modest endeavour along these lines already exists in various pan-European institutions plus such research foundations as Agnelli, Krupp, Nuffield and Volkswagen. None of the latter begins to rival the awesome might of Ford but quite a number are large by other standards.

But how far the Europe of the now enlarged Common Market should aspire to cultural identity in any more comprehensive sense is

9

doubtful. It is a question of what is desirable and also of what is feasible. The perennial struggle of the European film industries to preserve an effective autonomy, either separately or through co-production, has had mixed results to date. In television, on the other hand, European endeavours have been demonstrably successful. Yet in part this is because, at this early stage in the development of communications satellites, television is predominantly an intra-regional means of communication.

Arguably, in fact, the best hope for a distinctively European contribution to the wider world lies in international trade and aid, particularly apropos the Indian Ocean littoral. At present, the exports of EEC members to that all-important zone are over double the USA's and about 15 times the USSR's. All the same, any purposive co-ordination of effort would be a complex exercise in political economy.

In truth, political scientists have studied confederations too seldom over the years—preferring, as inherently neater topics, either federations or unitary states. And, in the virtual absence of definitive assessments, the myth has quietly arisen that confederations are bound to firm up with the passage of time. But they may be almost as liable to either collapse or fade away, particularly if external circumstances militate against them. For example, between Canada's achieving dominion status in 1867 and the Statute of Westminster in 1931, the British Commonwealth of Nations had strongly confederal attributes. But nobody would say that of the Commonwealth today.

All this being so, the best basis for working towards a firmly confederal EEC, one able to make a very positive contribution to the world of 1990, is a rejection of the euphoric assumption that such a consummation cannot but materialise. As Lord Snow once remarked, facile optimism is usually one of the chief barriers to genuine human progress.

Notes

1. E.g. *The Military Balance, 1975–76*, The International Institute for Strategic Studies, London, 1975, p. 11.
2. *The Economist*, 23 October 1976.
3. Richard F. Staar, *The Communist Regimes in Eastern Europe*, The Hoover Institution, Stanford 1967, pp. 278–9.
4. See "Economic Reform in Yugoslavia", *Political and Economic Planning*, Vol. XXXIV No. 502, PEP, London, 1968. Also Roy Moore, *Self-Management in Yugoslavia*, Fabian Research 281, Fabian Society, London 1970.

5. See the author's *European Security, 1972–80*, RUSI, London, 1972, p. 123.

6. See the author's "Towards the Superpower Deadlock", *The World Today*, Vol. 22 No. 9. September 1966, pp. 366–74.

7. Nils Sköld, *Defence Policy for the 1970's and 80's*, The Ministry of Defence, Stockholm, 1974, p. 11.

8. Ibid., p. 22.

9. *European Security, 1972–80*, op. cit. Chapter 5 (2).

10. Information Bulletin No. 4, The European Cultural Foundation, Amsterdam, 1973. Table 2.

11. Paul Bracken, "Urban Sprawl and NATO Defence", *Survival*, Vol. XVIII No. 6. November/December 1976, Fig. 1.

12. E.g. W. B. Reddaway, *The Economics of a Declining Population*, George Allen and Unwin, London 1939, and *Papers of the Royal Commission on Population*, Vol. III, HMSO, London 1950, p. 61.

13. Given its singular situation, the United Kingdom is undoubtedly right to rely entirely on voluntary enlistment. But, in fairness to its allies, it should accept unequivocally that the *quid pro quo* must be a comparatively large defence budget, measured as a percentage of GNP. The point is that, by definition, conscription entails considerable hidden costs.

14. G. M. Carstairs, *This Island Now*, Hogarth Press, London 1963. Chapter 6. Incidentally Professor Carstairs, though himself an Edinburgh psychologist, showed no interest on this occasion in political devolution.

15. E.g. William Wallace "Wider but weaker: the continued enlargement of the EEC", *The World Today*, Vol. 32, No. 3, March 1976, pp. 104–11.

16. See the author's "Turkey and the West", *RUSI Journal*, Vol. 121 No. 2, June 1976, pp. 63–7.

17

The Emergent Orient

Living as he did on the southern side of the great Asian cultural cleavage noted in the next chapter, the late Pandit Nehru of India was among the many sympathetic observers who misread the peculiarly East Asian departure known as Maoist Communism. He well realised that China would have the inner strength to modify classical Marxism-Leninism but clung to the callow assumption that it would thereby render it more eclectic and relaxed. In his case, the error was to be savagely mocked by the war of 1962.

All through the 20th century, in fact, the resilient toughness of the various East Asian peoples has been manifest in both their martial ardour and their economic dynamism. Crucial to it is a collectivist spirit which may itself stem from cultural homogeneity and from the absence, in this essentially agnostic civilisation, of the Church-versus-State and God-versus-Mammon dichotomies so familiar in the West.

Not that this trait is entirely beneficial. With it goes a certain inability to relate to other cultures except on a basis either of absolute rejection or else wholesale ingestion. Correspondingly, there are difficulties over the development of genuinely pluralistic modes within the body politic—e.g. the Western concept of constitutional opposition has yet to sink any very deep roots within this region.

Indubitably, the most remarkable element in the veritable economic miracle wrought by East Asia this last quarter of a century has been the achievement of Japan. At the end of World War II, the devastation and demoralisation were so severe that it was generally expected Japan would have to settle for living standards not very much above the Afro-Asian average. Instead, it got onto a secular growth curve which, though erratic, averaged ten per cent—probably the most dramatic example of large scale and sustained growth in the economic history of the world. Forecasts made several years ago suggested that the Gross National Product, measured at constant prices, would rise from 200 billion dollars in 1970 to anything between 1,500 and 4,500 billion at the turn of the century. Splitting the difference put the Japanese projection for the year 2000 close to the American one.[1]

Among the explanations are the immanent sociological ones identified by the late Ruth Benedict 30 years ago in her classic essay in cultural anthropology, *The Chrysanthemum and the Sword*. One says "essay" advisedly because one of the criticisms levelled against Miss Benedict, notably in a UNESCO survey of youth attitudes published in 1955,[2] was that she had wilfully discarded numerical survey techniques. Anticipating this objection, she herself had insisted that resolving the seeming contradictions in the underlying Japanese attitudes towards life could not be done by conducting opinion polls geared to Occidental parameters.[3] It is a dialectic that foreshadows in quite a striking fashion the one between the school which stresses literacy and that which stresses numeracy in modern futurology.

This being so, those of us who are disposed to play down the futurological value of "objective" mathematical techniques may make good cheer out of the impressive way some of Ruth Benedict's insights have stood the test of time. After all, it was she who foresaw that, as and when circumstances permitted, the Japanese would once again seek their "place of honour among the nations of the world" but this time through peaceful though purposive economic growth. One could fairly say, too, that, even in the 1970s, her sense of historical continuity is borne out in such major respects as the pliability of both the blue-collar and the white-collar labour force.

Not that such general considerations explain sufficiently Japan's prolonged boom. Some more specific and technical factors must be adduced as well. Although family planning has been promoted very effectively, the urban implosion has remained rapid, partly thanks to the sweeping land reform programme begun in 1946. Then again, OECD estimates that 39 per cent of the Japanese GNP was going into fixed capital formation in 1970, as against 25 per cent in West Germany, 18 per cent in the United Kingdom and 16 per cent in the United States. Other facets of applied economics could also be mentioned.

Be that as it may, many of the consequences of economic growth have been socially benign. Thus the average age at death has risen from 55 in the late 1940s to 74 today, whilst the infantile mortality record has become the best in the world; and all this despite the lack of adequate sewage disposal, a comprehensive public health service and a proper state pensions scheme![4]

On the other hand, there has been much to remind one of the Galbraithian contrast between private affluence and public squalor.

Not only sewage systems and social security but also water supply, recreational amenities and—above all—public housing finance have lagged badly; and with the sympathetic attitude towards business enterprise went, until recently, an utterly careless one towards pollution and congestion.

Nor have the ill effects of such imbalances in development been relieved in any wise by the ever mounting pressures on land space. One aspect of this is that the rural areas divide all too sharply into two types: stretches of steep and well-wooded mountain, very imposing but also hard of access, and coastal enclaves of farmland, husbanded too totally and exactly to leave much scope for recreation.

Yet despite the resultant exacerbation of social tension, the incidence of individual crime has remained tolerably low almost everywhere. But there are the big crime and protection syndicates which depict themselves as heirs to the Samurai tradition; and the young terrorists of the Japanese Red Army who seek to be equated with the *kamikaze* suicide pilots of 1944–45.

Kakuei Tanaka, the Prime Minister of Japan from 1972 to 1974, enunciated with singular fervour a comprehensive programme for "remodelling the Japanese archipelago" in which less emphasis would be placed on material expansion and more on such other human needs as "A congenial workplace, an emotionally rewarding life, and diverse opportunities for recreation". Among the particular objectives were a reversal of the drift of people from the countryside; the creation within industrial districts of spacious green belts, with shady parks and cattle pastures; and a general and drastic reduction in the proportion of industrial output from the Pacific Coast industrial belt—i.e. the area around a sinuous axis from Tokyo to Nagoya and Osaka in which half the population live.[5]

Alas, the ebullient Mr Tanaka was not blessed with the best of good fortune. Today he faces charges in connection with the Lockheed bribes scandal. Early in 1973 premature disclosure of his plans gave some extra twists to a land price spiral. Later that year Japan was to be hit especially hard by the energy crisis. Whereas in the previous three years industrial production had risen no less than 30 per cent, in the 12 months from June 1973 it actually dropped a little. Over the next two years a dramatic sales drive overseas was to spearhead a considerable recovery, this no doubt being facilitated by the strong underlying trend towards more knowledge-intensive exports.

Yet even through the second half of 1976, some symptoms of comparative stagflation persisted.

What this unsettling phase has served to highlight is Japan's extreme dependence on energy imports, over two-thirds being in the form of oil from the fractious Middle East. In 1970 only 17 per cent of its total energy supply came from domestic sources as against, for example, 55 per cent of Britain's and 91 per cent of the USA's. So it was not altogether surprising that at the end of 1973, acting explicitly in response to the Arab oil embargo, Tokyo altered substantially its declaratory policy on the Arab–Israel conflict.

Recent diplomatic realignments in the Western Pacific may have made the perennial Left–Right differences over foreign policy within Japan appear less stark than was previously the case. At the same time, however, they have aggravated the very real dilemmas this archipelago faces in respect of external security. On the one hand, it has proved exceptionally virile economically. Yet on the other, it would be very ill-placed to protect either its constituent islands or its vital sea-lanes against armed excursions from mainland territories perhaps beside themselves with material envy. The Russians, in particular, have not sweated and suffered the way they have since 1917 in order to come in third in the race to a trillion dollar economy.

Ever since 1952 Japan has sought to resolve this geostrategic contradiction by formal alliance with the USA. However, the anxieties the Japanese have always evinced about this nexus have lately been aggravated by the American swing towards introversion and by several particular episodes. Japanese susceptibilities were considerably ruffled by the unexpected *volte-face* in Washington's China policy in 1971. Then again, the bad taste left by Watergate was in no wise diminished by Japan having its own "clean politics" problem. Now the Lockheed scandal is tending to strengthen this association of ideas.

However, it cannot be said that much evidence yet exists of any switch to genuine self-sufficiency in defence, expenditure on which has still not risen to one per cent of GNP. What has been increasingly in evidence, on the other hand, is a resolve to lay firmer foundations in strictly economic terms for Japan's heavy imports of fuel and also of other raw materials. Thus contracts lately signed with Brazil provide for the construction there of a large aluminium smelter and for a big increase through 1980 in iron ore shipments from that quarter. Meanwhile, a wide range of other long-term arrangements are being explored. These might cover *inter alia* Australian uranium as well as Australian and Soviet natural gas and coking coal.

Even so, the general awareness that the world has entered an era in which international trade may be more prone to arbitrary interruptions, forceful or otherwise, inevitably casts some shadow over the hopes that have been expressed for this country's evolution, in the course of two or three decades, into the world's first post-industrial "garden society", a sociological and aesthetic gem. Even without this fresh uncertainty, indeed, the issue would be in some doubt. Thus two or three years ago, the Economic Planning Agency used its ultra-sophisticated Cosmo econometric model to work out the minimal pre-conditions for accommodating the burgeoning and variegation of national expectations to be anticipated in the period up to 1985. One conclusion was that a mean GNP growth rate of below seven per cent per year might place the requisite social expenditures acutely at risk; and yet now OECD is predicting an average growth rate for Japan of a relatively modest 6·2 per cent over the recovery period, 1974–80.

Nor has past dynamism guaranteed future tranquillity elsewhere in East Asia. On the contrary, nothing yet seen on this Earth bears more resemblance to *Nineteen Eighty-Four* than the way similarly oppressive regimes in South and North Korea perennially lean on each other in mutual self-justification. Invoking a threat of fascistic imperialism from the south, Kim Il-Sung continually strengthens his personal and familial grip on the means of persuasion and coercion in North Korea, perhaps his most spectacular purge being the virtual elimination of the army high command in 1968–69. Invoking the menace of alien communism, Park Chong-hui (who seized power in the South in 1961) uses a full panoply of repression (most notably, the Korean Central Intelligence Agency) to curb disaffected intellectuals, Christian activists and other pustules of dissent. Granted, his personality cult is not so pervasive as Kim's. Nor can he preclude infiltration so hermetically. But these are relatively minor qualifications to the common political reality.

In economic performance, too, the parallelism is close. Though in the first dozen years after the Korean War (1950–53), the North far outstripped the South, its growth abruptly retarded in the middle 1960s, bad agricultural policy and a tailing off of foreign aid being among the reasons. Meanwhile, the South boosted its averaged growth rate from an impressive eight per cent at the start of the

1960s to a remarkable 12 per cent at the decade's close. In addition, the birth rate was being brought well under control. Soon the indefatigable Herman Kahn was predicting that, come the turn of the century, South Korea, too, would enjoy living standards equivalent to those of the present day USA.

However, South Korea's economic boom has been export-led to a quite exceptional extent and has involved a deliberate switch to an oil-dependence amounting to 60 per cent of total energy needs. So, although South Korea did weather remarkably well the economic perturbations consequent upon "Yom Kippur", there must now be less assurance about the longer-term economic outlook. Obversely, both Koreas remain classic manifestations of the dangerous contradiction between economic dynamism and political immobilism. And this situation appears the more bodeful in the light of the historic role of Korea as a corridor of contact—peaceable and otherwise—between Japan and China.

Traditionally, China itself has tended to draw from the West either excessive praise or undue censure. Undeniably, during the 1950s and early 1960s, a negative stereotype was too prevalent, especially in the United States. To brand as "aggression" China's involvement in the Korean War was too simplistic. Gauche though Peking's intervention in Tibet clearly was, imputations by the Dalai Lama and others of calculated genocide should not have been accepted quite so uncritically as they were in some quarters.[6] And so on.

Nevertheless, we must resist the temptation just to replace the uglified stereotype with a prettified one, especially in the new situation created by the death of Chairman Mao. We do well to remember that our contemporary understanding depends too heavily on impressionistic reconnoitres by whistle-stop Marco Polos. For though the Bamboo Curtain may seem more graceful and translucent than the Iron Curtain ever did, it can block the free flow of facts and ideas every bit as effectively. Little comes out in the way of national economic statistics and there are good grounds for doubting the authenticity of such as do. Nor can the West really claim cognisance of a country in which the National People's Congress can meet for five days, as did China's in January 1975, without any Western correspondents being any the wiser until after the event.

Nor should we ignore a quite strong propensity to mutate the past, at least for the benefit of internal consumption. In the days before its split with Moscow and before the development of its own nuclear bomb, Peking solemnly wrote history as though the collapse of Imperial Japan was occasioned by, and only by, the Soviet Union's waging war on her.[7] More recently, the military contribution of Lin Piao has been drastically downgraded in the museums and elsewhere.

It would also be wrong to discount too glibly the more physical forms of repression. Towards the end of 1952 Peking averred that no fewer than two million "bandits" had been eliminated since the Communist take-over three years before. Perhaps it was more.

Since then such bloody repression has been absent from the Chinese scene. However, there may be a tendency to forget how savage individual maltreatment may be. Eric Chou, a political prisoner in the 1950s, has reported as follows, "For four years in Shanghai and later in Peking, I was alone in cells as small as seven feet by nine which contained only a wooden board, a blanket and a bucket . . . I was allowed no open air exercise and in my cell I was forced to sit all day with my back to the wall. Then, twice a day, came a sudden order 'Exercise!'. And for ten minutes I had to walk up and down the cell, whether I wanted to or not".[8] One is reminded of the prolonged physical and psychological torture of many United Nations prisoners-of-war during the Korean campaign. Also of the experience of various foreign hostages during the Cultural Revolution of 1966–69.

Indeed, the general excesses of this last-named episode are disturbing even in retrospect: industrial chaos, shattered universities, kangaroo courts in which young bullies terrorised their teachers, the thousands of casualties in street violence. . . . Nor could one feel at ease about a regime that went on saying how much it needed a masochistical purgation of this sort every few years. By the same token, it is hard to understand the view of Mrs Joan Robinson, Professor of Economics at the University of Cambridge, that "The Cultural Revolution makes the accusation of aggressiveness less plausible than ever".[9]

In addition, the Chinese Peoples' Republic has recurrently been prone to economic aberrations on the grand scale. Thus the intended Great Leap Forward in agriculture at the end of the 1950s was marred by wild over-optimism coupled with a flagrant disregard for ecological balance. Crop-planting densities were heedlessly doubled and forests ravaged. Purblind campaigns were launched against grain-eating birds, the massacre of sparrows reportedly passing the billion mark. An unduly cavalier attitude to the balance between Man and Natural Resources is also to be discerned in the failure to come properly to grips with family planning until 1969.

A similarly stark interplay of progress and regression is to be observed even within the narrower confines of scientific research and development. By the beginning of this decade some genuine and impressive advances had been registered, these in spite of the disruptions occasioned by the Soviet withdrawal of aid and then the Cultural Revolution. Electron microscopes and a radio-telescope had been built. A Space satellite was about to be launched. Thermonuclear military status had been attained. The first synthetic benzene plant in the world had been constructed. Nor is the above list of China's more exotic accomplishments in this sphere at all comprehensive. Nor has such progress been achieved through neglect of small and intermediate technology.

Yet against this must be set the negative connotations, not only for material well-being but also for political rationality, of the Maoist revival of traditional Chinese medicine. Included in this was herbalism, an approach that may well be of benefit in some cases. But included, too, was acupuncture: the sticking of needles into the skin at one or more of a 1,000 points distributed along a hypothetical network of "meridians" along which flow, according to ancient theory, the two complementary life forces—the Yin and the Yang. A specific disease is supposedly consequent upon a local imbalance of these forces, and hence susceptible to being cured by a puncturing of the appropriate meridian in the right place. A prick on the lobe of the left ear, say, might be deemed to pacify an inflamed appendix.

Nor does the evident fact that meridian theory may often serve as a most convenient idiom for hypnosis or allied psychological processes constitute a sufficient reason for retaining this superstition and all the needles that stem from it. Nor does its prevalence in some sportive circles elsewhere in the Far East and the wider world. By deliberately discouraging objective research and reformulation within the acupuncture school, the late Chairman Mao may have sown the seeds of a conflict between the political hierarchy and the medical profession every bit as damaging to Chinese biological science (and public rationality) as the Lysenko controversy was to Soviet in the 1940s.

Arguably, the dangers in any such acceptance of authoritarian obscurantism have been made all the graver in China by the volatile character of Education policy. Certain precepts are taken as axiomatic: the promotion of literacy; the creation of cadres which, being both "Red and expert", are able to spearhead the main axes of development; the ideological mobilisation and remoulding of the populace at large; and, of course, no private schools. Otherwise the turbulence has been great: "Types of schools, length of schooling, the nature of the schools on various levels, and the relations between schools are subject to constant change".[10]

At this stage, it is important thus to emphasise what an ideological typhoon modern China has so far been. For in the atmosphere of euphoria which prevails in the aftermath of the isolation and defeat of "the Gang of Four"—i.e. Madame Mao and her associates—hard upon the death of Chairman Mao, the presupposition is prevalent that the fanaticism they represent has been curbed decisively. What needs be remembered is that only a little while back received wisdom had it that the political thrust of post-Mao China was unlikely to be determined until after an interregnum of at least a year or two. And the experience of Chiang Kai-shek both before and after 1945 shows that it is not necessarily a conclusive advantage to start off on top in one of China's climacteric phases.

In fact, the eventual outcome (whatever that may mean) could well be determined by the malapropos progress of the Malthusian spectre: the pressure of population on, in particular, China's food resources. As regards the former, the birth rate does appear to have fallen during the 1970s at a rate which is quite unprecedented for a large territory. Nevertheless, authoritative estimates continue to be made which put the population of China in 1981 in the range 915 to 1,085 million, as against 540 to 555 some 30 years previously.

Official sources indicate that in 1971, and again in 1973, the aggregate yield of grain and potatoes was *c*. 250 million tons, though some Western analysts would say 225 was nearer the truth. Even on the former estimate, there has only been a 35 per cent increase since 1957 or 1963, to take two years which delimit the disastrous Great Leap Forward. It hardly constitutes a powerful recommendation for the "social transformation" especially associated with the introduction of the People's Communes in 1958. Nor was the way the 1975 National People's Congress felt obliged to endorse private or "sideline" agricultural plots as a constitutional right, this notwithstanding the vocal opposition of a purist faction evidently close to Madame Mao and, indeed, Mao Tse-tung himself.[11]

On the other hand, no Chinese below the age of 25 can recall life in the pre-People's Communes days. Therefore, the residual impact of the demoralisation this social upheaval caused could shrink quite rapidly from now on, especially if the limited but highly productive private plots receive more encouragement.

Furthermore, a form of the Green Revolution seems to be wending its way through China. Thus 90 per cent of the wheat land of Honan province was being sown with improved seeds by early 1974. By this time, too, the advance of land reclamation and water control throughout China was dampening down the crop fluctuations consequent upon climatic irregularities. This improvement is especially valuable in North China, traditionally the zone most plagued by droughts and floods and now that most susceptible to world climatic change.

Above all, there has been a big expansion in the use of chemical fertilisers. Already, the annual tonnage is likely to be comfortably in excess of 20,000,000 as against two or three million in the early 1960s. Even allowing for what may henceforward be a fairly steep decline in marginal returns, this trend is bound to be immensely beneficial, at least when combined with seed improvement.

But at the very heart of the Chinese rural revolution, in both its economic and its sociological dimensions, are still to be found the People's Communes. To be more precise, the massive reorganisation initiated in 1958 had three tiers. Typically, a commune had ten or twenty thousand people and worked perhaps 20,000 acres; and it was given a wide range of administrative, juridical and internal security functions. Within every such unit were established one or two dozen brigades and within every brigade up to ten teams. Evidently, a team or a brigade (depending on size) corresponds in general to a village and a commune to the hinterland of a market town.

Proof of the basic suitability of this triadic structure to date can be seen in the way it has survived, without drastic modification, the upheavals China herself has been through since its inception. One attraction has been its utility in mobilising labour (and to some extent capital as well) for a host of medium—and large-scale rural reconstruction projects. Among the examples observed by Han Suyin, ever a sensitive interpreter of the Orient to the Occident, has been a giant irrigation scheme begun in Anhwei province during the Great Leap Forward to link three rivers via numerous canals excavated among mountains and hills. Some 400,000 people from dozens of communes were involved in the basic construction.[12]

The obverse side of commune strategy is the quest for a large measure of single commune self-sufficiency, not only in food but in a range of basic and intermediate technologies. Two Australian scholars, E. L. Wheelwright and Bruce McFarlane, found that some of the communes they visited had a brick-and-tile or carpentry works whilst every one had a small manufactory for hand tools.[13] Furthermore the basic input–output accounting is currently devolved to team level.

On median assumptions, the Chinese grain output in 1973 worked out at 1·7 pounds per capita per day as against, for example, about 1·1 on the average for India in the 1960s and about 1·5 for China itself during the middle years of that decade. This being so, it is not unreasonable to anticipate that China will be at least self-sufficient in these staple foods in the 1980s, always provided it can avoid any very marked socio-political convulsions of the Cultural Revolution kind. Arguably, support is lent to this judgment by Audrey Donnithorne's deduction that, even in the 1960s, the prime factor behind grain imports was an uneven distribution regionally (because of transport and administrative impediments) rather than absolute dearth.[14]

As regards the social dimension, there can be little doubt that the Chinese Communists have already qualified drastically the immemorial concepts of family and of clan. And among the collateral trends have been the emergence of a generation gap, with the Red Guards as its most visible expression; the drive towards the full emancipation of women; the big diminution in private property; the sharp decline in ancestor worship and other traditional modes in religion and philosophy; and the belated yet now so fervent enthusiasm for birth control. All have been further advanced by and through the People's Communes.

Clearly, the future of China (and, by extension, of Mankind as a whole) hinges considerably on the future of the People's Commune and its subdivisions. How stable will this matrix prove in the long term? Assuming it does in essence survive, will it afford the peasantry a chance to sink new social roots from which to evolve a new autonomy? Or will it be instead a means of lifting them clean away from such roots as they may be said to retain, thereby leaving them helplessly susceptible to manipulation by arbitrary and capricious central authority?

Probably, much of the answer lies not within the communes themselves but at the further end of the Chinese institutional spectrum—

i.e. in the big national bureaucracies and maybe, in particular, the military. Today the status of the soldier per se is considerably higher in Mainland China than it was under the Kuomintang. For even the rawest draftee is among the small minority within his age chosen for the privilege of service in a People's Liberation Army with a very creditable record both on the battlefield and in public works.

Clearly, this transformation does not *ipso facto* make the present military leadership even more disposed to intervene in politics than was, to draw the obvious comparison, Generalissimo Chiang Kai-shek in his heyday. But it does mean that they recurrently find themselves in a position to hold the political ring.

As much was manifested clearly in the spring of 1969—i.e. amidst the dying embers of the Cultural Revolution—when the Ninth Party Congress elected a new Central Committee. For the upshot was an increase of from 25 to 40 per cent in the military element therein, a development that presaged a year or two of exceptionally overt military influence.[15]

At the Tenth Congress in 1973, the percentage was to drop to 25 once more. Even so, the military obviously played a major part in Hua Kuo-feng's triumph over the "Gang of Four" in October 1976. A pledge of loyalty to him from the Peking garrison on 16 October was followed the next day by a similar, and even more significant, declaration by the army garrison in Shanghai—the radicals' main power base.

Notes

1. Herman Kahn, *The Emerging Japanese Superstate*, André Deutsch, London, 1971, pp. 128–30.
2. Jean Stoetzel, *Without the Chrysanthemum and the Sword*, UNESCO, Paris and William Heinemann, London, 1955, pp. 16–17.
3. Ruth Benedict, *The Chrysanthemum and the Sword*, Secker and Warburg, London, 1947. Chapter 1.
4. Norman Macrae, "Pacific Century, 1975–2075?", *The Economist*, 4 January 1975.
5. Kakuei Tanaka, *Building a New Japan*, The Simul Press, Tokyo 1973, p. 191.
6. Felix Greene, *A Curtain of Ignorance*, Jonathan Cape, London, 1965. Chapter 13 makes this point cogently.
7. E.g. *An Outline History of China*, Foreign Languages Press, Peking, 1958, pp. 410–11.
8. Eric Chou, *The Sunday Times*, 16 February 1969.
9. Joan Robinson, *The Cultural Revolution in China*, Pelican Original, Harmondsworth 1969, p. 42.
10. Theodore Hsi-en Chen in Yuan-li Wu (Ed), *China, a handbook*, David and Charles, Newton Abbot 1973, p. 693.

11. See e.g. Yao Wen-yuan "On the Social Basis of the Lin Piao Anti-Party Clique", *Peking Review*, No. 10. 7 March 1975, pp. 5–10 and Chang Chun-chiao "On Exercising All-Round Dictatorship Over the Bourgeoisie", *Peking Review*, No. 14. 4 April 1975, pp. 5–10.

12. Han Suyin, *China in the Year 2001*, C. A. Watts, London 1967. Chapter 2.

13. E. L. Wheelwright and Bruce McFarlane, *The Chinese Road to Socialism*, Monthly Review Press, New York 1970. Chapter 10.

14. Audrey Donnithorne, "Why China Imports Wheat", *The China Quarterly* October/December 1971, No. 48, pp. 736–41.

15. "The East is Khaki", *The Economist*, 10 October 1970.

18

The Geography of Instability

The British Empire as reformed and extended after the loss of the American colonies was, first and foremost, an Indian Ocean empire. Correspondingly, India itself occupied a nodal place in its Grand Strategy. On the one hand, the security of the subcontinent—principally against a perceived threat from Czarist Russia—was a concern underlying much activity elsewhere. Yet on the other hand, India came after 1875 to serve as the locus of a key strategic reserve, a source of support for theatres as widely separated as France, South Africa and China.

Today this subcontinent is as nodal as ever it was. But now it is as the centrepiece of a rough-hewn quadrilateral of primary poverty with its corners in Manchuria, Senegal, Malagasy and New Guinea. Thus a World Bank map completed in 1972 showed no territories with average incomes per head of below $200 p.a. which lay outside that zone, save for Bolivia and the former British High Commission territories abutting South Africa—Botswana, Lesotho and Swaziland. Correspondingly, no territory that clearly lay within the zone had a mean annual income above $200, save for about ten small (and, in a sense, peripheral) territories in southern and eastern Asia.

Very generally, too, the latent threat of instability consequent on primary poverty is compounded by the quadrilateral zone in question being perhaps more prone to "future shock" than some other parts of the newly developing world. This is because what was, in many cases, fairly precipitate imperial withdrawal either coincided with or preceded an acceleration of cultural flux and of shifts in the communal balance. What is more, we may find that from now on, this effect is especially marked in the Arabian peninsula, the Himalayas and the remoter extremities of Indonesia—which, together with the archipelagos of Oceania, harboured the *shangrilas* of yester-year.

Before looking more closely at the landward fringes of the Indian Ocean basin, it may be appropriate to look briefly at Oceania—i.e. the fabled island chains of the Pacific and also Australasia. Since the 1940s names like Guadalcanal, Tarawa, Truk and Bikini have become symbolic of the advent of 20th century technocracy at its most bitter and abrupt. Now tourism is making a similarly sudden and big impact on some of the islands, an impact that may well not be stabilising in social and political terms.

In 1970 Hawaii embarked on "an experiment in anticipatory democracy" in the form of a Governor's Conference on the Year 2000, a futurology convention comprised not just of academicians but of hundreds of local laymen as well; and the task forces it established argued the importance of their island cluster as a relatively self-contained testing ground for ecological control and also for racial pluralism.[1] At that time, the population of this cluster was adjudged to be made up of 298,000 Caucasians, 269,000 Chinese and Japanese, 94,000 Filipinos and 110,000 of mixed or other descent. By then, over a third of all new marriages were across the standard ethnic boundaries.

Perhaps racial harmony is easier to promote in so multilateral a context than where the divide is virtually bilateral—e.g. that between the Indians and those of indigenous stock in Fiji. This Fijian dichotomy is, in fact, closely analogous to that between the Indians and the Creoles in the Indian Ocean island of Mauritius.

Further parallels between these two former British dependencies are their land hunger and their heavy reliance on sugar exports. But in both these respects the situation of Mauritius is the more serious, as witness the dispatch of British troops to curb communal clashes in 1965 and again in 1968. Fortunately, however, the population explosion is coming under control there, thanks to the positive concern evinced by the official administration and also by the Catholic Church.

Antipodal location coupled, in the latter case at any rate, with a goodly measure of economic self-sufficiency give New Zealand and Australia some immunity from the turbulence of the rest of the globe. But too much should not be made of this. The Labour governments returned to power under the late Norman Kirk and Gough Whitlam respectively in 1972 were very much the products of this turbulence. So was the inflation that dogged them in office.

As usual, the administration in Canberra was the one which attracted most notice abroad; and its Grand Strategy still merits perusal as a determining influence on the part *c*. 18,000,000 Australians will play in the world at large. Top priority was given to securing the social stability of the home base, especially through a doubling of the federal education budget. Meanwhile, more attention was paid also to the needs of the Aboriginal minority whilst the White Australia policy was modified a little further. At the same time, defence expenditure was pruned in the assumed absence of military threats during the next ten years, though various force structure options were kept open with a view to the longer term.

Arguably, the Whitlam government was altogether too anxious to cultivate a modish image of quasi-neutralism in external affairs. A precipitate granting of full independence to Papua-New Guinea might not prove the kindest service to the peoples concerned, given their polyglot tribal structure and lack of a broad administrative cadre. Berating Lee Kuan Yew because Singapore could not match the standards of democratic toleration achieved midst the untrammelled ease of Canberra accorded ill with the sharp reduction in Australia's involvement in the defence of the Malaysia–Singapore region. You do not make somebody more liberal by rendering him less secure.

Nor was Gough Whitlam's professed extroversion in some aspects of policy easy to reconcile, in terms of overall national psychology, with his studied introversion apropos Defence. A Fortress Australia, indifferent to the security of Commonwealth South-East Asia, might well turn careless, too, of the developmental issues which vex the Indian subcontinent and Southern Africa. The point gains importance through the probability that a case can be made for Australasia as a whole becoming, in the 1980s, the hub of a collective arrangement for maritime defence.

But for Australia and New Zealand, as for Papua-New Guinea and also Singapore and Malaysia, much hinges on the future stability or otherwise of the Indonesian archipelago, so vast and so lop-sided demographically. Of late its prospects have looked much brighter, thanks to a decade of good husbandry by the firmly anti-Communist regime that displaced Ahmed Sukarno. Nevertheless, the caveat must be entered that, thus far, economic growth has tended to benefit too exclusively the urban middle class of Java, in particular. Both corruption and an imbalanced pattern of foreign investment are partly to blame.

Some indication of the resultant tensions latent in the body politic can be gleaned from the racialistic riots on the occasion of the visit of Kakuei Tanaka, then the Japanese Prime Minister, in 1974. Symptomatic also has been the arbitrary detention of large numbers of political prisoners.[2]

Not that the ultimate promise of an Indonesian "economic miracle" is by any means dead. Thus though they be virtually uncharted as yet, the reserves of minerals, not least offshore oil and natural gas, are believed to be enormous. Furthermore, agricultural productivity may be increased greatly by grappling with such ecological problems as soil erosion. However, all may depend on whether the deep involvement of the army in government down through provincial to local level can be turned to better effect developmentally.

Between Indonesia and China lies an area kept disconcertingly fissile by physical fragmentation and by the continued paramountcy of ethnic politics. One remedy those concerned are groping towards is closer collaboration under the rubric of the Association of South-East Asian Nations (ASEAN), a body founded in 1967 and comprising Indonesia, Malaysia, the Philippines, Singapore and Thailand. However, tentative moves towards multilateral free trade could hardly be harbingers for the economic integration of the ASEAN region, seeing that only several per cent of the aggregate foreign trade of its members is intra-regional.

Moreover, Indonesia's advocacy of some measure of military collaboration has been greeted with little enthusiasm by its fellow-members. Instead, the current disposition is to rely on such tokens of China's restraint as the hero's welcome given in Peking in 1974 to the late Tun Abdul Razak, the conservative Prime Minister of Malaysia, and likewise in 1975 to Kukrit Pramoj, the engaging man for all seasons who was then Prime Minister of Thailand. Yet now the pro-Muscovite influences in Indo-China must also be reckoned with. At present, the Communist elements within the localised insurgencies in progress around the several borders of Thailand receive low-key assistance from various quarters.[3]

What the whole region needs, and may or may not get, is time to work through its developmental imbalances. In the main, the Malthusian pressure of population on land is not yet too oppressive within the four smaller states in ASEAN. However, the impact of the Green Revolution has been disappointing in Thailand, the most specialised grain producer of them all. Worse, Bangkok is fast becoming a classic instance of the metropolitan syndrome—the location of, for example, most of the 13,000 murders recorded last year.[4] Nevertheless, the post-1973 heirs to the old military dictatorship tried hard to cope with the tensions exposed and, indeed, exacerbated by their pursuit of two laudable aims: sinking firm the roots of parliamentary democracy and curbing the opium trade of the Meo tribesmen of the northern hills. But in the autumn of 1976 the military took over anew.

In West Malaysia, resentment against the economic prowess of the 35 per cent of the population which is of Chinese descent is subtly expressed through sundry forms of discrimination and more overtly through the zealous promotion of Malay as *the* national language and also of Islam. In the consequent alienation of the young Chinese can be seen a key to the recent revival of the long-moribund Malayan Communist Party, about 70 members of the security forces being killed in its terrorist attacks in 1975.

In the Philippines a classic stick-and-carrot combination seems to have gained some time: the stick being the tight state of emergency introduced in 1972 and the carrot a positive stress on rural ameliora-tion. Lately, a flickering Maoist insurgency has become much more subdued. So has the revolt by thousands of Moslem insurgents in Mindanao. Money to buy arms flowed to the latter from Libya through Sabah, the easternmost territory of East Malaysia and one long claimed by the Philippines.

Folk memories of long and inclement Malay ascendancy induce the non-Malay peoples of East Malaysia (i.e. over 85 per cent of the total population) to view with suspicion rule from Kuala Lumpur. More-over, the small but independent Sultanate of Brunei entertains anxieties that are similar in inclination even though their historical derivation is quite different. Relations between "KL" and the bustling city-state of Singapore are, at best, fragile.

Just how much time the non-Communist parts of the South China Sea region do get to consolidate themselves before major insurgencies build up again may depend on two exogenous factors. One is the future of the Sino-Soviet split. The other is how much time the three new Communist states of Indo-China find they need to consolidate themselves. Though the formal unification of the two Vietnams has now been effected, the difficulties Hanoi will face in fully digesting the labyrinthine politics and sociology of the South will undoubtedly be exacerbated by its own regime remaining very heavily Northerner. There are some signs that Hanoi is anxious to enlist Western tech-nology to further economic reconstruction. Unfortunately, however, there are rather more signs that it will eventually opt, first and foremost, for an illiberal and xenophobic "mass mobilisation" of a standard Marxist–Leninist kind.

Though in this immediate post-war period, Hanoi has remained disposed to play Moscow and Peking off against each other, it has obviously set most store by the kind of economic assistance the former has to give. Contrariwise, the Khmer Rouge in Cambodia have aligned themselves very exclusively with Peking, thereby giving a curious geopolitical twist to the cultural divide, identified by Richard Harris many years ago, between a Southern Asia embracing Cambodia and Laos and an East Asian Vietnam.[5] However, China may well be more than a little embarrassed by the orgy of fascisto-Marxist venom the Khmer Rouge have indulged in these last 21 months or so. Agreed, several million "reactionaries were liquidated" in China itself in the wake of the Communist accession to power in 1949. But, proportionately speaking, that was well over an order of magnitude less than the hundreds of thousands of fellow Cambodians the Khmer Rouge are feared either to have killed outright, with varying degrees of barbarity, or else wilfully left to starve since the fall of Phnom-Penh in April 1975.[6] Alas, what is also, after all, a militantly xenophobic regime may in due course resolve to try and export its macabre tensions.

West of the spinal watershed that can be traced down from the Tibetan plateau into Malaya, lies Burma, a country which seems perennially to be suffused with lassitude. What is more, one would have to say that such wells of political and social energy as it may be judged to possess have repeatedly been dissipated as an inherently weak central government has struggled to contain strong centrifugal tendencies of an ethnic or ideological kind. Inadequate though the data base is, there can be little doubt that Burmese living standards fell appreciably in the decade after the military coup of 1962. In one of his innumerable *tours d'horizon*, a bemused Herman Kahn cited Burma as a singular example of the rejection of the philosophy of economic growth.

Custom permits the commentator on political affairs, be he journalist or academician, to evince a lordly disdain for what he may plausibly depict as the stupidity of those engaged in public life. Necessary to his task though this prerogative is, however, it must sometimes be exercised with great moderation if it is not to appear callow and effete. Criticism of any Prime Minister of India is a clear case in point. For arguably this is quite the most daunting political job in the world: much harder most days, for example, than being Chairman of the Communist Party in China. Culturally, India is far more diverse than China has ever been. Furthermore, its form of republican government has been—and, for that matter, is—the more open, with all that this entails for the tactical vulnerability of those in power at any given time. Chairman Mao never had his familial idiosyncrasies internationally dissected the way Mrs Gandhi has. And we do not even know, at this point in time, whether his successor is married!

One can note all this. One can note also that the electoral corruption charges on which Indira Gandhi was found guilty by the Allahabad High Court in June 1975 were almost asininely petty in relation to the invalidation and six-year electoral ban imposed. Nevertheless, the blanket ruthlessness of the State of Emergency introduced a fortnight later continues to occasion legitimate concern; and now this is being exacerbated by planned amendments to the constitution, the effect of which would be much to strengthen the hand of the executive against both the legislature and the judiciary.

The crux of the matter is that an indefinite maintenance of any form of dictatorship, whether by the descendants of Nehru or anybody else, would be a disaster for India and hence for the world. To put the matter at its simplest, the bases for this solution have not been laid and cannot be. The British military tradition of political non-involvement pervades the Indian Army still. The extreme Left has been pathetically fissiparous for years; and the extreme Right is hardly less so. Besides which, one could never abide monolithic rule in a land with over 1,500 mother tongues: it would be worse than the USSR.

Hopefully, however, the current lurch into authoritarianism can be turned to some good effect by preparing the ground for a more balanced economic development than India has yet achieved. The halting economic progress that had been registered beforehand had done little or nothing to close the glaring gap between rich and poor. The influence of farmers and landowners within the Congress Party itself served to preclude the adequate taxation of their side of agriculture. Massive tax evasion by the upper classes had combined with a vast extension of official bureaucracies to necessitate repeated budget deficits. Above all, the urban implosion perennially looked menacing, despite the big improvement in the early 1970s in the management of notorious Calcutta. An authoritative essay published shortly before the political crisis of 1975 argued the need for India to break decisively from the narrow track of urban-impelled consumerism and to advance to the year 2000 on a broader front, both sociologically and philosophically.[7]

In retrospect, at least, Indira Gandhi has sought to justify the State of Emergency in terms of economic transformation, and to some extent her words have been backed by action. Corruption has been curbed, however unevenly. Family planning has been promoted more vigorously than ever before. More land has been distributed to landless labourers during this short time than over the previous two decades.[8] The accent of the much reiterated "twenty-one point" programme for reconstruction is firmly on more economic equality in both countryside and town.

Not that the task ahead is made any easier by the strategic vulnerability of India. Probably, it would be fair to say that the disposition of the first generation of statesmen who served this republic was to look out across their seaboard rather than across the Himalayan frontiers.[9] But since the bitter military defeats at the hands of China in 1962, about ten mountain divisions have been raised to try and screen adequately the 1,500-mile Himalayan sector.

However, the security of this exposed flank is not by any means an exclusively military question. On the contrary, the next ten years may show that a fragmented political geography plus the antiquated social and political structures has rendered the existing order in the Himalayas peculiarly vulnerable to cultural change, not to say "future shock". One instance may be seen in the tensions in Sikkim between the Nepali immigrants and the rest, tensions that in 1974 induced New Delhi to absorb this tiny kingdom as an Associated State.

The potential implications for India itself might have been less disturbing if only the 1971 triumph in war over Pakistan could have been used to make a generous settlement of the old Kashmir dispute. And if the juxtaposition of Nepal and Bangladesh did not pinch its territory into a waist less than 20 miles across at a point southwards from Sikkim. Also if Bangladesh had not sunk to so sorry a state. Also, one might add, if the prognosis for constitutional democracy was today good in Sri Lanka, formerly Ceylon.[10]

Lately, the territories which border the Persian Gulf have been quiet militarily apart from rebellions in two of their peripheral districts: the Dhofar province of Oman and Iraqi Kurdistan. Early in 1975 both rebellions still looked formidable, even though under heavy pressure. Then China disengaged from the international

Marxist front that was actively backing the Dhofari rebels whilst Iran ceased its support of the Kurds. Today the Gulf littoral seems almost at peace with itself; and this for all the foreboding these last 20 years or so as to what the near future held there in terms of collapsing dominoes.

Yet just because wolf has been cried a little too often, we cannot assume that the deepening contradictions of what is, in many ways, an increasingly dynamic situation will be held in check indefinitely, even given the absence of mischievous external interventions. In both Iran and Saudi Arabia, to take the two local giants, the approach being used to reconcile an accelerating economic boom with a deep-rooted traditional culture and tightly autocratic rule is basically a four-pronged one: remorselessly tough repression of radical dissent; the giving of top priority within the social programme to a distinctly conservative interpretation of modern education; an activism in foreign policy which may not be insincere but which does afford useful diversions; and a siphoning of some of the escalating oil revenue, either into overseas assets or else into a mushrooming defence budget. In fact, the defence expansion has been especially marked in the case of Iran: the land of high steppes and wide horizons that was the birthplace of chess, the original war-game.

In his 1973 Reith Lectures, Alastair Buchan warned that to expand militarily as fast as Iran was then doing was not only to generate a pall of fear among neighbours but also to create a new elite well adapted for mounting a coup some day.[11] However, if military officers do eventually come to play a determining part in the future of Tehran they may be men cast in the Atatürk mould. A more serious danger may lie in army assumptions of power within the Arabian peninsula in the middle 1980s. For there the cultural gap between past and present is so great, and several of the key infrastructures so weak, that the resultant synthesis of tradition and modernity could probably only be achieved à la Gadafi.

Likewise it would be fair to say that pronounced infrastructural weakness and unduly abrupt cultural change are the factors which have led already to the widespread displacement of the parliamentary forms of government generally bestowed on African territories before independence. No fewer than 15 of the 47 states in the Organisation of African Unity were under direct military rule in March 1976 whilst only three of the rest—Botswana, the Gambia and Mauritius—

retained some semblance of a pluralist political system. In the long-term, an especially dangerous strain will be that caused by the almost universal, and usually deepening, divide between the burgeoning urban-based elites and the mass of the people, both urban and rural. A lunch in some Nairobi hotels might cost the equivalent of a farm-worker's wages for six months!

Overall it is in East Africa that the prospect looks worst, in part because this whole region could all too easily become one across which the battle lines of the Middle East are extended to join those of Southern Africa: Marxist or fascisto-Marxist extremism being obliquely ranged against the forces of pragmatic moderation. Among the substantive bones of contention that could be either kept going or revived are the Southern Sudan, Eritrea, Ifar and Assars, and the arid march-lands between Ethiopia and Somalia. Among the other contingencies to bear in mind, assuming Idi Amin survives in Uganda, are that his schizoid sadism will induce him to take revenge for Entebbe on Kenya in the wake of Jomo Kenyatta's departure. Should any such ploy succeed, 150,000 Kenya Asians will be placed in danger of an expulsion as summary as that inflicted on their kith and kin in Uganda.

Mercifully, Zaïre looks more integrated, and hence more stable, than ever seemed possible a dozen or so years ago, even though it is not yet clear whether the recent developmental emphasis on agriculture and internal communications will preclude a further widening of intra-regional and intra-class disparities. Another big country that, aided by quite enlightened military governments and booming oil revenues, did recover relatively smoothly from fierce internal strife is Nigeria. But its future tranquillity will depend on a similarly smooth restoration of democracy (see Chapter 22).

West Africa and Brazil together define the waistband zone of the mid-Atlantic Ocean, a stretch of water identified by some (though not this writer) as a peculiarly critical strategic "choke-point". On the further side lies South America, for so long known as the continent of the "frustrated revolution" that all concerned may by now have been lulled into unwarranted complacency. Yet, even allowing for this and for the Argentina situation, one can discern positive grounds for believing that Latin America as a whole can once again look forward to several years during which revolutionary threats are unlikely to be so immediate as to inhibit constructive responses. Castro's Cuba and Allende's Chile did not prove inspiring exemplars.

Nor do Havana or Moscow or Peking seem much interested, at this particular point in time, in promoting subversion in the Western Hemisphere.

Furthermore, as various commentators have averred, the new migrants into the urban areas have not, in the main, developed at this stage a coherent radicalism such as might induce them to endorse protracted urban insurgency. And the fate of Che Guevara was testimony to the unsuitability for guerrilla warfare of so much of rural Latin America: the landscape is usually alright but the density of population is often too low. To which one might add that the counter-insurgency capabilities of South America's armed forces (which have an aggregate of *c.* 900,000 men with the Colours) have been steadily rising.

Nor is the old tradition of military intervention in central government yet dead. On the contrary, in 1973 the military intervened decisively in those two polities—Chile and Uruguay—in which this pattern had been thought outmoded. Different though the specific circumstances were, a desire to curb the extreme Left was a prime motive in each case.

Fortunately, grounds do exist for hoping that this breathing space from revolutionary upheaval will be used to good purpose. By and large, the officer corps is less cavalier about both its duties and its privileges than once it was. More of the clergy now act as pacemakers for social change as opposed to being mere apologists for the status quo. Meanwhile, the civil bureaucracies are tending to get stronger and more professional, whilst throughout the elite sectors the caudillo pattern of personalist rule is losing ground to less arbitrary and philistine leaderships.[12]

Yet against this promise must be set the complication that South America stands out as the area above all others where the maximisation of economic growth appears inappropriate as the basis for sustained and orderly progress. After all, the average real income in almost every state compares most favourably already with the levels obtaining over, say, most of Afro-Asia. But what continues to be highly unsatisfactory is the profile of income distribution. Indeed, analyses of the 1970 census in Brazil confirmed that, as a very general rule, the richer social groups and the richer geographical regions had materially increased their lead over the decade. Nor does it seem that these divergences have yet been checked. Meanwhile, even in the expansive environment of the São Paulo–Rio industrial axis "the contrast between private affluence and public squalor ... is unbelievable".[13]

Inevitably, one consequence of the big disparities has been to make elective democracy the more difficult to maintain or restore. All the same, the notion that elective democracy is, in the ultimate, the only legitimate form of government does run deep in the political culture of Latin America. Historically, the roots lie in the early 19th century and in the debt owed by the independence movement to revolution in France and evolution in Britain.

To turn north to the Caribbean is to enter an area wherein a multiple crisis of identity derived from geography and history is being accentuated, in manifold ways, by current economic and social developments. Tourism has been increasing quite steadily on the whole, and has become valuable thereby as a source of foreign exchange as well as a means of achieving the Keynesian multiplier effect on incomes. Contrariwise, it brings in its train seasonal unemployment, heavy extra imports and land price spirals.

Besides, it is always liable to spawn squalid commercialism of the sort too rampant in parts of pre-Castro Havana. Also to connote the master-slave relationship of earlier times. Similarly, one factor behind a very strong and destabilising drift from the land in various territories is the historical redolence of plantation life.

Conceivably, a sense of national identity, based largely on its size and its Hispano-Aztec heritage yet sharpened by rapid educational expansion, will enable Mexico soon to burst through the constraints of the moribund revolution of 1911. Otherwise, Central America stands desperately in need of some kind of Marshall Plan to grapple with the economic and social malaise reflected in severe unemployment and soaring crime rates in territories like Jamaica.

In the absence of some such concerted drive, many parts of the region may come to be plagued increasingly by radical millenarianism and cults of ethnicity, these perhaps culminating in fascist or fascisto-Marxist despotisms. To assume that the environment in question is too balmy and too diverse ever to favour any such general trend might be altogether too glib. The Guatemala of Castillo Armas and the Haiti of Duvalier, not to mention the Cuba of Batista, were classic studies in Rightist autocracy. And such West Indies names as Marcus Garvey, Stokely Carmichael and—at a rather more profound level—Frantz Fanon are prominent in the international annals of "Black Power".

In this ever-shrinking world Canada, too, has long had an external crisis of identity as well as an internal one, a root cause of the former being that half its population lies within 100 miles of a very extended and completely open border with the United States. Accordingly, in the first 20 years or so after the war, its sought to offset economic and strategic interdependence with the colossus to the south by acting as a "golden hinge" between the USA and Europe and also between the West and Afro-Asia. But although this aspiration has remained, during the late 1960s its strength was sapped by national introspection. Thus in April 1968, Pierre Trudeau, the new Prime Minister, explicitly gave top priority in defence to the security of Canada itself and especially of its coastal waters.

Yet within several years the "golden hinge" theme was being revived. This time its trans-Atlantic cornerstone is the "Framework Agreement for Commercial and Economic Cooperation" between Canada and the EEC.[14]

Notes

1. G. Chaplin and G. O. Paige, *Hawaii 2000*, The University Press of Hawaii, Honolulu, 1973.
2. Ronald Emler, "55,000 skeletons in Indonesia's cupboard", *The Times*, 14 May 1973.
3. Robert F. Zimmerman, "Insurgency in Thailand", *Problems of Communism*, Vol. XXV No. 3, May–June 1976, pp. 8–39.
4. *The Economist*, 18 September 1976.
5. Richard Harris, "Indo-China and the French", *History Today*, Vol. V No. 2. February 1955, pp. 84–94.
See also *The Times*, 12 December 1974 and 13 December 1974.
6. Michael Field, "The Reddest Revolution of All", *The Sunday Telegraph*, 15 August 1976. For the immediate background see Roger Kershaw "Cambodian National Union—A Milestone in Popular Front Technique", *The World Today*, Vol. 32 No. 2. February 1976, pp. 60–8.
7. J. C. Kapur, *India in the Year 2000*, India International Centre, New Delhi, 1975.
8. *The Economist*, 17 July 1976.
9. See e.g. K. M. Pannikar, *India and the Indian Ocean*, George Allen and Unwin, London 1945.
10. Christopher Dobson, "Family Misrule on Island of Discontent", *The Sunday Telegraph*, 14 July 1974.
11. Alastair Buchan, "Maintaining Peace in Asia", *The Listener*, Vol. 90 No. 2333. 13 December 1973, pp. 816–18.
12. Luigi R. Einaudi (Ed), *Latin America in the 1970s*, The Rand Corporation, Santa Monica, 1972. Chapter VI.
13. *The Economist*, 15 January 1973.
14. E. E. Mahaut, "Canada and the European Community: the New Policy", *International Affairs*, Vol. 52 No. 4, October 1976, pp. 551–64.

19

Southern Africa

Sir Karl Popper's remark about History being "a succession of attacks of intellectual madness, of all sorts of strange intellectual fashions" rings true in many situations in the febrile modern world. Yet to few is it more apposite than the Apartheid philosophy which has prevailed in South Africa ever since the victory of the Nationalists in the general election of 1948. In essence, its cardinal theme is that the several communities in South Africa should be separated as completely as possible, both territorially and otherwise; and that, whilst the development of them all will be facilitated, this will be under White supervision and in strict accordance with each one's original culture and traditions. Duly, the political and social affiliations of the Black peoples are presumed to be forever tribal.

Apartheid legislation has extended into virtually every aspect of life: marriage, residence, education, employment opportunities and rewards, leisure pursuits and even church attendance. What it cannot constrain, however, is the dynamic of economic evolution and expansion. Yet this incessant material change entails urbanisation, mechanisation, labour mobility and retraining, freer recourse to money, advertising and countless other tendencies, all of which erode every bit as incessantly the cultural differentiation between the different ethnic groups that is Apartheid's doctrinal point of departure. This is not to say that the doctrine is doomed to early and total collapse. But it is to say that, if vestiges of it do survive through 1990, they will have done so only by virtue of South Africa's having become still more actively repressive, by having rejected even more completely—at the political level—the liberal ideals which stand at the very centre of our post-Renaissance vision of progress.

At its outset, indeed, the implementation of this curiously utopian kind of authoritarianism was visibly interwoven with two other thrusts towards illiberalism, one direct and one oblique. The former was a McCarthy-style drive to "suppress Communism" and the latter a loosening of ties with Britain, the country seen by many descendants of the Boer-trekkers as a singular menace to White solidarity within South Africa.

Both thrusts have been sustained since then—so much so, in fact, that a cynic might be excused the quip that the elimination of individual freedom of expression is one sphere in which racial equality has obtained. True, the press fiercely retains an important measure of independence, certainly far more than in any Marxist state. At times, too, the judiciary has proved a stout bulwark of liberty. Nevertheless, some conspicuous milestones on the dark road to totalitarianism have already been left behind.

Among them is the Terrorism Act passed in 1967 and made retrospective to 1962. This permits the authorities to detain indefinitely anybody they have "reason to believe . . . is a terrorist or is withholding from the South African Police any information relating to terrorists or to offences under this Act". Moreover, terrorism is defined both broadly and vaguely; the onus of proof rests heavily with the defendant; and collective and repeated trials are permissible. Besides which, there is scope in this and similar legislation for interrogation in depth against a background of prolonged solitary confinement.

But central to the application of Apartheid as such is the drive to limit the number of Africans resident in the towns and cities, this notwithstanding Malthusian pressures in their rural homelands and the growing labour demands of urban manufacturing. Under legislation enacted by early 1976, no African could remain in an urban area for more than three days, except by special permission of a labour bureau, unless he or she could demonstrate that one or more of the following conditions obtained: they had lived there continuously since birth; they had worked there uninterruptedly for the same employer for no less than ten years or lived there with official approval for 15; she was the wife or he or she the child of someone allowed to be there. Basic to this tight control is a pass system made comprehensive in 1952.

Inevitably, intense misery has thereby been caused. Husbands and wives or parents and children are often separated for extended periods of time. By the end of the 1960s, pass law prosecutions were exceeding a million a year. Yet the result had merely been to retard the African urban implosion. Between 1951 and 1970 the African population in the tribal reserves all but doubled to reach nearly seven million. Concurrently, however, that in the urban areas more than doubled to over five million. Yet still special regulations inhibit the establishment of such "permanent" facilities as supermarkets, banks, cinemas or even service stations. This helps explain why vast conglomerations like Soweto, which houses more than a million people, are so utterly soulless.

The official response to this deprivation is focused on the Bantustans. Legislation passed in 1959 denied the Bantu—i.e. the Black South Africans—representation in the central parliament and made provision for the guided transition to internal self-government of their respective tribal groups. Among subsequent statutes has been the Bantu Homelands Citizenship Act of 1970 which made every Black South African a citizen of his tribe's designated homeland. One purpose has, of course, been to divert attention from the exclusive minority situation of the Whites as such: "Four million . . . of European origin, four million Xhosa, four million Zulu, two million Tswana, two million Sotho and so on. Each group is a minority—there is, in fact, no single majority group".[1]

No doubt tribal affinities continue to count for something among urban Africans. Increasingly, however, these ties are being dissolved by intermarriage and general cultural flux. Besides which, the geographical limits set for the Bantustans themselves are utterly inadequate. Altogether they extend across only 14 per cent of South Africa's total area, much of it sub-standard climatically and seriously over-grazed as well as over-peopled.

The sombre implications for economic viability can be more firmly grasped by taking a closer look at the Xhosa homeland, the Transkei, which in October 1976 became the first Bantustan to be formally accorded sovereign independence. Of the three million Bantu now registered as "Transkeian citizens", barely one and three-quarter million live on the 8,500,000 acres the homeland comprises, these mainly subsisting on maize, herding cattle in a time-honoured yet unproductive fashion, and surviving only by massive imports of maize coupled with the cash remittances of a migrant labour force which includes no less than 83 per cent of all the adult males.[2] In the fiscal year 1965–66, 62 per cent of the Transkei's total revenue came directly from the South African treasury. By 1974–75, the share had gone up to 77 per cent.

What is more, this imposed political regression to decaying tribal roots has been just as antipathetic to democratic evolution within the Transkei as outside it. After 13 years of existence, the Transkei legislative assembly approached independence with a membership composed of 45 elected representatives and 65 nominated chiefs. Before the pre-independence elections in September 1976, Paramount Chief Kaiser Matanzima, the head of the administration, arrested the entire executive of the opposition Democratic party and held them in prison without charge. A decree introduced after tribal disturbances in 1960 has been retained: it allows detention without trial and gives the chiefs power to confiscate the land of anybody who fails to obey them. Now allegations are being noised abroad that the top men in this protostate are starting to feather their own financial nests.

For all this, the Bantustan experiment can be regarded as a crab-like forward movement in some respects. For one thing, various of their chiefly leaders, most notably Gatsha Buthelezi of Kwazulu, have shown considerable aplomb in exploiting to the full such political leverage as their positions afford. Most of them are refusing to move towards formal independence on the terms currently envisaged, a pitch which corresponds to the one the Democratic party had adopted in the Transkei. Meanwhile, they have orchestrated protests against, for example, the iniquities of the pass laws and the disparities in wage rates between Whites and Blacks. Similarly, Chief Matanzima has insisted that Transkei should be multiracial internally and has joined with Chief Buthelezi in resisting the notion that English should be replaced by the given tribal language as the main medium of instruction in Bantustan schools. With this last point, they can be deemed to have complemented the key theme in the militant protest by Soweto students in June 1976: that they should not have to learn Afrikaans as well as English in their high schools.

The rising status of English as a *lingua franca* everywhere in an increasingly cosmopolitan world is one compelling reason why the Afrikaner hard core has been determined to raise, in both the police and other branches of the public sector, the proportion of Whites speaking Afrikaans as their first tongue. Yet, whilst there are grounds for concern over both this determination and its efficacy, it is a mistake to brand all Afrikaners as incorrigible extremists to a man. In preparation for the 1970 general election, an ultra-conservative *verkrampte* faction within the ruling Nationalist party broke away in order to challenge the pragmatism of Prime Minister Vorster over such matters as the inclusion of Maori players in a forthcoming rugby tour by New Zealand's "All Blacks". Also on account of their broader desire to make their Afrikaner Calvinism paramount once and for all, not only over the non-European communities but also over what they saw as decadent Anglophone liberalism. However, they failed to win any of the 78 seats they contested and forfeited their deposits in all but three.

Besides which, the Nationalists have had to accept the inner logic of their own Bantustan experiment. The way leading members of the party recently took to using the phrase "separate development" much more than Apartheid did suggest that the more supremacist interpretations of the latter—*baaskap* and all that—were implicitly being renounced, at least for the time being. Likewise late in 1974, South Africa's Ambassador to the UN went so far as to say that "Discrimination based solely on the colour of a man's skin cannot be defended". To dismiss such utterances as nothing but humbug may be to underestimate the power of humbug to force the hand of those who enunciate it.

What is more, by the time of the 1974 general election a fair amount had been done to remove the irksome pinpricks of "petty apartheid" especially in certain urban centres controlled by the opposition parties. Johannesburg City Council was, for example, throwing open its libraries, parks, museums and art galleries to the Black people who comprise 60 per cent of the population of this conurbation. Similarly, in Cape Town. Yet not only did the results of that year's general election fail to indicate any conservative backlash, but also they bespoke positive gains for a Progressive Party which was advocating a non-racial but qualified franchise within a federal constitution. Later the Progressives were joined by a Reformist splinter from the United Party, the official opposition. By the middle of 1976 the Progressive Reform Party, as the amalgamation was known, had 12 seats in Parliament as against the United Party's 36 and the Nationalist's seventy two.

On 29 November 1976 Chief Buthelezi formed another new party, to be known as the Black United Front and intended to form a bridge between whatever evolutionary reform elements survive within the urban ghettoes and those prepared to make use of the leverage the homelands policy affords. Among its aims will be the abolition of the pass laws and other means of influx control; the scrapping of the Bantu education system; and the transformation of the existing homeland governments into provincial assemblies.

In all this can perhaps be seen the rudiments of a multiracial alliance committed to a major transformation of the South African scene. Yet when acknowledging this, one should not forget the horrifying leeway to be made up before the country in question can even approach the multiracial ideal. The magnitude of the problem was highlighted by talks held, in the sanguine days of early 1975, between Mr Vorster and the leaders of the Bantustans and also the Coloured and Indian councils. He intimated that the government might soften the impact of the pass laws, would consider giving leasehold rights to urban Africans, and would also think further about trade unionism. In addition, he was prepared to see the executives of the Coloured and Indian councils sit on an "inter-cabinet council" with the leaders of the White government.

Evidently, Prime Minister Vorster felt he was pushing the interpretation of "separate development" to, if not beyond, its uttermost liberal margins. Nevertheless, it is all too easy to understand Chief Buthulezi's warning of the inevitability of civil disobedience and disruption in the absence of far more concessionary offers. Nor can one glean much reassurance from the reaction of the authorities to the spate of urban rioting and protest which began in Soweto in June 1976. The movement towards at least a qualified multiracialism in sport tentatively continues. But there has been no such mobility *vis-à-vis* the vital matter of improving the status and representation of the urban Blacks.

Meanwhile, the experience of the Transkei alone is enough to bear out the admonitions regularly issued these last 20 years that, quite apart from its inherent philosophical inconsistencies, separate development was doomed to failure because its pecuniary mechanics were insupportable. Since 1963 the South African government has pumped £250 million into the Transkei economy. Yet only several thousand new jobs have thereby been created, either in the homeland or on its periphery, whereas over 25,000 more Transkeians come onto the labour market every year.

Therefore, it seems clear that South Africa will stand no chance of tolerably smooth and balanced progress until its current political ideology has been superseded by one that stresses the development of the actual personality of each individual rather than the reassertion of the perceived personality of the communal group. In all probability, the best hope of initiating this would lie in English-speaking liberals forging a parliamentary axis with kindred spirits from the Afrikaans side.

But from wherever comes the lead, a multiracial economy and

society is going to be hard to realise, even as an approximation. Whilst per capita incomes for the different communities are difficult to come by, the average per capita income for South Africa as a whole in 1974 has been given as 925 rand. But in the all-important mining industry, for example, the average White worker's earnings were 6,700 rand that same year as against the average Black's 560.[3] Moreover, during the major strikes in Natal in 1973 not a few Black workers had been shown to be drawing wages that put them and their dependants well below the poverty datum line as officially reckoned— e.g. 1,000 rand per annum for a Bantu family of five.[4]

Worse, ministerial statements in 1972 indicated that the annual support from public education funds averaged 366 rand for each White child at primary school, 112 for each Indian, 91 for each Cape Coloured and 21 for each Black. Moreover, we are authoritatively advised that in the case of the Black children this estimate may have been too high.[5]

In other words, the elimination of economic Apartheid must either be very gradual or else must involve actual and considerable falls in White living standards. Unfortunately, too, attitudes may again be hardening up all round in such a manner as to make either accommodation less probable. A good deal of the running in townships like Soweto has lately been made by Black Power radicals. What is more, there are signs that the old resentment between the English-speaking and the Afrikaners smoulders in a fashion which could compromise a more open-ended political dialogue within White South Africa.

Undoubtedly a renewed sense of hopelessness about the urban crisis has encouraged a firming up of communal battle-lines. But so, too, has the way John Vorster's policy of *détente* with the Black states to the north has gone sour. As of the time of writing, the Geneva conference on Rhodesia holds out little hope of a peaceful transition to genuine majority rule, one obstacle being the encouragement the guerrilla hard-core receives from Moscow. Meanwhile, the MPLA regime in Angola, backed by the Cuban expeditionary force, continues operations against the remnants of the FNLA/UNITA guerrilla forces driven into the bush by the overwhelming firepower of heavy weapons in 1975.

The Angolan affair has, of course, been disturbing throughout. Early in 1975 UNITA looked set to lead in the independence referendum the three liberation movements were understood to have agreed to hold at the end of the year. The political flair of its leader, Jonas

Savimbi, was standing it in good stead. So was its political base within the large Ovimbundu tribal group. Moreover, both Zaïre and Zambia had made clear their view that FNLA/UNITA should be accorded a major stake in the independence settlement. This being so, the seizure of exclusive power by the MPLA must be acknowledged as a triumph of polarisation by Cuba and the USSR. In the light of which, the passage by the UN Security Council, in April 1976, of a resolution condemning only the South African army's temporary and much more tangential involvement might itself be condemned as discriminatory.

Not that this particular event was at all exceptional. One of the most disturbing features of the international scene since the 1950s has been the propensity of received opinion elsewhere constantly to use South Africa as the scapegoat for primitive group loyalties which are latent in all of us and which find expression, in sundry ways, in the policies of many countries. As a parliamentary candidate for the Progressive Reform Party, David Welsh—a lecturer at Capetown University—has known at first hand the weary sequence of arrest, interrogation and detention. Yet he has declared himself appalled by, in particular, "the callousness of the radical Left. When I was at a seminar in America a year or two ago . . . I suddenly realised that they didn't care if a whole generation was wiped out in the struggle as long as the glorious revolution took place in South Africa".[6]

Meanwhile, even moderate shades of Left opinion in the West tend to be adamantly hostile towards Pretoria, consistently grudging both in their praise of specific overtures and in their general sympathy. What makes the blanket negation all the more striking is that, at the time of the second South African War (1899–1902), the great bulk of the Left in Britain and elsewhere was solidly, in England often courageously, pro-Boer. In fact, they tended to endorse them absolutely, doing so in terms that correspond remarkably closely to all the more positive images of the Israelis projected in recent years: "straightforward, hard-working agrarians imbued with a splendidly tough but informal group solidarity, bags of martial zeal and initiative, and a fervent desire to live in peace".

This comparison is drawn because, in the wake of the 1967 "June war", the South African authorities started actively to explore the analogies between Israel's predicament and their own. Soon Defence Minister Botha was citing Israel's air raids against Fatah bases in Jordan to illustrate what his own country might do by way of "hard retaliation in the interests of self-respect and peace" if neighbouring territories harboured insurgent terrorists.[7] Early in 1974—i.e. not long after the slump in relations between Israel and Black Africa hard upon the latter's punitive offensive across the Suez Canal—the head of the South African Bureau of State Security was quoted as saying that as long as Israel survives, South Africa does. Soon, Israel was induced to raise its diplomatic representation in Pretoria to full ambassadorial level. Around this time, too, the secretary of the South African Board of Jewish Deputies was said to concede that Apartheid was valuable in that it allowed particular ethnic groups to preserve their cultural identity. In the spring of 1976, Mr Vorster paid an informal visit to Israel.

Still, the parallels implied have not as yet cut a great deal of ice in the West, mainly on account of two circumstances. The first is that Israel as strictly defined remains a thoroughly democratic state in almost every aspect of political decision-taking. The second is that, great though the social distance between Israeli Jew and Israeli Arab usually is, it is not preserved by an institutionalised panoply of privileges and proscriptions as harsh and bizarre as Apartheid. As is noted in the next chapter, however, the comparison could become more apt if communal relations within Israel and the occupied territories take a turn for the worse. In any case, a lot of South African Whites will glean their own lessons from Israel's resolve not to be driven into the sea.

Nor should we underestimate the capacity of White South Africa to fight for survival if such comes to seem the one and only course. South Africa has, at comparatively short notice, the military nuclear option. It is becoming considerably self-sufficient in the production and maintenance of the requisites of war: field artillery, strike aircraft, food, oil and so on. And this probably means that it could be hurt from outside only by a very broad diversity of economic sanctions.[8] Likewise, its internal security arrangements retain their grim efficiency, whilst its military manpower could, on full mobilisation, exceed a quarter of a million. Geography would be largely on its side, at least as long as it stood prepared to enforce closed borders in a thoroughly uncompromising fashion.

In summation, the policy of "separate development" has no future because logically it is a nonsense whilst pragmatically it is altogether too utopian. Hopefully, it will be transcended by what will inevitably be a gradual and uncomfortable progression towards a multiracial economy and society—a progression that, for all its traumas, could eventually do much to further the balanced development of the other countries in the region. Alternatively, the dynamic of the situation will induce a backlash into inter-communal hostility more blatantly illiberal on all sides than anything we have yet seen. And the South African Whites would be likely to retain the upper hand in the consequent race war through 1990 and well beyond.

Notes

1. *Progress through Separate Development*, The South African Department of Information, Pretoria 1973, p. 29.
2. *The Economist*, 20 March 1976.
3. *The Statesman's Year Book, 1976/7*, Macmillan, London 1976, p. 1295.
4. In September 1973 the official exchange rate was roughly two rand to three dollars.
5. *A Survey of Race Relations in South Africa*, The South African Institute of Race Relations, Johannesburg, 1974, p. 201.
6. As reported in *The Evening Standard*, 25 May 1976.
7. "In the steps of Dayan", *The Economist*, 3 June 1968.
8. See Chapters 7(c) and 9.

20

The Arab–Israel Question

Perhaps the most basic premise to establish is that, this side of 1990, none of the parties to this conflict will be able to impose its will by force of arms. The Israeli ability to do so will be circumscribed throughout by the Arab oil weapon. Also by the risk of a military victory proving pyrrhic, this by dint of casualty lists intolerable to a small nation rendered sensitive by the Jewish past to the need to preserve the future. A year or so ago a CIA study concluded that, whilst Israel should be able to defeat Egypt plus Syria in three weeks, it stood to incur thereby 36,000 casualties including 8,000 dead (this latter statistic being treble its sacrifice over the same interval in 1973).

Nevertheless, a fair summation of the balance of military advantage, in strictly operational terms, was that made by Major-General Mordecai Gur, the Israeli Chief of Staff, during the symposium held in Jerusalem on the second anniversary of the Yom Kippur war. He expressed confidence that the Israel Defence Force could win "a decisive victory in any conflict with the Arabs in the next five to ten years". Beyond that, he conceded, the weaponry to hand would make war too horrible for either side to contemplate.

To those who focus on Israel's persistent inferiority in numbers of tanks, artillery, warplanes and the like, the above expression of certitude about its military invincibility may be puzzling. Evidently, one element in its justification would be the defensibility of Israel's present battle lines. Even so, this situation would not necessarily be affected materially by another concessionary agreement on disengagement. Thus irrespective of the specifics of any such accord in the Sinai, the Suez Canal (with or without an underpass or two) would remain a source of weakness to any Egyptian army deployed beyond it. More than two millennia ago, Sun Tzu—the Chinese scholar and general who is often spoken of as the first strategic theorist of all time—said that an army should never oblige itself to fight with its back to a waterline.[1]

Another consideration is that Israel, being Israel, will never again be taken by strategic surprise the way it was in 1973. Here the maxim that History does not repeat itself (because those who are unfolding the present plot witnessed the preceding denouement) is not just relevant: it is conclusive.

Admittedly, Israel's superiority in the air, which until 1973 was the unassailable coping stone of its constant ascendancy in land and also naval warfare, will be further qualified by the advent in Arab hands of more advanced surface-to-air missiles, warplanes and related systems, Soviet or other. However, the geometric truism that you cannot cover everywhere with the narrow envelopes of fire a SAM-6 presents to low-flying aircraft is of considerably more moment over the wide, flattish, bare and sunlit coasts and hinterlands of Egypt and Syria than over the North German plain. Nor are any shipments from the Soviet Union and so on likely to offset in kind the 300 F-15 and F-16 advanced fighters Israel should have in service by 1985.

Besides which, in this sphere of military activity even more than others, one can be sure that the expected shrinking of the technology gap between the USSR and the West's main arms exporters will not be matched fully by a closure of the indigenous gap between Israel's Arab neighbours and itself. In other words, the former will continue to find the operation and maintenance of sophisticated equipment quite a tough proposition.[2] The fact that we over-estimated this factor before 1973 must not lure us into under-estimating it now.

Then again, in spite of such grim though isolated incidents as the massacre of children at Maalot in 1974, the Palestinian guerrilla movements have never looked like posing a physical threat to Israel's survival, not even at their military zenith. Let us take, for example, the myth that only King Hussein's armed intervention against the guerrilla bands in East Bank Jordan in September 1970 stopped the West Bank from becoming a second Vietnam. In reality, it was obvious down in the Jordan valley in the months beforehand that the Israeli interception rate against infiltration was crushingly high.[3] The September showdown did not cause the collapse of the guerrilla campaign across the Jordan valley: it was itself a consequence of it.

One thing the guerrilla campaign did do in the late 1960s was induce the Israelis to adopt a series of harsh security measures in the West Bank and the Gaza. A bitter controversy recurrently erupted within the West's intelligentsia, notably inside Amnesty International, about the methods of interrogation in depth used against key suspects. Other contentious measures included severe curfews and the arbitrary demolition of hundreds or thousands of homes in which guerrillas had been harboured, willingly or otherwise.

With the easement of the security situation the occupation regime has become far more relaxed, as witness the very open West Bank elections of 1976. But one quasi-permanent legacy of the previous phase has been a heightened awareness on the part of the Israelis themselves of their vulnerability to insurgent terrorism. Another does seem to have been a certain radicalisation of political opinion on the West Bank, a radicalisation that has since been supercharged by the civil wars in Jordan and the Lebanon. Each of these shifts of attitude has further complicated the search for a peaceful accommodation.

Since 1967, the situation in the occupied territories has been a cardinal theme in the propaganda war between Arabs and Zionists. The war is one that, between 1917 and 1973, the former lost as regularly as they did the trials by combat. Partly this outcome was a function of a big differential in technical competence. Yet it was also because Arab publicists proved far more prone to fabrication and hyperbole.

For one thing, they operated against the background of what was still a weak tradition of modern scholarship. Perhaps, too, this in its turn encouraged the erroneous belief that sensationalism was the best way to break down the partiality for Israel so deeply embedded in Western, and especially American, opinion. Clearly, they also felt extravagance was essential to the political mobilisation of peasant communities heavily preoccupied by a primordial struggle against starvation and disease. No doubt, too, the script-writers were themselves impelled by a powerful subjective urge to mask the daunting facts about Israel's military and economic prowess.

However, several of these factors have been modified substantially in the wake of "Yom Kippur". In consequence, Arab journalism and broadcasting already show strong indications of a greater technical awareness and presentational moderation. In all probability, this trend will gain momentum in the 1980s as, for example, public services all over the Middle East draw into their upper echelons growing numbers of officials who have benefited from some higher education in the West.

Occasionally, it is suggested that the new-found moderation may be more than cosmetic, that it will involve a fundamental revision of attitudes towards Israel. Usually, the Egypt of Anwar Sadat is cited as a putative pacemaker in this direction.

However, such inferences may be altogether too glib. So far as Egypt is concerned, there is no guarantee that the Sadat regime will long survive. Subject to the results of the 1976 census, the population of Greater Cairo (now *c.* 9,000,000) seems to be growing at four per cent a year, an urban implosion that cannot but exacerbate what is already a highly combustible state of congestion and deprivation. To make matters worse, the new middle class that has gained so much from the economic liberalisation of the last two years flaunts its spending power altogether too brazenly. Meanwhile, Egypt remains in need of about two billion dollars worth of aid a year, at least until tourism, oil and canal dues come good around 1980. Given these and other indications of persistent and severe economic strain, we cannot exclude the possibility of a reversion to a more thoroughgoing authoritarianism, perhaps in the form of a martial puritanism inspired by the Moslem Brotherhood.

Moreover, the decisive political force in Egypt, even as things stand, is neither the Arab Socialist Union nor Anwar Sadat himself. Instead, it is a military establishment 350,000 strong. Whatever happens, persuading the combined Egyptian forces to accept the drastically reduced role (and therefore size) a definitive peace with Israel would involve would be difficult enough. To get them to do so without the historical vindication that the national aspirations of the Palestinians had been largely met would be flatly impossible. For virtually the sole rationale behind the original Egyptian military build-up was a triumphal solution of the Palestinian question. Similar considerations apply with Syria, this notwithstanding the pro-Christian weighting of its intervention in the Lebanon in 1976.

Therefore, the scene seems set for a continuation of the current confrontation between the Arabs and the Israelis for some years to come: no war but no peace either. What has to be recognised, on the other hand, is that, in its non-territorial aspects, this status quo is not static but highly dynamic. Israel faces, in an unusually acute form, the universal dilemma about national and ethnic identity, the dilemma caused by cultural flux or "future shock".

In this situation, the basic problem is compounded by the fact that, although Israel is defined as a Jewish state, over a third of the 4,500,000 people living in the territories it currently controls are Arab. Even without this complication, however, the pressures towards social and hence political change would be relentless. One authoritative projection put the income per capita of Israel proper at

$3,000, at constant prices, in 2000 AD as opposed to $1,330 in 1965. The self-same source guestimated the number of television sets at 300 per thousand people then as against 75 in 1970.[4]

Here again the "puritan paradox" rears its sardonic head: the fruits of the "back to the land" puritanism of early Zionism ineluctably corrode the ethic from which they stemmed. Thus, today the kibbutzim tend to hire cheap Arab labour to do the menial tasks, a disposition that Golda Meir was always anxious about yet powerless to curb. Meanwhile, their members come to expect such consumer durables as television sets and cars, each of which is admitted to have particularly negative implications for the intense and exclusive social interaction that is the *sine qua non* of kibbutz life.

Then again, whilst the young generation in Israel is as yet much less obviously alienated than its peers in many countries, it is not only vigorous and wilful but also alive to the cosmopolitan youth culture that has spread throughout the West and far beyond. This being so, one is bound to wonder how much longer some of the more assertive young people are going to acquiesce in, for example, the more restrictive of the sabbatarian taboos or the absence of a civil marriage code.

What is more, the young sabras (i.e. native born) have often turned out to be less bound than were their forbears by their ties with the Jews of the Dispersion: "I am not a Zionist, I am an Israeli". In a sense, of course, the embryonic Israeli nation had already started to turn its back on the Dispersion when it rejected the gentle "refugee jargon" of Yiddish in favour of a renaissance of Hebrew, a tongue which "has no half-tones or modulations of key or timbre".[5]

True, the challenge and triumph of 1967 was to reforge the links awhile. Even so, only a few months afterwards Rabbi Elmer Berger, the Executive Vice-President of the 20,000-strong American Council for Judaism, was arguing that a prerequisite of peace would be Israel's relinquishment of her role as the focus of a Zionist ingathering. Soon, too, the tensions between Dr Nahum Goldmann, President of the World Jewish Congress, and Israel's new Prime Minister, Golda Meir, were to betoken a wider divergence. Not irrelevant in this connection is the fact that, come 1990, very few Israelis below the age of 50 will remember first-hand the birth of their state. Relevant, too, is a long-term tendency for immigration to decline, despite a resurgence (largely from the capricious USSR) between the climacteric years of 1967 and 1973. In 1966 there had actually been a net outflow; and by 1975 the net movement was again back to zero or thereabouts.

Meanwhile, cultural convergence between the various communities is likely to gather pace within Israel's *de facto* frontiers, this being a key dimension in the cultural flux referred to earlier. In particular, the contrast in life style between the average Israeli Arab youth and the average Israeli Jewish youth may be neither very evident nor very meaningful by 1990. Furthermore, that between young Israelis and young West Bankers may have started to diminish fast.

By the same token, the longer the occupation of the West Bank lasts the harder will it be to separate the territory in question from Israel proper. In fact, we may already be very close to the point of no return to anything like the 1967 status quo ante, quite irrespective of what any politicians say. East Jerusalem apart, the number of Israeli civilians settled in the occupied West Bank is still only 7,000. Nevertheless, the geographical spread of their sundry outposts has been such as to render disengagement from "Judaea and Samaria" excruciatingly difficult in terms of Israeli politics.

Yet some of the more benign aspects of the occupation regimen also tend to gravitate the West Bank (and, more ambivalently, the Gaza) towards Israel rather than East Bank Jordan. Among them are the modest strength, good personal behaviour and normally low profile of the garrison force; the acknowledged fact that the local Arab press has usually been freer than under Jordanian rule; the appreciable sums spent on development, even outside East Jerusalem; the encouragement of a sustained agricultural boom; and the permits granted to tens of thousands of Arabs to take up manual work in Israel. To which may be added the "Open Bridges" scheme whereby trade continues across the Jordan River and whereby each year visitors can come to the West Bank and the Gaza and thence, if they wish, go into Israel.

Besides which, there can be little doubt that Israel's general staff makes a militarily sound appreciation when it says that, given the inherent threat of terrorism and with technological progress raising the military dividends to be gained from sudden armoured thrusts, the permanent location of the strategic frontier along the River Jordan has become imperative. Agreed, that stipulation would not in itself rule out an Israeli withdrawal from the West Bank within the context of a demilitarisation agreement. But, as things stand, it does serve to cap all the other pressures towards an indissoluble nexus.

Yet what this means is that, in 1967, Israel got itself more or less inextricably landed with a proportion of Palestinian Arabs so high as to make it logically impossible for the resultant polity to remain at once distinctively Jewish and genuinely democratic. Therefore, when certain commentators have spoken of the West Bank and the Gaza Strip as bargaining counters to be traded in to obtain peace, they have grasped absolutely the wrong end of a very awkward stick. Israel always had a far more basic need to offload the greater part of this territory than any Arab leader had to receive it back. Though little explicit reference to this inverted trump card is ever made by either side, some account was being taken of it in Amman well before the "Yom Kippur" watershed.[6]

Within Israel itself, a proper coming to grips with the demographic contradiction created by the events of 1967 has been delayed by two special factors. One has been the on-going state of belligerency. The other is a preoccupation with the still underprivileged situation of the Oriental Jews—those from such Arab countries as Morocco and Iraq plus a few from non-Arab Asian states. Although these people and their children comprise half the population, barely a tenth of the Knesset was drawn from their ranks in 1972. Similarly, their per capita income is scarcely half that of the European Jews.

But, serious though this problem is at this point in time, it should iron itself out fairly smoothly in the course of the 1980s as the third generation of Oriental immigrants approaches manhood. At least it poses no question about the identity of the Jewish state anything like as fundamental as that raised by the Palestinian presence.

Underlying anxiety about the latter situation goes far to explain the criss-cross nature of the debate which developed after 1967 about Jewish settlement in the occupied territories. Thus within the Labour-Mapam alignment, which won 56 of the 120 Knesset seats in the 1969 election, every gradation from near minimalist to near maximalist was to be found, the prime justification ranging at each and every point from historic destiny to tactical necessity.

However, representing as they corporately did the main fount of Israeli social democracy, almost all the Members of the Knesset within Labour-Mapam seemed initially to take for granted that full political rights would be extended to any Arabs brought permanently under Israel's jurisdiction. Yet by the early 1970s this presumed axiom was being actively challenged from within the Israeli Left. Thus one ostensibly Marxist analysis of the socio-economic revolution under way on the West Bank concluded by advocating the creation there of a client state in which only local self-government would be allowed.[7] Then again, shortly before the Arab summit conference convened in Rabat in the autumn of 1974, Foreign Minister Yigal Allon said that, if the said conference took decisions adjudged to preclude peace, Israel would "find a way to protect its political and military interests while doing justice to the Arab population living in the occupied areas".[8]

Shades in such statements of what would assuredly be intended as a liberal interpretation of the "separate development" philosophy implemented by successive Nationalist governments in South Africa. Moreover, this subtle shift of emphasis in Israeli official circles was being matched at the grass-roots level by a greater profusion of comments similar to those long heard from the White minorities in Southern Africa: "this land was more or less empty when we first came in"; "our Arabs are better off than any others in the region"; "our enemies are mere terrorists who cannot even agree among themselves". . . . The plain truth is that all advanced minorities caught up in so agonising a situation are prone to reactions of this sort.

The inference might be drawn that victory in the general election to be held in the spring of 1977 is destined effectively to go to a Rightist axis, most of whose members would be firmly in favour of the gradual but complete absorption of the West Bank without the due extension of political rights to its indigenous Arab inhabitants. Arguably, too, the likelihood of this outcome has been increased by the way the social deprivation of the culturally conservative Oriental Jews is being accentuated by Israel's economic strains: a 40 per cent inflation rate in 1975 and an external debt of nine billion dollars by the middle of 1976. Nor have the corruption scandals helped in this connection.

Let it be said straightway that if such does come to pass it could lead to a rupturing of Israel's underlying political consensus, one result perhaps being that its responses to military challenge might be judged less nicely than in the past. In addition, were Israel to pass politically into the hands of men like Beigin and Sharon this would be an acute embarrassment to the whole Atlantic community, given that the latter's very survival may increasingly depend on its forceful reaffirmation of the tenet that democracy is indivisible. To which one might add that the ascendancy of the Israeli Right might also stultify the embryonic quest for a new political dialogue in South Africa, seeing how much South Africa is now inclined to take its cue from Israel (see the last chapter).

However, the odds may still be against this happening, either in 1977 or at any time in the foreseeable future. Collectively, the Labour Party very much remains the keeper of the ark of the Zionist covenant, the founding father of the state and the mainspring of much of its high degree of social and technical innovation. Furthermore, the obvious retort that indefinite rule by one party is itself a denial of democracy can always be parried by reference to the rumbustious unruliness of the Labour leadership, hardly the makings here of a monolithic caucus. Besides which, there are splits within the Right which have potentially much more negative implications, concerning as they do such divisive issues as secularism versus theocracy.

Certainly, it would be a dreadful mistake for the international community to push in 1977 and 1978 for a speedy yet definitive solution to the Arab–Israel dispute, lest the opportunity passes by forever. What this means, in particular, is that it would be a blunder to oblige the Israelis and the Palestinians respectively to accept, whether provisionally or unconditionally, the creation of a Palestinian state in the West Bank and the Gaza, even if this artefact was blessed at its inception by countries like Egypt and Jordan. Surely, Israeli ministers have been right in their insistence that there is not enough room to squeeze in such a state. Nor would it do much for the Palestinians in East Bank Jordan: modern Amman is, after all, 80 per cent a Palestinian town.

Nor would the polity envisaged be cohesive internally. No matter that PLO supporters swept the board in the West Bank municipal elections of April 1976, the social structure of this territory is still quasi-feudalistic and therefore contrasts sharply with the flotsam society of the Gaza Strip. Within two years of its establishment the fledgling state would have sundered, leaving the Gaza to become a shop-window for Cuba and North Korea. Nor would federation with Israel, as advocated by one of Israel's most respected publicists,[9] actually meet this particular point.

An important corollary is that such an entity would be useless throughout as an anvil on which to hammer out a solution of what is perhaps the thorniest aspect of this whole problem, Jerusalem. Not that any civilised being wishes again to split this sacred and lovely city with barbed wire, à la 1948–67. On the contrary, there would now be wide endorsement of a joint municipality, underpinned by international guarantees: "a city of peace and cooperation between the three great monotheistic religions", to quote King Hussein talking to *Le Monde* in November 1972. But he went on to explain that this formula would have to involve formal recognition of Arab sovereignty over the Old City as it had obtained before the June War. What is more, the customary character of the conurbation as a whole would have to be preserved by tight control of its demographic growth and the maintenance of the existing numerical balance between the two chief communities.

Clearly, these stipulations would not be easy to reconcile with the master plan for Jerusalem promulgated by the Israelis in 1969. Within the city proper, the population increase predicated between then and 2010 AD was from 200,000 Jews and 70,000 Arabs to 440,000 Jews and 160,000 Arabs. And by the end of this phase, the total number of people in the Jerusalem metropolitan area was to roughly treble to 900,000, the great majority in the new suburbs being Jews.

Above all else, progress towards a stable settlement in the Middle East depends on a growing acceptance on the part of Israeli Jews and Palestinian Arabs that their respective destinies are closely and positively linked. At the time of Willy Brandt's visit to Israel in 1973 Vera Elyashiv, an Israeli authoress, wrote of the special bond between her own people and the Germans: "We are the two sides of a tragedy . . ." Much the same could be said, albeit in a lower key, of her people and the Palestinians. Many of the first-generation Israeli leaders, notably David Ben-Gurion and Golda Meir, were altogether too indifferent to their measure of responsibility for the very real injustice the Palestinian people have suffered. They have been too ready to discount the not inconsiderable part that terrorism, especially by the Irgun, played in the initial exodus of refugees in 1948. They have also been too quick to set against it, *lex talionis* fashion, the numerically comparable inflow of Oriental Jews.

As regards the latter, their main flight did not occur until after that of the Palestinians. Nor were the Palestinians instrumental in effecting it. Nor was this "coming up to Israel" entirely involuntary. Nor was it a dispersion to desert fringes.

Not that the Israelis would find a genuine dialogue with an authentically Palestinian leadership at all easy to sustain. Over the years the top men in the guerrilla movement have mainly been of dismal quality, utterly effete or hopelessly embittered or both. You could not look for a worthwhile or even congenial exchange with crude racists like Amin Husaini or Ahmed Shukairy. My own view was that Kamel Nasser, the PLO spokesman killed by Israeli commandos in 1973, represented some improvement.[10] But it was a moot point.

All the same, many of the Palestinian professional people today at work in Amman and other cities are manifestly of superior calibre. Among the specific signs of progress several years ago was the advent of the Journal of Palestine Studies, an objective—and indeed, scholarly—publication emanating from Kuwait University and the Institute for Palestine Studies in Beirut. One must hope that it has survived the Lebanese civil war and that it and other benign influences will flourish in the several years of peace that now seem likely within the region. Some thought on where a dialogue might lead is taken in Chapter 22.

Notes

1. Sun Tzu, *The Art of War*, translated by Lionel Giles, Civilian Publishing House, Taipeh 1953. Chapter 8.
2. Antoine Zahlan, "The Science and Technology Gap in the Arab–Israel conflict", *The Journal of Palestine Studies*, Vol. I No. 3, Spring 1972, pp. 17–36.
3. See the author's "The Jordanian Civil War", *The Military Review*, Vol. LI No. 9, September 1971, pp. 38–48.
4. *The Middle East in the Year 2000*, The Association for Peace, Tel Aviv *c.* 1971.
5. Arthur Koestler, *Promise and Fulfilment: Palestine 1917–49*, Macmillan, London 1949, p. 313.
6. See the author's "L'idée d'abandonner la rive occidentale du Jourdain gagné du terrain dans la royaume hachémite", *Le Monde Diplomatique*. September 1972.
7. B. Shaicovitch, "Dialectical Paternalism: Marx on the West Bank", *The New Middle East*, No. 55, April 1973, pp. 21–5.
8. *The Guardian*, 23 October 1974.
9. Uri Avnery, *Israel Without Zionists*, Macmillan, New York 1968. Chapter 11.
10. "Kamel Nasser: Terrorist or Man of Peace?" *The New Middle East*, No. 56, May 1973, pp. 17–18.

Part V

A Synoptic Appreciation: Inferences and Remedies

21

A Menacing Interaction of Trends

Notwithstanding what was said at the outset about the hollow character of the actual advances thus far made towards disarmament, it can be claimed with some justice that the conceptual foundations for future progress have been laid. Thus one beneficent development has been a very widespread down grading of General and Complete Disarmament (GCD) in the scale of policy priorities. Today the vast majority of commentators overtly acknowledge that, in a world as plagued as ours is by conflicts of attitude and interest, GCD can only represent a false utopianism. Probably, too, there is tacit acceptance of the likelihood that certain kinds of military power will have a legitimate part to play in world affairs for centuries, if not millennia, to come.

With this down grading of GCD has come, too, a wide even if tentative endorsement of two other propositions. The first is that defence policy and the quest for arms control and phased disarmament are best seen as twin aspects of the same theme: "not contradictory but complementary", to quote a study launched within NATO in 1966 by Pierre Harmel, the Foreign Minister of Belgium. The second is that mutual reassurance, through military and political measures, is likewise the *alter ego* of mutual deterrence.

Among the milestones of this new approach have been the inauguration in Helsinki in 1973 of the multilateral Conference on Security and Cooperation in Europe. Also the commencement in Vienna shortly afterwards of negotiations on Mutual Force Reductions in Central Europe. Also, too, the Arab-Israel disengagement agreements reached, with the coercive encouragement of the Superpowers, in the wake of "Yom Kippur".

Even so, we ought now urgently to consider whether we may not have substituted one form of false utopianism with another, thus raising expectations which may then be shattered all the more completely. Much store has been set by *détente* between the Superpowers plus their respective alliances. Yet, after nigh on ten years, the fruits of this ramified dialogue are neither tangible nor stable. Meanwhile, various trends on the global plane—ranging from the crime wave to plutonium—point to the world of 1990 being more violent than today's.

Furthermore, one does not have to accept too simplistic a rendering of the old axiom that peace is indivisible to see how, in the international arena just as more locally, violence begets violence. In particular, Limited World War (see Chapter 2) could become a recurrent pattern of conflict once certain thresholds of restraint had been pierced. Not the least of the reasons for apprehending this is that it could plausibly be deemed to fit a loose interpretation of the Marxist-Leninist dialectic.

On the other hand, the most crucial point about Limited World War is that, almost by definition, it is likely first to break out not through deliberate and massive aggression on any nation's part but on account of instabilities within an interlocking framework of collateral deterrence. Needless to say, too, such instabilities may be either triggered or accentuated by the misperceptions to which any era of flux and tension is prone: a failure to understand the "action-reaction" phenomenon being a standard case in point.

For instance, an afterglow of the post-1950 propensity to assume the worst about China could be observed when some read undisguised expansionism into the article of September 1965 in which Lin Piao stretched the classic Maoist model to envisage insurgency in the "world countryside" (i.e. the newly developing regions) as encircling the "world city" (i.e. the Atlantic area). But by that time, there was a steadily extending American commitment to major operations throughout Vietnam, a commitment which was being explained partly in terms of a postulated need to minimise China's influence. Therefore, this and all the other talk in Peking then about "setting Asia ablaze" might fairly be regarded as no more than countervailing deterrence. In short, the "active defence" school there was prudentially invoking a presumed capacity to foment insurgency in order to offset the nuclear-capped might of Washington.

Almost certainly, too, there was a close connection between the Vietnam war and the intensified skirmishing along the armistice line in Korea in 1967 and again in 1968. Nor is it inconceivable that a wish to divert American attention from Vietnam lay behind those curious machinations by the USSR in the Middle East in May of the former year, though this is not to say it actually wanted the all-out war which ensued.

However, there can be little doubt about Western Europe's being the theatre placed most at risk by the logical and dialectical possibility of Limited World War. The new spirit of rationality apparently suffusing the Soviet officer corps (see Chapter 24) is unlikely to modify greatly a very special and long-standing Russian interest in the European theatre, less than entirely rational though the manifestations of this interest may sometimes have seemed.

For one thing, the USSR has proved itself to be by no means unaware of the hostage connotations of the Western European region. One case in point, though perhaps purely token, was Bulganin's warning, delivered towards the close of the Suez campaign in 1956, about rockets being fired at London and Paris. Likewise during "Cuba" Khrushchev alluded to a possible invasion of Turkey. Meanwhile, plans were being laid in several capitals lest action be taken against West Berlin. Similarly, the physical albeit non-violent pressures applied to West Berlin during the early months of both 1965 and 1968 were ominously coincident with sharp escalations of the Vietnam conflict, even though the given reasons were couched in terms of the local situation. What is more, the military vulnerability of Western Europe will be exacerbated in the 1980s by the extra premium accorded sudden and massive non-nuclear attack by yet another surge of technological innovation, its axial theme being what has been adjudged tantamount to a revival of artillery. A special factor is that the increasing accuracy of ordnance is to the net advantage of he who strikes first.

The basic point would not have been lost on Napoleon Bonaparte, as is well illustrated by the most definitive study of his generalship yet written.[1] For he was imbued with a burning conviction that the key to success lay in sudden, swift and decisive attack; and he was no less persuaded that, "Missile weapons are now become the principal ones" or again that "It is with artillery that war is made". To pray Napoleon in aid may not be inappropriate. Not only was he an unsurpassed master of tactics. He was also appraised of the need, extolled throughout this study, to let Grand Strategy embrace a whole range of intellectual disciplines.

Evidently, a combination of topography and the ratio between troops and linear space does leave the Northern Army Group of NATO especially susceptible to the technological change anticipated. Among other scenarios for aggressive action which are by no means implausible within the time-scale here under review, and to which similar tactical considerations apply, are these: the Soviet Union versus Poland or parts of North China; the Warsaw Pact versus Romania or Danubian Yugoslavia; and Syria or Iraq versus Jordan.

Clearly, the military threat to Western Europe and the other territories just mentioned will be further heightened by the dogged progress of the USSR (or perhaps one should say COMECON) in terms of quality of technology, the exotic mix of skills required in cruise missile and advanced fighter development probably remaining signal exceptions through 1985. To some extent, too, differential changes in the volume of heavy industrial output may be unhelpful to the West and its friends.

Historically, the output of steel or sulphuric acid or industrial products at large has been taken as the best index of this latter aspect of military potential. Obviously, strong arguments can be adduced today, and even more particularly tomorrow, in favour of using computer installation additionally or instead: one of these arguments being that it does full justice to the economic strength of the USA. Nevertheless, the statistics of steel output seem set to remain quite appropriate criteria of most nations' material ability to manufacture the diverse paraphernalia of modern mechanised war. Besides which, they are a good deal easier to obtain and summate.

In the boom year of 1973 North America produced $c.$ 150 million tons of crude steel; and so did the nine members of the EEC. Meanwhile, all the full members of COMECON turned out $c.$ 178 million tons, almost three-quarters of this being Soviet. Japan produced 120 million tons.[2]

Doing some extrapolations through from 1953 and 1963, and feeding in certain approximate corrections, one gets the following impression of the steel balance in the middle 1980s. North America plus the EEC will have an annual output close to 400 million tons, rather over half then coming from the European side of the ocean. Meanwhile, between 250 and 275 million tons are likely to be registered by COMECON, the Soviet proportion having dropped to two-thirds. In other words, COMECON will have narrowed the percentage gap between itself and the Atlantic region to an appreciable extent.

Seeing that its output quadrupled between 1953 and 1963 and then again between 1963 and 1973, it is hard to see how Japan can fail to exceed 250 million tons in 1985, even when big allowances are made for possible alterations in that country's economic configuration and socio-political milieu. More is the pity that national attitude still combines with geographical eccentricity to inhibit Japan from playing its full part in either the defence of the West or world economic development.

Communist China actually has something of an iron and steel crisis, and this for the third time round. During the Great Leap Forward the annual output of what passed for steel roughly quadrupled to *c*. 18,000,000 tons, thanks mainly to a frenetic cult of backyard charcoal furnaces. In 1961 it slumped almost to the previous level, yet was to recover within five years to *c*. 15,000,000 tons—the general quality of which was tolerable. But then the Cultural Revolution arrested expansion for several more years.

Since 1971 the estimated figure has hovered a little above 20 million tons, some four million tons of pig iron and finished steel being imported annually by 1974. Apparently, one factor hindering the growth of indigenous supplies is the extreme energy-dependence of Chinese blast furnaces. Accordingly, we may find that China's steel production does not exceed 50,000,000 tons in 1990, even be it spared damaging political strife in the interim.

What then of those countries that are more likely to import the great bulk of their so-called "conventional" weaponry? Here the most critical question is the width of the technocratic base on which armed services are built. Probably the number of motor vehicles in civilian employ is the best single measure of this, even though it discounts far too completely electronic facilities and skills and even though, too, it does play down those countries—e.g. most of the Marxist ones—in which the political culture has been antipathetic to the private car.

But to focus thus is to highlight in this context, as well as others, the rapid spread of mechanised land transport in poor countries as well as rich. Across the African continent, exclusive of the Republic of South Africa, *c*. 1,800,000 motor vehicles were registered in 1963 and *c*. 4,000,000 in 1974. In the Indian subcontinent the total rose from about one to just over one and a half million across the same interval. Within South America the increase was from 3,850,000 to 10,500,000.[3]

The trend these figures reveal is collateral with that of the global distribution of supersonic warplanes referred to in Chapter I, even though it is neither as dramatic nor as directly ominous. Since the growth in vehicle ownership tends to remain almost exponential for some time, it is reasonable to infer that many of the nations in question will at least triple their vehicle ownership between 1970 and 1990. And such would be in line with the projection to the year 2000 quoted in Chapter 6.

Still, one cannot stress too much that quite the most serious aspect of the ramification of arms potential lies in the diffused accumulation of plutonium. For the great majority of prospective nuclear powers, the attraction of nuclear warheads will be that they constitute a strategic deterrent: a weapon of last resort, intended to preclude total annihilation or subjugation. This being so, the closest analogy which presents itself historically is the main battle fleets in the classic naval balances of the pre-nuclear era. In 1914, for example, the Grand Fleet at Scapa Flow and the German High Seas Fleet at Kiel lay in a relationship of mutual and very stable deterrence quite akin to that of the American and Soviet strategic nuclear forces in 1976 or 1990.

However, even as late as 1939 only about one dozen navies around the world possessed any capital ships—i.e. the battleships, battle-cruisers and fleet carriers that comprised the core of every main battle fleet. Yet by the early 1980s there will be up to several dozen potential or actual nuclear powers in the world. The exact calculation simply depends on where one elects to draw the arbitrary line as to what is a "significant" reactor capacity (either installed or planned) in regard to plutonium accumulation; and on how much attention is also paid to the spread of reprocessing plants. Moreover, that decade seems set to witness the emergence of the centrifuge and jet nozzle as autonomous sources of highly enriched uranium for several of the above-mentioned states, South Africa included.

For these reasons alone, nuclear control has become a good deal more difficult than ever warship reductions proved to be in the great naval conferences of the inter-war years. Therefore, it is just as well that, from Sweden to California, reports trickle in of a burgeoning public debate about nuclear energy.

But what must be hoped is that, as this debate gathers momentum, international security will at last displace industrial pollution as the paramount theme within it. What must also be hoped is that disputation does not polarise, as anxieties heighten, into a dialogue of the deaf: utopian absolutism versus raw pragmatism.

Unfortunately, what should be a rationally conducted and empirically-based discussion about this and every aspect of world resource strain and environmental impact seems all too prone to swing to extremes, much as arguments about Defence are. The widespread protest about ecology which peaked around 1969 afforded numerous instances throughout the Western world, partly because it was considerably bound up with the New Left and the counter-culture. An example may be seen in the study of food prospects for the United Kingdom published in 1974 by a Friends Of the Earth group. Having investigated various facets of the problem with no little finesse, the authors insist that "the annexing of agricultural land for *any irreversible development should cease forthwith*" (my italics).[4]

No doubt they were persuaded that nothing less than a totally uncompromising declamation could attract attention to their cause. Yet a less shrill advocacy of conclusions more in accord with both the actual situation and their own analysis thereof might have permeated the policy-making community. Shock tactics are always more likely to stiffen it up.

Even in the field of climatic research, a tendency towards such destructive divergence can occasionally be discerned. Yet there is no factor appertaining to the world food balance that more urgently requires thoroughly objective investigation.

In particular, we want more definitive guidance on whether Man's economic activity is liable to modify the Earth's climate appreciably over the next decade or two. In principle, it could do this by altering either the reflectivity of the Earth's surface or else the gaseous or solid particle content of the Earth's atmosphere. However, some of the effects are either self-compensating or mutually correcting.[5] More knowledge must be obtained on all this, not least because some areas most crucial to the world food balance—e.g. the Volga basin, North China and the Lower Ganges valley—could be acutely susceptible to climatic vagaries.

We could also do with a fuller international debate about the non-ferrous metals outlook. Granted, any very great concern about impending shortages could, in certain circumstances, become self-fulfilling because of intensified stockpiling or reserve conservation. But this nettle must be grasped sometime; and better now than ten years hence.

However, it may be no less important to curb an inclination to discuss the physical resource balance as if it were on a quite different plane, not to say planet, from the human factors in global change. Certain ineluctable physical realities will influence greatly the availability of resources in the years to come. There are also determinants on the demand side, the two most general being population pressure and the revolution of rising expectations. But there is, too, the evolving infrastructure of development; and, as the economic history of Communist China has demonstrated as well as that of anywhere, these three strands interact incessantly and not always constructively.

Unfortunately, the more negative interactions could be aggravated in the 1980s, as much of Afro-Asia plus the Caribbean approaches a quasi-organic crisis of political development. As, in the new states, the generation which gained independence passes on, the impetus to nation-building will be liable to wane. In some cases, either the sheer size of the territory or population or else the firmness of its roots will make a nationhood so distinctive as to hold this tendency in check. But often a waning will occur, thereby allowing fissiparous forces freer rein. Concurrently, these forces could be strengthened by other adverse trends. Among these may be a spread of bureaucratisation, factionalism and corruption linked with the growth of a drastically underemployed urban intelligentsia.

Against which it could well be said that the high export earnings which not a few newly developing countries are at last deriving from their primary products should enable this impasse to be avoided or broken through. With some this may indeed be the outcome. After all, a prime reason for a crystallisation of the attitudes of an urban and national bourgeoisie into a venal cynicism may often be a sense of futility, a sense that irrespective of effort and sacrifice the crisis of development will never be surmounted. Given the financial wherewithal, optimism and idealism may revive.

However, the prospect could be very different wherever augmented revenues are pouring into the coffers of a regime too ill-attuned to modern life to utilise them properly. Maybe it is too deficient in the relevant expertise. Maybe it is afraid that Education and other reforms will generate more expectations than they satisfy. At all events, such a political and social order might have stood a better chance without such pecuniary lumber. It is a thought which could prove uncomfortably germane to the Arabian peninsula by the middle of the decade ahead.

As regards the advanced industrial democracies, the current disposition is to speak of Britain and Italy as the countries whose stability is most in question. But it is probable that Britain and quite possible that Italy will, by the turn of this decade, be breaking out of the worst of the crisis syndrome that has plagued each of them since the late 1960s. North Sea oil should be acting as a moderately strong catalyst for the British economy. Meanwhile, the economic emancipation of the Italian South, which thus far has been disappointingly slow, may be accelerating in line with vigorous economic growth almost everywhere else on the Mediterranean littoral. And the consequent boost to national morale could conceivably act in conjunction with the challenge from the Communists to induce a more profound and less localist civic consciousness.

Although its 1976 general election was a notable victory for moderation, the large industrial democracy most liable to be disturbed by social and political tensions in the 1980s is probably Japan. One strand in this apparent paradox is simply that various patterns of indiscipline and dissent do seem curiously little in evidence as yet, bearing in mind the degree of urban congestion within the Pacific Coast belt. From this some would argue that a breaking point is bound to come fairly soon, unless big programmes of urban renewal are launched in the meantime. Another energy crisis could be this point. So, alas, could a major earthquake.

A further consideration is that a kind of counter-cultural revolution still appears to be making headway among Japanese youth. One theme within this is a qualified acceptance of limits to economic growth, a return to traditional notions about harmony with nature. Another is a rather egocentric hedonism. A common denominator can, of course, be found in an at least partial rejection of the puritanical devotion to hard work and high investment which has characterised the last 30 years—a rejection, if you like, of *The Chrysanthemum and the Sword* (see Chapter 17). Not irrelevant is the fact that *c.* 2,000,000 Japanese made pleasure trips abroad in 1975, roughly an order of magnitude more than ten years previously.

Yet the obverse side of this particular coin may be that, in reality, Japan's social stability continues to be geared to the expectation of high economic growth; and also that any serious attempt to remodel the archipelago through urban renewal and in related ways would itself make big incremental demands on resources. Therefore, any trend across the Western world, as the 1980s progress, towards a slow-down of economic growth might have more worrisome implications for Japan than for Britain, to cite a conspicuous example of a nation more or less habituated to low growth already.

However, it is not really helpful to speculate as to which of the open societies of the West may be most prone to instability. We understand too inadequately the variables that determine alienation. Likewise the further variables that transmute this alienation into political dissent. For one thing, we are perennially confused by the paradox that one factor in the virulence of many of the more youthful dissenters is a covert (and quite erroneous) belief that, in the final analysis, "the system" is massively unshakeable.

Besides, although every advanced nation (and, for that matter, every newly developing one) is *sui generis* to quite an extent, there is a commonality of problems across the genre as a whole. A disagreeable admixture of inflation and unemployment may have become more endemic throughout the West than ever it was for the first quarter of a century after 1945, this deterioration being due both to technological advance within industry and to the more difficult circumstances now prevailing in world trade. As the 1980s progress the lower birth rates of recent years should ease the teen-age impact of unemployment. At the same time, earlier retirement and shorter working weeks may be more generally alleviative, as may a calculated fostering of the labour-intensive service trades. Even so, the structural fault in question may go too deep to eliminate entirely.

Meanwhile, technological change will widely diminish job satisfaction. This is why, for example, Sweden continues to be beset by rising absenteeism, in spite of the great endeavours made there to "humanise" the shop floor.[6]

Here we see one contradiction inherent in our post-Renaissance idea of progress which has got to be resolved, or at any rate contained, if the open societies of the West are to avoid destructive gyrations to political extremes. Another is that, whilst we are cultivating decision-making talents in more and more young people sundry mechanistic trends strongly favour an ever-narrower concentration of the decision-making process. Obviously we ought to offset the latter by deliberately making democratic representation more genuine and efficacious not just in legislatures and other organs of government but also in trade unions, student councils and consultative bodies of all kinds. Nor is this need gainsaid by the fact that, certainly as far as governmental reform is concerned, the best way of meeting it is never easy to identify.

However, these challenges are underlain by what, if crime rates in the relevant age bracket are anything to go by, remains the growing alienation of teenagers virtually throughout the ever more urbanised and mechanised civilisation of the West. In this exceptionally synthetic milieu, the young generation tends successively to lose primordial satisfactions which it may then yearn for vaguely but intensely. As one British specialist on drug abuse has put one aspect of it, "Few modern teenagers have ever been physically extended. Walking under a hot sun until exhausted, swimming in a cold river instead of a heated pool, cycling home soaked to the skin, running across country on a cold winter's day . . .".[7]

Correcting this imbalance is one thing educationalists may have to pay more attention to if democratic society is to flourish. Laying a better foundation for good citizenship in terms of solid and appropriate factual knowledge is among the others. Educational philosophy may indeed be the key issue in public debate by the year 2000, if not well before.

But the parliamentary democracies of the West do not have a common destiny solely in that they will all have to grapple with the imbalances or contradictions of advanced development. It is common also in the more direct sense that the fortunes of one affect those of all. The balkanisation of Canada that some now fear would be a disaster for the Atlantic Alliance. Correspondingly, a political crisis in, say, Belgium or Denmark culminating in their withdrawal from the EEC and NATO would have the most traumatic repercussions throughout the West.

These particular examples are deliberately chosen to reflect another elementary truth. We are prone to ignore unduly the role of the less powerful members of the Western Alliance system, both within the Atlantic area and beyond. Thus we speak as if the fate of EEC hinged on Britain, France and Federal Germany, with Italy as a kind of outrider. In fact, of course, every single member of EEC will have a critical influence on its future and *vice versa*.

Not that anybody would deny that the United States will have a uniquely determining influence on the overall picture. And what makes this reality so centrally relevant at this point in time is the large number of imponderables surrounding President Carter's accession to office. His personality is rather inscrutable and his intellect very eclectic. His electoral success owes much to the multifarious backlash against what has been seen as the Washington Establishment, the backlash induced by the unprecedented traumas of Vietnam and Watergate. By the same token, he himself constitutes a remarkably novel bridge between the conservative and liberal wings of the American body politic. Moreover, he comes to power at a time when the liberal internationalist tradition seems to be ebbing, not least on Capitol Hill. To put it another way, he finds himself situated on the descending phase of a Klingberg cycle. Meanwhile, some of the USA's social ills continue to worsen whilst certain others may not ameliorate as fast as expectations rise.

In short, Jimmy Carter's ensuing term of office could be unusually climacteric in the history of his country and hence of the rest of this planet. To find a plausible parallel with this dark horse personality approaching a turbulent scene, one must go back to Harry Truman. Fortunately, the comparison does a lot to reassure.

Irrespective of all the imponderables, however, it is likely that, all across the Western world, the interaction of internal and external stress will induce a reaction against the rather utopian liberalism that became modish in the 1960s. Depending on exactly what pattern of law and custom then obtains in any particular territory, the themes might include the following: limiting the right to strike in key occupations; a reversion to more formalised discipline in educational establishments and in certain armed forces; a reversion to stricter assessment and streaming in education; a greater reluctance to use legal reform to promote social change; a harsher penal code and maybe tougher prisons; capital punishment for convicted terrorists and the more forceful interrogation of terrorist suspects; tighter political screening within the public service; and the firmer censorship of pornography.

Every single one of these possibilities would cause a fair amount of political anguish. Nevertheless, they can all be seen as legitimate bones of contention within an open society. Much more alarming would be a closed-minded withdrawal into what Pierre Trudeau has dubbed "the wigwams of the past"—i.e. primitive communal sentiments. For one thing, the point has earlier been made that the local ethnic revivals of recent years—e.g. the Basques and the Quebecans—have been built on corroding foundations. Therefore, if there is a really powerful upsurge of ethnic sentiment it will be on a grander scale. In other words, it will take the form of a Fortress Atlantica syndrome—a belief that the shrunken realm of White civilisation is beleaguered by the looming forces of darkness and decay.

A collective backlash of this essentially defeatist kind would be a godsend for the forces of totalitarianism everywhere. For this reason alone, it has to be avoided at all costs. Yet the task of ensuring this is in no wise made easier by the continuing fragility of the world economic system. One aspect of this is the marginality of world stocks of certain key commodities, among them the staple grains. Between 1961 and 1965 the basic level fell from an estimated 65 days' world consumption to barely forty. Then the trend was arrested awhile, thanks to the Green Revolution and the mobilisation of idle American cropland. But around 1972 it resumed, the basic level dipping below 30 days' early in 1974.

Nor does the monetary situation much improve. To my mind, there is a quite unacceptable air of *déjà vu* about demands that we return to some kind of gold standard. Even so, it would be impossible to refute, as solid historical fact, the correlation drawn by those who make the said demands between the retreat from gold and accelerated inflation: "Since 1968 the link with gold in the world monetary system —the convertibility of the dollar into gold—has been broken in fact, and since 1971 has been broken completely. That has been the period in which the world inflation has accelerated from unsatisfactory but tolerable to unprecedented and intolerable levels".[8]

The danger now is that, in the absence of a fundamental restructuring of the international liquidity base, there will be a progressive degeneration into a chaotic reserve pattern in which the dollar is supplemented by a whole range of other national currencies, various of them enjoying (or enduring) a quasi-reserve status. Meanwhile, recurrent disruptions will be threatened by armed conflicts, commodity shortfalls, fiscal mismanagement and OPEC impulses. Even as 1976 drew to a close, one could see some ill-omens, a general one being an early retardation of the late 1970s boom and a specific one the marked propensity of OPEC financiers to transfer out of sterling in times of anxiety.[9] A particular hazard is that the big holders of liquid assets will periodically feel tempted to stockpile commodities vigorously; and this hazard may increase as countries like Saudi Arabia expand their port capacity.

Still, the nub of the problem of preserving a creative interdependence, in economics and in other matters, between the West and the newly developing nations may lie in the evolution of attitudes within the latter. To strike a sanguine note, it could be argued that, whereas ten to 15 years ago the "steadily increasing hostility between White and non-White"[10] pointed to the battle-lines of racial conflict being

11

drawn on a world plane, most of the signs have become less inauspicious in the interim. We have seen the end of the Indo-China conflict, one that many sought to depict as straight White versus Yellow. The notion of a cohesive Third World holding the balance, morally as well as materially, between the West and the USSR has lately looked a sight less convincing than it did between the Bandung Conference of 1955 and 1960, the year Mr Khrushchev used the Russian metaphor of the *troika* (a sledge pulled by three horses) to advocate the reorganisation of the UN secretariat along tripartite lines. In fact, when the "energy crisis" broke in 1973, some actually started to speak of a "new Third World" comprised of OPEC and other newly developing primary producers in oligopolistic bargaining positions. This they firmly differentiated from an ever impoverished "Fourth World".

But the new terminology did not catch on. Nor does the full sequence of events lend itself to so neat a reinterpretation. Overall, the income gap between the "rich" nations and the poor—or, as some would say, between "North and South"—widened appreciably between 1960 and 1973. Moreover, whilst some of the territories many still collectively entitle the "Third World" may be amassing monetary wealth, this in itself serves to emphasise further their persisting deprivation as far as life opportunities are concerned. Paris or Heidelberg or San Francisco, let us say, looks very much like a golden city on a hill to an aspiring young person from Kuwait or Lagos or Tehran. He will therefore share some of the "us versus them" feelings of his opposite number in Bangladesh.

However, the real significance of the Afro-Asian solidarity movement that achieved some eminence through 1955 and 1960 was not that it showed how Afro-Asia, with or without Latin America, could tread a genuine middle way. It was to be found instead in the endeavours of certain of its ideologically more radical or fascisto-Marxist leaders, notably Nkrumah and Sukarno, to mobilise widespread support for a multi-pronged offensive against the West, this being launched under the cover of non-alignment. Herein lies one of several good reasons why any further employ of this dated term "Third World" should be actively discouraged.

To which one may add that there are various particular foci of tension where it is very much in the interest of the West, and hence of Humanity at large, to seize or retain the initiative as against the USSR. Among several near the periphery of the Bamboo and Iron

Curtains are Taiwan and Thailand; Bangladesh and India; Saudi Arabia and Turkey.

Even more obviously, Israel and South Africa are destined to stay in the international front-line. This being so, we must expect all the more extremist of the elements disposed against them to play continually on their sense of ethnic exclusivity and strategic isolation. Blanket condemnations of them, in the United Nations and elsewhere, as "racialist" have this as one of their aims. So do successive acts of terrorism within or near their borders. So too, did the malicious polarisation of the situation in Angola these last 15 months by a Cuba prodded and aided by its great economic benefactor, the USSR.

In like manner, the Palestinian guerrilla leaders have never as yet overtly afforded very much political encouragement to moderate opinion within Israel. According to mood and audience, the "democratic State of Palestine" they envisage can be modelled on China or on Switzerland. Correspondingly, the consequent fate of the Jewish inhabitants of present day Israel may vary from reversion to May 1948 to either Arabisation or acceptance on equal terms, perhaps within a federal or confederal framework. Furthermore, one is bound to observe that the 8,500-word speech Yasser Arafat, speaking as Chairman of the PLO, delivered to the UN General Assembly in November 1974 threw precious little light on these points. Nor was there even much in it to dispel Israeli forebodings of genocide. All that it did make clear was that Arafat's own *weltanschaung* is more Marxist than we had sometimes been encouraged to believe.

Unfortunately, there is among the liberal intelligentsia in the West an inclination to play down the gravity of the Middle East conflict, especially as compared with that in Southern Africa. Liberal Christian leaders, for example, tend to exercise themselves much more about the latter situation, to assume that a global race war (nuclear or otherwise) would start along the Zambesi rather than along the Jordan.

Now there is one respect in which this preoccupation is well justified. Thanks to an interaction of History and Geography, most of the non-Marxist states of independent Black Africa are considerably softer, in the Gunnar Myrdal sense, than are the Arab ones. This means *inter alia* that they are more vulnerable to insurgent subversion, a situation which is in no wise eased by a willingness in some Western circles to lend charitable succour to guerrilla groups. To make the

most obvious comparison, Zaïre has more cause to fear the gunpower
of the MPLA in Angola than ever Syria has that of the PLO in the
Lebanon.[11]

In other respects, however, the Middle East is a far more dangerous
tinder-box, as witness its continuing emergence as a fount of the two
most strategic energy sources: nuclear fission (see Chapter 25) and
oil. To my mind, the biggest particular threat of a Limited World
War being initiated in the Middle East is that latent in the belated
yet breathless development of Saudi Arabia. Suppose a Gadafi does
come to power in Riyadh in 1985? Around that time Arab economic
leverage may be at a peak in terms of both oil and liquid capital. The
USSR may be waxing more belligerent; and the Arab–Israel conflict
is likely yet to be outstanding. Here are all the ingredients for the
ramification of a conflict which begins with a political use of the oil
weapon.

Moreover, a crisis in the Middle East is far more likely than one in
Southern Africa to bring about a split down the middle of the
Atlantic Alliance. Not that there is any basis for this in political logic.
North American opinion is not totally and unconditionally pro-
Israeli; and Western European is most certainly not pro-Arab in
anything approaching a comprehensive or absolute sense.

However, this question is not one of mere logic. Indeed, it dips well
below the surface of mere politics, exposing as it does so some very
complex cultural cross-currents. Several strands in pro-Zionism (e.g.
in parts of Western Europe and the American Deep South) represent
an inversion of the anti-Semitism which has been one of the ugliest of
the bends sinister across Western society since long before the
Renaissance. Some strands in anti-Zionism (e.g. in the more fascistic
sectors of the New Left[12]) are a straight continuation of this grim
lineage. The contemporary admiration for Israel as a patriotic
young democracy fighting for survival in the ancient Holy Land
reflects in no small measure profound, if incoherent, reservations
about affluent industrial society in the late 20th century—that
penultimate expression, if you like, of the ambiguities of Renaissance
Man.

Under these confused circumstances, there is a very real risk that,
in the context of another Middle Eastern crisis, seemingly marginal
differences between the two sides of the Atlantic (e.g. over the volume
and urgency of arms supplies to Israel) could lead to a fatal rupture of
the alliance. In the aftermath of "Yom Kippur", in fact, there were

some acute spasms, even from within the ranks of such embattled upholders of Truman-style globalism as the senior leadership of the AFL-CIO, the American trade union confederation. For instance, in the autumn of 1974 Lane Kirkland, the Secretary-Treasurer of AFL-CIO, spoke thus apropos trans-Atlantic differences over the Middle East, anything but clear-cut though these were: "Our old allies in Europe are in the process of surrendering control of their honour and destiny to their former puppets. It is time to force their choice of which side they are going to be on, and nothing is to be gained by further evasion, temporising or delay. If we are to stand alone, with Israel, we may as well know it now".[13]

Needless to say, a sundering of the Atlantic Alliance over Israel, Eurocommunism or anything else would be a disaster in the most direct and immediate sense, not only for all the European members of NATO but also for every country in Europe and the Near East whose own security depends heavily on a NATO-Warsaw Pact equilibrium. However, it would be little less of a disaster for the United States and Canada. No doubt a Fortress America might hope to survive geostrategically by playing off against each other Russia, China and other Marxist states. But even if this much were achieved, it could only be so through a lapse into a pathetically narrow and illiberal variant of Pacific Firstism with the most damaging consequences for the morale and hence the social cohesion of North America itself.

If a continual and comprehensive dialogue between the USA and Western Europe is essential to world peace, hardly less so is a gradual easement of the bonds between the USSR and an Eastern Europe which is gaining ground on it economically. Clearly, Yugoslavia is especially nodal in this connection. Equally clearly, we would be most unwise to accept without reservation recent assurances by Mr Brezhnev that the USSR has no intention of instigating an invasion of Yugoslavia after the departure of Tito. Mr Brezhnev will not last much longer himself. Furthermore, once the invasion of Czechoslovakia was over and done with, the said gentleman was quite prepared to dismiss as a fable the very notion of "the limited sovereignty of a Socialist Commonwealth" adduced to justify that adventure. Nor did this, in its turn, stop the Warsaw Pact leaning menacingly on Romania—with border manoeuvres and aggressive propaganda— hard upon Nicolae Ceauşescu's visit to the Far East in June 1971 and his invitation to Richard Nixon in July. The truth of the matter is that the USSR has always been reluctant to use naked force in

Eastern Europe. But rather that than accept the risk of falling dominoes.

Besides which, Yugoslavia is exceptionally vulnerable to pressures and intrigues which stop well short of full-blooded invasion. As much can be shown by comparison with China, the other great centre of deviant Communism. Unlike China, Yugoslavia is decidedly multinational. Like China, it has been too dependent unduly long on a founding father born in the 1890s. Similarly, too, it relies considerably on a tradition of partisan defence in depth, the relevance of which is diminished by its national capital lying directly under the shadow of the hostile border.

This comparison with China is pertinent in another respect. It demonstrates, through the career of Lin Piao, another truism which tends to get overlooked. This is that those elements within the leadership of a secondary Communist power who are most infused with the spirit of authoritarian puritanism are the very ones whose alignments within the international Communist fold are likely to be the most subject to abrupt change. In the 1930s Lin Piao had led the vanguard on the epic Long March from Kiangsi to Yenan, the phase that above all others was the trial by ordeal of the Communist heresy we know as Maoism. In 1959 he was very deliberately brought out of semi-retirement, just as the Sino-Soviet split was developing, to take charge of the People's Liberation Army (PLA). In that capacity, he master-minded both a renovation of the PLA's traditional strategy of guerrilla resistance and the development of what could be taken, in their respective ways, as the dialectical counterpoints to this: the nuclear bomb and the military-cum-heavy industrial complex. During the Cultural Revolution, Lin was set against Liu Shao-chi as the exemplar of the true Maoist way. Yet we are quite reliably advised that, in 1971, he was killed in a plane crash in Mongolia whilst endeavouring to escape to the USSR.

By the same token, we can surmise that, contrary to what is often supposed, it is the faction in Peking and Shanghai closely associated with Madame Mao which would be the most likely to rebuild the ideological bridges between Peking and Moscow. And if this be so, we can draw cheer from the worsting of the "Gang of Four" in the autumn of 1976. Even so, we must be alert to the possibility that this matter may not yet have been finally resolved. Changes in either the Kremlin or the outside world, to say nothing of China itself, could prove unhelpful in this regard.

One dire result of a Sino-Soviet realignment could be the consolidation of a common front of hostility towards, and simulated disdain for, Japan along with South Korea and Taiwan. A more extended one would be an informal division of labour between these Communist giants, in furtherance of ideological expansion, across the world at large. Arguably, the rudiments of this can already be discerned in the realm of economic assistance, in that aid agreements arrived at by the USSR and China have not, as a rule, been competitive in the blatant way Soviet and American ones often have.[14]

Nevertheless, the most serious connotations might not lie within strictly geopolitical parameters. More likely, they would be found in a corruption of the doctrine and practice of Chinese Communism as evinced internally. Maoism does possess several traits which might be cultivated with advantage not just to China but to Mankind as a whole. Among them are its stress on agrarian life, grass-roots participation, low-level technology, mass education and socialisation, and continual combat against bureaucratic inertia. Yet it also embraces proclivities of quite another kind: bureaucratic centralism, technological gigantism, martial puritanism, social conformism, secretiveness, the manipulation of dissent, the mutation of the past . . . And one cannot but apprehend that if a Muscovite cabal ever did achieve dominance in Peking, the latter set of alternatives are the ones which would come out on top. To put it in a nutshell, "big is beautiful" would triumph over "small is beautiful".

In fact, of course, there is much in Soviet experience to suggest that "big" can be either tawdry or downright ugly. In *European Security* it was argued that the USSR is the residuary legatee of a peculiarly rigid North Eurasian political culture, one that missed out on the Renaissance and Reformation and then waxed too large geographically.[15] In Chapter 14 of this study attention was drawn to Soviet dilemma of the subject nationalities—one that successive observers from Rosa Luxembourg in 1918 to Zbigniew Brzezinski in 1968 have recognised as fateful. Everything considered, one would have thought it difficult to avoid the logic of the argument that, as the 1980s progress, the immobile Soviet body politic will approach a crisis which will be all the more convulsive for having been so long delayed. Also that as it does so, its external policy is likely to become ever more erratic and more frequently bellicose.

Yet such logic does get overlooked because the average intelligent Westerner has acute difficulty in making the imaginative leap into the mind of the average Soviet *apparatchik*. Usually, for example, he takes it for granted that the latter is just as firmly committed to ushering in the affluent society—what Mr Khrushchev liked to extol as "Goulash Communism"—as he would be himself in the Soviet situation. Yet the *apparatchik* most certainly is not. His persisting ambivalence towards the private automobile is indicative of that.[16] So is a continuing equivocation about the absorption of Western technologies.

Another understandable but invalid assumption is that, since the Soviet regime has failed in human terms, it no longer poses a strategic threat. As a *New Statesman* leader writer put it on one occasion, "The once militant army has become a conservative institution, concerned above all with maintaining itself in good order ... there is really nothing to be scared of; the fears and fulminations of Dulles now belong to the past as much as do the hopes of Lenin".[17] No matter that the Soviet challenge has been apprehended by many people who could claim to divine its nature better than Mr Dulles did.

On first examination, Russia is an enigma. It is so because it is a paradox. Since long before the Bolshevik revolution, those concerned to predict the future of the world order have been markedly at variance in their long-term prognoses for it. Thus to read Andrei Amalrik, James Burnham, Sir Halford Mackinder, George Orwell, Alexis de Tocqueville, Sidney and Beatrice Webb, and H. G. Wells (to say nothing of the great Russian novelists) is to be presented with every possibility from near-invincibility to inchoate stagnation.

What this spread does suggest, of course, is that the USSR retains the latent potential to be dangerously strong in some respects and dangerously weak in others. Oddly enough, Karl Marx was among those who perceived this dualism in Czarist Russia. Unfortunately, he became rather too phobic about it.

Notes

1. David G. Chandler, *The Campaigns of Napoleon*, Weidenfeld and Nicolson, London, 1967. See especially Part Three.
2. *1974, Statistical Yearbook*, United Nations, New York, 1975. Table 126.
3. *1975, Statistical Yearbook*, United Nations, New York, 1976. Table 157.
4. Michael Allaby et alia, *Losing Ground*, Earth Resources Research, London, 1974, p. 33.
5. See the 1976 Symons Memorial Lecture, *Quarterly Journal of the Royal Meteorological Society*, Vol. 102, No. 433, July 1976, especially pp. 494–496.
6. "Sweden's absentee workers", *The Economist*, 28 August 1976.

7. George Birdwood, *The Willing Victim*, Secker & Warburg, London 1969, p. 162.

8. William Rees-Mogg, *The Reigning Error*, Hamish Hamilton, London 1974, p. 68.

9. *The Economist*, 16 October 1976.

10. Ronald Segal, *The Race War*, Jonathan Cape, London, 1966. Chapter I.

11. Lord Chalfont, "When will the West remove its blinkers and see what is happening in Africa?" *The Times*, 22 November 1976.

12. See Seymour Martin Lipset, "The Return of Anti-Semitism as a Political Force" in Irving Howe and Carl Gershman (Ed.) *Israel, the Arabs and the Middle East*, Bantam Books, New York, 1972, pp. 394–426.

13. *Free Trade Union News*, Vol. 29, No. 11. December 1974.

14. Pierre Galoni, "Sino-Soviet Commercial and Aid Agreements to Africa: Assistance or Clientship?" *Pan-African Journal*, Vol. VL, No. 3. Autumn 1973, pp. 349–368.

15. Neville Brown, *European Security, 1972–80*, RUSI, London 1972. Chapter 1.

16. John M. Kramer, "Soviet Policy Towards the Automobile", *Survey*, Vol. 22, No. 2 (99) Spring 1976, pp. 16–73.

17. *The New Statesman*, 26 June 1969.

22

Politics: The Coordinative Dimension of Strategy

(a) THE CARDINAL CHOICE

One could be tempted to deduce from the history of the last four decades that our nuclear world is inexorably subject to rhythmic alternations of tension and *détente*. Taking 1944 as effectively the beginning of this nuclear era, it must surely be admitted that the ensuing nine years (i.e. to 1953) were far more bitter and, indeed, violent than the great majority of observers anticipated in the initial year just cited. Also that the succeeding nine (i.e. 1953 to 1962) were more relaxed than seemed probable at their outset. Then again, that the next nine were less agreeable than had generally been expected in 1962, whereas this decade now promises to run its course a sight freer from terrorism and other forms of violence than some of us thought likely in 1971.

Far be it from me, however, to suggest at this late stage that the forward projection of this pattern leads irresistibly to the conclusion that the period 1981–90 will be unexpectedly violent. Too categoric a stand was taken earlier in this study against the neat superimposition on reality of quasi-mathematical over-simplifications. Even so, the above retrospection does serve to alert one to the possibility that the approaching decade will prove tenser than the present, as the general world crisis of imbalanced development interacts with the particular Soviet one of political immobility. To which one could add that almost all surprise events—e.g. earthquakes and assassinations—are liable to aggravate matters.

In the search for a comprehensive strategy for coping with this prospect, one soon runs up against the residue of the derisive reaction against "globalism" mentioned in Chapter 2. Among its manifestations has been the contention that all aid is imperialism and that the kindest way to treat the newly developing countries is to let the situation within each of them take its revolutionary course.

Such an abdication would, in fact, be a recipe for disaster. Virtually all the revolutionary ideologies this century has spawned—be they Left or Right or hybrid—can be traced back to the essentially totalitarian theorisings of Hegel and Rousseau. So not only are they devoid of any thoughts about how best to accommodate the aspirations of individual citizens as these rise in line with economic and social emancipation. They are prone as well to grave distortions of outlook in other respects. Among these are a prickly disinclination to work at all closely with the world at large, other revolutionary regimes not excluded. Also an especially strong propensity to err massively in internal planning because of an inadequate data flow and insufficiently open, frank and rational discussion.

But what also merits emphasis is that, paradoxical though some may find it, revolutions tend to yield their best fruits altogether too slowly for modern purposes. The American revolution was not at all radical in social or philosophical terms. Even so, it took about 20 years to ferment and secure independence from Britain. The Bolsheviks did not gain control of Russia until nearly 40 years after the first Marxist cells had formed in that country. The Communist Party of China took 30 years to come to power. Nor can we assume, in the last mentioned case, that events would have moved faster in the absence of adverse alien interventions. Quite possibly, the reverse.

Now it is true that, even allowing for our customary ignorance as to their inception, *coups d'état* often seem to be staged at short notice. Moreover, that genuinely spontaneous uprisings *en masse* do occasionally occur, an apparently pure example being the Hungarian revolt of 1956.[1] However, neither kind of event necessarily amounts to revolution in any sense an ideologue thereof would recognise. And even when it does, it may soon succumb to a counter-revolutionary backlash, as did the Paris Commune in 1871. Alternatively, the subsequent phase of consolidation will tend to be exceptionally chaotic and prolonged.

This phase is liable, in any case, to extend over years rather than months: the classic sequence—as delineated by Crane Brinton—being a series of lurches to ideological extremism and "strong man" rule, a process in which a Reign of Terror plays a salient part.[2] Furthermore, even when all this is more or less over and done with, the special propensity to err on the grand scale will remain, as witness the way the Communists in Peking recklessly launched the Great Leap Forward and the Cultural Revolution but took 20 years to go firm on family planning. In short, given the speed at which the world crisis is developing, there would not be enough time for widespread recourse to revolution, even if the rest of Mankind could trust the revolutionaries and their dogmas.

What there is just about enough time for is far-reaching but evolutionary reconstruction on the world plane; and, within each individual state, the main thrust of this evolution should be towards the achievement or maintenance of an effective parliamentary democracy in some shape or form. The general argument in favour of this averment was advanced in Chapter 2. To it must be added several more specifically related to the contemporary world scene.

One is the need to engage in a wide and tough-minded dialogue with the newly developing world about political means and ends—in particular, the promotion of liberal democracy, at least as an ultimate ideal. By and large, it is difficult to dissent from Professor Gregor's judgment that, on the record to date, "African socialism and Arab socialism share far more specific traits with paradigmatic Fascism" than they do with the pristine visions of the European socialist pioneers of the last century.[3] One of the least agreeable of the recurring traits is a Rousseau-like obfuscation whereby the notion of individual political freedom gets intermingled hopelessly with that of psychological liberation through mass mobilisation.

To insist on the principles at stake is crucial to a stable yet dynamic political process, not merely at state level but also at that of the street-corner or village pump. Alleviation on a "self-reliance" basis of the extra infrastructural burden (drains, pavements, public buildings etc.) occasioned by the urban implosion would involve, among other things, entirely new patterns of community politics. The redistribution of land tends to be truly economic only when accompanied by the development of voluntary cooperatives for production and marketing.

Then again, Woodrow Wilson's old precept of self-determination through democratic participation has a determining relevance to several issues that act as major fulcra in the international scene today. Presumably, the indigenous people of Taiwan have as much basic right to a determining say in their own future as other former subjects of colonial rule have been conceded. Evidently, too, for the Whites of South Africa or the Jews of Israel to be driven into the sea would be a morbid crime per se. Besides which, any settlement in these areas which failed respectively to ensure a future for these large and talented communities would almost certainly not be "majority rule" in any meaningful sense. All it would be is domination by a fascisto-Marxist cabal.

Similarly, the stability and security of the advanced industrial democracies of the West directly depend upon the fierce reaffirmation of their democratic values, a reaffirmation perhaps informed by the sort of personal leadership a Winston Churchill or Charles de Gaulle or Franklin Roosevelt or, of course, a Bertrand Russell or Alexander Solzhenitsyn may provide at his most inspired. Confrontational politics in countries like Britain and Italy, to say nothing of Australia or Canada or Japan, may be suitably circumscribed if all factions can be brought to acknowledge that more is at stake than relative incomes or the cultural differences between various occupations, social classes, ethnic groups or regions. It may also prevent too careless an approach both to regional devolution and to the geographical extension of the EEC. This side of the Atlantic, such carelessness owes much to a quasi-historical romanticism which encourages the belief that together these two tendencies could be the precursor of a spontaneous harmonisation of a European family of nations extending from Brest to Brest-Litovsk if not Vladivostok.

The chief point to be nailed apropos a "wider Europe" is that what always used to be called the Iron Curtain coincides almost exactly with what is, or ought to be, quite the most critical divide within political science: that between those states which rely on a secret police to retain internal cohesion and those which do not. Indeed, with the recent liberalisation in Greece, Portugal and Spain, only Yugoslavia (plus, if you like, Albania) stands out as anomalous in this European context.

By the same token, the gradual emancipation of Eastern Europe will depend not inconsiderably on Western insistence; and by this is meant, most immediately, an insistence on the application of the liberalising provisions of the 1975 Final Act of the Helsinki Conference on Security and Cooperation in Europe. In the absence of such rigour, above all in regard to wider contacts and "Non-intervention in internal affairs", Helsinki will verily become "the funeral of Eastern Europe" as Solzhenitsyn apprehended. Clearly, the 1977 follow-up conference will be a touchstone in this regard.

Eastern Europe is important in more than its own right. Its quiet liberation is basic to another departure needed to ensure that recurrent Communist participation in the governments of such countries as

Iceland, Italy, Finland and France could never lead to a Muscovite takeover. This departure is nothing less than a Marxist Reformation, an open acknowledgement that Moscow—historically, the "Third Rome"—contains within itself the seeds of its own decay. And that, in consequence, it is in the process of becoming, objectively speaking, a bastion not of progress but of reaction. Furthermore, as its internal contradictions deepen, it is liable to become a more active or direct threat to world peace.

A further respect in which Eastern Europe is nodal is that many of its intelligentsia adhere to the classical liberal values with a passion rarely evidenced in the West of late. This is because of their mortifying experiences these last two centuries; and because of links preserved with Western liberals across most of this time. In Czechoslovakia, the embers of constitutional liberalism glow warmly in spite of a huge overburden of monolithic repression. They flicker resolutely in Poland rather closer to the surface. Much the same may be true of Eastern Germany and elsewhere.

This being so, the intelligentsia of Eastern Europe could one day make a signal contribution to the realignment of young people in the West. In an influential passage on "The End of Ideology in the West", which was published as early as 1960, Daniel Bell spoke of the "restless search for a new intellectual radicalism" on the part of sharp young intellectuals: "They cannot define the content of the 'cause' they seek, but the yearning is clear".[4] Meeting this yearning may depend on the generation concerned being staunchly reminded, perhaps by Poles and Czechs, that political freedom is a *sine qua non* of the wider freedom they seek. Weight is added to this consideration by the reliance we would always place on young manhood for the military defence of our land and values.

Not unrelated is the future of the commitment to parliamentary democracy on the part of the intellectual leadership within the West itself. As was acknowledged in Chapter 14, the standing of the Soviet Union has never been lower in the eyes of this fraternity, notwithstanding parts of it having lately come more under the generalised influence of a somewhat turbid Marxism. Nevertheless, traces of undue indulgence have persisted, as reference to the work of two British scholars shows all too well. In a major study, Dr David Lane, a Cambridge Fellow and leading authority on the Soviet bloc, once delivered himself of the thought—one part banality; three parts absurdity—that the role of the KGB in "suppressing anti-Soviet literature" is similar to that of the British police in respect of "pornography and pornographers. All police forces try, of course, to repress activities which threaten a given social order"![5] More recently, A. J. P. Taylor, a doyen of modern historians and by no means a Communist, has reiterated the old canard that logistic exhaustion "produced the tragedy of Warsaw ... It would have demanded resources which, at the time, the Russians had not got to penetrate Warsaw" in support of the Polish Home Army in the summer of 1944.[6] How can such broad-brush considerations excuse the failure of the veterans of Stalingrad and Kursk to lift even a little finger in support of the Home Army's heroic rising, until such time as it faced certain defeat?

The plain truth is that, whilst only a very low proportion of the West's intelligentsia is "pro-Soviet" at present, a significantly higher fraction is too intractably "anti-anti-Soviet". Perhaps one approach to this problem should be to tackle those concerned on the subject of internationalism, a precept by which they normally set store. No one could ever describe the Soviet polity as remotely internationalist so long as lingering ideological shibboleths inhibit it from joining such United Nations affiliates as the Food and Agriculture Organisation, the International Monetary Fund and the World Bank. Nor when it stays so obstinately impressed with the virtues of gold as a means of international payment. Nor when it not only declines to help finance United Nations peacekeeping but also refuses to permit the UN ever to exercise its due prerogatives within the confines of the Iron Curtain. Nor when it will not countenance arms control inspection on its own territory. Nor when its foreign aid record is so patchy.

Nor, for that matter, when its spokesmen regularly evince a thoroughly cavalier attitude towards the population explosion and other economic problems faced by territories less well endowed with natural resources than is their own.[7] Nor when it endorses the maximisation of economic growth as brazenly as would the most bloated of capitalists. Nor when, acting in tacit collusion with Japan, it has obliged the International Whaling Commission to make "compromise after compromise to the detriment of whale stocks".[8] Nor seeing that its attitude towards the ecological control of its own vast environment has been utterly casual across the years. Nor when it strives to maintain a nexus with Eastern Europe which can only be described as a singularly systematised and extensive manifestation of neo-colonialism. One could go on and on.

Any debate on such issues of political principle will have big strategic implications just as have various others in the historical experience of Britain alone: the search for a *via media* after the English Reformation; the handling of the American colonies; deciding our response to the French Revolution; Gladstone's "bag and baggage policy" in the Balkans; responding to the threat from European fascism . . . Still, it is absolutely vital to the health of an open society that this kind of debate always be conducted between private individuals and groups, without benefit of official manipulation or patronage.

Having said this, however, one does have to acknowledge that, if a wide reaffirmation of democratic values is the upshot of this debate, the projection of this new commitment further afield will depend on a fair measure of official support especially in broadcasting. In fact, the West has lost out badly in the recent past just because of the *blasé* stance adopted by its governments in this sphere. Between 1960 and 1973, the hours broadcast weekly to foreign countries by the USSR almost doubled to 2,000 whilst Eastern Europe registered much the same advance. China expanded from just over 600 to 1,600, not the least of her targets being the minority nationalities within the USSR. Meanwhile, the American networks increased their effort merely from 1,500 to 1,800 whilst the BBC's stayed well-nigh static around 600.[9]

Yet this is a sphere in which the West can be much the more effective, hour for hour. Independent surveys show, for instance, that the BBC has 15 times more listeners for its Hindi broadcasts in India's large urban areas than has the USSR. It is an ascendancy not unconnected with the way Indian social scientists, though Leftist as a genre, regularly display a disdainful indifference to what they regard as turgid and mediocre Soviet scholarship.[10]

The evidence is, too, that Western audience ratings in Eastern Europe zoom whenever the situation there gets more repressive. Herein lies one reason for the recurrent Soviet campaign against Radio Free Europe and Radio Liberty. Another may be that millions of people inside the USSR itself regularly listen to such transmissions.

(b) THE EXPANDING CONTEXT

Obviously, any intensification of the West's propaganda offensive would provide some ammunition to whatever elements within the

Kremlin are avowedly opposed to *détente*. But, if the analysis set out earlier be correct, *détente* on the Soviet bloc-Atlantic Alliance axis is unlikely, in any case, to yield much in the way of arms control or anything else until a far-reaching transformation has been effected in the Soviet body politic. Better perhaps that we direct a higher proportion of our political energies to the cultivation of closer understandings with the newly developing world.

The Strategic Arms Limitation Talks may be taken as something of a test case. We wait month after month for a SALT 2 agreement. This is intended to codify the understanding reached at the Vladivostok summit in 1974, and it was originally hoped for by the end of 1975. Yet US President Jimmy Carter is among those who have regularly protested that the Vladivostok ceilings were too high. Meanwhile, some more specialist commentators have come to doubt whether the SALT dialogue can any longer be justified in any terms.[11]

So could not the USA seize the moral initiative by withdrawing from SALT and then levelling off its strategic inventory on a unilateral basis? A new departure of this sort might not only be beneficial in the competition with the Soviet Union for superior prestige. It could also make a big contribution to a nuclear non-proliferation strategy. Nor would this strategic inventory then be placed seriously in danger of losing its assured capacity for second strike. The size and ever-improving quality of its submarine component would alone be enough to guarantee that (see Chapter 10).

Another choice that may be worth making firmly is the one between a perhaps sterile *détente* with Russia and a more fruitful rapport with China. And the basis of the latter might be to preserve Peking from the bouts of paranoia about geopolitical encirclement to which continental powers seem perennially susceptible. In China's case this means ameliorating conditions on her maritime flank; and an integral part of any such strategy must be a resolution of the acute dilemmas posed by Taiwan and Hong Kong.

In the Sino-American communique issued at the conclusion of President Nixon's visit to Peking in February 1972, the United States rather carelessly allowed "that all Chinese on either side of the Taiwan Strait maintain there is but one China and that Taiwan is a part of China". By way of qualification, it merely reaffirmed "its interest in a peaceful solution of the Taiwan question by the Chinese themselves".

But the Wilsonian principle of self-determination would, in this situation, specifically require that the 15,000,000 people indigenous to this island be asked, at some stage, whether or not they do currently regard themselves as Chinese first and Taiwanese second. Moreover, there would be severe practical difficulties in anything more than notional integration with the mainland at any time in the foreseeable future. At the heart of them lies the fact that the dynamic Taiwanese economy achieves average incomes roughly quadruple those on the mainland.[12]

Similarly, the four million inhabitants of Hong Kong enjoy a high rate of economic growth, whilst trade through this enclave brings in a third of Communist China's foreign exchange. Nevertheless, it is widely assumed that the fate of this British colony is already sealed in that the lease of its New Territories will not be extended in 1997, which means that Hong Kong proper will thence forward be an utterly inviable offshore island.

Not that anybody dare take for granted the stability of this enclave in the interim. Were 1997 to draw near without some new understanding between London and Peking being at least sought, a social crisis could be precipitated by a collapse of business confidence. There may, in any case, be an accelerating escalation of internal tension as affluence aggravates the pressure of population on space. Even now, the recorded incidence of crime has started to rise, a circumstance which ought to astonish no one, considering how many people have been crowded into less than 400 hilly and fragmented square miles in an often hot location. Nor can we discount violent interactions between the colony and its hinterland. After all, in 1967 the violence of the Cultural Revolution overspilt into Hong Kong, in spite of the restraining influence of local units of the Peoples' Liberation Army.

If either Hong Kong or Taiwan or both were to be handed to Peking on a plate, encouragement might thus be given to the ideological hard-liners in the Chinese capital. Conversely, however, the hard-liners also stand to gain if years go by without any sign of a negotiated settlement of either question.

The happy medium probably lies in obtaining for each what would amount to an Outer China status, an acceptance of overlordship from Peking sufficiently loose to allow the existing inhabitants a goodly measure of genuine autonomy. Not merely would this be tolerably in line with the precepts of self-determination subscribed to elsewhere. It would also introduce into the Chinese Communist polity a heterodox element that could not but augur well for its gradually becoming more pluralistic.

Not that an active search for such a solution would be at all easy to conduct. In the case of Taiwan it would presumably be essential to break, at an early stage and conclusively, the Kuomintang commitment to *Fan-kung Ta-lu*: "To counter-attack the mainland!" One way to do this would be to insist on the abandonment of its key forward positions, the offshore islands of Quemoy and Matsu. Concurrently, an effort might be made to gain for the indigenous Taiwanese people more executive influence and freedom of expression within their own homeland.

Hong Kong could be a still more ticklish issue, even allowing that a tradition of quiet—and thus far effective—diplomacy has built up around it over many years. At one time the establishment there of a special legation from Peking was at least casually mooted. Now doubt prevails as to whether this would serve the interests of those concerned any better than such informal nexi as the New China News Agency and the Bank of China have done.

Maybe one answer lies in exploring with Peking how Hong Kong might best dovetail into its own long-term plans—e.g. by installing fertiliser factories in the near future and offshore oil support in the more distant. This in its turn might phase into a broader endeavour to expand continually China's trade with the non-Communist world. The omens here are not at all bad. The annual value of this trade, as estimated by the CIA, rose quite steadily from 3.5 billion dollars in 1971 to 12·0 billion dollars in 1975.[13]

More specifically, it may be possible to induce China to export, on favourable terms, some of the food surpluses it may eventually be accumulating. Indeed, in a speech to the UN World Food Conference in November 1974, the head of the Chinese delegation did give some encouragement to this thought. After ritually deriding "the long-discredited Malthusian theory of population" and dutifully placing the blame for the food crisis squarely on "colonialism, imperialism and the Superpowers", he did go on to say that, whilst his people were thus far making only a small contribution to a solution of this crisis, they did hope "gradually to change this state of affairs".

Yet if it would be foolish just to wait upon events where the Far East is concerned, it would be even more so apropos the main Middle East conflict. Here it does seem to me that the imperatives of human and strategic geography interact with those of democratic philosophy to favour strongly a triple solution. One part would be for Israel and the West to press for the transformation of Jordan as it now is into a social democratic East Palestine. The second is for Israel to accept the ever-greater interpenetration of itself and the old West Bank of Jordan by gradually assimilating into its own polity, on a free and equal basis, the Arab peoples domiciled there. The third is for Israel and others to promote the economic regeneration and local self-government of the Gaza Strip community, pending a decision on its political future being taken by all concerned. To clinch everything, there would need to be a solemn guarantee that a conditional "right of return" would apply to Jewish and Palestinian individuals actively threatened by religious or political persecution elsewhere. Also firm assurances against any attempted Anschluss across the Jordan river.

In principle, Israel is not ill-suited to press for the gradual transformation of East Bank Jordan into a social democratic East Palestine, perhaps with Hussein as a constitutional monarch. Israel itself is by far the closest approximation to a social democracy anywhere in the Middle East and has close ties with social democratic movements in Europe and elsewhere. It has a pronounced national flair for innovation, social as well as technical. The antipathy the Palestinian masses evince towards it is not, in my observation, a constant factor: it is ambivalent and volatile.

Even so, a full 15 years might be required for this metamorphosis, not least because of the perverse suspicion it would arouse in such authoritarian Arab regimes as Syria and Saudi Arabia. Needless to say, too, much the same applies to the incorporation of the West Bank and the transformation of the Gaza. For what is here being proposed is, in a sense, the transcendence of Zionism to a broader plane than renascent Hebrew nationalism—its translation towards the universalist ideal men like Albert Einstein always held it should attain.

Straightway many would retort that so bold a voyage into the unknown can "never" be made. But categoric rejection can often be the very attitude which immediately precedes peaceful compliance. There is much within the richly liberal traditions of the Jewish intelligentsia world-wide that would be conducive to such a reconstitution. It would be in line, too, with the cultural homogenisation that, for good and ill, seems inseparable from progress in the modern world. Granted a few years of peace, the possibilities latent in the current situation could begin to ferment along these lines, given the likely absence of a feasible alternative.

If such a process of adjustment could take a good 15 years in the Israel-Palestine situation, we would do well to allow longer still in the South African: perhaps as much as a quarter of a century, save on the extremely sanguine assumption that Zimbabwe (*alias* Rhodesia) turns out to be a reassuring example of communal harmony. One justification for saying this i. that the dominant community would be taking even more of a gamble in many ways. It has a lot to lose in terms of superlative living standards. It could expect to end up a decidedly outnumbered minority within its own polity. Opening the country's long and tortuous borders, which would have to take place at some stage in the movement towards a truly multiracial society, could have a peculiarly dramatic effect on the internal security situation.

Besides, the resurgent liberal challenge lately evident within the White community as yet lacks breadth and cohesion. In particular, one must wonder whether the Progressive Reform Party and others of like persuasion have recognised how heavily any major advances on the race front would depend on changes in other aspects of economic and social policy. The tax structure is a case in point. Thus a young bachelor enjoying a gross unearned income of 90,000 Rand (*c.* $125,000) in 1974 would have paid barely a third of this in income tax, even though millions of his compatriots were living no higher than the bread-line.

An added complication is the delineation of the ultimate goal. Probably most commentators would agree that a South African multiracial democracy would have to have a federal configuration. However, given the intricate political and social structure of this whole region, it would be futile so much as to hazard a guess as to what this configuration might be.[14] Nor are the uncertainties on this score diminished by the failure of federal experiments in various other parts of the former British Empire, among them Central Africa. Nor by potential conflicts between the tendency for a needful movement towards economic equality to depend on centralisation, whereas that towards political and cultural equality will require pronounced devolution.[15]

Still, none of these impediments is justification enough either to wash our hands of South Africa or always to treat it as the prime global scapegoat. The contradictions inherent in the separate development policy it is now embarked on do afford the outside world ample leverage to promote its internal liberalisation. Thus an international programme of selective aid to the Bantustans might be highly beneficial in certain circumstances—e.g. by promoting the English language in education. Maybe, too, aid for Pretoria and the provincial administrations could be so deployed as to further land redistribution and other ameliorative measures. Assistance in external security could also be appropriate were it to encourage Pretoria to be more adventurous *vis-à-vis* political emancipation. So would a reappraisal of the disposition to ostracise South African universities on account of their enforced racial exclusivity. Better to essay all this than to resign ourselves without further ado to a "war of liberation" that would most likely extend across more than 25 years and culminate in utter misery all round.

This is not to say that the sundry sticks with which South Africa has regularly been belaboured by the international community should forthwith be discarded forever. Merely that a few carrots should be to hand as well. Never to alternate the latter with the former would be irresponsible, pharisaical and unscientific. So would blank disregard of the White's fear of genocide, exaggerated though this may seem when viewed from afar.

To a large section of public opinion throughout the Western world, this line of reasoning will still appear low farce. What is noticeable, however, is the stress on the need to adopt a more open-minded approach being laid of late by some individuals with detailed knowledge of the South African scene and impeccable credentials as advocates of liberal reform. A case in point has been Mrs Merle Lipton of the Royal Institute of International Affairs. In December 1974 she spoke as follows, "It is important, both psychologically and morally, to be fair—to be seen to be fair—towards White South Africa. This does *not* mean the abandonment of principles nor the removal of pressures. It does mean the abandonment of double standards and of the practice of continually shifting one's ground and 'raising the ante'—practices that convince Whites that their critics want to punish, not reform, them and that exacerbate their security fears which are a major obstacle to further progress. It means, too, a willingness to concede points and acknowledge progress".[16]

In applauding these axioms, one might add that adherence to them does not have to alienate Black Africa. Gaullist France had a close—and, indeed, distinctly expedient—relationship with South Africa.

Yet it the while preserved a close rapport with almost all the franco-phone territories to the North. To which one might further add that legitimised leaders like Kaunda and Mobotu have a real, if sometimes muted, interest in evolutionary as opposed to revolutionary progress within their continent.

Indeed, across the developing world as a whole this remains very generally true. What can also be said is that there is widespread acceptance, in principle, of the proposition that "democracy" is a superior form of government. Moreover, by this is often meant democracy in the classical liberal sense, not some kind of organic or Rousseau-ish sense: mass mobilisation through a political religion.

The manifestations of this acceptance are various. Phrases like "majority rule; one man, one vote; and self-determination" have wide currency, so wide that even the political religionists regularly pay lip-service to them. Not infrequently, in fact, a totalitarian regime goes through electoral motions. Even Cuba has at long last started to do so.

What can also be said is that, however badly they may lapse themselves, the great majority of countries endorse the ideal of individual liberty that seems historically to be very closely associated with Western-style democracy. Although the UN Declaration of Human Rights may be honoured all too often in the breach, it continues to count for something as a yardstick of comparison. Likewise to dismiss as mainly humbug such General Assembly votes as that in November 1974 condemning the use of torture by 125 to nil may again be to underestimate the potential use of humbug to force the hand of its purveyors.

Furthermore, Mankind at large is by no means insensitive to the West's being much more pluralistic than the Soviet bloc. Therefore, President Kennedy's avowal that the world would be kept "free for diversity" was of a sort that can always make a powerful appeal.

Even so, progress towards democratisation has been too unsteady these last few years to justify any complacency about the facility with which it might be further encouraged. Thus towards the end of 1974, the Shah of Iran seemed to view benignly the activities of Mardom, the official opposition, as it girded itself for a renewed struggle at the polling-stations with Iran Novin, the parliamentary majority. Yet early in 1975 he intimated that all established political factions should dissolve so that their members could enlist in a new National Resurgence Movement, essentially based on Iran Novin.

Similarly, within a year or so of the ending of the Nigerian civil war in 1969, General Yakubu Gowon had set 1976 as the target year for a return to civilian rule. From then on, he recurrently laid stress on the need for "free and fair elections", "properly elected governments", "genuinely national parties" and "the eradication of corruption". Being a member of a minority tribe himself, he was plainly eager to work for an open plurality.

Yet, by the beginning of 1974, the great majority of ordinary Nigerians, reassured by the oil boom, did not appear as worried by the continuance of a military government as was that government itself. On the contrary, there was a fear abroad that, were politics to become open again, ethnic and class tensions over various policy issues—e.g. education—would cause renewed internal disruption. Then again, the regime often presented to popular eyes what the Sandhurst-trained would call a "mufti" image: civilians as administrators and heads of statutory bodies, rather than soldiers or policemen. Contrariwise, few people believed any government, whether elective or no, could readily reduce the 225,000-man army left over from the conquest of "Biafra".

In the event, General Gowon announced on 1 October the formal abandonment of the plan to return to civilian rule by 1976. The next July Gowon himself was deposed. The successor administration duly arranged local elections for the autumn of 1976, these being seen as a pilot scheme for national hustings at some unspecified date in the future. Reportedly, too, extensive military demobilisation is now being planned.

Elsewhere, the reckoning for 1976 is uneven. The retreats from democracy in India, the Lebanon and Thailand have been remarked already. Hypersensitive to pan-Arabist dissent, the Ruler of Kuwait partially suspended his country's constitution and dissolved its parliament in August, intimating that an amended constitution should be approved by referendum within four years. On the other hand, Egypt made a tentative move towards a guided though not entirely bogus democracy. In March the dominant Arab Socialist Union was divided into three wings: Rightist, Centrist and Nasserist-cum-Marxist. Accordingly, the parliamentary elections held in the autumn "were about the best yet—which is not to say all that much".[17] Meanwhile, preparations were being made in Bangladesh for multiparty elections early in 1977. Since when, they have been deferred.

Obviously the portents for a sustained evolution towards democracy are made less good in some cases, Bangladesh and Egypt among them, by economic marginality. But a more universal difficulty is that Sir Harold Wilson's quip about a week being a long time in politics holds good in the wider world no less than in Westminster. In consequence, the governments of emergent states are just as inclined to think too tactically as are others. Therefore they may rate the short-term advantages of, let us say, silencing a contentious newspaper more highly than the long-term value of a free press. Interference with the judiciary often comes within the same bracket.

Nor is such a disposition entirely irrational or totally blameworthy. After all, any polity may be never so vulnerable as in the initial stages of liberalisation. One is reminded of de Tocqueville's judgment that the *Ancien Régime* fell in France in 1789 because it was an inconsistent mix of repression and toleration.

In the light of which, one is bound to ask whether military governments might not be the ones best suited to guide newly developing countries towards parliamentary democracy. However, the first thing to recognise here is the absence of anything approaching a common pattern. Thus Gadafi in Libya and Amin in Uganda run personalist despotisms which have had precious little in common with the successive military governments in Nigeria or, for that matter, with the Marxist regime in Somalia.

Nevertheless, certain themes may be very recurrent. Morris Janowitz has identified the main ones thus: a strong sense of national statism and a consequent playing down of tribalism and sectionalism; a rigorously martial regard for the puritan virtues and hence a stolid hostility to corruption and decadence; the acceptance of collective public enterprise as a vehicle of economic, social and political change; and a disdain for, and distrust of, organised political expression.[18] To all of which may often be added ideological agnosticism or, at any rate, eclecticism.

Circumstances are not difficult to envisage in which this set of attitudes may prove more conducive to real progress than either fully-fledged but premature parliamentarism or the ill-sorted shibboleths of the quasi-Leninist political Left. Moreover, this thought is one which draws succour from the discernible trend towards authentically civilian elements occupying key posts in governments originally established through military coups. Not only Nigeria but also Egypt and Zaïre have lately been conspicuous cases in point. Still, Turkey remains the archetypal example of a beneficent interaction over time between civilian tribunes and military guardians,[19] this notwithstanding her heavy-handed response (since 1974) to the extremism sustained by the old EOKA faction in Cyprus.

Whenever a broader dialogue with Afro-Asia and Latin America is mooted, one has to ask whether this should primarily be through United Nations channels. True, nobody could pretend that the UN today commands the prestige it seemed poised to acquire, say, 15 years ago. Nor that it seems well-prepared, in either spirit or structure, to meet the global challenge of the 1980s. On the other hand, to allow the UN to fall into desuetude could be to render a grave disservice to the future. The history of Europe and the world since the Thirty Years' War indicates that comprehensive arrangements for regulating the international order are only likely to be established in the immediate aftermath of convulsive conflict—1648, 1815, 1919, 1945. Yet the world of the 21st century will have to have an overriding authority of some kind.

Nor are the agonies of choice thus posed diminished by the groundswell that has set in so strongly against the medium for dialogue the UN has relied on most these last five years. This is what the sardonic call the "mega-conference", a very multinational and very public gathering convened with a view to discussing "the environment" or some other loosely defined subject of concern. Strikingly enough, this groundswell has been evident even in circles that one might expect to be innately sympathetic: "Whatever the subject, it is always the same conference".[20]

Evidently, it is desirable to limit the global polarisation of rich and poor. Evidently, too, one way to do this is to encourage the required dialogue to ramify into more intimate and specialist channels. Closely related as an aim should be the exploration of the sundry points of contact between politics and economics—if you like, to revive political economy on the international plane.

Not that anybody should delude themselves that this would be easy either. Plumb in the centre of the intellectual arena in question are the anxieties being engendered by accelerating environmental decay and sustained population growth. Manifestly, the advanced countries are nowadays according a higher priority to ecological protection than do most of those still wracked by primary poverty. Likewise, they cannot but press the view that lowering the birth rate must be a top governmental priority across by far the greater part of Afro-Asia and Latin America all through the 1980s.

However, their ability to do this persuasively is undermined by the way, ever since the late 1960s, their own birth rates have very generally been falling, and this without official encouragement. The rub is that they are thereby rendered vulnerable to the charge of requiring less sophisticated and fluid societies to do *de riguer* what they themselves are doing out of hedonistic preference.

Nor will the parrying of this riposte be made any easier by the probability that, in the 1980s, the West will feel obliged to arrest in one politically sensitive field the global trend towards greater economic interdependence. This field is the trans-national migration of labour.

Even during the 1973–75 recession, in fact, various Western European countries began to curb the inflow of "guest workers" from further afield. Likewise in the United States resentment burgeoned against the six to eight million "wetbacks"—illegal immigrants from Mexico or elsewhere in Central America—said to be in the country.

Fear of unemployment, cyclical or structural, will always be one motive for exclusion. Fear of terrorism may often be another. A further consideration is that, except in a few of the smaller territories, the quantitative easement afforded by liberality is negligible. No "open door" policy could ever make any positive impact on the Malthusian problem of the Indian subcontinent. On the contrary, it would most likely exacerbate it by much accelerating the outflow of the more skilled and motivated.

Even so, a tougher attitude on quotas and their enforcement would be bound to occasion resentment, especially if adverse political developments in regions like the Caribbean, sub-Saharan Africa or South-East Asia made whole communities anxious to leave. No matter that no Communist state need be expected to open up its borders to any displaced peoples.

In the main, however, the immigration question will be consequential only within the context of a much broader one—that of the total distribution of the world's resources. Increasing difficulty will be experienced in getting, say, Brazilians or Indians to limit any of their aspirations so long as they can see the United States alone, with but five per cent of the world's population, consuming anything between 20 and 50 per cent of a wide range of primary products. Among the grounds for saying this is an incipient movement in Afro-Asian and Latin American political and social philosophy away from Rousseau's more immoderate derivatives and towards more traditional and fundamental human values. For an integral part of this embryonic trend, from Brazil to India and—by no means least—Tanzania, is an assertion that newly developing countries must not attach too much priority to economic growth. Obviously, however, a corollary is going to be that advanced countries do not have to either. Shades yet again of the "alternative society".

As might be inferred from Chapter 5(b), we must not allow the romantic optimism of certain "anti-growth" intellectuals within the West to lure us into underestimating the difficulties that would be involved in evoking any very positive response to arguments along these lines. In 1970 OECD predicted that, whereas in the decade just ended the mean growth rate of its then members had been 4·8 per cent per annum (i.e. 55 per cent altogether), in the one just beginning it would be 5·2 per cent per annum or 65 per cent compound. Since then this particular expectation has been vitiated by the way a sharp recession has been succeeded by a tremulous boom. Nevertheless, a smoothly exponential growth of that order would still be endorsed as optimal, even though only a three to four per cent average is actually anticipated for the second half of the 1970s.

Nor could this mode of thought be lightly cast aside. The advanced industrial economies of the West continue to be geared, first and foremost, to internal and external market forces, not just because competition is a spur to efficiency but also because a predominantly market economy is almost certainly a prerequisite of an open society. Probably the only restrictive mechanism which could be employed by Western nations collaterally, and without unacceptable damage to free markets, is a general tax on energy use.

Not that our experience to date suggests that multinational solidarity may readily be achieved in this sphere, even were the aim not retardation but faster expansion. Certain facets of energy production (e.g. oil-refining and hydroelectricity) featured in the ill-starred attempts by the European beneficiaries of the Marshall Plan to coordinate their investment plans. In 1973 an Arab attempt to weaken the unity of EEC by a differential application of the oil embargo made disturbing headway. Later an EEC attempt to hammer out a common energy policy (backed by much heavier investment in this direction via the Commission itself) was severely impeded by the United Kingdom's determination to keep effective autonomy over its North Sea oil.

Behind what seem, at first sight, essentially technical difficulties about coordination lie, of course, very vexed social and political questions. Growth modulation would necessitate many awkward adjustments embracing the whole of our social ethos. Among them would be matters concerning the dynamic of world trade, the internal spread of incomes, the future of the free market and the limits of government intervention. So all things considered, it is improbable that the West could make a political commitment to continual growth restraint until sometime after 1990—i.e. at a relatively late stage in the dialogue about the politics and economics of a new world order. Perhaps then it could successfully be sold to electorates as the agreed alternative to the risk of repeated bouts of international economic warfare.

Yet the seeming remoteness of this prospect would be no justification for delaying further public discussion of it. Despite what has been said above about a burgeoning interest in long-range indicative planning, Western democracies still tend not to be strong on foresight. Nor can matters appertaining to energy policy yet be deemed any great exception. In 1965 the then British government enunciated an energy plan that involved *inter alia* the accelerated closure of coal mines. Not long afterwards it slashed by half a promising national programme for nuclear fusion research. Similarly, Alastair Buchan related how in April 1973 he was advised at the White House that they "had not yet begun to focus on the energy problem".[21]

Another respect in which the challenge of the 1980s will be formidable is its sheer complexity. In politics and economics, to say nothing for the moment of military strategy, the issues to be tackled will be manifold and endlessly interwoven. Hence the situation overall will run counter to a human propensity, which extends well beyond the corridors of governmental power, to focus all too single-mindedly on whatever is seen as *the* key issue: "the energy crisis", "the Bomb", "the Communist threat", "Chile", "racism", "inflation" or whatever. As a bedouin proverb fatalistically puts it, "A hand can only hold one melon".

But that is just too bad. We shall be obliged to hold or juggle with many rather awkward melons between now and 1990: political, economic, military . . . Herein lies an added reason why our Grand Strategy needs urgently to be suffused with a reaffirmation of constitutional democracy and its *alter ego*, the rule of law. We are most unlikely, for instance, ever to build a new economic order in the world without a prior commitment to enlarging political freedom: a commitment, if you like, to the proposition that the most important question in public affairs is whether any two citizens can hold a conversation without either having to wonder whether the other is an informer.

Notes

1. Carl Leiden and Karl Schmitt, *The Politics of Violence: Revolutions in the Modern World*, Prentice-Hall, Englewood Cliffs, 1968, p. 58.
2. *The Anatomy of Revolution*, Prentice-Hall, Englewood Cliffs, 1952, pp. 266–283.
3. A. James Gregor, *The Fascist Persuasion in Radical Politics*, Princeton University Press, Princeton, 1974, p. 408.
4. Daniel Bell, *The End of Ideology*, Free Press of Glencoe, New York, 1960, pp. 369–375.
5. David Lane, *Politics and Society in the USSR*, Weidenfeld and Nicolson, London, 1970, p. 255.
6. A. J. P. Taylor, *The Listener*, Vol. 96, No. 2472, 26 August 1976, p. 235.
7. E.g. Galina Kiseleva, "A Soviet view: the Earth and population", *Development Forum*, Vol. 2, No. 4. May 1974, p. 9.
8. Joanna Gordon Clark *et alia*, "Whales: time for a fresh start", *The New Scientist*, 23 January 1975, pp. 7–23.
9. "The Radio War", *The Economist*, 30 March 1974.
10. Stephen Clarkson, "The Low Impact of Soviet Writing and Aid on Indian Thinking and Policy", *Survey*, Vol. 20, No. 1 (90). Winter 1974.
11. E.g. Colin S. Gray, "SALT: Time to Quit", *Strategic Review*, Vol. IV, No. 4. Fall 1976, pp. 14–22.
12. Robert W. Barnett, "China and Taiwan: The Economic Issues", *Foreign Affairs*, Vol. 50, No. 3. April 1972, pp. 444–458.
13. *The Economist*, 18 September 1976.
14. Leo Marquard, *A Federation of Southern Africa*, Oxford University Press, London, 1971, p. 124.
15. *South Africa's Political Alternatives*, Study Project on Christianity in Apartheid Society, Johannesburg, 1973, pp. 218–220.
16. Godfrey Morrison (Ed), *Change in Southern Africa*, Miramoor Publications, London, 1975, p. 17.
17. *The Economist*, 6 November 1976.
18. Morris Janowitz, "The Military in the Political Development of New Nations", *The Bulletin of Atomic Scientists*, 20, October 1964, pp. 6–10.
19. See the author's, "Turkey and the West", *RUSI Journal*, Vol. 121, No. 2, June 1976, pp. 63–67.
20. *Development Forum*, Vol. IV, No. 6. July–August 1976, p. 1.
21. Alastair Buchan, "The Irony of Kissinger", *International Affairs*, Vol. 50, No. 3. July 1974, p. 378.

23

The Economic Priorities

Nothing would be gained from the most imaginative programmes for the international coordination of resource development and redistribution were these to be launched within the context of currency collapse. For that matter, a strong NATO would be of little avail if the multilateral global trade on which Western Europe so critically depends could no longer be soundly financed.

Nor does the history of the last ten years, in particular, indicate this sphere to be one in which decisions of lasting merit can be expected in time of crisis. On the contrary, it is so fraught with technical complexity and yet so susceptible to psychological disturbance that, in a crisis situation, there is either overreaction or else no reaction at all. With the reform of the international monetary system, anticipation is everything. If you like, strategy ought always to retain a commanding influence over tactics in this interplay of economics and politics.

By 1975 a strong consensus did seem at last to be emerging, both in official circles and in academic, that the answer to the liquidity problem in the medium- to long-term cannot be found in a latter-day revival of gold. Instead, the Special Drawing Rights were slowly but, it appeared, surely gaining favour among experts as the best way to provide for an orderly expansion of world reserves, one which would not oblige all countries to seek to build up payments surpluses that are simply other countries' deficits. Several of the newly-rich oil producers had revalued their currencies in SDRs rather than dollars, whilst Egypt was denominating its new canal dues in them too. Above all, the commitment of the IMF gradually to sell off 23 billion dollars worth of gold betokened the triumph of the view that this precious metal should at long last be demonetised. In other words, firm American insistence had prevailed over a crumbling French reluctance.

Yet still the indications are that SDR expansion will be uncomfortably, not to say dangerously, retarded by considerations which, seen in relation to the magnitude of this problem, border on the otiose. Anxieties have been expressed lest the SDR sector proves difficult to cut back if needs be, a requirement that looks decidedly theoretical in the light of all our recent experience. Deflection of aim has also been effected by a contention that, instead of being tied to IMF quotas, the successive SDR issues should be made to the poor nations as an act of positive discrimination. Also connected with the sluggish progress has been the stipulation that SDRs can only be used by central bankers to make settlements among themselves and with the IMF.

In an abrasively explicit statement at the IMF conference in Nairobi in September 1973, George Schultz of the US Treasury adjudged a period of United States balance of payments surpluses to be "indispensable for full restoration of confidence ... and for implementing any lasting monetary reform". Hopefully, one could stretch the point and hence infer that anticipation of such surpluses in the 1980s could soon make the USA willing to push harder for SDR expansion and also for a regularisation of the exchange rate mechanism.

Within informed circles, the conviction has been growing for some time past that both rigidly fixed exchange rates and freely floating ones may be unduly disruptive. The former can be altered but occasionally and abruptly in clumsy response to what are perforce the continual shifts in the relative competitiveness of national economies; and the latter are all too liable to cause paralysing uncertainties, partly because they do not correct imbalances in current accounts anything like as smoothly in practice as they do in theory. Yet neither are the surreptitious "managed floats" currently in vogue an ideal compromise.

Therefore one solution strongly favoured these days, especially by the academics, is the hybrid system variously known as "crawling peg" or "gliding band" or "snake". Under this, the exchange rate of a given currency in terms of, say, the dollar may regularly fluctuate within a relatively wide band, the mid-point of which can alter by maybe one or two per cent a year. Unfortunately, experience with the "snake" some Western European countries started to operate in 1972 has not been encouraging. For one thing, the membership of it has chopped and changed in a most erratic fashion.

But the most urgent necessity in the international monetary field of late has been a more complete recycling of the extra 70 billion dollars per annum (to cite one estimate for 1974) the oil-producers have been gleaning from the post-"Yom Kippur" price increases. After all, the peak predicted value of OPEC liquid reserves in 1980 quoted in Chapter 8 would be about twice the net aggregate value of the long-term capital investments the United States of America has accumulated abroad as of this point in time. Apprehensions of deliberate economic warfare apart, it would be far better for the stability of the international exchanges if a really high proportion of this wealth were instead to be invested in solid and productive projects in the advanced industrial countries (whence it would mainly have derived), rather than left to swill around in short-term funds. However, this ideal would be a hard one to approach even if attitudes on every side had proved unequivocally positive.

Nor do the said attitudes show much sign of waxing this favourable. Though the Arab boycott of firms that deal with Israel remains haphazard and half-hearted, it still engenders genuine antipathy, particularly in the United States. What is more, as it becomes clear that a stable solution of the Arab-Israel dispute will only be effected over a much longer time-scale than "shuttle diplomacy" has ostensibly assumed, Arab governments may grow all the more aware of the tactical advantages of purchasing short-term bonds. At the same time, the advanced industrial nations may remain determined to preserve legal and bureaucratic obstacles to foreign investment in general—the Rome Treaty provisions being, of course, a major exception.

The situation in this last respect may be illustrated by two or three examples from an overview obtained about a couple of years ago. Any Swedish firm making a fifth or more of its shares available to foreigners was not entitled to own real estate. In the USA, there were some key industries which could not be even partially owned by aliens: domestic aviation, shipping, communications, hydroelectric and nuclear power, and—by implication at least—the prime defence contractors. Whilst France had no blacklist of industries denied to foreigners, in practice much the same sectors were protected as in the United States. In addition, any stake which would result in 20 per cent or more of a company being foreign-owned needed the finance ministry's seal of approval.

Furthermore, there was then a disposition in some countries to tighten controls, a disposition that drew added succour (perhaps especially in the United States) from an undertow of popular resentment in the wake of "Yom Kippur" and all that stemmed from it. But we may always do well to remember that the annals of history

12

are laden with instances of a fundamentally sound desire for economic sovereignty expressing itself in ways that are sterile if not actively self-destructive.

Let us draw, by way of example, a parallel with 1938 and 1939. As one looks back over the tabulations of the balance of power in Europe hastily being concocted, one usually finds a solemn reference to gold reserves as presumptively critical indicators of national economic resilience. Yet gold was very generally to play a minimal part in financing the ensuing war efforts. Likewise, the day after tomorrow, whatever economic stranglehold the Arabs or anybody else is able to exert on the West is most unlikely to result from the ownership of real estate, a few small but nodal sectors just possibly excepted.

Indeed, a strong case can be made for creating a whole series of trusts to attract OPEC investment through the market mechanism but in accordance with broad guidelines agreed by both sides. Hopefully, the emergence of some such pattern for continual negotiation rather than sporadic confrontation will have been furthered by the general producer-consumer dialogue since 1974. But it is very much a matter of descending from high politics to grass-roots political economy.

However, all discussion of how surplus revenues on the OPEC scale might be most expeditiously and beneficently "mopped up" perforce gets round eventually to the question of international economic aid. But that big subject has wider implications for the West. On the far Right aid is condemned as enervating and conducive to *étatisme*. On the New Left aid is condemned as neo-colonial and conducive to *étatisme*. Nevertheless, the mainstream of informed opinion has always adjudged these objections to be either insufficient or plainly wrong-headed, especially as seen against the background of rising expectations. It would argue, for example, that a newly emerging nation may best achieve consolidation by passing through an *étatist* phase.

Yet even if one starts from the full acceptance of this view, it is far from easy to estimate how much aid is actually required. In particular, how close to the true optimum was the aid volume the OECD countries disbursed in, for example, 1974? This consisted of 12 billion dollars of official development assistance, together with as much again in the form of private investment and export credits plus grants by voluntary agencies.

In 1961, P. N. Rosenstein-Rodan combined models of absorptive capacity and of savings gaps to calculate requirements in the 1960s as six billion dollars annually. In 1964, the Secretary-General of UNCTAD presented a report in which a foreign exchange gap of 20 billion dollars was predicted for 1970. The next year, the then President of the World Bank suggested at a ministerial meeting of the Development Assistance Committee of OECD that the newly developing countries would be able efficaciously to absorb 14 billion dollars a year by the second half of the 1970s.[1]

When evaluating projections of this sort and vintage, four considerations have to be borne in mind. The most obvious is that, over the last decade, the value of money in the newly developing world has fallen by an average of two-thirds or thereabouts. The second is the way, in many of these countries, the balance of trade has lately worsened, owing to the oil price rise and the collateral world recession. A third is that an appreciable fraction of any aid-sponsored investment programme will assuredly be either incorrectly oriented or else misused. Lastly, absorptive capacity is these days acknowledged on all sides to be hard (very probably, increasingly hard) to calculate; and also to have been underestimated, as a general rule, in the past. In any case, it tends to grow fairly rapidly over time, thanks not least to urbanisation.

Certainly the accelerating urban implosion is feeding a major extra dimension into this whole problem. From the data cited in Chapter 6, one might fairly surmise that every additional urban dweller requires, in due course, roughly 1000 dollars worth of investment in basic amenities, not to mention for the moment facilities for employment. Multiply that by an average urban growth of 50,000,000 a year within Afro-Asia and Latin America through the 1980s, and one begins to dwarf most previous estimates of aid requirement.

On the other hand, at the Habitat Conference at Vancouver in 1976, emphasis was placed on the philosophy of self-reliance (at either family or precinct level) in such matters. And quite possibly this approach may, when adopted with conviction, ease greatly the budgetary strain occasioned by the provision of basic amenities. But even then one has to reckon with all the investment, public or private, that will have to be financed from somewhere to create, in the course of the coming decade, hundreds of millions of extra jobs. The orders of magnitude involved moneywise are such that many of these territories would find it impossible to cope without pretty massive external aid. After all, the United Nations estimated the aggregate national incomes of this whole zone at below 500 billion dollars a year before "Yom Kippur".

To all of which must be added the complication, alluded to in Chapter 8, that the recent swings in the balance of trade have seriously aggravated the medium-term debt burden of many newly developing zone. In the middle of 1974 an "oil facility" was set up within the IMF. What this has amounted to is an arrangement to borrow, mainly from OPEC states, money which can then be lent onwards to countries (especially within the newly developing world) very adversely affected by the jumps in the posted prices of crude oil. But by the end of 1975 the oil facility commitment to the newly developing states as a whole was more than a factor of ten less than the 60 billion deficit they had collectively accumulated in the two calendar years in question. Even allowing that half the deficit in question had been run up by half a dozen essentially dynamic economies, the disparity was disturbing. Needless to say, too, all other "soft loan" arrangements appear grossly inadequate in this new situation.

Presumably such deficits will taper as world recovery proceeds, generating the while a renewed bullishness in raw material prices. But inevitably the probability now is that they will recur periodically, at least for many of the states concerned.

So there can be little gainsaying the proposition that economic aid programmes will have to expand considerably through 1980 if the poorer countries are to stand any serious chance of sustaining the balanced development essential to their stability and world peace. At first sight, one is tempted to think that a triangle of money flow could come into being and remain stable: petro-dollars to OPEC; commercial investment by OPEC in the West; official aid and commercial investment by the West in the newly developing world.

But the politics of the business apart, it is improbable that the respective flows would equate so agreeably. In the light of this and of the uncertain international liquidity outlook, we should not allow ourselves to become too hidebound by progressive orthodoxies apropos the terms on which aid is offered. Private enterprise (multinational or otherwise) has a valuable role to play still, provided it can be honed rather than debilitated by the now continual patter of home-based criticism. Furthermore, what some depict as a crucial distinction between grants and mere loans in the official sector may, in reality, be less important than the specific terms in each case. Above all, we might be well advised to act more conservatively in the matter of "tied aid"—i.e. those grants or loans which have to be expended in the country of origin—if, as a result, the total flow can be sustained the better.

Usually, three objections are raised to aid being tied. It obstructs the optimum allocation of resources, a notorious example being the way in which recipients of Soviet aid have been obliged to buy Soviet capital goods which are either inappropriate or else plain inferior. It connotes "mercantilism" or "neo-colonialism", negative images that History renders the West (as opposed to the Soviet bloc) especially prone to. Finally, it is a largely superfluous stipulation in that a lot of aid will be spent in the country of origin, later if not sooner.

Just how pertinent is this last point, in particular, seems chiefly to correlate with whether or not the volume of aid from a given country stays low in relation to the sum total of its exports to the newly developing world. Thus, whereas in the period 1964–68 the net flow of official development assistance from the OECD area as a whole was equivalent to 22 per cent of its exports to the newly developing countries, in the case of the United Kingdom it was only fourteen. Correspondingly, well over half the gross drain on the British balance of payments was eventually being recovered.

Contrariwise, for the USA the aid/export ratio was as high as a third. Correspondingly, a relatively low proportion of the outlay was automatically being recouped through a boost in exports.[2] So it was only to be expected that Washington was strongly disposed to tie aid contractually whereas London had assumed a more "liberal" posture in this regard.

Inevitably, such differences in circumstance will persist into the 1980s and, indeed, beyond. This being so, some commentators might be well advised not to wax too moralistic if certain donor states do continue to tie. The world of the 1980s should look a good deal more polycentric, not least so far as aid outlets are concerned, than did that of the 1950s and 1960s. And the consequent option of wide source diversification over time ought to make agreements to tie in specific instances less disagreeable to recipient states. To repeat, the most vital thing will be to augment the flow of aid all round.

As regards its geographical distribution, one of the most contentious issues over the next five to ten years may be the extent to which India and the countries which flank it should be accorded special consideration. Writing in 1960, Andrew Shonfield, now the Director of the Royal Institute of International Affairs in London, urged that India, along with Brazil and Mexico, be placed on a priority list for aid allocation because all three had the managerial skill and material infrastructure to move, given such support, into a stage of self-sustaining economic growth.[3]

These days the distinction between those territories that are poised ready for economic "take-off" and those which are not looks less clear-cut than once it did. In terms of enlightened Grand Strategy, however, the case for preferential treatment of the whole subcontinent may actually have been made stronger by the succession of crises which culminated, in the summer of 1975, with Indira Gandhi's sudden introduction of a very thoroughgoing state of emergency and then the coup against Sheikh Mujib in Bangladesh. Thus, were pluralist democracy to disappear once and for all from the republic of India, the entire region (and hence the world at large) would find itself teetering on the brink of a major disaster. Basically, this is because, irrespective of its political complexion, the uncompromisingly authoritarian rule of so large and polyglot a nationhood would almost inevitably cause differential strains sufficient to trigger off a succession of communal blood-baths.

Nor should anyone be too quick to turn this argument against Mrs Gandhi by contending that, when she suspended democracy, she ruled herself out of court in this regard. As of the time of writing, we cannot be sure what political strategy she will eventually favour, this for the very simple reason that she is not yet sure herself. For that, matter, we do not know the part she personally will play in formulating and implementing whatever strategy is actually chosen. Hopefully, however, the state of emergency will prove to have been only a temporary retreat from freedom, a breathing space used to buttress the economy and so to adjust the working of the constitution as to make the executive stronger without rendering the elective legislature impotent.

Besides, whilst much can be said for supporting most firmly in the long run those regimes which seem the best adapted to the pursuit of democratic ideals, it is surely wrong to switch aid on-and-off as if conducting some kind of Pavlovian experiment. Considerations of national and personal pride apart, newly developing states must feel able to make at least medium-term assumptions about aid receipts. India is among the countries which have already been inconvenienced quite enough in this and related spheres.

It could be said, of course, that a redoubled effort thus to back the republic of India is rendered futile in advance by the contiguity of a sump of human misery in the form of Bangladesh. Yet there, too, the situation might not be hopeless. At least one study has envisaged a per capita growth rate of two to three per cent per year being achieved even before the population explosion has been brought properly under control and without generating an inordinate demand for foreign capital inputs.

Basically, the economic strategy whereby this might be effected would, it was thought, have two strands. One would be a progressive extension of the Green Revolution in agriculture. The other would be the absorption of the labour surplus into small-scale, labour-intensive industry. This would mainly be geared to the agricultural sector and might depend critically on innovatory technology plus a favourable tariff structure.[4] Now the new regime there is at least trying to encourage family planning and has launched some imaginative schemes for communal self-improvement.

As regards the guidelines for economic development overall, the all-important thing is to avoid glib catch-phrases which allegedly encapsulate profound insights of universal validity. To my mind, a bad example of this error being made was the cult of "intermediate technology" that blossomed in the 1960s. Many of the questions it posed were, of course, pertinent ones. Was it sensible to build massively capital-intensive prestige projects which then become distinctly unprestigious in the absence of adequate markets or back-up facilities? Might not lots of tube wells and windmill pumps be better than one giant dam? Would not a broad spread of small and medium-size firms act as seed-beds for enterprise and ladders for advancement?[5] In short, is it not more beautiful to be smaller?

But the truth of the matter always was that there could be no absolute answer to any of these questions. For one thing, the very concept, "intermediate technology", is itself an unsatisfactory abstraction, possessing neither inner coherence nor exact delimitation. For another, the circumstances of the newly developing lands are so various that no generalisations so sweeping apply. Just because some progress is being made in Tanzania along the lines here indicated, it does not follow that they are as suitable for India. After all, Mahatma

Gandhi made a tremendous effort to revive both the handloom and the spinning-wheel by according them mystical significance. Yet, as Arthur Koestler reminds us in his caustic revaluation of the Mahatma's life and thought, "The spinning-wheel found its place on the national flag but not in the peasants' cottages".[6]

Inevitably, the best solution in most situations lies in a complementary mix of large and small. One classic example of this approach in a backward region has been the work of the Tennessee Valley Authority established under Franklin Roosevelt's New Deal, whilst some of the more recent instances are to be found in Maoist China. But to cite such ideologically-contrasting environments is really to imply that there is no single blueprint for developmental progress.

Nevertheless, several general precepts can be identified. One need is to insist that population control is almost everywhere important, notwithstanding the resistance this averment may encounter at governmental level and below. Another is to ensure that the mechanics of development do not result in the poorer strata of any society suffering not just a relative but an absolute drop in their living standards.[7]

What also is evident is that a general precondition of dealing with the urban implosion is a reduction in the all too persistent developmental lag of the rural areas. Whilst agricultural expansion is as requisite as ever, it is becoming more important that this should revivify rather than disintegrate rural society: shades here of the enclosure controversies in English economic history. In many situations, one of the best ways to achieve revivification will be to give much more functional (and therefore political) power to the local administrative echelons. Certainly, the widespread reluctance of well-qualified young men and women to go and work up-country may be partially overcome if they can see this as a step, not to near oblivion, but to exciting responsibilities.

Arguably, however, the 1975 White Paper on British aid placed too much stress on the rural challenge by comparison with its dynamic *alter ego*, the urban.[8] All the same, there are certain spheres in which the two aspects are not merely complementary but considerably coincident; and one of these may be, in fact, administrative training. Here the advanced nations could do a great deal more at minimal extra cost if only the academic communities concerned could rid themselves of inertia, formalism, and petty chauvinism. Too often, "in the past staff have gone all over the world to different countries where, from the world supermarket of courses, something attractively packaged and priced has been selected. There is no cooperation between centres, courses may have been inaugurated as an exercise in academic development or be quite out of date, and the essential component of a continuing relationship leading to a feeling of responsibility and an increase in effectiveness resulting from under-standing, is lost amidst the welter of ill-adapted programmes".[9] Such is the stated opinion of a leading British expert in this field.

As regards the non-monetary aspects of world trade, the primary producers (not least the poorer ones) have a genuine grievance in the continued manifestation of the old historical tendency for food and raw material prices to be exceptionally unstable. Thus throughout the industrialised West public opinion has become conditioned to believe that no prices ever come down at all appreciably in the contemporary world. Yet the fall in the price of copper on the London Metal Exchange from £1,400 a ton in May 1974 to under £500 a ton in early 1975 showed just how invalid this generalisation remains for many primary products. In fact, of course, such instability may be no less disadvantageous to consumers in the long run, especially in view of the latent risk of sudden and arbitrary interventions in commodity markets by currency-rich rogue elephants.

In any event, the West does seem well justified in its deep reluctance to countenance some of the remedies being proposed by the more obviously aggrieved parties. In particular, suggestions that commodity prices be indexed to general international price levels might, if adopted, compound most disagreeably each and every inflationary surge. Naturally, the same objection can be levelled against proposals advanced, notably by the Shah of Persia, for linking oil prices to those of perhaps two dozen other primary products.

Almost certainly, the best medium-term answer for most com-modities lies in the creation of world buffer stocks sufficient to cushion all but the most apocalyptic swings in supply and demand. Unfortunately, the International Tin Council has found stocks of its metal normally equivalent to one or two months' consumption insufficient to contain price oscillations on several occasions these last 20 years or so. Correspondingly, the vulnerability of the inter-national market in foodstuffs to increased demand pressures in the early 1970s was indubitably accentuated by the fact that, in the spring of 1970, the estimated global stock of grain was already at the relatively low level of ten weeks' consumption.

12*

Early in 1975 a study by the UNCTAD secretariat estimated that the initial cost of building extra stockpiles for 18 staple foodstuffs and raw materials equivalent to six weeks' world consumption all round would, at 1970–74 mean prices, come to ten billion dollars. Still, everything that was said above about the inadequacy of existing buffers in the face of the market pressures resulting from short-term inelasticities in supply and demand does rather suggest that four months' would be a safer target to aim for. Nor would the sums of money thereby involved (essentially on a once-for-all basis) be beyond the means of some of the big consumers, to say nothing of the OPEC membership.

My own view is that evolution in this direction would make a big, perhaps vital, contribution to world peace in the 1980s. Yet in this, as in other sectors of international economic planning, no service is done by playing down some of the non-monetary obstacles. Even the elementary matter of the geographical distribution of the stockpiles could raise some prickly political hackles. Nor is it at all certain that a comprehensive approach is best, particularly in view of the prior existence of various individual commodity agreements. To which one must add the irony that, in ten years' time, some of those primary producers who are keen for buffer stocks today may be deploring them as a "neo-colonial" artifice: buying futures on an increasingly bullish market. Arguably, the West should go it alone in this regard, presumably under the rubric of OECD and maybe taking as an example the long-established policy of prescribing minimum oil stocks. Thus the EEC Commission called for 90 days' supply as early as 1971, whilst reportedly South Africa has now amassed four years'.

As was also noted in Chapter 8, the advanced industrial nations are likely to come under increasing pressure to liberalise their industrial trade ever further. To quite an extent, they ought to be able to adjust to this prospect spontaneously. For one thing, the progressive industrialisation of the newly developing world will create or widen many markets as well as threaten many. Nevertheless, it is worth thinking of certain sectors in which countervailing expansion may be to the long-term benefit of individual Western nations and the world at large but may require at least indicative planning on the part of the governments concerned.

The more extensive recycling of raw materials is one. The 1974 Green Paper on this subject reported that already Britain was recovering, for example, 26 per cent of its aluminium, 37 per cent of its copper and 62 per cent of its lead.[10] But it also insisted that this subject merited far more examination than it has yet received, in the realms of political economy no less than those of applied technology.

In addition, there would appear to be a case for a much more determined effort to expand coal production. In June 1975, the then US Secretary of Commerce warned a Congressional panel that the United States would be running "great risks" if it failed to boost its annual coal production from 600 to 1,000 million tons by 1985. Similarly, planning projections made by OECD in 1974 for all its member states had envisaged an aggregate expansion of 60 per cent (i.e. to c. 1,600 million tons) by 1985, this at an additional capital cost of $40 billion. Alas, however, as of early 1977 OECD is anticipating that only about 1300 million will, in fact, be mined eight years hence.

Granted in various parts of the world, notably North America and Australasia, the secular trend in coal output was still upward on the eve of "Yom Kippur". Nevertheless, one does have to confess to scepticism as to whether any revival of coal can be so very dramatic even after 1985. All else apart, the environmentalist lobbies that have become so articulate in the freer societies will everywhere oppose the open-cast mining on which a renewed expansion would heavily depend.

But that coal could stay competitive with oil in a wide range of uses—e.g. in electrical generation, as a chemical raw material, and in domestic heating—now seems beyond doubt once again. What remains very uncertain, on the other hand, is how soon it will become commercially attractive to convert coal directly into oil, the nub of the problem being that the calorific conversion ratio is still only about 40 per cent. Much will depend on the success of current work in South Africa and the United States and the extent to which the relevant experience is shared. Anyhow, the former country is due to be producing six million tons of synthetic oil soon after 1980 and the latter fifteen million soon after 1985.[11] In some states (South Africa perhaps included) balance of payments considerations may advance the day when this option comes to appear economically as well as strategically attractive.

Meanwhile, the prospects for the 21st century ought to be guaranteed as firmly as possible by according the quest for nuclear fusion all possible backing (see Chapter 26). At the same time, the environmentalists have got to be made to realise that, germane though some of their apprehensions undoubtedly are, they cannot convincingly couch opposition to nuclear fission power in absolute terms. For one thing, the atmospheric pollution occasioned by the normal operation of a nuclear power station is far less than for a conventional model.[12] More importantly, to accept the energy gap a complete abnegation would create would be to suppose that our Western civilisation could fully revert to a low-energy technology about 20 times as fast as it converted to a high-energy one in the first place. By extension, to resist both coal and nuclear fuel is tantamount to saying we can retrace the path to the New Stone Age in not a hundredth of the time which has elapsed since then.

Another priority concern for the advanced industrial nations must be the expansion of food supply. Straight industrial remedies may provide part of the answer in two directions. One is the accelerated development of foodstuffs that are, to a greater or lesser extent, synthetic. The other is an added emphasis on the expansion, both in home territories and overseas, of nitrogenous fertiliser. Pursuit of this objective, which is perhaps most suitable to regions rich in natural gas, would serve to correct progressively a chronic and desperate short-fall in Afro-Asia and Latin America. As yet, barely a fifth of the 100 million tons of the chemical fertiliser mined and manufactured each year is utilised within that zone, China conspicuously excepted.

Over and beyond these considerations, however, is the strong case which can today be made, on broad economic and strategic grounds, for a reversal of the slowing down of agricultural expansion within the OECD zone. But that might require a further shift of emphasis away from *laissez-faire*, within both lay and specialist circles. Thus in 1972, Professor D. Gale Johnson of the University of Chicago argued forcefully and, indeed, authoritatively in favour of the industrial countries accepting a continuing retardation of their agricultural sector as a precondition of a liberalisation of the world food trade.[13] In Britain a 1975 White Paper advocated merely an arresting of the levelling-off in growth.[14] Often the EEC has been lambasted for being too keen to protect its farmers. Yet there may be much to be said at this stage for professional analysts paying less regard to short-term competitiveness where farming is concerned.

Public attitudes may need to change as well. All round the world there persists a marked disposition to treat material progress as linked inexorably to intensive industrialisation, this in spite of such contrary examples as Denmark and New Zealand. Furthermore, there is also quite a bit of ambiguity in many parts of the western world about agricultural advance per se. On the one hand the food problem is deemed so acute that every urban encroachment on "invaluable farmland" is deplored as veritable sacrilege. On the other, many of the modern "industrial farming" methods for securing quick boosts in land productivity are roundly condemned, certainly in part with reference to ecological equilibrium but also on aesthetic and social grounds. Nevertheless, it may prove possible to reconcile these several considerations more satisfactorily in the 1980s, thanks to scientific advance and changing global circumstances. In particular, an agricultural pattern that was relatively labour-intensive and diversified might be able to respond flexibly to major food emergencies and yet also be very acceptable in non-material terms: a partial reversion, one could say, to the tradition of the yeoman and the homesteader.

Notes

1. John White, *The Politics of Foreign Aid*, The Bodley Head, London, 1974, pp. 120–121.
2. David Wightman, *The Economic Interest of the Industrial Countries in the Development of the Third World*, United Nations, New York, 1971. Table IX.
3. Andrew Shonfield, *The Attack on World Poverty*, Chatto and Windus, London, 1960, pp. 61–64.
4. Austin Robinson, *Economic Prospects of Bangladesh*, Overseas Development Institute, London, 1974.
5. See e.g. Keith Marsden, "Progressive Technologies for Developing Countries", *International Labour Review*, Vol. 101, No. 5. May 1970, pp. 475–480.
6. Arthur Koestler, *The Heel of Achilles*, Hutchinson, London, 1974, pp. 221–224.
7. Irma Adelman and Cynthia Taft Morris, *Economic Growth and Social Equity in Developing Countries*, Stanford University Press, Stanford, 1973. Chapter 4.
8. Cmnd. 6270, *The Changing Emphasis in British Aid Policies*, HMSO, London, 1975.
9. Henry Maddick, "Assistance to Local Governments during the Second United Nations Development Decade", *The International Review of Administrative Sciences*, Vol. XXXVII, 1971, No. 3, pp. 229–239.
10. Cmnd. 5727, *War on Waste*, HMSO, London, 1974, p. 18.
11. "Coal from Oil", *The Economist*, 8 May 1976.
12. See e.g. *Scientific American*, Vol. 234, No. 1, January 1976, p. 31.
13. D. Gale Johnson, *World Agriculture in Disarray*, Macmillan, London, 1973. Chapter 10.
14. Cmnd. 6020, *Food from Our Own Resources*, HMSO, London, 1975, p. 8.

24

The Military Shield

By the middle 1950s, a framework of containment effectively equivalent to that the West preserves today was an accomplished geopolitical fact. And, between then and now, the conceptual problems of deterrence have been kept relatively simple by one overriding perception. This has been that, thanks to a benign political evolution, the threat of major conflict has been receding more or less continuously. Granted, technological change has periodically made some elaboration of the panoply of deterrent options seem either feasible or needful—e.g. Limited Strategic War in 1962 and, albeit a shade belatedly, Flexible Response in 1967. But most commentators have felt able to subscribe pretty consistently to the following assessment: "If the options we have are sufficient now, they will be more than sufficient a few years hence. This is because the inhibitions against illicit international behaviour are binding tighter the whole time".

However, if the prognosis summated in Chapter 21 be valid and we are now entering an era that is liable to be ever more tense and less orderly, deterrence theorists and defence policy-makers are going to find themselves presented with dilemmas that not only are more urgent than before but also require sharper intuitions. The latter is stressed principally because it is likely to become harder to keep enough alternatives in hand to permit flexibility without thereby appearing positively to invite adversaries to try on new aggressive ploys. If one does allow that the taboos against a variety of illicit acts are weakening again, the question remains as to how fast this is happening and along what particular lines. How sure could we be that any of the more specific of the defensive precautions taken would not be read by prospective adversaries as a prior commitment regularly to meet certain patterns of international violence strictly on a *pari passu* basis?

Minesweeping at sea may serve to illustrate the point. If maritime violence is destined to increase, the mine could have a peculiarly sinister and potent part to play. Therefore, for the nations of the

West to disregard the need for countermeasures would be to leave themselves dangerously exposed to any sally of this sort. Yet to seek a full panoply of defence in this one sector could be held in hostile quarters to betoken a willingness to accept war, perhaps prolonged war, within the confines thus set.

Seeing that the USSR is bound to remain the ultimate major threat, the difficulty the West will perforce find in striking the right balance will always be aggravated by the former's extreme predilection for official secrecy and by the Clausewitzian bent of her geostrategic thought. Moreover, there are two elementary reasons why little amelioration can be expected in either regard. The first is that the USSR has a certain amount to gain in functional terms from preserving each trait. The second is that both have become, in any case, quasi-instinctual.

On the other hand, we may be witnessing already a refinement of Soviet military doctrine at tactical level. Not that this has ever before been anything other than turgid and banal. Objectivity has been sullied by emotive jargon and verbal genuflections to Marxism–Leninism. The generalised postulate—half platitude, half falsehood—has been offered in place of the concrete fact. Little has been done to relate tactical axioms to actual scenarios.

To my mind, the acme of this banality was reached in 1962 and 1963 with the publication in Moscow of successive editions of a synoptic review of modern defence by a syndicate of young and presumptively free-thinking officers working under the chairmanship of the late Marshal Sokolovsky, one of Zhukov's close colleagues in World War II. Through these volumes, the first comprehensive Soviet works on such matters to appear since 1926, wove a most odd admixture of hidebound conservatism and whimsical radicalism. Thus there was an extravagant insistence on the enduring worth, in this missile age, of the warplane and the battle-tank. Yet, at the same time, some of the silliest of the West's science journalism or science fiction was alluded to in talk about anti-gravity techniques, lasers and so on.[1]

Underlying this dichotomy there was, of course, a common denominator. This was a resolve implicitly to deny any need for basic alterations in the existing military posture in the light of technical innovation: "In the short-term there will be no change worth worrying about; and the long-term need not exercise the present general staff".

Hence anybody perusing the texts here cited can the better understand why, time and time again, the Wehrmacht was staggered by the way the Red Army squandered men and material. Also why, in the continental air warfare environment of the 1950s, the USSR evinced a ludicrously strong bias in favour of the defensive side of operations; and why it casually neglected to build up its ICBM force in the wake of Sputnik I. Also why it has always been extraordinarily complacent about military logistics. Nor did the appearance of a third and final edition in 1968 advance matters as much as it should have.

Soon afterwards, however, students of Soviet defence policy were drawing attention to a general burgeoning of interest in the use of cybernetics to rationalise troop dispositions.[2] But, if such were the case, the departure in question should be dismissed as otiose. After all, the largest surpluses of fat in the Soviet military corpus have never needed a computer to delineate them: they might readily be picked out by any intelligent person with no bureaucratic axe to grind. Under which circumstances, the computer serves not as an aid to revaluation but as a substitute for it.

Here one is forcibly reminded of Gunnar Myrdal's insight into the reason why the Soviet authorities have allowed Econometrics to flourish these last ten years or so. Good minds can be lured into its abstract and apolitical theorisings, released thereby from the normal obligation to genuflect to Marx and Lenin but rendered harmless as well.[3]

Even so, it would be quite wrong to allow these and other false red dawns to date to lull us into a false sense of security. Following on from Chapter 12(a), there are numerous signs now of a ramifying Soviet debate about military postures and doctrines at the tactical level, the upshot of which could be armed services much better tailored to modern operational requirements—especially sudden and major offensive operations below the nuclear threshold, presumably in the context of Limited World War. Accordingly, we might do well to discard rapidly our comforting images of the nimble NATO Davids slaying at a blow the clumsy Communist Goliaths.

Nor is all this so very astonishing. Undoubtedly, Soviet technological advances in the military sphere will have boosted the confidence of the officer corps. So must have the virtual disappearance of any questioning by the political leadership of the relevance of a large military establishment in the thermonuclear age, questioning that

Khrushchev (and, even more particularly, Malenkov) used to engage in occasionally. Probably these two factors alone do much to explain why current discussion about, for example, mobile armoured warfare is characterised by an empiricism, incisiveness and panache virtually absent in the days of the Sokolovsky studies.[4]

An enhanced Soviet enthusiasm for surprise and momentum is bound to accentuate a number of already needle questions faced by tactical analysts in the West. Some of these will concern the extent to which tactical command and control can or should be computerized, on land as well as at sea and in the air. Inevitably this debate extends into such further enigmas as the battlefield vulnerability of cybernetic networks and the delegation of nuclear control. But the nub is how far an electronic artificial intelligence will ever be able to interpret and hence predict and so determine the awesome complexity of modern battles. Some clue as to the general answer may be found in what, in Chapter 18, was incidentally acknowledged to be the first war-game of them all: chess.

After about a quarter of a century of work on computer chess programmes, the most competent are barely as good as strong amateurs in the human league. Not that their limiting factor is to be found in the speed and accuracy with which they interpret knowledge. On the contrary, computers can now "think" millions of times faster than humans, chess-players most certainly included. Their weakness lies instead in their memory banks, in their too limited ability to store patterns of knowledge and present them to themselves for synoptic scanning. Unfortunately, the number of possible outcomes to a chess game is roughly 10 to the power 120: one with 120 noughts after it!

Nevertheless, the experts exude confidence that this ignorance barrier will be broken through in the relatively near future, thereby enabling computers *inter alia* to outplay Grand Masters on the chessboard. But still they will be dealing with a grossly oversimplified rendering of even a bipolar confrontation in real life, to say nothing of the diverse, multilateral and indeterminate relationships more characteristic of a whole range of armed conflict situations from insurgency wars to nuclear crises. Thus chess operates in but two dimensions as opposed to several and, in its classic mode at any rate, is concerned only with data that can be exactly defined and measured. Since there is always much that is incommensurate and intangible in the real world of either war or peace, this could never lend itself as well to such mechanistic monitoring.

Besides, even in chess tournaments between human adversaries, there may be a growing tendency for the psychological factor to override, as witness the Fischer-Spaasky marathon. Correspondingly, there may be increasing acceptance of the random factor throughout. A non-player likes to ask, "How many moves can you see ahead?" A Czech master is said to have replied, "One or maybe two".

True, tactical aviation is one environment which does look pre-eminently well suited to computer involvement at various levels. The great bulk of the relevant data is commensurate and tangible, whilst closing speeds which are often of the order of a mile a second place a fantastically high premium on swiftness of reaction. Yet even here it is possible to discern a burgeoning debate in professional circles as to how far automatic command and control should go.

However, this particular problem merges inseparably with the wider one of the future of independent air arms. A bluntly expressed but highly authoritative American view is as follows. Now that manned aircraft no longer reign supreme as a "means of getting an explosive charge from here to there . . . the only reason for having separate Air Forces has . . . disappeared. But we have them and therefore should plan to use them as effectively as possible. They do seem to be somewhat less rigid than the other services in their think-ing. In my country, for example, the Air Force is in the forefront of developing new ways of doing things".[5] Evidently, if this generalisa-tion be universally applicable (and some corroboration can be found in British experience), then the aviation professionals could soon be called upon to shoulder a most daunting task, that of pioneering the right mix of a rich diversity of exotic new weapons: manned aircraft with broadcast ordnance; manned aircraft with stand-off missiles; rocket-assisted shells; cruise missiles; tactical anti-missiles; recon-naissance drones; and so on.

Taxing and urgent though these technical questions are, it is important none the less not to evaluate them entirely in esoteric terms. Almost certainly, more attention should henceforward be paid to the ambient political factors than air forces, in particular, have sometimes given in the past.

This though is especially germane to the manifest need to replace manned aircraft by mobile surface-to-surface missiles as the in-theatre nuclear deterrent against the escalation of conflict in Central Europe. In the light of the geopolitical analysis here conducted, one might fairly deem it imperative that this be completed before what may well be an era of heightened world tension in the middle 1980s. Yet it is far from clear that any such deadline will be met. Sheer complacency could be one braking factor. Another will be the legacy from the way cruise missile development has thus far focused predominantly on the strategic air and naval roles. Related to this may be an undue disposition to wait upon the advent in the land environment of the tactical cruise missile, rather than opt immediately for a full-scale revival of an eminently suitable tactical ballistic missile in the form of the Pershing: a step that purists might condemn as technologically retrograde, irrespective of any short-term operational imperatives.

One interface which, in British experience at any rate, is always liable to be neglected is that between air and sea power—meaning, most particularly, the Long-Range Maritime Patrol aircraft. Here we have, in fact, one of the key instruments whereby the Western powers may continue to exploit one of their great geographical advantages: the collective possession of very extensive coastlines plus not a few oceanic islands. Let us assume, for example, that it is agreed that the maritime trade routes across and from the Indian Ocean do need special protection but that unconditional dependence on South Africa in this aspect of defence is politically inappropriate. Then the LRMP might have a leading role to play in a network of protection for the "east-about" exit routes, at least as an emergency alternative. This network would be geared to Diego Garcia, the Cocos Islands, North-West Cape and other parts of the Australasian littoral. It might also serve to screen Indonesia.

Perhaps the central premise to work from where naval power is concerned is that, in the 1980s, it will become more exclusively committed than in the recent past to the preservation of the freedom of the High Seas against pressures from landward, pressures that will draw strength from changes in the overlapping spheres of politics and economics and also in that of war technology. Given this premise, what general inferences follow? Among the most weighty is the rising importance of the submarine as a prime weapon of sea-control or interdiction, notably in those narrow or distant waters (e.g. the Norwegian Sea, the Eastern Mediterranean and the Sea of Japan) which are vital but in which Western surface ships may become uncomfortably vulnerable. Conversely, however, the gradual trend towards a diminished status for the surface ship as a genre will be retarded or modulated in some measure by what may prove a growing requirement for individual police actions in support of fishery protection, innocent passage, pollution control and so on. Armed confrontations over such issues have tended since 1945 to be only occasional and low-key. But some of them—e.g. about fishing rights in the Sea of Japan—have given rise to no little bitterness.

Both for submarines and for surface ships the issue of nuclear propulsion will soon have to be faced more squarely. One considera-tion is that the cost-differential is diminishing: so much so, indeed, that the indefatigable Admiral Rickover is now able to insist that the lifetime cost for a fully nuclear task group (a carrier plus four escorts) is only six per cent above that of a similar force, conventionally propelled.[6] The riposte has been that such calculations presuppose the escort ships are rather large ones. But wherever the point of fiscal balance may lie, the tactical advantages of being able to equate cruising speed with maximum speed are very real, below the surface and also on it.

This being so, no one should abide the muddled thinking that, for instance, leads New Zealand dockers to believe that the arrival of a nuclear-driven frigate is tantamount to a visitation of the plague or that leads American congressmen to equate the supply of naval reactors with the dissemination of nuclear warheads. As early as 1957, the Netherlands Navy listed a nuclear-powered attack submarine among its longer-term requirements, only to find the project repeat-edly stalled not only by budgetary difficulties at home but also by a persistent disinclination in Washington to modify the 1958 Atomic Energy Act so as to permit the relevant reactor technology being supplied to allies other than Britain. Yet one cannot but wonder whether there is much gain in such significant NATO naval partners as the Netherlands, Italy, Greece and Turkey making a submarine contribution to collective security after 1985 unless the boats in question are nuclear-propelled And arguments that are hardly less compelling may apply to some core elements in their respective surface fleets.

Then there is the question of amphibious warfare, the viability or otherwise of which is bound to depend heavily on the specifics of the given naval task. No doubt moderate-size landings to evacuate refugees or to lend moral and physical support to small states under threat in, say, the Caribbean will remain possible at all events. What may demand more agonising reappraisals, however, is whether to stand ready for a major intervention to break a crippling embargo of oil or some other vital resource. Given that only the United States is likely to retain anything approaching the full panoply of power for so bold an enterprise, the problem presents itself to such countries as the United Kingdom and France in something like this form: "Should we deliberately retain a capacity to betoken our political support by making a modest though not negligible contribution to any American effort of this sort?" The Korean War stands as one obvious precedent for such betokening. So, in an inverted sense, do the unsuccessful overtures by the United States government for a symbolic European involvement in Vietnam.

What must be conceded straightway is that any operation along these lines would be a very serious matter indeed. Let us look a little more closely, for instance, at a scenario of intervention against one or more of the extremist regimes that could come to power in the Persian Gulf. Even under optimum circumstances the waterway in question might be difficult to enter, perhaps in the face of such weapons as pressure mines or surface-to-surface missiles and with the nearest Western baselet at Diego Garcia, over two-and-a-half thousand miles away. Were the USSR or, not inconceivably, Iran to obstruct movement, recourse to the threat of nuclear escalation might perforce be had at an early stage. Meanwhile, retaliatory currency manipulation could extend the conflict into the international money markets. Worse still, systematic sabotage of the oilfields themselves could easily cause a several month delay in the resumption of large-scale production.[7] Moreover, such considerations might apply with much the same force in the case of Libya, at any rate if she and Egypt were closely aligned at the time.

Besides which, one would be entitled to enquire whether the mere contemplation of such an imbroglio was not incompatible with the plea made in Chapter 22 for a more positive quest for dialogue with Afro-Asia and Latin America. But the answer could fairly be, "Not if this option is seen only as the last alternative to industrial strangulation". The tolerable stability of the West's relations with the Soviet bloc these many years are always assumed to have owed much to the very thinly veiled capacity of each side to obliterate the other at half an hour's notice. Likewise our dialogue with the newly developing world may not suffer from the candid realisation that a total breakdown of this dialogue could produce a situation of great danger for all parties, leading at best to extreme bitterness and confusion and at worst to total havoc. Out of such a realisation may come a stronger will to work for mutual understanding.

So far as what one may term straight Army matters are concerned, three issues seem to me destined to assume greater importance. The first is one of delineation and arises out of the prospective ascendancy of indirect fire: the *métier* of the modern artillerist. When, 60 years ago, armoured mechanisation initiated a revival of the cavalry, it sparked off, too, intense altercations (the embers of which still glow) about the interplay between cavalry and infantry, plus the implications for artillery and aviation. In like manner, we can now expect much discussion about where exactly to draw the functional divides between artillery and armour on the one hand and artillery and aviation on the other. Fervently must one hope that attention is focused on the right mix of actual weapons, rather than on organisational rationalisations which are all too liable to prove distracting and premature.

Then there will be the difficulties inherent in preparing men in peacetime for warfare which, if it ever does come, may break upon individuals more suddenly and ferociously than ever before, the Sinai in 1967 not excepted. One derivative but important theme must be the desirability of having available in such open warfare environments as Central Europe substantial formations of *élite* troops that can rapidly move (presumably by air) to defensive positions ahead of an incipient enemy thrust. Closely concordant with this stratagem might be the tactical sowing of minefields across the axis of advance. And it would be a pity if remnants of the old prejudice against "defensive" weapons and stratagems led to a disregard for the usefulness of the helicopter in this particular role. In fact, its employment thus would require great *élan*.

Lastly, at the other end of a modern army's spectrum of operational tasks lies the curbing of terrorism, especially urban terrorism. The word "curbing" rather than "defeating" is used advisedly because, in the great majority of cases, the key to the decisive defeat will lie in political and economic reforms designed to separate the tiny minority imbued with the morbid terrorist psyche from the great silent majority who may, under certain circumstances, be indulgent or acquiescent but who could never bring themselves to perpetrate any of the psychopathic atrocities of which we have heard so much from Kenya, Vietnam, Ulster and many other places in turn. To invert Maoist doctrine, "The fish must be isolated from the sea".

By the same token, the incidence of urban insurgency worldwide is most unlikely to be kept even tolerably low unless the mounting problem of urban deprivation is tackled effectively. For quite apart from anything else, the security forces have usually lost half the battle the moment they feel obliged to overreact.

One must insist on this last point because of the sort of thing one occasionally reads about the way the technology of counter-insurgency may "progress" in the years ahead, especially as regards crowd control. We are told of dart guns that can hit individuals in a crowd with marker dyes or tear gas or tranquillising drugs; novel and highly disconcerting varieties of foam; sprays which render road surfaces hopelessly slippery;[8] and psycho-chemical gases that temporarily induce delirium, drowsiness, irritability or panic. Such devices are not congruent even aesthetically with any degree of open government. An outward appearance of low-profile amateurism, such as the British police and Army have traditionally preferred, leaves far more scope for moderating dialogue with the populace at large.

With the increasing internationalisation of fascisto-Marxist terrorism, the connections between this vexing matter and another one—the operation of intelligence services—have inevitably become closer. As regards the latter, it is ever more apparent how intricate is the task of attaining a pattern of democratic control that is genuine without being stultifying. In the current American debate the best-informed protagonists of the intelligence community freely concede that abuses have occurred and that control must therefore be tightened. But they are acutely worried lest this might lead to endless security leaks.[9]

However, this circle will never be squared without a broad consensus on aims and methods being maintained or—as in the United States at the moment—rebuilt. Clearly, too, the bedrock of this consensus must be a vibrant conviction that liberal democracy is a priceless asset. Above that, there must be a set of guidelines for the *modus operandi* of the Secret Service and those who direct it. In this regard, we may all owe a considerable debt to John Bruce Lockhart for a recent succinct exposition.[10]

As regards the strategic purposes of intelligence, something like the following set of precepts may be appropriate to the 1980s. The covert though peaceable collection of data (including, on occasion, in allied domain) should be tacitly accepted as routine, condoned by international custom if not international law. On the other hand, active intervention within a foreign territory should be resorted to only when the authorities therein are struggling either to preserve a truly democratic system or else to move towards one, yet are being frustrated in their endeavours by the violently disruptive and polarising interference of the KGB or some other adversary service. Such methods should never be used simply to buttress reactionary regimes. Nor to instigate insurrection anywhere. Nor to track down international terrorists illicitly, unless these are deliberately being harboured. Nor should intelligence services concern themselves with the ideological struggle at the global level.

When laying down any such precepts it is relevant to remember that there are several reasons why the KGB might be expected to wax stronger abroad in the 1980s. Such a trend would be in line with a general ramification of Soviet power, not least in and around the comparatively soft states of Black Africa. Also with a Marxist perception of the mounting world crisis. In addition, it could serve to maintain a balance within the KGB itself between the internal arm (which will probably be obliged to expand) and the external.

Of course, the big attraction of intelligence services for all countries is that they can be almost breathtakingly cost-effective. To which the sardonic might reply that it is just as well something in Defence can. Even approximate long-term costings for Defence as a whole, on the basis of the inferences drawn above or any other, would be an elaborate statistical exercise; and one which, in any case, would almost certainly be vitiated considerably by the actual course of events. All the same, it does today seem rather obvious that the levelling-off of cost-escalation on the procurement side, which some of us were looking forward to only a few years ago, is not going to materialise.

But maybe this much can be said. Yesterday, the problem was mainly one of securing a marginal superiority of like over like: a tank with slightly tougher armour or a fighter able to travel 20 miles an hour faster. Tomorrow the quest will be more for equipment which is adequate in relation to the full mix of hostile and friendly systems to be expected in a total battlefield environment characterised by continuous innovation.

In fact, the maritime arena may be the one in which the strains of this innovation prove especially severe. This is partly because naval technology seems once more to be entering a particularly revolutionary phase. It is also because marginal shortfalls in equipment cannot be offset at sea by resting on the defensive in well-chosen terrain. The oceans are strictly neutral.

Whether or not the West can afford to sustain a Defence burden of at least the same magnitude (measured as a percentage of GNP) as the present one, does largely depend on whether it is resolved so to do. Israel spent almost a third of her GNP on Defence in 1974. Britain spent up to half during World War II. It was spending over ten per cent in the early 1950s, and still carrying a conscription burden to boot. So the 5·2 per cent Britain was spending in 1974 can be said to have been determined by political choices disguised as economic necessities.

Still, when all the non-Communist states of Europe and North America are considered, it is far from certain that the downward drift in national defence efforts will long continue. In ten countries the GNP percentage fell between 1972 and 1975 but in two it stayed constant whilst in nine others it rose.

Measured as a percentage of public expenditure, on the other hand, it fell in 13 but rose in only six.[11] And some would say that this was the critical test, because most Western democracies are currently experiencing a public expenditure crisis. Thus there was, in a number of Western countries at least, a fairly close cause-and-effect relationship between the inflationary spiral of 1974–75 and a concurrent expansion or persistence of the public sector deficit. In Italy, for example, this rose from 5·4 to 11·1 between the two years in question, and in Britain from 5·3 to 5·7.[12]

At the same time, however, pressures for ever more civil government expenditure persist. To cite future-oriented Sweden again, one might have assumed that the Swedes already had a sufficiency of public health facilities. However, the number of physicians in service in that country is expected to grow from 10,500 in 1970 to 27,000 in 1990.[13]

On the other hand, the competition for priority between such sectors and Defence is much blunted by a secular tendency for the realm of government as a whole everywhere to expand. Looking at the OECD zone synoptically, one finds that the percentage of the combined GNPs spent within the public domain rose between 1955 and 1969 alone from 41·8 to 48·4.[14] Furthermore we can assume this trend will gradually progress, notwithstanding periodic crises of over-stretch and recurrent expressions of anxiety—and not only from the political Right—about the implications for pluralist democracy of the overmighty spending power of officialdom.

A dimension to all this which one must not forget is the relationship between the armed forces and social flux. Obviously, the image and status of the martial virtues and the profession of arms will be affected, for good or ill, by shifting attitudes towards a whole range of diverse notions—mortality, free will, libertarianism, masculinity, hierarchy, a career for life ... What needs to be remembered, however, is that even the erosive flux of the last ten years has been well adjusted to on the whole. For instance, although armies have rated historically as a well-nigh exclusive male preserve, various of the Western ones have of late considerably extended the role of women.[15] Indeed, there is a somewhat ironic comparison to be drawn between this pragmatism and the extreme cult of *machismo* subscribed to by some of the more fascistic elements within the New Left, a trait which can be traced back at least as far as the "man and his chick" syndrome of the Beat Generation hipsters of the early 1950s.

Nor should armed services be too self-conscious about being, to some extent, a channel for *émigration intérieure*, a retreat for those who do not entirely identify with the "spirit of the age". Every profession from village postman to university lecturer has something of this angle to it. Furthermore, the political danger inherent in an army becoming so isolated socially that it sees itself as the sole repository of national virtue is less, in the context of the modern communications explosion, than formerly it was prone to be.

Furthermore, we can find in the German Federal Republic a particularly striking example of constructive response by one Western country to its own manifestation of the contemporary social flux. During the late 1960s, the morale of the Bundeswehr slumped: the chief index being an increase in the number of conscientious objectors from 2,800 in 1964 to well over 30,000 in 1972. But then the great German tradition of military staff-work was applied in full force to every relevant question from the hard drugs culture to alternative service and the philosophy of deterrence.[16] Now commentators remark on how revitalised the Bundeswehr is.[17] One might add that similarly favourable comments can be heard about the American army, as its reconstitution proceeds carefully but apace in the aftermath of Vietnam and Selective Service.

Nevertheless, many would insist that the habitual military distinction, legal and social, between commissioned and non-commissioned ranks remains too much at variance with a dominant trend in modern industrial society—i.e. the burgeoning of a new middle class through the convergence in values and life style of blue- and white-collar workers. Arguably, however, relations between officers and other ranks, in particular, are more extensive and relaxed in any British infantry regiment today than they are between "Staff and Works" in most of our factories; and undeniably they are more so than between the academic and non-academic staff of any of our universities. Thus to depict the average NCO, in the British Army or anywhere else, as being in the "obscure, confined, comfortless, and precarious position" de Tocqueville perceived him to be a century-and-a-half ago would be an obsolete parody. None the less, the nuances may be worthy of continual attention in an era of incessant social and technical change.

Notes

1. V. D. Sokolovsky, *Military Strategy*, Revised edition, Moscow, 1963, p. 394.
2. See David Holloway, *Technology, Management, and the Soviet Military Establishment*, Adelphi Paper No. 76, The International Institute for Strategic Studies, London, 1971.
3. Gunnar Myrdal, *Against the Stream*, Macmillan, London, 1974, pp. 311–312.
4. See e.g. Phillip A. Karber, "The Soviet Anti-Tank Debate", *Survival*, Vol. XVIII, No. 3. May/June 1976, pp. 105–111.
5. John H. Morse, "Advanced Technology in Modern War", *RUSI Journal*, Vol. 121, No. 2. June 1976, pp. 8–13.
6. Admiral H. G. Rickover, "Nuclear Warships and the Navy's Future", *The United States Naval Institute Proceedings*, Vol. 101, No. 1/863. January 1975, pp. 18–24.
7. "Out of the Fire", *An Economist Survey*, May 1975, p. 36.
8. See e.g. Rex Applegate, *Riot Control—Material and Techniques*, Stackpole Books, Harrisburg, 1969.
9. E.g. Hanson W. Baldwin, "The Future of Intelligence", *Strategic Review*, Vol. IV, No. 3, Summer 1976, pp. 6–24.
10. "Secret Services and Democracy", *RUSI and Brassey's Defence Yearbook 1975/6*, Brassey's, London, 1975, pp. 67–83.
11. *The Military Balance 1976–1977*, IISS, London, 1976. Table 2.
12. *The Economist*, 31 July 1976.
13. *Swedish Medical Care in the 1980s*, The Federation of Swedish County Councils, Stockholm, 1973. Table 3:4.
14. *The OECD Observer*, No. 59. August 1972, p. 5.
15. See "The Military: Some Amazing Gains", *Time*, 5 January 1976 and "More or Less Equal, but no guns yet", *The Economist*, 10 January 1976.
16. *E.g. White Paper 1972/3: The Security of the Federal Republic of Germany and the Development of the Federal Armed Forces*, Federal Press and Information Office, Bonn, 1972.
17. E.g. Richard Cox, "A New Self-Confidence in the Bundeswehr", *RUSI Journal*, Vol. 120, No. 4. December 1975, pp. 58–61.

25

The Quest for Arms Limitation

An axial proposition throughout this analysis has been that there is a diverse and continual interplay between the arms race, on the one hand, and economic and social stress, on the other, especially as reflected in international attitudes and actions. In many ways, of course, it is a disagreeable tenet. Nevertheless, it does have a brighter side. Quite simply, this is that the arms race is not subject only to the impulsion of its own inner logic. At all times, the actual state of play is much influenced by a complex mix of political motives and perceptions.

This truism is particularly applicable to the spread of nuclear weapons. As Leonard Beaton and John Maddox observed in what perhaps was the first study synoptically to blend the technical considerations with the political, "Nations do not decide to manufacture weapons merely because they realise it is feasible and the spread of nuclear weapons is obviously not as inexorable even as the spread of the juke box".[1] In other words, governments are well aware that independent nuclear deterrence ineluctably raises a host of subtle and contentious questions: technical and ethical, internal and external. But for this awareness, indeed, such countries as Canada, India, Japan and Sweden would have had "the Bomb" many years ago.

What then of the proliferation risk in the Middle East, the region in which technical capability and political will are most liable to reinforce each other repeatedly? In June 1974, the United States offered both Egypt and Israel industrial reactors. In each case the application of safeguards was made a condition, even though Israel already had—at Dimona in the Negev—one reactor not subject to safeguards. But doubts were soon expressed in Congress and elsewhere as to how effective any inspection routines might be.

Nor was unease assuaged at all by the fact that, four days after Presidents Nixon and Sadat had reached provisional agreement on this point *inter alia* during their talks in Cairo, the latter's foreign minister, Ismail Fahmi, warned in a newspaper interview that Egypt would not ratify the Non-Proliferation Treaty until Israel had both signed and ratified it. Moreover, he went on to say that if Israel introduced nuclear weapons into the Middle East, Egypt would match them.[2] Not long after "Yom Kippur" two exceptionally well-informed British commentators had endorsed the view that Israel did have nuclear devices already and stood ready to use them if its very existence was threatened.[3]

Another twist to this inauspicious spiral was effected in December 1974 when Ephraim Katzir, Israel's scientist-President, opined that the United Nations' decision to give Yassir Arafat a hearing marked the beginning of the "real destruction of Western civilisation by Middle Eastern Arab countries". At the same time, he reminded all and sundry that "It has always been our intention to provide the potential for nuclear weapons development. We now have that potential. We will defend this country with all possible means at hand. We have to develop more powerful and new arms to protect ourselves". When asked whether this would cause world concern, he reportedly replied, "Why should the subject worry us? Let the world worry about it".[4]

What some read as an Arab riposte to President Katzir's declamation was delivered by Colonel Gadafi a few weeks later. In an interview with the Lebanese newspaper *An Nahar*, he foresaw "that nuclear power will one day be as essential as electricity. And while people now say that this country has 50 planes and that country 500 planes, the day will come when they say that this country has three nuclear bombs and that country has ten, and so on".[5] Later that year Libya was promised a ten megawatt reactor by the USSR. Early in 1976 France agreed to supply Libya with a much larger one: it was, in fact, unofficially reported to be in the 600 megawatt range. True, Libya ratified the NPT in 1973. True also, however, that around the end of that same year it did illicitly transfer to Egypt some Mirage Vs procured from France for its own defence. Perhaps, too, one should not discount altogether the plea for a collective Arab deterrent made in *Al-Ahram* in November 1973 by Muhammad Hasanain Heikal.[6]

Not that it is only in connection with the Arab-Israel dispute that the menace of a nuclear Middle East is looming. Thus whilst Iran has no intention of going nuclear under present circumstances, it is studiedly reserving its options lest the regional situation changes. Let us refer, by way of example, to a press conference given by the Shah in the autumn of 1974. He received sympathetically a question suggesting that one way to avoid "nuclear blackmail" (which some might read as "adequate safeguards") was to base nuclear reactors on natural uranium as India had done, this notwithstanding either the critical view official circles in Tehran had taken of New Delhi's decision to do an underground test or the recent conclusion by Iran of an IAEA safeguards agreement.

The Shah went on to say that his country had already made plans to install 23,000 megawatts of nuclear generating capacity. Also that, whilst several reactors were being bought from France, "We will buy everywhere, both from the Western countries and from the East if they are ready to sell. So it is a complete diversification of markets that we envisage".[7] Early in 1975, practical confirmation of this strategy was afforded when a 15 billion dollar trade pact, to be implemented over five years, was signed between Iran and the United States. Included in this package deal was the supply of eight nuclear reactors.

In short, Iran is moving into a position where it will be able to resist attempts to monitor its nuclear fuel cycle too closely, no doubt arguing the while that the most advanced industrial nuclear powers do not submit to such constraints themselves. This being so, it may well be that the key to a non-proliferation strategy in respect of Iran lies in ensuring that the alliance links which the West retains with it continue to seem both credible and acceptable.

Much the same applies to endeavours to dissuade Turkey from taking up a nuclear option in the course of the 1980s. It has had a research reactor in operation since 1962. Moreover, though this particular facility is subject to an IAEA safeguards agreement, it has thus far resisted diplomatic pressure (e.g. from Britain) to ratify the Non-Proliferation Treaty. Furthermore, in February 1975 the Turkish Minister of Defence specifically said that "There are plans to manufacture atom bombs and nuclear reactors". Agreed, this bald assertion came three weeks after the US Congress had voted to impose an embargo on the sale of arms to Turkey, the Cyprus dispute being the reason. All the same, it did bespeak a burgeoning resolve in Ankara somehow to become less dependent on American arms supplies.

Inevitably, very similar considerations are being weighed in the balance in Yugoslavia, a newly developing state that may not be part of the Middle East as such but which certainly occupies a pivotal place in the tortuous geopolitics of the Eastern Mediterranean.

Suffice to note that Yugoslavia has three research reactors in service now, plus a 600 MW industrial reactor under construction and due to go critical in 1979. Also how, in December 1975, an article in *Borba*, the Communist party newspaper, argued that "Cheap and easy manufacture of 'mini-nuclear' weapons, capable of destroying entire units or headquarters of the aggressor, would have a sobering effect on anyone contemplating invasion of our country . . .".[8]

Still, the immediate problem is not really nuclear deterrents for Israel, Egypt, Libya, Iran, Turkey, Yugoslavia and so on. Rather it is the heading off of such ultimate possibilities by strengthening the matrix of international nuclear control before the ramification of nuclear agreements and installations has gone so far that such strengthening becomes impossible. Recently, several bi-national agreements have highlighted how urgent this aspect of the situation is. Thus, West Germany and France have undertaken to sell to Brazil and Pakistan respectively complete nuclear fuel cycles—not just reactors but plants for uranium enrichment and uranium or plutonium separation as well. Meanwhile, the United States plans to supply nine tons of fuel-grade uranium to India and a big nuclear reactor to Spain. Every one of the four recipient countries here cited is on the list (given in Chapter 10) of states which have not even signed the NPT.

The problem of devising a more adequate world strategy against nuclear proliferation is one that has to be approached through several layers of concern, each of which is distinct and important. The first is the failure of a very large part of Afro-Asia and Latin America, in particular, to sign and ratify the NPT. The next is the freely admitted flimsiness of this treaty itself, as measured by any criteria of binding commitment.

More particularly, we have to bear in mind how unsatisfactory the safeguards procedures still are. Thus at the 1975 NPT review conference those states with civil nuclear technology available for export—Britain, Canada, France, West Germany, the United States and so on—refused to give an undertaking to supply nuclear equipment only to those non-nuclear states which agreed to place all of their nuclear material and activities under International Atomic Energy Agency safeguards. "By refusing to go that far, they preserve the absurd situation whereby non-parties to the Treaty are in a more advantageous position than are parties . . ." because Article III firmly stipulates that so total a commitment as this is required by those who accede.[9] Then again, although it was agreed in principle in 1973 that the EURATOM wing of EEC should monitor nuclear development within the Community as a surrogate of the IAEA, implementation is being impeded by French non-cooperation.

Perhaps the most direct measure of the extent of IAEA coverage is the number of power and research reactors subject to its safeguards. In July 1973, these covered 52 under the auspices of the NPT and 82 via other channels, 134 altogether. By December 1975, the respective figures were 65 and 81; and of the new combined total of 146, not quite a third were power reactors.

Evidently, this gradual upward trend affords little prospect of ever matching the spread of reactors among those states not as yet members of the military "nuclear club". Thus they already had 230 reactors in operation by December 1975, just over a fifth of them being power generators. Five years later, it is expected they will have 330, getting on for a half of which will be for power production.

But if the lag thus indicated were to be corrected through a more comprehensive and rigorous application of the NPT, a big expansion of the IAEA safeguards organisation would thereby be necessitated. Increasingly, indeed, the comment is heard that the inspectors the agency employs (70 at the time of writing) are becoming subject to serious overstretch.

Of late the annual IAEA budget has been *c.* $30,000,000 (at 1975 prices). However, less than a sixth of this appropriation is being spent directly on safeguards. Well over a half is spent on technical assistance and other services of a promotional kind whilst the remainder goes on overheads.[10]

In the light of which, *The Economist* has strongly argued the need to make an institutional separation between attempts to preclude military nuclear proliferation and endeavours to promote the civil application of nuclear energy. In doing so, it has deployed the following analogy: "In 1974, the American Atomic Energy Commission was disbanded, and in its place two new bodies were created, one to license and regulate nuclear power plants, the other to encourage their construction through research and development. Since then, the new Nuclear Regulatory Commission has proved far stricter in its regulatory duties than the old commission had ever been, much to the displeasure of the nuclear industry and of electricity producers. Their resentment is perhaps the best barometer of the success of the commission as a regulatory body".[11]

Given the urgency of the problem of nuclear control and the ramshackle character of the international arrangements thus far made for it, an initiative was taken in January 1976 in London by seven countries actively concerned with the export of nuclear materials and technology: Canada, France, West Germany, Japan, the Soviet Union, the United Kingdom and the United States. This initiative took the form of confidential exchanges of letters whereby the various signatories pledged themselves to modulate their export policies in such a manner as to limit the spread of nuclear weapons. Eight other states involved in nuclear exports—Belgium, Czechoslovakia, East Germany, Italy, the Netherlands, Poland, Sweden and Switzerland—have since aligned themselves with this "secret London club". Soon one or two importer states may.[12]

Alas, it is an approach which has been subject to searching criticism on several counts. The club shows little sign thus far of evolving an effective common strategy. It may be divisive within EEC. Above all, its operation behind closed doors has been diametrically at variance with the open diplomacy precepts of the NPT.

Perhaps more promising is the emphasis Dr Kissinger has been placing, throughout his last year at the State Department, on concentrating all facilities for the reprocessing of nuclear waste in regional centres under multinational control. At any rate, in mid-December, the promise was underscored by President Giscard d'Estaing's announcement of a French embargo on future deals to export nuclear reprocessing plants.

However, it would be otiose to pretend that, in this world of bureaucratic inertia and petty chauvinism, implementing the Kissinger precept would not be fraught with difficulties. Jealous dispute over geographical location could often occasion delay, an apprehension that seems all too well borne out by a close parallel from within the EEC. Thanks to the competitive yearnings of Britain, France, West Germany and Italy to act as host country, the commencement of work on the Joint European Torus (JET) has now been brought to the brink of cancellation; and yet this esoteric installation is something that must be built, and sooner rather than later, if Western Europe's valuable research into thermonuclear fusion is to continue. Suffice to add that the incipient public debate about the control of reprocessing ought now to be informed by more technical guidance on—for example—the feasibility or otherwise of various states independently building their own separation facilities.

13

Then there is the vexed question of how to establish an international regime for peaceful nuclear explosions. During the "atoms for peace" euphoria that gripped it in the middle 1950s, the United States initiated a programme for such detonations. Duly, this was entitled Plowshare, as per the Book of Isaiah: "They shall beat their swords into ploughshares, and their spears into pruning-hooks".

As noted already, in 1974 India used this objective as the alibi for her first nuclear explosion. Today Egyptian sources hypothesise the nuclear blasting of a channel to flood the Qattara depression from the Mediterranean. France has done some work in this field. The USSR has done a lot though at times the Academy of Sciences seems less enthusiastic than does the military lobby!

Meanwhile, Argentina and Brazil have cited autonomy in this regard as a reason for not signing the NPT. Yet Article V of the Treaty does provide that an "appropriate international body" should ensure that all non-nuclear signatories can have explosions carried out for them on a non-discriminatory basis. Also that, additionally or alternatively, they can seek comparable bilateral arrangements. Both these principles were reiterated in the final declaration of the 1975 Review Conference.[13]

Undoubtedly, one factor inhibiting their implementation is genuine uncertainty about the real commercial dividends. Everybody recognises that if a single detonation in, say, the high kiloton range is required, a nuclear charge is two orders of magnitude less expensive than a chemical. Also that, in theory at least, this shock tactic is occasionally relevant. Among the occasions may be the creation, under the appropriate geological conditions, of underground chambers for the disposal of toxic waste; the extraction of a higher than normal proportion of a natural gas or oil deposit; and radical civil engineering to blast out routes to be followed by motorways, railroads or canals. Nevertheless, these last few years the feeling has become widespread (at least outside the more macro-minded Soviet circles) that, the risk of radioactive venting or seepage apart, too much was initially claimed for this manifestation of "atoms for peace".

Clearly, this matter is another which merits much fuller international discussion. Equally clearly, however, no resolution of the strictly pragmatic considerations would *ipso facto* reconcile countries like Argentina, Brazil and India to reliance on "borrowed power". Needless to say, the same goes too for proffers of nuclear protection in exchange for the renunciation of nuclear weapons. Speaking as

Prime Minister to the Parliamentary Labour Party in June 1966, Harold Wilson advanced as one justification for Britain's retaining a military presence East of Suez that it would give countries like India a third nuclear alternative to reliance on the Superpowers or making "the Bomb" themselves. In June 1968, the Security Council passed a resolution along similar lines though, of course, of more general import. Alas, there is as yet little evidence of such overtures making much impression in places like New Delhi.

Nevertheless, the threat of the military "nuclear club" continuing to expand might be turned to some advantage here. Presumably, if the choice of guarantors was at least prospectively rather wider, situations of dependence on any one of them would be less *infra dig* than might otherwise be the case. Perhaps, indeed, the key to a viable anti-proliferation strategy lies in extending this argument thus. The less exclusive the status and security connotations of possessing an independent nuclear deterrent, the less vigorous will the proliferation trend be.

Nor will this sense of exclusivity necessarily be governed solely by diminishing marginal returns in a simple numbers game. In other words, it does not have to depend on an alarming degree of nuclear proliferation having already occurred. Thus whilst the development of an industrial nuclear programme may afford an *entrée* to a military nuclear force, it may contrariwise serve—at any rate in prestige terms—as a substitute for it. Likewise, the installation of nuclear propulsion units in submarines, warships and other vessels may impart an aura of nuclear sophistication which extends beyond the purely practical advantages thereby conferred and which is akin to that associated with nuclear warheads.

Then again, to move close to the military nuclear threshold may sometimes be an alternative to crossing it; and to cross it quietly may often be much less destabilising than to do so with pomp and circumstance. Whilst India moved across the nuclear threshold in the early 1970s using ill-defined peaceable activities as its pretext, Israel moved at least up to it without formally admitting as much. Neither departure was consonant with the precepts of open government essential to any democracy. On the other hand, it would be hard to indict either Tel Aviv or New Delhi for nuclear bombast.

Some stress, too, that there is great merit in eschewing the diplomatic prerogatives presumptively consequent upon any kind of nuclear status. On this argument, it is just as well that, in contradistinction to 1963, the United Kingdom was not "at the top table" for the 1974 treaty limiting nuclear tests. By the same token, a *prima facie* case can be made for having her and France alternate as the incumbents of what would then become a European permanent seat on the UN Security Council. The place thus vacated might, for instance, be filled by Japan, a country which, after all, did have a permanent seat on the League of Nations' Council until her withdrawal in 1933.

As a Japanese specialist in international relations has put it: "That the permanent members of the UN Security Council are all nuclear powers is undesirable because it gives the impression that nuclear armament is the passport to big-power status and gives prestige to the possession of nuclear weapons. It is encouraging to note that a considerable number of countries, including the United States, seem to favour the idea of seating Japan as a permanent member of the UN Security Council".[14]

Obviously, such advocacy is worthy of our serious attention. To my mind, however, it is faulted by a fortuitous conjunction between technology and politics. Every single one of the five permanent places on the Security Council is filled not by a mere nuclear power but by a thermonuclear one—i.e. by a state that has mastered the much more difficult task of developing the hydrogen bomb. Obversely, no other state seems at all likely to achieve this, not between now and 1990 at any rate. Therefore, permanent membership of the Security Council can plausibly be read as an accolade which highlights the huge difference in potency between nuclear and thermonuclear weapons, thereby sapping—at least in some cases—any enthusiasm for the former.

Another false trail may be any renunciation in advance of the first use of nuclear weapons. Not that much was heard of the brasher forms of this proposal at the Geneva conference. All present seemed to accept that, for instance, NATO could never withstand, without recourse to tactical nuclear release, a full-scale and prolonged non-nuclear attack on Western Europe by the combined armed forces of the Warsaw Pact.

However, Romania, Yugoslavia and nine newly developing states did suggest at Geneva the adoption of a protocol which would lay down the following principles. The nuclear members of the NPT would undertake "never and under no circumstances" either to use or to threaten nuclear weapons against non-nuclear-weapon states which were party to the Treaty and whose territories were "completely free from nuclear weapons". They would also be pledged to refrain from the "first use" of nuclears against any other non-nuclear-weapon parties to the treaty.

Unfortunately, even these judiciously chosen ground rules would be so restrictive as to compromise stable deterrence. Thus the defence of maritime trade could not invariably be ensured without the employment of nuclear warheads against submarines of uncertain national origin; and similar arguments apply to air defence in theatres like Central Europe. Nor might forceful intervention to break embargoes on supplies of vital raw materials succeed without invoking the nuclear threat. Then again, however incongruent the proposition may sound, the peculiarly nasty mirror-image relationship which persists between the authoritarian regimes of North and South Korea makes it all the more imperative that the USA (and the 15 other UN members at least notionally involved) keep a wide range of military options open apropos the 1953 commitment to uphold the armistice in Korea. Nor are these by any means the only crisis scenarios which might be adduced.

But this most certainly does not mean that there are no concessions that the existing members of the nuclear club can make to meet the point, reiterated frequently at Geneva, that the NPT does contain a commitment to work "in good faith" for actual nuclear disarmament, as opposed to mere arms control. Thus the coordination of the British and French strategic deterrents could commend itself on arms control grounds as well as military operational ones.[15] Then again, is there sufficient reason why Britain, France and the USA should not release figures for their stockpiles of military materials, fully fabricated or otherwise? And might this not be a suitable preliminary to the voluntary and explicit limitation of same? And so to the opening for inspection of other nuclear installations?

As was at least implicitly admitted in Chapter 21, dynamically to pursue towards such matters policies that were at all enlightened would usually be to part company with the USSR. However, there is one sphere in which it might actually be helpful to align more closely with customary Soviet predilections. It concerns the possibility of a total ban on underground nuclear tests.

Formally, at any rate, these were excluded from the 1963 partial test ban treaty because the sponsoring nations were unable to agree on the necessity or otherwise of on-site inspection. The USSR insisted that the recording of shock waves on seismographs obviated what was to it a decidedly unwelcome stipulation, whilst the United States and Britain contended that, with warheads in the low kiloton range, a shock wave might effectively be muffled and would, at all events, be hard to distinguish from the seismic signatures characteristic of earthquakes. Accordingly, no further steps were taken along these lines until the summer of 1974 when President Nixon and Secretary Brezhnev signed in Moscow the treaty precluding military nuclear tests of over 150 kilotons yield—i.e. anything more than seven times the strength of the Hiroshima bomb and so without doubt susceptible to purely seismic surveillance at the present state of the art. True, in a complementary treaty signed in May 1976 the USSR did concede that on-site observation of peaceful nuclear explosions could occur. Even so, there is no reason to assume that this avowedly special case heralds any general relaxation of the atavistic aversion to foreign observers, military and otherwise, trampling over Mother Russia.

But should not reconnaissance from Space be able to ascertain whether a pinpointed yet ambiguous seismic signature might have derived from other than natural causes? Surely, one could not carry out a meaningful nuclear test without a few vehicles and other paraphernalia in the general vicinity.

As regards those very low kiloton or sub-kiloton tests which might avoid seismic detection altogether, there are these considerations to bear in mind. The United States has had warheads in the quarter of a kiloton range in service (notably in air-to-air missiles) for some 15 years now and, what with that and all the low yield tests in the recent past, must be at the stage of steeply diminishing returns where warhead miniaturisation is concerned. The USSR is unlikely to have progressed as far in this direction but is also unlikely to be concerned to do so, given that its tactical nuclear philosophy has always been less intricate. Similarly, actual or prospective secondary nuclear powers, with more elementary nuclear strategies, need not be expected to take much interest in the esoteric art of deliberately making a basic fission explosion ever less efficient in order to force its energy yield further and further below the Hiroshima level.

Admittedly, other difficulties would also be posed by extending the scope of the international ban on nuclear weapons tests. For years to come, not to say indefinitely, there would be some conspicuous absentees from the list of signatories, much as with the NPT. Furthermore, such a proscription would be difficult to define, let alone enforce, in the absence of a codicil to the NPT designed to effect the comprehensive regulation of peaceful nuclear explosions. Yet, when all is said and done, it is hard to imagine a viable anti-proliferation strategy not including a comprehensive ban on the testing of nuclear weapons.

What also is hard to imagine is any substantial progress on so-called "conventional" disarmament or arms control until nuclear proliferation is being curbed satisfactorily. For one thing, the technical hurdles that present themselves apropos the panoply of conventional war are usually more diverse and intricate than those of nuclear deterrence. For another, the USSR is more unequivocally in favour of checking nuclear proliferation than it has been about halting conventional arms races in Europe, the Middle East, South-East Asia and so on.

Where some scope for early progress may exist is in the evolution of more systematic and ethically sensitive policies apropos arms exports. Yet even this laudable aim is bedevilled by conflicts of priority. Maybe the chief questions to ask in given situations are these. Would a general embargo on arms exports to an actual or prospective conflict zone have an asymmetrical effect as did that of the proscriptions applied by the League of Nations to China and Japan alike during the Manchurian crisis and then to Italy and Ethiopia alike during the former's invasion? Might any such asymmetry be a good thing or would it automatically favour the aggressors, just as it did when it handicapped China and Ethiopia more than their sophisticated adversaries? Is the given situation one in which it may be possible to preserve some distinction between defensive and offensive weapons or between external security and internal? If internal security is involved, would it be essentially a matter of bolstering legitimate and beneficient authority or of sustaining a repressive regime? To what extent would weapons supply to a country stimulate the growth of its indigenous military establishment and would this be good for its national development? Would any act of abstention merely encourage the USSR or other external suppliers to move in? Might not the associated supply of spare parts and ammunition afford the best opportunities for constructive leverage? Would the withholding of arms encourage the proposed recipients, and maybe others, to develop their own capacities for weapons manufacture? And might these weapons include nuclear ones? Unfortunately, numerous technical developments—not least the cruise missiles and the new means of electronic warfare—are making some of these questions harder to answer.

Notes

1. Leonard Beaton and John Maddox, *The Spread of Nuclear Weapons*, Chatto and Windus, London, 1962, pp. 81–82.
2. *Arab Report and Record 1974*, p. 247.
3. Christopher Dobson and Ronald Payne, *The Sunday Telegraph*, 30 December 1973.
4. *The Times* and *The Daily Telegraph*, 3 December 1974.
5. *The Daily Telegraph*, 14 January 1975.
6. See *Arab Report and Record 1973*, p. 536.
7. *Kayhan International*, 12 October 1974.
8. Reprinted in *Survival*, Vol. XVIII, No. 3. May/June 1976, pp. 116–117.
9. William Epstein, "Nuclear Proliferation: The Failure of the Review Conference", *Survival*, Vol. XVII, No. 6. November/December 1975, pp. 262–269.
10. *The Annual Report For 1975*, IAEA, Vienna, 1976. Table 12.
11. *The Economist*, 28 February 1976.
12. *The Times*, 29 March 1976.
13. For the full text see *SIPRI Yearbook 1976*, Almqvist and Wiksell, Stockholm, 1976. Appendix 9A.
14. Kei Wakaizumi, "Japan's Role in a New World Order", *Foreign Affairs*, Vol. 51, No. 2, January 1973, pp. 310–326.
15. See the author's *European Security, 1972–80*, RUSI, London, 1972, p. 66.

26

The Further Outlook

Even if things do go every bit as well as we can reasonably hope, the world of 1990 does not promise to be particularly paradisiacal so far as the great majority of its inhabitants are concerned. The grim communal conflicts of the Levant and Southern Africa will almost certainly not have been conclusively resolved. On the contrary, they are all too likely to have reached the kind of intermediate stage towards a settlement in which the interaction of impatience and fear is at its most combustible. By the same token, whilst we may well have observed the commencement of the USSR's crisis of fundamental transformation, the crossing of this deep and unavoidable Rubicon will probably be incomplete.

Nor will we yet have conquered the problem of nuclear proliferation, even if we have made in the interim great progress—along the several lines indicated above—in evolving a specific strategy for dealing with it. For according to the IAEA projections, nuclear generating capacity world-wide can be expected to double during the final decade of this century to become in the year 2000 no less than ten times what it was in 1980.[1] If so, the number of potential plutonium warheads being generated each year as we enter the third millennium will be around 200,000; and the subsequent decay rate will, of course, remain negligible in human historical terms, plutonium having a half-life of over 20,000 years.

The sad irony is that ultimately it should be possible to solve the energy crisis once and for all by the one form of nuclear power that causes comparatively little nuclear pollution and which poses no military or terrorist menace—namely, controlled thermonuclear fusion. Research into this began more or less simultaneously in the USA, the USSR and Britain some 20 years ago; and since a 1958 agreement, the international exchanges of data on this subject have remained remarkably open and extensive. Today something well in excess of £100,000,000 per annum is being spent to this end, Japan having joined the Superpowers and Western Europe as a significant contributor.

Already fusion research has had its fair share of false dawns. Furthermore, as the Director of the Institute of Physical Problems in Moscow has lately acknowledged freely, the experts as yet understand far too little about the dynamic behaviour of a plasma of heavy hydrogen isotopes being thus confined and energised.[2] Nevertheless, the great majority of these experts continue to be quite optimistic about reconciling, in due course, the two parameters crucial to inducing within a plasma self-sustained and exothermic reactions. One is the temperature being achieved within it; the other is the density at which the plasma is held, multiplied by its containment time.

By 1974 or thereabouts, the prospects looked good for the 30,000,000°C needed to initiate these reactions being registered within a few years. However, the prognosis was much less encouraging in respect of the multiple of density and containment time, the best performances to date being between ten and a hundred times below what was sought. So it was beginning to look as if the desired results would not be achieved on both parameters together until some fundamental changes in technique.

Across the years much work has been done on the use of pulsed currents of electrons to transmit the bursts of energy required to activate a plasma, this being then held within a strong magnetic field; alternatively, on the use of converging laser beams to both activate and confine it. Now much attention is being paid to another approach, the employment of ion beams rather than laser ones for this dual purpose.

Still, if all does go reasonably well these next few years in the basic research and also in the engineering, one or more fusion-driven Experimental Power Reactors (EPRs) in the 25 megawatt range should be in service by the late 1980s. Another six or seven years on, second generation EPRs of around 100 megawatts capacity should be operational. Hopefully, these will be succeeded by pilot plants of the order of one or two thousand megawatts apiece around the year 2000; and then, after several years more, fully commercial models in the several thousand megawatt range should make their appearance.

These successive stages have been spelt out here to demonstrate that fusion reactors stand little chance of giving a significant boost to world electricity supplies this side of the year 2010. Nor should we forget that progress will not be even as rapid and assured as this, unless technical genius and good fortune are nurtured by a benign political and cultural environment. International collaboration will have to be sustained in the face of upwellings of nationalist sentiment, as has perhaps been evidenced in the somewhat extravagant talk already heard about military objections to pooling the relevant aspects of laser research. The resentment of some mighty nuclear fission lobbies, especially research and development lobbies, may have to be curbed. Some major problems of funding and administration will have to be tackled, not least in less developed countries, as we move towards and into the commercial production phase. All of which will depend heavily on widespread recognition of fusion research for the heroic intellectual adventure, in various branches of applied science and technology, that it undoubtedly is.

Sometimes one is given to understand that fusion power will be dirt cheap, a kind of philosophers' stone of the energy world. Alas, the strain of capitalisation will alone be sufficient to ensure that energy costs will not diminish so dramatically. Nevertheless, the situation should eventually improve sufficiently to enable the margins of exploitation of this Earth's food and mineral potential to be considerably extended, thereby alleviating the more desperate shortages in those spheres. But eventually probably means after 2025.

Nor should we expect much assistance in the meantime from solar power, the reason being simply that the capital investment required across the board would be quite impossible to justify as an interim measure. Calculations indicate that, even on the decidedly optimistic assumption of a 10 per cent efficiency, an array of solar cells sufficient to supply the USA's electricity needs in 1990 would cost over time seven or eightfold its GNP for that particular year.[3]

This is a pity because no form of power could be less polluting than solar. Would that the same could be said of coal, the fuel that, around the turn of the century, is likely to regain from petroleum pride of place among the hydrocarbons. Not only are coal-products sure to remain expensive as sources of energy, this notwithstanding technical advances apropos gasification *in situ*, hydrogenation to oil, and so on. In addition, the climatic effects of the accumulations of dust and carbon dioxide from coal-burning, in particular, are bound to cause concern, at least until two or three decades of close monitoring have established whether or not the net effect is liable to prove intolerably deleterious.

Herein lies one geophysical factor that could oblige Mankind to restrain the growth of the world economy through the year 2000 more than it may be restrained automatically by certain material shortages. Another could be a more generalised anxiety about the diverse and still indeterminate consequences of an ever-expanding output of goods and services, irrespective of the energy spectrum which sustains it. Admittedly, a lot of nonsense was talked by "ecodoom" radicals a few years ago about "thermal pollution"—i.e. the sheer volume of heat energy produced by Man wrecking the biosphere, allegedly within a generation or two. Nevertheless, there may genuinely be quite a number of more particular environmental trends which could prove markedly adverse and which do correlate closely with global economic growth. Perhaps the most extraordinary possibility seriously aired of late has been that the upward drift of fluorocarbons used in aerosol sprays is wreaking havoc with the ozone layers in the stratosphere, the layers that protect us against excessive ultra-violet radiation and which may modulate our climate. Once again the most worrying aspect is the margin of uncertainty, years more research being needed.

So in this broader sphere, too, the overall impact of ecological disturbance may be to reinforce political pressures to restrain economic growth everywhere, at any rate until the relevant data bases are more complete and key control measures determined. True, any retardation in the rise in total output should increasingly be offset by a progressive slowing down of that in the world population. Even so, it is clear that Mankind as a whole will tend not to have any great surpluses of disposable resources, at the very least until a return to relatively cheap energy with nuclear fusion has facilitated the extraction of less accessible or lower grade minerals, the cultivation of more arid zones and the like.

What makes this prognosis the more sobering is that the era to which it refers may also be unusually difficult in terms of social and political adjustments. Thus the required scale and configuration of military force will inevitably be a matter of continual debate. Then again, dealing satisfactorily with the manifold economic problems to be expected is liable to involve a large measure of global economic management along something approaching confederal lines. Yet that is a pretty gargantuan stipulation in itself. Suppose the United Kingdom was a confederation with 120 constituent territories, culturally most diverse and with some over 50 times as rich as others. Would not the question "Is Britain governable?" be asked even more urgently than in the recent past?

To pose this rhetorical question is merely to aver that, even on optimal assumptions, the next half century or so is bound to be a testing time in many ways: a period of great stress and no little danger that may one day be seen in stark contrast with the halcyon era which has succeeded it. Disturbing though this interpretation may seem, however, it implies the kind of challenge that appeals profoundly to the courageous and altruistic sides of our human nature. Proof can be seen in the recurrence at many times and in many places of folk-memories, myths and prophecies about near-to-cataclysmic crises that have to be surmounted in order to attain promised lands of affluence, leisure and peace. An early example was, of course, the Sumerian story of the Flood in which the Gods ordain the human race to perish only to be frustrated by Noah's building an ark in which to preserve "the seed of humanity". As is well-known, this saga, which may have had some historical foundation in abrupt climatic change, was perpetuated in Babylonian, Hebrew, Hittite and other ancient literatures. Close parallels also developed in pre-Columban South America.

Similarly, evoking images which read curiously like premonitions of a nuclear holocaust-cum-population crash, the Norse and Germanic legend writers foretold the "Twilight of the Gods". But even this horrendous scenario is succeeded by a most salubrious regimen in which "The fields bear crops though no seed has been planted". The meadows are green; birds circle above; fishes disport in the waters. The cycle of life is resumed.[4]

The Israelites wandering for "forty years" across the inhospitable Sinai towards the "land flowing with milk and honey" was an epic real-world essay in what today would be called "nation-building". The first part of John Bunyan's *The Pilgrim Progress* is an allegorical and individualistic rendering of the same theme in a nonconformist setting: Christian's troubled passage to the Celestial City on the hill. The long and colourful tradition of millenarian thought is permeated by a sense of deepening crisis which will be resolved gloriously though only through convulsive upheaval. Then again, Karl Marx naively looked forward to a post-revolutionary era in which money, bureaucracies and all such coercive nexus would be replaced by a "classless" society in which all would live "abundantly" and collaborate fully. Be they factually based or no, these and countless other epics of desperate struggle and final triumph reveal much about the instinctual side of our psychology. We have always been inwardly glad to blend the actuality of taxing conflict with the prospect of bounteous bliss.

But this is not to deny that the next generation or so may require, both in politics and elsewhere, what will veritably amount to a new order of leadership: one in which constancy of ultimate purpose is combined with great mental agility apropos the endless kaleidoscope of immediate issues. And, as the New Frontier era in the United States was to demonstrate in some ways, this combination is hard to sustain. Not many of History's greatest architects of change have been philosopher-kings, forever weighing the pros and cons of the passing scene with entirely open minds. Much more typically, they have been men of intense and narrow passions, more concerned with a few rigid loyalties and fixed objectives than with the scholarly virtues. Indeed, many would have dismissed the latter as a dilettante indulgence.

Related to this is another problem. Right across the positivist humanist tradition which has built up in Western literature since the Renaissance, there is a disposition to disregard the diminution of challenge and excitement inherent in much that we are pleased to dignify as Progress. Exceptions can be found,[5] but they are few and far between.

Granted an alleged need to "find a substitute for war" has become too easy a popular *cliché*. Nevertheless, evidence accumulates daily in such fields as anthropology and ethology which appears to confirm that Mankind as a whole, and especially the young generation, does demand more from life than the constant burgeoning of affluence and the endless extension of leisure. So unless the decidedly cornucopian open society that seems to await large sections of Humanity in the second quarter of the 21st century can promise more, we may be beguiled *en route* by the sado-masochistical fantasies of fascism and fascisto-Marxism.

Avoidance of so sombre a lapse is likely to depend on a revaluation of our moral and social philosophy as diverse and searching as any these last five centuries. As such, any prevision of it would extend far beyond the purview of this study. However, there is one question which does cover a good deal of common ground. Should not the international community now be planning a much bigger and well coordinated programme for extension into the last of Man's grand physical frontiers—that of Outer Space? Could this be the counterpart for the 21st century of the discovery of the Americas by the Renaissance?

One says "international community" advisedly. For though the signal American and Soviet achievements in this sphere have often received wide acclaim, it is hard to believe that much international goodwill can indefinitely be sustained unless participation in the major Space endeavours can become multilateral. But this in its turn will depend on the preservation in regions like Western Europe, the Far East and Australasia of those exotic technologies that bear directly on such objectives.

Weight is added to this thought by two further ones. The first is the self-evident one that no country or region will be at all well placed for participation in Space research unless it is maintaining also an aeronautics industry. The second is that the 1980s look set to be an exceptionally decisive decade for the aeronautics industry world-wide. Military aviation and missilery will be in a state of rapid flux. In addition, development work will probably start on exotic new models for introduction into civil service in the 1990s. Among them may be a hypersonic transport (HST) able to carry 300 passengers at 3000 mph; a subsonic nuclear transport able to carry 600; and a jumbo freighter intended to lift minerals recovered in such inaccessible places as the mountains of Antarctica.

Meanwhile, about half the $45 billion expected to be spent on new aircraft between now and 1985 will be to update existing capacity and the other half to expand services. True, the number of passenger-miles flown in the non-Communist world is generally expected to rise at barely half the rate achieved in the 1960s. Even so, the result should be c. 825 billion in 1985 and c. 1·10 trillion in 1990, as against 400 billion in 1975.

Accordingly, the chances for the survival of a capability for aircraft manufacture in Western Europe, in particular, through 1990 are better than once they seemed. But in the event, all will hang on whether the region is determined to ensure this. And one element in this determination will or should be whether a linked capacity for Space research should be maintained: in other words, whether mere aeronautics should not elevate itself into Aerospace.

Seeing that the potentialities of Space for military observation have already been largely realised by the two Superpowers, the case for a big and multinational Space programme through the turn of the century stands or falls almost entirely by its impact on civil affairs.

Innumerable purveyors of science fiction, H. G. Wells episodically among them, have visualised Mankind easing simultaneously its twin burdens of congestion and tedium by colonising the Moon and other planets. Yet so far as the congestion part goes, this notion is as purely a pipe-dream today as ever it was.

Let us take, by way of confirmation, the opinion of Isaac Azimov, an author whose credentials as a Space-age visionary are as firmly established as are anyone's. He has gone so far as to anticipate a Moon colony being a 21st century Japan in miniature, a settlement able to pay its way by technological excellence facilitated—in this context—by the extent to which microengineering may be enhanced by near-perfect lunar vacuo, and electrical conductivity by the low lunar temperatures.

But that essay in *avant garde* futurology itself lends force to his solemn caveat that, "If anyone thinks that the important reason for exploring Space is to find outlets for our expanding population, let him think again". The time-frame is hopelessly extended whilst the cost-effectiveness balance is ludicrously unfavourable. Nor could any group of lunar settlements ever contain so very many inhabitants, irrespective of timing and outlay.

On the other hand, the continued exploration of Space may yield invaluable psychological and hence political benefits. As much was fiercely claimed for it by, for example, *The Economist* around the time of Neil Armstrong's historic touchdown in 1969. Thus, "When Man became a toolmaker, he ceased to be a monkey. The human race's way of sublimating its highest aspirations has been to build the greatest and grandest artefact that the technology of the time can achieve ... Oddly—or perhaps not so oddly—the Churchmen with their unstinting praise of the astronauts have recognised this where the liberally-educated rationalists with their bored carping ... have not. Spiralling to the planets expresses something in human nature that relieving poverty, however noble a cause that is, does not".[6] In particular, the journal in question felt that the Moon "offers a new frontier" to dynamic and intelligent youth, people who have tended to find modern terrestrial existence "intolerably confining".[7]

My own recollection would be that, though attitudes may not have polarised in quite the manner thus indicated, most of the alumni of the Western intelligentsia did react to Armstrong's visit to the Moon in a manner more or less in line with this "liberally educated rationalists" stereotype. Resentment against official circles within the

United States over Vietnam and the ghetto crisis undoubtedly contributed. Maybe, too, jealousy emanating from residual Russophilia played a part in some quarters.

The late Bertrand Russell was not incapable of being crudely anti-American. But nobody could sensibly accuse him of ever having been a Russophil. Nor was he in the least antipathetic to Science as such. Nevertheless, he deplored the lunar expedition as just another example of "our silly cleverness", and as part and parcel of a modish disposition to "cause people to spend more time in locomotion and, therefore, less in thought".[8] Yet once the argument is generalised to this extent, the same objection applies as with the anti-growth intelligentsia. Exceptionally peripatetic intellectuals should never protest too immoderately at a certain amount of movement by the masses, whether actually or via their telescreens.

What, then, are the options before us? Sir Hermann Bondi, the leading British cosmologist who is currently chief scientist at the Ministry of Defence, always stresses the desirability of the much more vigorous development of remote control vehicles, so that these may become the exclusive spearheads of a new wave of interplanetary exploration. But other experts would still attach great importance to the flexibility achieved in direct human exploration, the work of the Apollo 15 crew in 1971 being deemed an especially noteworthy example. Besides which, an Outer Space colony inhabited solely by remote control vehicles is really hard to imagine.

However, a manned landing on, for instance, Mars could, if launched direct from the Earth's surface, require a lift-off an order of magnitude above what was needed to send Neil Armstrong off to the Moon in 1969 or even above that of the Viking unmanned probes to Mars in 1976. Moreover, a round trip extending over two or three years could pose serious problems apropos the physiological effects of prolonged weightlessness; and it would, too, in time lags of up to 45 minutes in each conversational exchange between the astronauts and the Earth.

Even so, a prognosis widely subscribed to in the United States during the late 1960s was that, were the current Space programme to continue flat out after all, within 20 years a man could be set down on Mars and safely recovered. Presumably, much the same time span still applies. To which may be added the prospect that, within 25 to 50 years, it could prove practicable to provide some primitive but permanent sealed accommodation on the Moon, perhaps at a direct cost per acre not vastly in excess of what the Dutch have lately expended on reclaiming land from the sea. Eventually, such lunar outstations might mount astronomical telescopes (radio as well as optical) which, there being no atmosphere to contend with, would enable the uttermost limits of the universe to be explored more definitively than hitherto, thereby making invaluable contributions to the great debates about cosmology. For the time being, however, attention is being focused, both in the USA and in the USSR, on the assembly and maintenance of manned Space platforms just beyond the fringes of the Earth's own atmosphere.

My view would be that, whilst no decision should be taken yet about when to establish the first lunar outstation, the onward march of Earth-based radio-astronomy should receive every encouragement. Meanwhile, the United States should take the lead in a coordinated drive by the members of OECD and all other interested parties to land a man on Mars on the earliest astronomically-suitable occasion in the third millennium. In terms of the consequent strain on world resources, 2025 AD or thereabouts might be a better deadline. Quite apart from the quasi-mystical significance some otherwise sophisticated people do seem to attach to the year 2000, however, it may be desirable psychologically to have this goal set at such a distance in time that it comes well within sight during what could prove an especially critical decennial span in world affairs: namely, 1985 to 1995.

To those who would deplore any such sortie as an essentially primitive diversion, the answer could be "So be it". If a monumental exercise in pyramid-building is the best means available of canalising some basic and potentially harmful instincts, then surely it should be resorted to.

By the same token, we should not be inhibited unduly by those who would warn us against any repetition of the "politics of expectation" launched by the New Frontier. As Henry Fairlie put this argument, "For three years after 20 January 1961, the American people were persuaded that, metaphorically as well as literally, they could shoot for the Moon ... When the expectations of a people ... are so aroused, and are then not realised, frustration grows and disillusion follows".[9] However, this rather negative connotation may chiefly apply when the venture in question is undertaken by one nation largely to upstage another. If the effort is more truly international, the nobler aspect may become dominant with the result that popular expectations are sublimated rather than spurred.

For let no one doubt that a voyage to Mars would have its nobler aspect. The experience of being in direct touch with a celestial body in an independent orbit anything between 34 and 240 million miles away might do much to enable Humanity to see its Earth-bound tensions and conflicts in proper proportion. After all, even the first lunar landing did something to enhance our awareness of a common destiny on Spaceship Earth. And to that extent, it measured up to Werner Von Braun's description of it as the greatest evolutionary event since Life left the Sea.

Notes

1. *The Annual Report for 1975*, IAEA, Vienna, 1976. Table 7.
2. Academician Peter Kapitza, "Energy—the fusion solution", *The New Scientist*, 14 October 1976.
3. Gerald Foley, *The Energy Question*, Penguin, Harmondsworth, 1976, p. 210.
4. Harald Hveberg, *Of Gods and Giants*, Johan Gmudt Tanum Forlag, Oslo, 1969, pp. 82–86.
5. E.g. George Orwell, *The Road to Wigan Pier*, Victor Gollancz, London, 1937. Part 2.
6. *The Economist*, 26 July 1969.
7. *The Economist*, 19 July 1969.
8. *The Times*, 15 July 1969.
9. Henry Fairlie, *The Kennedy Promise*, Eyre Methuen, London, 1973, pp. 12–13.

Index